Birth as an American
Rite of Passage

Birth as an American Rite of Passage

Robbie E. Davis-Floyd

UNIVERSITY OF CALIFORNIA PRESS
Berkeley · *Los Angeles* · *Oxford*

University of California Press
Berkeley and Los Angeles, California

University of California Press
Oxford, England

Copyright © 1992 by
The Regents of the University of California

Library of Congress Cataloging-in-Publication Data

Davis-Floyd, Robbie.
    Birth as an American rite of passage / Robbie E. Davis-Floyd.
        p.   cm.—(Comparative studies of health systems and medical
    care; no. 35)
    Includes bibliographical references and index.
    ISBN 0–520–07439–4 (cloth: alk. paper)
    1. Childbirth—Social aspects—United States. 2. Childbirth—
United States—Psychological aspects. 3. Rites and ceremonies—
United States. I. Title. II. Series.
    [DNLM: 1. Holistic Health. 2. Labor. 3. Pregnancy. WQ 300
    D261b]
    RG518.U5D38   1992
    618.4′01′9—dc20
    DNLM/DLC
    for Library of Congress   92–402
                                                                   CIP

Printed in the United States of America
1   2   3   4   5   6   7   8   9

The paper used in this publication meets the minimum requirements
of American National Standard for Information Sciences—Permanence
of Paper for Printed Library Materials, ANSI Z39.48–1984 ⊗

To my husband, Robert N. Floyd, with all my love forever.

Contents

Tables

Acknowledgments

My deepest thanks go to Brigitte Jordan for her invaluable help—for her commitment of time and energy to careful editing of this book, for her own work, which provided the inspiration for mine, and most of all for her enthusiasm for and belief in my abilities and the worth of my contribution. Heartfelt thanks also to Beverly Stoeltje for the inspiration, encouragement, and care she lavished on the first phase of this work—my dissertation—and for her continuing friendship.

Series Editor John Janzen, as well as Carol McClain, Rayna Rapp, Carole Browner, Carolyn Sargent, Nicole Sault, Ellen Lazarus, Peter Reynolds, and Richard Bauman provided invaluable editorial assistance from an anthropological perspective. Michelle Harrison, Marshall Klaus, and most especially Susan McKay made enormous contributions to the accuracy of the medical information. Lisa Chatillon, Rae Fortunato, and Julie King (who awaits the imminent birth of her child as I write) gave useful feedback on earlier drafts, as did Jay Hathaway and Mary Brucker on Chapter 4, and historian Kevin Roddy on Chapter 2. Sheila Kitzinger, Michel Odent, Emily Martin, Barbara Katz Rothman, Carol Laderman, Harriet Hartigan, Gayle Peterson, Marimikel Penn, and Janet Isaacs Ashford provided much-needed encouragement and support at various stages of this project. To all of them, I express my gratitude.

I also wish to thank Kip Koslowski and Lisa Bradley for assistance with the sections on childbirth education. Special thanks to Kip for understanding my work so well that she could go out and take just the photographs I needed; although it was not possible to include most of them in this book, they have enlivened every talk I have given on the subject of birth and I am deeply grateful for them. And many thanks to Stan Holwitz at the University of California Press for being a patient and steady source of support.

I am also grateful to Pauline Kolenda, Polly Perez, Karen Michaelson, Susan K. Baker, Eddie Kolb, Margie and Jay Hathaway, Bruce Jackson, Robert Hahn, Tom Verny, Barbara Rylko-Bauer, Phillip Whitten, Nicole Sault, Diony Young, and Candace Fields Whitridge for the opportunities they have given me to share my work and thus to expand and deepen it. And, of course, to Barbara Kirshenblatt-Gimblett for encouraging me, twelve years ago, to make women's issues the focus of my graduate research.

Sincere and special thanks go to the childbirth professionals (who wished to remain unnamed)—physicians, midwives, nurses, and childbirth educators—who so willingly gave me their time and so freely expressed their thoughts and shared their experiences.

I offer warm appreciation to Janis Claflin, Cindy Thomason, Joy Jones, Pat Otis, and Frances Terry for providing me with nurturing environments in which to write, to Rima Cunningham, Megan Biesele, Ginger Farrer, and Nicole Sault for the emotional nurturance they consistently offered me, and to Sandy Zitkus and Adela Popp for their invaluable assistance with tape transcriptions.

Heartfelt thanks and love go to my family—my husband for his belief in me and for his unflagging support for my hopes and dreams, and my children—my daughter Peyton, age 12, and my son Jason, age 8—for being themselves and for loving me even when I work long hours and am distracted.

I feel tremendous gratitude to all the women who so willingly shared with me their time, their emotions, and highly personal stories about some of their most significant life experiences. Many of them said, as they looked at their busy schedules, "I want to find time for this because it's for other women." I hope this book gives something back to them.

Introduction

Birth as a Rite of Passage

... if we consider the sparse ethnographic record, we find
that there is no known society where birth is treated, by the
people involved, as a merely physiological function. On the
contrary, it is everywhere socially marked and shaped.
—*Brigitte Jordan,* Birth in Four Cultures

Across cultures and throughout history, humankind has used rites of
passage to transmit cultural beliefs and values to the individuals participating in those rites. In non-Western cultures, specific rituals, often
involving the entire community, accompany such life-changing events
as birth, puberty, and death. Such rituals generally serve to imbue individuals in transition with a sense of the cosmic importance of the group
and of the place of the individual within that group. Although pregnancy and childbirth are life-changing events, in our technologically
oriented society there appears to be no society-wide spiritual or humanistic rite of passage to initiate newborn mother and child into
American life. There is, however, a surprising standardization of medical procedures for childbirth across this country—a standardization
most reminiscent of the standardized rituals that make up rites of passage in traditional societies.

A common tenet of modern thought holds that the transfer of the
birthplace from home to hospital which has taken place in American
society represents the deritualization of what in other, more "primitive"
societies has traditionally been a process laden with superstition and
tabu. Originators of this belief, the members of our medical profession
hold that obstetrical procedures are determined by physiological reality.
On the contrary, however, I suggest that the removal of birth to the
hospital has resulted in a proliferation of rituals surrounding this natural physiological event more elaborate than any heretofore known in

the "primitive" world. These rituals, also known as "standard procedures for normal birth," work to effectively convey the core values of
American society to birthing women.

As increasing evidence of the unnecessary and often harmful nature
of obstetrical procedures accumulates and is published by the medical,
psychological, anthropological, and lay presses, many individuals involved with birth are asking how it is possible that a medical specialty
that purports to be scientific can appear to be so irrational. I hope to
demonstrate in this book that these obstetrical procedures are in fact
rational ritual responses to our technocratic society's extreme fear of
the natural processes on which it still depends for its continued existence. Cumulatively, routine obstetrical procedures such as intravenous
feeding, electronic monitoring, and episiotomy are felt by those who
perform them to transform the unpredictable and uncontrollable natural process of birth into a relatively predictable and controllable technological phenomenon that reinforces American society's most fundamental beliefs about the superiority of technology over nature. My
focus in this book will be on the cognitive transformation of birthing
women through these rituals of hospital birth.

RESEARCH METHODS
AND THEORETICAL CONCERNS

This book is based on research conducted in home and hospital interviews with 100 pregnant women and mothers primarily in two cities,
which I shall call Centertown and Anycity, and with many of the midwives, nurses, childbirth educators, and obstetricians who attended or
assisted these women. (In order to fully protect the privacy of my interviewees—a privacy for which many of them expressed a strong need—I
have changed the names of both the individuals I interviewed and the
cities in which I worked.) I chose these two cities simply because I lived
in them for extended periods and because they seemed to me to offer
a good cross-section of the United States: Centertown is a very conservative industrialized southern city with a high level of unemployment;
Anycity is a liberal southwestern city, organized economically around
high-tech industry.

When I began my searches in Centertown and Anycity for mothers
to interview about their births, and for pregnant women to query about
their expectations for birth, I did not specifically seek out women who
believed in any particular type of birth, I simply followed the "mother

trail" wherever it led. In both cities I made contact with several obstetricians and midwives who gave me the names of some of their clients who might be willing to talk with me. I got other names from childbirth educators, La Leche League leaders, and, of course, many of the women I interviewed sent me on to their friends. Most of these interviews were conducted in the homes of the women, who had given prior consent over the telephone. However, I learned to carry my mini tape recorder at all times; a number of my interviews were conducted on airplanes and at conferences in various cities across the nation, and once I even accosted a friendly looking pregnant woman in a store. Whenever possible, I interviewed women both before and after their births. (A listing of interview questions can be found in Appendix A.) Although most of my interviewees had more than one child (so that I ended up with data on 194 births), in this book my primary emphasis is on the cognitive transformations experienced by these women during their first births. (Reinterpretations of first births and the meanings of subsequent births are addressed in Chapters 6 and 9.)

Although I conducted interviews with only 100 women (who may not be statistically representative of the U.S. middle-class population), this book is intended to be a broad overview of birth in the United States for middle-class women. I therefore will cite national statistics, when available, to ground the experiences of the women in my study in the context of the wider culture. As I analyzed my interviews I was working inductively, rather than deductively, to determine patterns and generalizations. Near the vicinity of the final sample size, I realized that I had come to understand the pattern of responses, that I was no longer being surprised by the experiences and reactions the women were reporting. At the same time, I honor the uniqueness of every woman's birth experience. It is my hope that the individual voices of the women who taught me about these general patterns will not be lost in this book, but instead will speak strongly of the emotional and psychological ramifications of these patterns throughout my presentation and analysis.

In my interviews I grasped the reality of what recent national statistics confirm: women all over the United States are subjected to a series of obstetrical interventions so standard that they are difficult to avoid in most hospitals, under the care of most obstetricians. The vast majority of women giving birth in American hospitals are dressed in a hospital gown, placed in a hospital bed, hooked up to an electronic fetal monitor, and ordered not to eat; they have an intravenous needle inserted into their arm, are anesthetized to some degree, receive the synthetic hormone pitocin if their labor is not progressing rapidly and regularly, and have an episiotomy (a surgical incision of the vagina to widen the birth outlet). Nearly one-quarter of all women giving birth in this country will do so this year by Cesarean section, perhaps the ultimate technological intervention.

A number of researchers have pointed out that factors of social class and ethnicity shape both women's reproductive experiences and the meanings women attach to these experiences (Lazarus 1988a; Martin 1987; Nelson 1983; Rapp 1988a, b; Shaw 1974). The subjects of my study were well-educated mainstream middle-class white women who, given the realities of American life, could be expected to receive the best that the American obstetrical system has to offer. It is a well-documented sociological phenomenon that poor women giving birth in hospitals must accept prenatal care from the hospital clinic, are assigned for birth to whatever residents happen to be on duty, and are usually given little or no choice as to how their births are managed, and that black and Hispanic women often receive unfavorable medical treatment (Fraser 1988; Lazarus 1988a; Martin 1987; Nelson 1983; Scully 1980; Shaw 1974).[1] Therefore, I focused my research on women who were able to go to private obstetricians and to pay for private (i.e., non-hospital sponsored) childbirth education classes, because of the greater number of options presumably open to such women for exercising individual choice in their childbirth experiences. The existence of birthing options among the women I sought to interview seemed critical for my research, since much of the initial impetus for this research stemmed directly from the following questions: *given the possibility of individual, informed choice, why is the pregnancy/childbirth experience ritualized in such consistent and uniform ways in doctors' offices and hospitals across the country? What is the significance, for the individual who can choose how and where to give birth, of the "standard American hospital birth," and what are the cultural factors that underlie that standardization?*

To address these questions, I apply a model derived from symbolic anthropology to the pregnancy/childbirth process in the United States which interprets this process as a year-long initiatory rite of passage. The answers to these questions emerge from decoding the symbolic messages conveyed to birthing women by the rituals of hospital birth, and from a detailed consideration of the responses of individual women to these birth messages.

In arriving at these answers, I journeyed not only through anthropological works on birth and on ritual, and the medical and alternative literature on pregnancy and birth, but also through the feminist writings—anthropological and otherwise—on birth and the women's health movement, in particular via the books and articles of Suzanne Arms (1981), Gena Corea (1979, 1980, 1985a,b), Barbara Ehrenreich and Deirdre English (1973a,b), Michelle Harrison (1982), Emily Martin (1987), Adrienne Rich (1977), Diana Scully (1980), Nancy Stoller Shaw (1974), and Barbara Katz Rothman (1981, 1982, 1989). The feminist revision of birth as presented in these works has immense power and value. These writers have explosively and consistently exposed the intense patriarchal bias in the American Way of Birth and in the medical treatment of women and their bodies. Their work led directly to my own initial questioning of that system and provided much of the inspiration for this book.

Yet the more I immersed myself in these works and their point of view, the more I was forced to notice the dissonance between this feminist critique of birth and the beliefs, desires, reactions, and behaviors of the women I was interviewing. It took me years to be able to hear that most of these women were not raising their voices in resistance and re-visioning of the American Way, but in varying degrees of harmony and accord with that Way. I have therefore tried in this book to move beyond the perspective that sees women's choices for birth technology as "false-consciousness" waiting for the feminist conversion, to a perspective that views such choices as embedded in the hegemonic cultural model of reality that most of us to some degree embrace, in part because that model is consistently presented to us through our most basic cultural rituals.

This book is addressed to a multiple readership. It is written as a work of anthropology with an intended audience not only of social scientists but also of health care practitioners, childbirth educators, feminists, pregnant women and mothers, and students of ritual and of American society. In this effort to serve such diverse interests, I take support from George Marcus and Michael Fischer, who envision "writing single texts with multiple voices exposed within them, as well as with multiple readerships in mind" as "the sharpest spur to the contemporary experimental impulse in anthropological writing, both as ethnography and cultural critique" (1986:163). Among the many voices speaking in this book is my own voice. The choices in favor of technocratic birth made by the majority of women in my study are in conflict with my personal beliefs and values. That I am highly critical of the American way of birth, and an advocate of birth under a wholistic, not a technocratic, model will be evident throughout. Yet, although I question the cultural factors that shape the birth choices made by contemporary American women, I strongly support their right to those choices. I have taken seriously Marcus and Fischer's point that "the statement and assertion of values are not the aim of ethnographic cultural critique; rather, the empirical exploration of the historical and cultural conditions for the articulation and implementation of different values is" (1986:167). I have endeavored to refrain from allowing my advocacy to interfere with my analyses of the responses of the women in my study who accept, to one degree or another, technocratic birth and its accompanying ideology, and have tried to explore some of the historical and cultural conditions for the articulation and implementation of that ideology. That done, I have allowed myself, in the final two chapters, the luxury of speaking my mind, my heart, and my hopes for a future with more real alternatives for birth and more conceptual freedom to choose.

Chapter 1 will discuss the pregnancy-birth continuum of experience as a year-long rite of passage for the mother. Chapter 2 focuses on the paradigm that provides the rationale for the medical conduct of this rite, which I call the technocratic model of birth. Chapter 3 demonstrates step-by-step how obstetrical procedures work to map this technocratic model onto the woman's perceptions of her labor and birth experience, with the goal of aligning her individual belief system with that of society.

The beliefs about birth held by my interviewees reflect the tension in the wider society between the technocratic model and the "natural childbirth" ideal. Chapter 4 seeks to provide a conceptual framework for understanding the relationships of various nationally known forms of that ideal—in particular, the "natural childbirth" of Grantly Dick-Read, the "prepared childbirth" of Ferdinand Lamaze, and the "husband-coached childbirth" of Robert Bradley. These alternative paradigms are points along a spectrum of possible beliefs about birth in American society. One end of that spectrum is defined by the extreme form of the technocratic model of birth, the other by the extreme form of what I call the wholistic model of birth.

Chapter 5 investigates in depth the responses of individual women to their socialization through birth rituals. I find here that the single factor that most influences how a woman responds to her socialization process is the degree of correspondence between the technocratic model dominant in the hospital and the belief system she herself holds when she enters the hospital. This belief system may be upheld, or overthrown, by the rituals of hospital birth. When it is upheld, she will generally perceive her birth experience as positive and joyful; when overthrown, as negative and traumatic. Subsequent reinterpretations by some women of the meaning of these experiences are presented in Chapter 6.

Chapter 7 briefly examines medical school and residency as an eight-year-long rite of passage for nascent physicians in order to show how medical practitioners themselves are socialized into the technocratic model, thus ensuring that the system will continue to perpetuate itself in its present form. Chapter 8 investigates the cultural consensus on and futuristic significance of the increasing technocratization of American birth, and Chapter 9 considers other potential directions in American birthways, including the cultural significance of the systems-based wholistic model of birth.

This book is as much about ritual—how ritual enacts models of reality and how individuals respond to those enactments—as it is about birth. The theoretical grounding for Chapters 1 through 9 is provided in the remainder of this introductory section, in the form of a discussion of the nature and characteristics of ritual and rites of passage. This discussion is not meant to be exhaustive, but to clearly present the anthropological concepts upon which the rest of the book depends.

RITUAL AND RITE

Noted anthropologist Edmund Leach (1976) distinguishes between rational-technical behavior on the one hand, which "produces observable results in a strictly mechanical way," and "communicative" and "magical" behaviors on the other hand, which operate symbolically and do not stand in a cause-and-effect relationship to reality. It is the overt cultural stance of the medical profession that obstetrical procedures are determined by physiological reality, thus qualifying as purely "rational-technical" behavior. Yet, as I hope to show, these "scientific" procedures more than meet the anthropological criteria for ritual behavior, and their primary functions have at least as much, if not more, to do with the culturally appropriate socialization of the birthing woman as with her "rational-technical" medical care.

Much of this argument will rest on anthropological theories about ritual. Clear presentation of these theories will lay the necessary foundation for the reader to make the cognitive leap to the interpretation of obstetrical procedures as rituals. Marcus and Fischer have written:

> Disruption of common sense, doing the unexpected, placing familiar subjects in unfamiliar, or even shocking contexts are the aim of this strategy to make the reader conscious of difference. . . . In anthropology . . . the defamiliarizing effect is only a springboard for sustained inquiry. For example, modern doctors may be compared to tribal shamans as the opening of an ethnographic and critical investigation of medical practice. However, in what we will define as the stronger version of such projects of criticism in anthropology, defamiliarization is more than an attention-grabber, but is a process that should entail a critical reflecting back on the means of defamiliarization itself—using our example, considering not only how we think about doctors, but also how we think about shamans. (1986:137)

In keeping with this definition of the defamiliarizing process, this book will seek to place familiar images of American birth—women in hospital gowns hooked up to machines, families staring at newborn babies in plastic bassinets through nursery windows—in the unfamiliar, perhaps even shocking, context of purposive socialization through an initiatory rite of passage. Such placement, as a springboard for sustained inquiry, engenders reflection not only on how we think about hospital birth, but also about the means of defamiliarization—ritual itself. This section, therefore, presents a reformulation of ritual/rite of passage theory. I include here not a broad survey of the literature but a specific definition of ritual and a description of its chief characteristics and most important functions in rites of passage.

CHARACTERISTICS OF RITUAL[2]

A *ritual* is a patterned, repetitive, and symbolic enactment of a cultural belief or value; its primary purpose is transformation. The consistent performance of ritual is an integral part of every known human culture. The characteristics of ritual explicated below are integral not only to its role in hospital birth, but also to its myriad roles in other aspects of human cultural life. These characteristics include (Davis-Floyd 1990*a*):

1. The symbolic nature of ritual's messages.
2. Its emergence from a cognitive matrix (belief system).
3. Its rhythmic repetition and redundancy.

4. The cognitive simplification that ritual works to engender in its participants.

5. The cognitive stabilization that ritual can achieve for individuals under stress.

6. The order, formality, and sense of inevitability established in ritual performances.

7. The acting, stylization, and staging that often give ritual its elements of high drama.

8. The intensification toward a climax that heightens ritual's affective (emotional) impact.

9. The cognitive transformation of its participants that is ritual's primary purpose.

10. Ritual's importance in preserving the status quo in a given society.

11. Ritual's paradoxical effectiveness at achieving social change.

It is not necessary to look at every ritual as doing each of these things equally; however, these are all salient features of ritual in general, all part of the capacity of ritual as a symbolic form. Ritual is a powerful didactic and socializing tool. To grasp its inner workings is to have a choice in our response to the rituals that permeate our daily lives.

Symbolism   Ritual works by sending messages to those who perform and those who receive or observe it. These messages are not presented as straightforward verbal "rational-technical" communication, but symbolically. A *symbol,* most simply, is an object, idea, or action that is loaded with cultural meaning; following Geertz, it is "any object, act, event, quality, or relation that serves as a vehicle for conception— the conception is the symbol's meaning" (Geertz 1973:93).

Recent neurophysiological research has demonstrated that straightforward verbal messages are received by the left hemisphere of the brain, which decodes and analyzes these messages, thereby enabling the recipient to either accept or reject their content. In contrast, symbols are the appropriate vehicles for ritual's messages because they are received by the *right* hemisphere of the brain, where they are interpreted as a gestalt (d'Aquili 1979:173–177; Lex 1979:124–130; Luria 1966:90; Ornstein 1972).[3] In other words, instead of being intellectually analyzed, a symbol's message will be *felt* in its totality through the body and the emotions (e.g., the Marine basic trainee being required to sleep with his rifle).

The practical result of this characteristic of symbols is that their messages are often received by individuals on unconscious levels; although the individual may remain unaware of his/her incorporation of the symbol's message, its ultimate effect on the recipient may be extremely powerful, acting in the immediate situation to "map changed or adjusted perceptions of the possibilities inherent in a situation onto the actor's orientation to it" (Munn 1973:593). On a more fundamental level, Munn continues, "ritual symbols may be said to regulate and affirm a coherent symmetrical relationship between individual subjectivity and the objective social order" (Munn 1973:606). In other words, rituals work to align the belief system of the individual with that of the social group conducting the ritual.

In Chapter 3, I will demonstrate how routine obstetrical procedures can work to map a technocratic view of reality onto the birthing woman's orientation to her labor experience, thereby aligning her individual belief and value system with that of the larger society.

A Cognitive Matrix   A matrix (from the Latin *mater* = mother), like a womb, is something from within which something else emerges. Rituals are not arbitrary; they come from within the belief system of a group. Each symbolic message that a given ritual sends manifests an underlying cultural belief or value. Sometimes these are made explicit in ritual, but most often these deep beliefs that the ritual expresses are unconsciously, rather than consciously, held. Ritual's primary purpose is to symbolically enact and thereby to transmit a group's belief system into the psyches of its participants (Wallace 1966; McManus 1979b).

Because the belief system of a culture is enacted through ritual, analysis of ritual can lead directly to a profound understanding of that belief system. Analysis of the rituals of hospital birth reveals their cognitive matrix to be the technocratic model of reality which forms the philosophical basis of both Western biomedicine and American society. This model will be fully presented in Chapter 2.

Repetition, Rhythm, and Redundancy   For maximum effectiveness, a ritual will concentrate on sending one basic set of messages which it will rhythmically repeat over and over again in different forms. What is repeated in ritual can include the occasion for its performance (as in a ceremony that happens every year at the same time); its content; the form into which this content is structured, or any combination of these. This redundancy enhances ritual's efficiency in communicating whatever messages it is designed to send; as Redfield (1960:358) points out, the Mayan farmer who hears the shaman chant the names of the gods twenty times in one hour, several times a day, is not likely to forget them.

Rhythmicity has long been recognized by anthropologists as a key feature of transition rituals (Needham 1979). Rhythmic, repetitive stimuli affect the central nervous systems of ritual participants, generating a high degree of limbic arousal, coordinating emotional, cognitive, and motor processes within an individual, and synchronizing these processes among the various ritual participants (d'Aquili 1979). According to recent neurobiological theory, under proper conditions repetitive stimuli may bring about the unusual neural state of simultaneous high discharge of both the excitation and relaxation nervous systems in humans (normally, one or the other predominates) (Lex 1979; Gellhorn 1968, 1969, 1970; Gellhorn and Kiely 1972). Under stable social and environmental conditions, this simultaneous discharge of both nervous systems produces an intensely pleasurable, almost orgasmic sensation (indeed, both subsystems do simultaneously discharge during orgasm). Under conditions of stress, the sensations so produced are more likely to be those of calm, reassurance, and a sense of control.

Redundancy and repetition are two of the most noticeable characteristics that hospital birth rituals, also known as routines, utilize to ensure that their messages will be received and remembered. Although the intensely pleasurable sensations that can result from successful rituals are not a key feature of hospital birth, such sensations are often experienced by home birthers who consciously create rituals to foster group unity among themselves and their friends and helpers. In the hospital, the calming and reassuring effects of ritual are generally paramount.

Cognitive Simplification   In any culture, ritual participants will differ from one another both in intellectual ability and in conceptual structure. (Individuals of high cognitive complexity, for example, may adopt a relative view of reality tolerant of many interpretations of a given phenomenon, whereas individuals with simpler cognitive systems will tend to insist on one correct interpretation.) Straightforward didactic communications must take these differences into account if their messages are to be understood. Ritual, however, overcomes this problem by simply reducing its participants, at least temporarily, to the same cognitive level. At this level of cognitive functioning, which John McManus (1979b:217–218; after Harvey, Hunt, and Schroeder 1961) calls "stage one," individuals see the world from within the confines of one particular cognitive matrix and tend to think in simple either/or patterns that do not allow for the consideration of options or alternative views.

The advantage of this cognitive reduction of ritual participants to stage one functioning is that only one ritual structure is now sufficient to communicate social norms and values to a wide variety of individuals. In other words, even complex thinkers can be reduced by ritual to simple either/or thinking; thus they may not tend to question the symbolic messages they are internalizing. This process is most clearly visible in the performance of religious rituals such as the Catholic Mass, which can be deeply and equally convincing to individuals of all levels of cognitive complexity.

Such cognitive simplification must precede the conceptual reorganization that accompanies true psychological transformation. The most common technique employed in ritual to accomplish this end is the rhythmically repetitive bombardment of participants with the symbolic messages described above. In rites of passage, the additional techniques of hazing, strange-making, and symbolic inversion also effectively work toward the conceptual reorganization of the initiate, and will be discussed later on.

In hospital birth, the cognitive focus of the birthing woman can be narrowed to stage one simply by the rhythmicity and pain of the labor process; this narrowing can be enhanced by her repetitive bombardment with technological stimuli. However, the most interesting effects of ritual's ability to narrow individual cognitive functioning can be seen in the process of medical training, in which repetitive hazing techniques such as overwork, rote memorization, and exhaustion combine to ensure that the medical student will not question the basic tenets of the belief system he is constantly internalizing during the course of his or her eight-year training (see Chapter 7).

Cognitive Stabilization When humans are subjected to extremes of stress, they are likely, at least temporarily, to retrogress cognitively into a dysfunctional condition that McManus terms "substage," becoming panic-stricken, unreasonable, or simply out of touch with reality. Whenever the danger of such retrogression is present, ritual plays a critical role, for it stabilizes individuals under stress by giving them a conceptual handle-hold to keep them from "losing it." When the air-plane starts to falter, even those who don't go to church are likely to pray! The simple act of rhythmically repeating "Dear Lord, please save us," can enable terrified passengers to avoid the panic behavior that might increase the likelihood of disaster.

Ritual mediates between cognition and chaos by making reality appear to conform to accepted cognitive categories. In other words, to perform a ritual in the face of chaos is to restore conceptual order. Even a little bit of order can enable individuals to function under the harshest of conditions. Think of the earthquake victim who sweeps off her front steps when the entire house lies in ruins around her: those steps represent one ordered cognitive category. To make them clean is to ground oneself in a little piece of the known and the familiar. From that cognitive anchor, one can then begin to deal, a little at a time, with the surrounding chaos. Rituals (such as prayer, or even the handshake and standard "Nice to meet you" we give to unfamiliar strangers) provide their participants with many such cognitive anchors. Ritual thus has high evolutionary value; it was a powerful adaptive technique our hominid ancestors probably utilized to help them continue to function at a survival level whenever they faced conditions of extreme environmental or social stress.

The birth process itself can generate extreme stress. The pain, strength, and intensity of contractions can leave a laboring woman floundering. This natural and sometimes chaotic process is also stressful for medical personnel. Obstetrical routines can structure the birth process to fit accepted cognitive categories and to make birth happen in an orderly way, thereby providing cognitive anchors for both laboring women and their hospital attendants.

Order, Formality, and a Sense of Inevitability   Order is the dominant mode in ritual. Its exaggerated precision and careful adherence to form and pattern set ritual apart from other modes of social interaction, enabling ritual to establish an atmosphere that feels both inevitable and inviolate. One would find it hard to imagine, for example, interrupting a church service to argue with the minister. According to Moore and Myerhoff:

> In its repetition and order, ritual imitates the rhythmic imperatives of the biological and physical universe, thus suggesting a link with the perpetual processes of the cosmos. It thereby implies the permanence and legitimacy of what are actually evanescent cultural constructs. (1977:8)

To perform a series of rituals is to feel oneself locking onto a set of cosmic gears which will safely and inevitably crank the individual right on through the perceived danger to safety on the other side. The Trobriand sea fisherman who makes elaborate offerings and incantations in precise order before embarking into perilous waters believes that, if he does his part with precision, so must the gods of the sea do their part to bring him safely home (Malinowski 1954).

The establishment of such a sense of inevitability is particularly important in the performance of obstetrical procedures. Although a culture may do its best through ritual to make the world appear to fit its belief system, reality may occasionally perforate the culture's protective filter of categories and threaten to upset the whole conceptual system. When obstetricians and nurses see babies being born and dying in spite of their predictions and technologies, they know that ultimate control over birth is beyond them, and they recognize their powerlessness in the face of birth's mysteries. In such circumstances, humans have always used ritual—often in the form of elaborate prayers or religious sacrifice, as a means of giving themselves the courage to carry on. Serving this purpose, the initial performance of many of the obstetrical procedures analyzed in Chapter 3 often entails the application of other procedures, providing a strong sense of cultural order as imposed on and superior to natural chaos.

Acting, Stylization, and Staging Ritual's set-apartness is enhanced by the fact that it is usually highly stylized and self-consciously acted, like a part in a play. According to Moore and Myerhoff, "These qualities of acting, stylization, and staging enable ritual to command the attention of participants and audience, while at the same time serving to deflect questioning and/or the presentation of alternative points of view" (1977:7). Its stylization thus enhances the inevitable and inviolate atmosphere that ritual seeks to establish.

Affectivity and Intensification Behavioral psychologists have long understood that people are far more likely to remember events, and to absorb lessons from those events, if they carry an emotional charge. Recent research in the health sciences has succeeded in defining the physiological chain of events through which emotional learning takes place:

> Memory is created in a highly charged emotional experience due to a registering of significance through the limbic system of the brain. . . . [Out of the

ordinary experiences] are transferred electrochemically (acetylcholine is the neurotransmitter) through the hippocampus which acts as a bridge between the limbic system and long-term memory storage. If events are not perceived as carrying value or significance to the individual, the data is kept approximately seven hours, never to be encoded in long-term memory storage. (Peterson and Mehl 1984:194)

The repetitious bombardment of ritual participants with symbolic messages will often intensify toward a climax, working to create the high emotional charge that ensures long-term memory storage. As Victor Turner has shown, the rhythmic intensification of the ritual performance can produce "a concentration so extreme that there is a loss of self-consciousness, and a feeling of 'flow'" (1977:36–52). Neurophysiologist d'Aquili postulates that this feeling of flow results from the simultaneous discharge of both subsystems of the autonomic nervous system mentioned above. He states:

> The ecstatic state and sense of union produced by ritual are usually very brief (often lasting only a few seconds) and may often be described as no more than a shiver running down the back at a certain point. This experience may, however, be repeated at numerous focal points during the ritual . . . [and is available] to many or most participants. (1979:177–178)

In simpler terms, we experience this "shiver down the back" feeling during a ritual when our physical and emotional experiences of the symbolic messages we are receiving become one—when, for example, the goose bumps pop out as we stand to salute the banner-bearing choir marching down the aisle on Easter Sunday, or the American flag passing by in a parade.

Their rhythmic repetition, evocative style, and "precise manipulation of symbols and sensory stimuli" (Moore and Myerhoff 1977:7) enable collective rituals, including those of hospital birth, to focus the emotions of participants on the calculated intensification of their messages. The intensification of rituals performed on the laboring woman as the moment of birth approaches parallels the natural intensification of the labor process, increasing the affectivity that this state naturally produces, and enhancing the chances that the symbolic messages conveyed by these rituals will be stored in long-term memory.

Cognitive Transformation   The goal of most initiatory rites of passage is the profound cognitive transformation of the initiates. Less shattering kinds of transformation can be said to occur in *all* types of ritual. The ritual handshake and "hello, how are you?" open a previously nonexistent channel of communication between two individuals, resulting in almost immediate "entrainment" of their bodily rhythms (Condon and Sander 1974). But ritual's true potential for transformation, of course, goes much deeper than this example, entailing profound possibilities for individual interior change.

Transformation for ritual participants occurs when "symbol and object seem to fuse and are experienced as a perfectly undifferentiated whole . . . and insight, belief and emotion are called into play, altering our conceptions . . . at a stroke" (Moore and Myerhoff 1977:13). When a ritual succeeds at triggering this type of profound cognitive transformation, the individual's entire cognitive structure will eventually reorganize itself around the newly internalized symbolic complex—a process better known to students of religion as a "conversion experience." (Such profound transformations must usually be preceded by the cognitive simplification described above.)

In hospital birth, as I will argue in Chapter 3, this fusion occurs when reality as presented by obstetrical procedures, and reality as perceived by the birthing woman become one and the same, thereby making her birthing process one of cognitive, as well as physiological, transformation. Alternatively, if this perceptual fusion never occurs during the woman's labor and delivery, or if it preexists entry into the hospital, her cognitive transformation during birth may have more to do with individual empowerment (by "empowerment," I mean enhancement of the individual's self-image and sense of personal capability) than cultural entrainment (see Chapter 5).

Preservation of the Status Quo   Through explicit enactment of a culture's belief system, ritual works both to preserve and to transmit that belief system, and so becomes an important force in the preservation of the status quo in any society. Thus one usually finds that those in power in a given social group have unique control over ritual performances. They utilize ritual's tremendous effectiveness as a didactic mechanism to reinforce both their own importance, and the importance of the belief and value system that sustains them in their positions (Burns and Laughlin 1979:264). In Chapter 2, we will briefly investigate the historical process by which physicians, notably obstetricians, gained control over birth rituals and utilized this control to institutionalize and augment their self-defined positions in society as the only people capable of maintaining cultural control over the birth process.

Effecting Social Change Paradoxically, ritual, with all of its insistence on continuity and order, can be an important factor not only in individual transformation but also in social change (Geertz 1957; Turner 1969, 1974). New belief and value systems are most effectively spread through new rituals designed to enact and transmit them. Even if a ritual is being performed for the very first time, "its stylistic rigidities and its internal repetitions of form or content make it tradition-like" (Moore and Myerhoff 1977:9), thus giving entirely new belief systems the feel and flavor of being strongly entrenched and sanctioned by ancient tradition. Moreover, entrenched belief and value systems are most effectively altered through alterations in the rituals that enact them. Indeed, ritual represents one of society's greatest potentials for the kind of revitalization that comes from internal growth and change in response to changing circumstances (Wallace 1966).

Since the 1960s childbirth activists have been involved in efforts to transform many of the technocratic rituals through which hospital birth is conducted into rituals that enact a more humanized view of birth and the female body. At the same time, advocates of home birth have been working to create entirely new rituals for birth—rituals that enact profoundly alternative beliefs about the nature of both birth and reality itself. Often operating in conflict with the use of ritual by those in positions of control to maintain the status quo, such groups are actively engaged in tapping the alternative power of ritual to effect social change and expand our options for cultural diversity in both practice and belief. Some of their efforts will be investigated in Chapters 4 and 9.

RITES OF PASSAGE

A rite of passage is a series of rituals designed to conduct an individual (or group) from one social state or status to another, thereby effecting transformations both in society's perceptions of the individual and in the individual's perception of her- or himself (van Gennep 1966; Turner 1967, 1969).

Ritual's role in rites of passage is fourfold:

1. To give humans a sense of control over natural processes that may be beyond their control, by making it appear that natural transformations (e.g., birth, puberty, death) are actually effected by society and serve society's ends (Malinowski 1954).

2. To "fence in" the dangers perceived cross-culturally to be present in transitional periods (when individuals are in between social categories and therefore call the conceptual reality of those categories into question), while at the same time allowing controlled access to their energizing and revitalizing power (Douglas 1966; Abrahams 1973).

3. To convey, through the emotions and the body, a series of repetitious and unforgettable messages to the initiate concerning the core values of the society into which he or she is being initiated through the carefully structured manipulation of appropriately representative symbols, and thereby to integrate those values, as well as the basic premises of the belief system on which they are based, into the inmost being of the initiate (Turner 1967, 1969). As Abrahams says, "what distinguishes a full-blown rite from all other ritualized behaviors is the number of [central symbols] resorted to, and the willingness—indeed the felt necessity—to repeat so often the message of the enactment through these [central symbols]" (1973:24).

4. To renew and revitalize these values for those conducting, as well as for those participating in or merely watching, the rituals through which these transformations are effected, so that both the perpetuation and the vitality of the belief and value system of the society in question can be assured (Turner 1967, 1969; Geertz 1973; Abrahams 1973).

Rites of passage generally consist of three principal stages, outlined by van Gennep as: (1) separation of the individuals involved from their preceding social state; (2) a period of transition in which they are neither one thing nor the other; (3) a reintegration phase in which through various rites of incorporation they are absorbed into their new social state (1966). Van Gennep states that these three stages may be of varying degrees of importance, with rites of separation generally emphasized at funerals, and rites of incorporation at weddings.

Yet the most salient feature of all rites of passage is their transitional nature, the fact that they always involve what Victor Turner (1967, 1979) has called "liminality," the stage of being betwixt and between, neither here nor there—no longer part of the old and not yet part of the new. In the "liminal phase" of initiatory rites of passage, "the ritual subject passes through a realm that has few or none of the attributes of the past or coming state" (1979:237). Of this liminal phase, Turner writes:

> The passivity of neophytes to their instructors, their malleability, which is increased by submission to ordeal, their reduction to a uniform condition,

are signs of the process whereby they are ground down to be fashioned anew and endowed with additional powers to cope with their new station in life. . . . It is the ritual and the esoteric teaching which grows girls and makes men. . . . The arcane knowledge, or "gnosis" obtained in the liminal period is felt to change the inmost nature of the neophyte, impressing him, as a seal impresses wax, with the characteristics of his new state. It is not a mere acquisition of knowledge, but a change in being. (1979:238–239)

One of the chief characteristics of this *liminal,* or transitional period of any rite of passage is the gradual psychological "opening" of the initiates to profound interior change. In many initiation rites involving major transitions into new social roles, this openness is achieved through rituals designed to break down the initiates' belief system—the internal mental structure of concepts and categories through which they perceive and interpret the world and their relationship to it. Ritual techniques that facilitate this process include *hazing*—the imposition of physical and mental hardships (familiar to participants in fraternity initiation rites), and *strange-making*—making the commonplace strange by juxtaposing it with the unfamiliar (Abrahams 1973). A third such device, *symbolic inversion,* works by metaphorically turning specific elements of this belief system upside-down or inside-out, so that the high is brought low, and the low is raised high, and the world in general is thrown into confusion (Babcock 1978:13–32):

As this process is continued over time, the cognitive reality model begins to disintegrate. Learned versions of reality and previously instrumental responses repeatedly fail the initiate. Confusion and disorganization ensue . . . introducing a relatively entropic state. At this point the individual should be searching for a way to structure or make sense out of reality, and in terms of the initiation, his search constitutes the launching point for the transformation of identity. (McManus 1979*b*:239)

The breakdown of their belief systems leaves initiates profoundly open to new learning and to the construction of new categories. Any symbolic messages conveyed to an initiate during this opening process can thus be imprinted on his or her psyche as deeply "as a seal impresses wax" (Turner 1979:239).

For example, in the rite of passage of Marine basic training, the initiate's normal patterns of action and thought are turned topsy-turvy. He is made strange to himself: his head is shaved, so that he does not even recognize himself in the mirror. He must give up his clothes, those expressions of individual identity and personality, and put on a uniform indistinguishable from that of other initiates. Constant and apparently meaningless hazing (e.g., orders to dig ditches and then fill them up) break down his cognitive structure. Then through repetitive and highly symbolic rituals (such as sleeping with his rifle), his physical habits and patterns of thought are literally reorganized into alignment with the basic values, beliefs, and practices of the Marines.

Cross-culturally, the most prominent type of rites of passage are those dealing with life crises. They accompany what Lloyd Warner has called

> the movement of a man [sic] through his lifetime, from a fixed placental placement within his mother's womb to his death and ultimate fixed point of his tombstone . . . punctuated by a number of critical moments of transition which all societies ritualize and publicly mark with suitable observances to impress the significance of the individual and the group on living members of the community. These are the important times of birth, puberty, marriage and death. (1959:303)

The sequence of these life-crisis events which Warner uses refers to the baby's birth and not to the *woman's* giving birth nor to *her* transition into motherhood. Thus this sequence reveals a strong male bias that may be one reason for the general anthropological overlooking of the significance of the rites of childbirth across cultures. Arranged from a female-oriented physiological perspective, the sequence would have to read: birth, puberty, marriage, childbearing, menopause, death.

Arnold van Gennep, pioneer of the anthropological study of rites of passage, did not fail to recognize the importance of childbirth as a rite of passage for the woman. In 1908, he stated:

> The ceremonies of pregnancy and childbirth together generally constitute a whole. Often the first rites performed separate the pregnant woman from society. . . . [T]hey are followed by rites pertaining to pregnancy itself, which is a transitional period. Finally come the rites of childbirth intended to reintegrate the woman into groups to which she previously belonged, or to establish her new position in society as a mother, especially if she has given birth to her first child. . . . [T]he return to ordinary life is rarely made all at once; it too is accomplished in stages reminiscent of initiation steps. Thus the mother's transitional period continues beyond the moment of delivery, and its duration varies among different peoples. The first transitional period of childhood . . . is grafted to its latter stages. (1966:41–43)

In the following chapter I discuss the three stages of separation, transition, and integration of the pregnancy/childbirth rite of passage into motherhood, in order to demonstrate (1) why I consider the three seemingly separate events of pregnancy, birth, and the newborn phase of motherhood to be part of one single rite of passage; (2) the significance of this oneness for the pregnant woman, namely, that during birth she is at the most intensely liminal and sacred—and therefore at once powerful and vulnerable—phase of the rite; and (3) the gradually intensifying nature of the relationship between this rite of passage and the American medical system. Although the focus of this book is on the rituals of hospital birth, this overview of the stages of the entire rite is presented as part of the cultural and individual context in terms of which these hospital birth rituals must be understood.

One Year

*The Stages of the Pregnancy/Childbirth
Rite of Passage*

I didn't know I was an adult until I had a child.
—Linda Moore

SEPARATION: "OH MY GOD, I THINK I'M PREGNANT!"

The phase during which the newly pregnant woman gradually separates herself from her former social identity has its beginnings in her very first flutterings of conscious awareness of the possibility of pregnancy. For a time she will probably live with the intensely personal experience of the wondering; finally, wary of misinterpreting what her body tells her, she will usually seek the scientific confirmation of the drugstore test. If the results convince her, her next moves will usually be to tell the baby's father and call the doctor, not always in that order.[1]

The first days of beyond-a-doubt pregnancy will be ones of inner turmoil—maybe excitement, maybe anguish, certainly some panic and much self-questioning. Already her conception of self is being tested—her body is doing things on its own, and she must cope with her total lack of control over these changes. By the time she has fully accepted the reality of her pregnancy and gone public with the news, neither she nor those close to her will see her quite as they did before.

That this separation process is a structurally discrete phase of the pregnancy/childbirth rite of passage can be understood by a look at the steadily increasing number of women who opt for amniocentesis (a medical test in which the amniotic fluid is drawn out with a needle and tested for evidence of genetic defects). These women experience separation phases that are considerably longer than usual, for the amnio-centesis can only take place in the fourth month of pregnancy. In her recent study of the psychological effects of amniocentesis, *Tentative Pregnancy* (1986), Barbara Katz Rothman documents the agonizingly uncertain attitudes these women must take toward their pregnancies until the test results are in. For if the tests indicate genetic defects, most women will opt for abortion. To say that the long period of waiting on the test results can drag out the length of the separation phase considerably is not mere academic hairsplitting: the woman's full acceptance of her pregnancy, or lack of it, can have a definite effect on her relationship with the baby and on her ability to psychologically prepare herself for birth and motherhood (Bowen 1983; Chamberlain 1983; Rothman 1986). Thus, this process of separation from her former structural identity can be considered complete only after the woman herself has fully accepted the pregnancy.

TRANSITION: PREGNANCY AS TRANSFORMATION

One interesting thing about pregnancy viewed from a Turnerian perspective is that it is both a state *and* a becoming. (Webster's gives the etymology of "pregnant" as L. *praegnans—prae* "before," *gnans* "being born," and defines pregnancy as "the state of being pregnant." Translated literally, that would be "the state of being before being born.")

The liminal phase of pregnancy, this lengthy "state of being before being born," can be best understood as lasting from the woman's final acceptance of her pregnancy until three to six weeks after her baby's birth. During this phase the pregnant woman fully experiences the cultural overlays on her physiological process of becoming a mother.

John McManus (1979a) discusses "*alternation*" between models of reality, and "*resolution*"—ultimate acceptance of the model of reality presented by ritual—as chronological features of ritual transformation; and indeed these processes are so experienced by pregnant women. "Becoming mothers" in this society usually find themselves living out their pregnancies in near-constant alternation between the contradictory paradigms (in the sense of "model of reality") of pregnancy extant in several different and clearly separate experiential domains, which I have labeled *personal, public, medical, formally educative,* and *peer group* (Davis-Floyd 1983). Each domain will present the pregnant woman

with a different type of ritual and symbolic response to the physiological reality of pregnancy, which will be based on the paradigm of
pregnancy and birth peculiar to that domain. These often-conflicting
perceptions offer the pregnant woman a set of possibilities from which
to choose how she will interpret her own unique experience of becoming a mother. Her ultimate resolution of these paradigmatic conflicts,
as we will discuss in Chapter 5, will be heavily influenced by the type
of rituals which ultimately surround and shape her perceptions of her
birth experience.

TRANSFORMATION IN THE PERSONAL DOMAIN

> Suddenly, everything is so different! I don't know
> who I am any more.
>
> —Elise Pearsall

What Turner calls liminality, pregnant women experience as a sense
of change, of growth, of detachment, fear, wonder, awe, curiosity,
hope, specialness, simultaneous alienation from and closeness to themselves and their families, irritation, frustration, exhaustion, resentment,
joy—and a trembling sense of unknown, unknowable potentiality. Inner emotional and physiological transformations are reflected almost
daily in outward changes. Old habits and patterns drop off and new
ones develop as pregnant women struggle to find new ways of doing
something as simple as tying their shoelaces, and as complex as balancing their increasing needs for peace and emotional support with the
daily demands of their marriages and careers.

Rapid psychological growth and change are possible in pregnancy
as they are not in usual structural life. Psychologists have noted the ease
and speed with which pregnant women can benefit from psychothera-
peutic techniques (Brazelton 1973; Peterson 1981), for the near-constant inner and outer flux of pregnancy keeps the category systems of
pregnant women in a continuous state of upheaval as old ways of thinking change to include new life. For example, growing a baby inside, as
well as mothering a newborn, puts a woman in much closer touch with
her own childhood experiences, allowing old, deeply buried thoughts
and emotions to surface. Hopes and fears from the past and for the future merge at the surface of her daily consciousness, as time compresses
in the physical experience of pregnancy, and past, present, and future
together are carried in her womb.

Because of the psychological state of openness and receptivity that pregnancy tends to induce, the manner and direction of a woman's personal transformation is very likely to be heavily influenced by the sort of treatment she encounters in the public domain.

TRANSFORMATION IN THE PUBLIC DOMAIN

Is it just my imagination, or is everyone staring at
my tummy?
—Suzanne Gladstone

In order to understand better the cultural and individual significance of pregnancy as a liminal process of becoming, we need only recall that in our society pregnancy has but recently been accepted as appropriate to the public domain. Before World War II, pregnant women were examples of the "structural invisibility of liminal personae" (Turner 1979:236)—very nearly as hedged about with ritual and tabu as Turner's Ndembu initiates. They were expected to remain secluded in their homes, as their presentation in public was somehow felt to be improper. When in public their pregnancy was to be disguised. Even the word "pregnant" was too pregnant to be used. Just as people did not die, but "went to sleep" or "passed away," pregnant women were "with child," "p.g.," "in the family way," "expecting," or "baking a bun in the oven." The mysterious procreative powers of nature, made undeniably manifest in the visibly pregnant woman, were apparently too threatening to a society that wanted to believe it had ultimate control. These euphemisms helped to mask the fact that it is nature, not society, that controls the creation of new human beings. Moreover, the pregnant woman, unlike all other human beings, holds two individuals in one body. This undeniable but highly anomalous phenomenon of nature refutes at least two of our culture's most powerfully held categories—the cultural idea of one individual per body, and the mathematical law that one does not equal two. As the Ndembu youth, no longer boy and not yet man, is both sacred and contaminating to society, so the pregnant woman, neither childless nor mother, public proof of a sexuality properly kept private, walking representative of nature in a culture that seeks to deny nature's power, structurally resident in a liminal period for nearly one whole year, still crosses too many categories for comfort.

In the last four decades pregnancy has "come out of the closet."

Today we see pregnant women everywhere, from the classroom to the executive office, from the night club to the formal dinner, and it is only a few old die-hards who mutter under their breath about unseemly display, or raise eyebrows at Loretta Lynn singing "Pregnant Again" on "The Tonight Show." Concurrent with this rise to respectability has been pregnancy's redefinition from a private and feminine to a public and medical event (Rothman 1982:29; Oakley 1984). (In the United States, in 1900, "less than 5% of women delivered in hospitals . . . by 1939 half of all women and 75% of all urban women were delivering in hospitals" [Wertz and Wertz 1989:133]. Today, the figure is 99 percent [Pritchard et al. 1985:xx].) As the rites and rituals of pregnancy and childbirth have been moved out of the home and away from the tutelage of the pregnant woman's family and midwife, and into doctor's offices and hospitals, the announcement has been made to society-at-large that these forces of nature are now "under control," and society has lost some of its fear of them. Yet, though accepted as a state, pregnancy as a "becoming" is still tabu-laden and ritually hedged, only now the tabus are cast as medical necessities, and the rituals are thought of as scientific or educational procedures pertaining to the state. In other words, I suggest that pregnancy's recent rise to status and respectability serves to disguise the still forceful perception of it as a ritual process.

Turner stresses that an important aspect of liminal phenomena is that their symbols tend to have common emotional meanings for all members of a given group (1968:2). A common experience of the women in my study was that in the public domain, the visible physical fact of pregnancy frequently turns women into symbolic objects. Many find that their public symbolic transformation is sometimes negative. Some men, formerly friendly, begin to avoid them as their bellies grow, occasionally admitting openly that the big stomach embarrasses them. Some women find that during conversations, people stare at their stomachs instead of their faces, increasing their sense of being made into objects. Sometimes it is other women who withdraw, viewing the pregnant one as a symbol of female subjugation by males or as a slave to her own body and to the forces of nature.

Other common experiences, mostly seen as positive, are of being viewed as Mother Nature Personified, as the Venus of Willendorf (i.e., as a fertility symbol), as Earth Mother, or as representing Motherhood or the Essence of Womanhood, or the Creative Force at Work in the Universe, the Future Incarnate, the Continuation of Mankind, the Mystical Union of the Male and Female Principles, Yin and Yang, the Oneness of Humankind. Many pregnant women eventually come to perceive *themselves* in one or another of these ways:

> I enjoyed it. People treat you very special—you'll notice that. That's fun, a lot of fun. And the glow. I don't know if I believe that but there were quite a few people who say there is a special glow, you can just tell. Well, and sometimes I could look at myself in the mirror, and I would be feeling really in touch with my body, in touch with my baby, and I could sort of see what they mean. (Patricia Hellman)

> One of the days we were there, I went out into the ocean by myself. It was a glorious day, and I just settled deep into the water and the sand, and let the waves lift me and float me around. All of a sudden I became aware of the baby in my womb, floating in his own salty water in the amniotic sac. I had such a powerful sensation—how can I describe it? It was a real physical sensation of the water within and without, and the life within and without— I was in the water, inside of the ocean—inside of the womb of the earth, my mother, and the baby inside of me was in that same water—I felt like the child and the mother of the universe all at once. For just a few moments, I felt totally at one with myself, my child, the water and the earth—I really physically experienced the unity of all of life. (Elizabeth Davis)

Reinforcing these perceptions of specialness is the behavior of men (and sometimes other women), who rush to open doors and pick up dropped coins, who tote suitcases across the airport and give up seats on the bus, sometimes sheepishly admitting that nowadays pregnant women are the only ones to whom a man can safely offer his chivalric services. Apparently pregnancy increases the force of the stereotype of the weak female, or at least combines it with the cultural tabu against women lifting and carrying heavy things. The combination seems to open the door to a chivalry nowadays oft-suppressed. To these sorts of ministrations, the barely showing pregnant woman may at first react with scorn and disgust. Pregnancy has not weakened her one bit, and "I can carry my own suitcase, thank you!"

But by the seventh or eighth month, whether delighted or simply resigned to the inevitable, she has adapted to her new symbolic status and the social rituals that accompany it. She probably no longer even flinches when strangers reach out to pat her stomach, having learned and accepted the social reality that her belly is now a part of the public interactional domain. She may come to regard with more sympathy those who avoid her—sometimes she would like to avoid herself! Many pregnant women find it ultimately very comforting to adopt and utilize the cultural beliefs encoded in the symbols thrust upon them as a framework within which to conceptualize and interpret their new physical realities.[2] This process seemed to become an integral part of their rite of passage, of their separation from their former conceptions of self, as anthropologist Michelle Rosaldo described:

> One thing that struck me was how, when pregnant, an aspect of taboo/liminal status was becoming, as it were, public property: in a shoe store, the saleswoman told me not to buy stack heels; hands-on-tummy; concern (don't reach, lift); then "your baby will get a cold if you don't put a hat on" when I was walking; comments/concern around my failure to observe the seclusion rule on return from the hospital . . . the "end" of it all was that loss of the public eye, the recognition that pregnant women no longer looked at me and my baby and smiled. (Personal correspondence, Sept. 15, 1981)

TRANSFORMATION IN THE MEDICAL DOMAIN

The first time I heard the heart beating through that
thing he put on my tummy, I thought I would die from
the joy.

— Sandra Kowalski

The paradigm of pregnancy dominant in the medical domain is the technocratic model of pregnancy and birth, which is explicated in detail in Chapter 2. Implicit in this model are the assumptions that the baby develops mechanically and involuntarily inside the woman's body, that the doctor is in charge of the baby's proper development and growth, and that the doctor will deliver (produce) the baby at the time of birth. Although the vast majority of their pregnant time is lived out in the personal, public, or peer group domains, most American women experience this medical paradigm as providing the overarching conceptual and structural framework for their experience of pregnancy, whether or not they espouse its basic tenets.

Thus, the pregnant woman will seek official confirmation of her pregnancy from her obstetrician and will mark its progress in routine monthly visits to his office. She will be reassured when he[3] assists her to hear her baby's heartbeat. She will tell the doctor when she first feels the baby move, and he will tell her that she is now halfway through the pregnancy. Her first baby picture will be from the ultrasound machine in his office, which may also tell her whether she carries a girl or a boy. She will eagerly await the due date her physician sets with his standardized formula (even if she is sure the baby was not conceived when the chart says it must have been). As her due date approaches, her visits to the obstetrician will intensify to every two weeks or more. If the due date comes and goes with no sign of labor, she will grow increasingly anxious with each passing day in which she does not conform to standardized expectations. If she goes more than two weeks past her official due date (one week, in some places), her labor will be artificially induced. She will call the doctor when labor begins, enter the hospital for labor, birth, and the early neonatal period, and take the baby to the pediatrician at around one week of age to make sure he or she is all right. Finally, she will go for a postnatal checkup at the obstetrician's office six weeks after the birth.

Because pregnant women perceive these events as *the* defining, or framing (Goffman 1974) elements of their experience, from a rite of passage perspective it becomes clear that doctors in this society have taken on the role of the ritual elder in many cross-cultural initiation rites, with one important difference. Among the Ndembu whom Turner studied, the primary role of the elders is to impress upon the youths undergoing initiation into manhood the sacred knowledge about themselves and the cosmos they inhabit that is felt to be necessary to their ultimate competence and self-responsibility as full members of society. Eliade describes this knowledge as follows:

> Every primitive society possesses a consistent body of mythical traditions, a "conception of the world," and it is this conception that is gradually revealed to the novice in the course of his initiation. What is involved is not simply instruction in the modern sense of the word. In order to become worthy of the sacred teaching, the novice must first be prepared spiritually. For what he learns concerning the world and human life does not constitute knowledge in the modern sense of the term, objective and compartmentalized information, subject to indefinite correction and addition. (1975: 27–28)

Instead, what the initiate learns constitutes the formation of a subjective inner state that is the result of the transformative rituals performed throughout the course of the initiatory rite of passage; these rituals produce "not a mere acquisition of knowledge, but a change in being. [The initiate's] apparent passivity is revealed as an absorption of powers which will become active after his social status has been redefined in the aggregation rites" (Turner 1979:239).

However, a necessary condition for the initiate's absorption of sacred knowledge is the elders' willingness to impart it to him. Although our physicians are quite willing to exercise the authority accruing to this ritual elder role, and to effect through their birth rituals a true "change in being," it is the experience of many pregnant women that these physicians seem reluctant at best to impart the sort of empowering knowledge that pregnant women are most desirous of receiving. Commonly, pregnant women are not even allowed access to the information recorded on their own charts.[4]

Many women in American society have been socialized since early childhood to give more attention than they receive, to "go along" with an unpleasant situation rather than create a scene, to be "good" (Derber 1979; Graebner 1975)—a set of characteristics that has much in common with the sort of patient behavior considered ideal by medical personnel (Beuf 1979; Parsons 1951). It never occurred to most of the women in my study to try to read their charts, even when they had pressing questions. Two women did report "sneaking a peek" while waiting in the examining room, and then feeling terribly guilty, as if they had no right to the esoteric information the charts contained. The intimacy of this information could not override the vast conceptual distance between the information and the women it directly concerns—a distance created by the clipboards, standardized charts, and technical jargon that symbolically shout "off limits" to the uninitiated. As Marx and Weber point out, the holders and guardians of traditional authority in society are often protective of the special knowledge and training that is supposed to legitimize authority; they have a vested interest in the continuing mystification of that knowledge (Gerth and Mills 1958: 233).

Of even greater relevance here, of course, is the deeper political and feminist issue of information as power, and of the centuries-old efforts of men in Western society to shut women out of access to intellectual sources of power by defining spheres of "authoritative knowledge" (Jordan 1989, 1990) and women's spheres of social activity as mutually exclusive (Dubois et al. 1985:25–28, 68–75; Ehrenreich and English 1973b; Wertz and Wertz 1989). Indeed, obstetrics had its beginnings in the exclusion of female midwives from male guilds that claimed exclusive access to esoteric knowledge and instruments such as forceps, presumed by men to be beyond women's intellectual abilities and physical skills (Donegan 1978:28–29; Donnison 1977). As we shall further investigate in Chapter 2, the attitudes and beliefs of these early "man-midwives" about the male's right to exclusive control over information regarding women's bodies and reproductive processes have been fundamental to the development of modern obstetrics.

One of the very first sensations experienced by most of the first-time mothers in my study was panic at the realization of their near-total lack of knowledge about birthing and babies. The quest for such knowledge can be identified as a major theme of their pregnancies. Yet it is significant that much of the knowledge they sought is *scientific knowledge about medical birth*. Most of these women seem to equate knowledge with *information*—to place their trust in intellectual knowledge, and not in intuitive, emotional, or bodily knowledge—and to equate only this sort of knowledge with power and control. Thus, for example, although a woman may "feel" or "just know" that she is pregnant, until objective science (the obstetrician or the drugstore test) confirms that knowledge, she isn't "sure."[5] One woman in my study "just knew" the sex of both of her children; no one believed her until ultrasound "proved" her right. This split between highly valued "objective" or "scientific" knowledge and culturally devalued internal knowledge is significant because it is precisely on these "lower" levels that obstetrical rituals work.

In the OB/GYN's office, women experience some of the effects of these rituals early on in their pregnancies. One brief example will suffice, an excerpt of one woman's description of her first visit to the "OB":

> They got me undressed; they laid me on the table and put my feet in the stirrups with a sheet over my knees, and told me the doctor would be in in a minute. After they left the room, I sat up. When one of the nurses came back in, she said, "You sat back up!" I said, "I'm not about to meet a doctor lying down." (Melinda Simpson)

This particular doctor's response to Melinda's questions about his management of the birth process was, "Don't you worry about a thing—I'll take care of everything. All you have to do is trust me." Although many obstetricians do try to answer all questions, their practices are usually structured in such a way as to render lengthy discussions either difficult or impossible (Mendelsohn 1981; Carver 1984). Most pregnant women in my study were keenly aware that they needed to learn, to mature, to be more in command of themselves and their lives in order to prepare to be responsible for the life of another. Realizing that the knowledge that is respected, that enables one to be a competent player of our cultural game, is primarily factual and intellectual in nature, these women turned to the formally educative domain of books, and of classes in "childbirth education."

TRANSFORMATION IN THE FORMALLY
EDUCATIVE DOMAIN: PREGNANCY AS
A QUEST FOR KNOWLEDGE

> I read everything I could get my hands on!
> —Jan Jones

> I read so that I would *know*. When [I found out]
> this baby was breech, I checked out every single book
> that had anything about a breech delivery. I got hold
> of a nursing manual and found out what kind of for-
> ceps they use to deliver the head. . . . Everything, so
> that when they came at me with something I wouldn't
> be stupid and not know what was going on. And also
> I knew what my options were. . . . What I could have
> and what would be best and all that.
> —Debbie Kelso

Childbirth education classes, in which women *do* receive much of
the technical information they seek, have become an integral part of
the pregnancy/childbirth rite of passage for many American women
(Rothman 1981, 1982; Sargent and Stark 1989). Occurring as they do
during the last six or seven weeks of the pregnancy, they constitute the
beginning of the cultural process of ritual intensification which will culminate in the birth of the child. In this intensification, these classes are
paralleled by, and counterbalance, the intensified frequency of visits to
the obstetrician in late pregnancy. The focus of childbirth educators in
general is on providing the pregnant woman and her partner with as
much knowledge and advance preparation for childbirth as they desire
to receive. In so doing, childbirth educators can either foster independence of thought in pregnant women, or socialize them further into the
technocratic model (see Chapter 4). In general, classes taught in hospitals are geared toward such socialization; in the words of one Centertown hospital instructor:

> I just want my couples to have as good a hospital experience as possible, so
> I make sure they understand everything that's going to happen to them so
> they won't be shocked or scared. If I talked too much about alternatives, I
> would just set them up with expectations that are not going to get fulfilled.
> Besides, I like this job and I don't want to lose it.

Some out-of-hospital classes do tend to present alternatives and to encourage women not to be passive recipients of hospital procedures.

Whatever their orientation, from a rite-of-passage perspective childbirth education classes play several other important roles besides that of intellectual preparation for birth: (1) they draw the pregnant woman's partner or husband into increased participation in her (and his own) transformative process, thus serving the same functions as rituals of "couvade" in many primitive societies; (2) they focus the attention of the pregnant woman and her partner on the supremely transformative upcoming event of birth, thereby heightening their awareness of the impending transition; as July Saunders put it, "Lamaze classes help you get to your high"; (3) they provide the pregnant couple with a wider network of couples in the same liminal stage as they, thereby increasing their opportunities for socializing one another into the shared experience of pregnancy; (4) they provide the pregnant woman with a cognitive matrix in terms of which she can interpret and make sense out of the often bewildering events of late pregnancy, labor, and birth; (5) they furnish her with specialized breathing techniques and other rituals that she can utilize to ground herself within this cognitive matrix during labor. This cognitive matrix and its accompanying rituals enable the pregnant woman and her partner to make their passage into parenthood without the psychologically disruptive fear that so often accompanies the journeys of new parents into the painful physiological unknowns of labor and birth.

When pregnant women turn to the formally educative domain for their individual empowerment through knowledge, one of the first things they encounter is the wide range of paradigms for pregnancy now available in childbirth education classes and the burgeoning literature about pregnancy and birth. "Childbirth without fear," "painless childbirth," "husband-coached childbirth," "natural childbirth," "prepared childbirth," "assertive childbirth," "wholistic childbirth," "spiritual childbirth," and "active birth" are but a few of the paradigms on bookstore shelves and in telephone directories through which women can choose to interpret their pregnancy and birth experiences. Some of these contrasting approaches will be analyzed in Chapter 4. For our purposes here, the one critical factor common to all of these paradigms is that they tend to present the pregnant woman with a preformulated *ideal* of what childbirth could and therefore should be like. Faced with such a bewildering array of conceptual choices, many pregnant women turn to the peer domain for emotional support and the reassuring sense of perspective that can come only from those who have "been through the fire, and survived":

We read. Dan would go to the library every month and he would get five or ten books and we would read them all. So we did a tremendous amount of reading the first three or four months. I pretty much knew what I wanted by then. We had Lamaze classes. I talked to friends. That is another place that I got information. They told me how it was at City Hospital and at Memorial, and I really got them to be specific. I wanted to hear from my friends that had been through labor—to tell me step by step just what it was like and what happened. So by the time that I actually had mine, I had heard probably ten to fifteen firsthand accounts. With the books that I read, with the classes, and with what they said, then I knew what to expect, and what I didn't want. You know, like IVs and a prep, episiotomy and stuff like that. It was all kind of gearing toward the natural way of having a child. Also, I just socialized more in general. I met more women for lunch. I reached out more to talk, especially about my pregnancy. (Patricia Hellman)

TRANSFORMATION IN THE PEER DOMAIN

One day early on in my pregnancy, it dawned on me that I was actually going to have a baby. Shortly after that I realized with a thud that I didn't know anything about babies, much less about having them. And so I thought, well who is there to talk to who does know? And then I realized that I didn't even know *anyone* who had a baby.

At a party I discovered that a woman I had just been introduced to had a two-year-old. As I confessed my fears and my sense of isolation, she smiled. "Don't worry," she said. "There's an underground network of mothers in this town, and you'll find it!"

—Elise Pearsall

Victor Turner places great emphasis on the collective, shared nature of liminality. That special, spontaneous unity shared by those initiates who pass through the ritual process together, Turner calls *communitas* (1969, 1979). Although this concept is useful as a takeoff point from which to begin to understand the nature of the special bond shared by women who are "pregnant together," it does not carry over completely, as the relationships between these women tend to be much more structural than Turner's original use of the term implied.

Elise felt her sense of strong bonding with other pregnant women as a "secret sisterhood," Michelle as a "special sense of sharing." Janice said, "It's like belonging to a private little club"; and Dee put it this way, "Whenever I saw another pregnant woman, and our eyes met, I knew that she knew that I knew—you know?—and we would smile."

Although the extent of this secret sisterhood as experienced by individual women seems to vary a great deal, it generally includes all pregnant women encountered, both strangers and friends, and usually extends to mothers of tiny infants as well. Some women reported experiencing this sense of bonded mutuality with mothers of young children, and a few reported feeling it for all women who had given birth, saying they felt their pregnancy placed them "on the other side" of womanhood in general. First-time mothers seemed to experience this feeling of community more intensely than others, often commenting with amazement on this unfamiliar sense of kinship with other mothers.

Cultures get created and spread through language. Pregnant women must know that, for they talk to each other—as much and as long as they can. First-time mothers, equal in their inexperience, search together for the means to cope with this suddenly topsy-turvy world. It becomes a common feature of their experience that two members of the sisterhood, even if mere chance-met strangers, will choose to discuss above all other topics the subjects of pregnancy, childbirth, and children, no matter who else is there or what else may be happening.

They rapidly learn the "pregnant people getting acquainted" ritual that replaces the standard "Hello, who are you, and what do you do?" It goes like this:

Look at belly, smile, raise eyes.

"How many months are you?"

"Seven."

"Gosh, you don't look it."

"I know, but I sure feel it."

"I know what you mean."

"When is yours due?"

"In April."

"Really—that's soon! What kind of delivery do you plan to have?"

"Well, we're taking Lamaze classes, but I don't know . . . "

"So are we! Who's your teacher/Who's your OB?"

"Really? What do you think of her/him?"

—and they're off.

What these women are engaged in is far from idle talk. It is the serious business of socializing each other into the culture of shared pregnancy, which also means helping each other to prepare for the birth. Ridington (1979) has shown how hunter-gatherers carry elaborate

technological knowledge in their heads as pattern, code, artifice instead
of artifact, and pass it on to others in story, symbol, and example. Just
so do women encode their growing knowledge of pregnancy and
childbirth in what Labov and Waletzky (1967) called "personal narratives"—especially and specifically narratives about the traumas of
pregnancy, the giving of birth, and life with the newborn. As a network
of mothers and mothers-to-be develops, these narratives become, as one
woman put it, part of the "repertory of the group" (see Chapter 5 for
examples).

Encoded in them is a vast amount of information, grounded in experience, which, in spite of its devaluation by physicians, can serve to
counterbalance the technocratic model of pregnancy and childbirth, as
well as the educative ideal (Bromberg 1981; Keeler 1984). Here we see
the dialogue between the official and the informal: "The doctor says
you're too fat? Don't worry, Sybil gained fifty pounds and lost it all in
two months." "Your teacher said you can't do Lamaze if you develop
toxemia? Well, I did, and it worked out just fine." In their study of 84
couples, Sargent and Stark confirm the importance of such informal interactions, stating that although "childbirth classes influenced responses
to delivery less than preexisting beliefs, values, and expectations . . .
personal experience and non-idealized accounts of birth by family and
friends do significantly affect orientations toward pregnancy, labor, and
delivery" (1989:41–42).[6]

About the only event in pregnancy that is generally recognized as an
important ritual in the United States is the baby shower usually given
for first-time pregnant women by a close relative or friend. Most of the
women in my study were given baby showers—usually these were attended by women only, but occasionally, in recognition of the transitional status of both parents, they would be couples' events. These
events carry tremendous emotional importance for the nascent mother.
Said Susan Jeffers:

> There's just nothing like it. There you are, hugely pregnant, surrounded by
> all your best friends and your mom and your aunt. And everybody is laugh-
> ing and bringing you tea and you open all these wonderful presents. It makes
> you feel so special, so loved and appreciated. And you know these people
> will love and appreciate this new life you are bringing as well.

Elise Pearsall agreed:

> I was so worried that no one would think to give me a baby shower that I
> flat out asked two of my best friends to do it. I knew I would be devastated

if no one acknowledged me that way. I love my women friends so much, and it was so important to me to have them all together with me to celebrate and to look forward to the birth of my child.

These baby showers are worthy of study in their own right. For one thing, they are forums for communication of accumulated childrearing strategies and wisdom. Many women consciously choose to give the items they personally found the most useful for their own newborns—the perfect diaper bag, the best baby swing, the most stimulating crib toy. And as the gift is opened, they will explain its rationale; the result is often an exchange of parenting strategies. Moreover, unlike the hand-knitted clothing of yesteryear, most of the gifts in today's baby showers are products of considerable technological sophistication. As such, they constitute a sort of grammar of modern baby-raising techniques, communicating not only the love with which they are given, but also cultural and individual notions about the appropriate roles of mother, father, and child in relation to one another. For example, gifts of plastic bottles and nipples acknowledge that even the breast-feeding mother will have to leave her baby in the care of others for parts of the day. Crib equipment, decorations for the baby's room, infant rockers, playpens, car seats, strollers, and teddy bears that play recorded womb sounds express the physical separation of mother and child generally taken as a given in our culture. In contrast, the gift of a cloth baby carrier encourages the physical contact typical of most non-Western cultures, suggesting that the mother will want to keep her baby close to her body for long periods of time. Subtle differences in economic status and class-related values are expressed through the choice of Luvs or Huggies over Pampers, Aprica over Perego strollers, whereas environmental awareness can be encouraged through gifts of cloth (instead of disposable) diapers and diaper covers.

Whatever the symbolic messages communicated by the gifts (and these deserve further investigation), the baby shower itself communicates strongly to the mother that she is loved, valued, and appreciated by her relatives and peers. Especially for most of the first-time mothers in my study, such acknowledgment was an important step in developing a sense of capability as a mother. The gifts themselves were generally perceived as enhancing this sense of preparedness and capability—to have the (culturally) necessary clothing and equipment available was, for most of them, an important prerequisite to psychological preparedness for the birth.

TRANSITION: BIRTH AS TRANSFORMATION

> After nine months of having fun being pregnant out
> in the world, I have to admit that walking into the
> hospital and putting on that gown was something of a
> shock.
>
> —Georgia Adams

Unlike the larger year-long rite of passage of which birth forms the climax, the birth process itself is rarely lived out in the public or peer domains; its cultural treatment is, with the exception of the early stages of labor, almost entirely medical. In this medicalization, we see a narrowing of the sets of symbols and meanings that our culture offers to pregnant women for interpreting their experiences to those representing the most essential core values and beliefs which form the conceptual basis of our society, and which, as will be discussed below, are represented by the medical profession.

Anthropologist and childbirth educator Sheila Kitzinger, after observing the cultural treatment of birth in many countries, noted that "in any society, the way a woman gives birth and the kind of care given to her point as sharply as an arrowhead to the key values in the culture" (1980:115). The high visibility of a society's key values, or *core values* (as they are usually referred to in anthropology) in birth rituals reflects birth's key importance to the future of that society. But birth is not enough to ensure a society's future. Full social members are not just naturally born; they must also be culturally made.

Socialization, according to John McManus, is "the imposition of culturally sanctioned beliefs, values and ways of acting upon the members of the social group." Through the socialization process, the world becomes known in a culturally acceptable way. "The task of socialization," McManus continues, "is to persuade or coerce each member of the society to accept the group-cognized environment and to follow the behavioral dicta implicit in that reality model" (1979b:229).

If the belief and value system of a given society—the "group-cognized environment"—is not passed on to its children, that society will undergo radical changes and/or will eventually cease to exist. In a sense, the birth process creates not just one but four new social members: the new baby, the woman who is reborn into the new social role of mother, the man reborn as father—and the new family unit they form. Each must be properly socialized to ensure cultural continuity. But because mothers are generally most responsible for socializing their children, their absorption of the "group-cognized environment" and its implicit behavioral dicta must be so thorough that they cannot help but teach those systems of behavior and cognition to their children simply by their patterns of daily living. Such unconscious and thorough absorption can be very effectively achieved by the cultural treatment of the woman during the "opening" process of birth.

The "opening" that occurs during birth is quite literal—a birthing woman's cervix must dilate to a diameter of ten centimeters in order for her baby to be born—while the stress, anxiety, and pain of the labor process are often enough in themselves to ensure simultaneous category breakdown and psychological opening. Many new mothers have commented on the reduced cognitive state and openness to outside suggestion which accompanies labor:

> Hesch (who never moved from his seat opposite me) suggested I deal with the contractions [of transition] by using two pants and a blow. That was the smartest thing I've ever heard in my life. I was impressed by how clever and insightful he was—it sounds silly, but that's just the way I felt: how clever an idea. That, I gather, is what they mean when they say you need strong direction during labor. (Rothman 1982:20)

The natural rhythmicity, intensification, and emotionality of the labor process is enough all by itself to put the laboring woman in a far more intensely affective state than all but the most grueling male initiation rites can produce. As those critical hours of transition and transformation open both her cervix and her category system, they render the becoming mother far more receptive to new messages than she will be before or after the birth. As is characteristic of liminal experiences, after the birth is over, the peculiar intensity of its feel and flavor will remain indelibly imprinted on the mother's mind and body:

> I think it was the height . . . the highest emotional experience I have ever had. When I knew they were born and I heard them cry, I could not speak. The two doctors who were there both times knew me. By the second one, they knew what the problem was. My throat would just catch and tears would come. I couldn't even get words out. It was just happiness beyond what I can explain. (Linda Perkins)

> It's amazing the power that experience has, that we remember it so clearly. I can still feel the emotions I felt on the operating table two years ago. And I have talked to other women whose daughters or sons are fifteen years old, and they will be telling me about their birth experiences fifteen years ago, and tears will come in their eyes—tears of joy, or tears of sorrow, whichever

it is. This one woman talked about how she gave birth in a Catholic hospital thirty years ago and how she was so lucky because they let her be awake and they didn't give her any drugs, they just loved her. And she said it was the most fantastic—the triumph of those moments when she pushed her baby out, and then reached down and caught it herself—well that triumph was still with her and her eyes were just shining, and then she started crying at the thought of it—thirty years later! (Elaine Johnstone)

I had a Cesarean too. That was forty years ago—imagine! And you know— I've never gotten over it. You're the first person that's asked me how I felt about it in years, but no, I've never gotten over it. I still remember that mask coming down over my face, and I still feel as angry as I did then, when I woke up. Those people took my birth away from me. I don't know why and I don't know how, but I've never felt the same about myself since. It's something I just can't—I just really don't understand it. (Joan Klimer)

By making the naturally transformative process of birth into a cultural rite of passage for the mother, a society can take advantage of her extreme openness to ensure that she will be imprinted with its most basic notions about the relationship of the natural to the cultural world as these two worlds meet in the act of birth. She will then indeed receive the knowledge she has been seeking—in the form of an enactment of the belief and value system of the society that she must help to perpetuate.

TRANSITION: THE IMMEDIATE POSTPARTUM PERIOD

Those newborn days—so beautiful, so special, so
scary. I would go from the top of the world to the bottom and then back to the top in seconds.
—Leah Wilson

To the feel and flavor of the birth experience, the days immediately following the birth add a special feeling of their own. Although the special intensity of these days does not match that of the birth itself, many women have noted their unique quality, saying that they long once again to experience that particular feeling of freshness and specialness. These newborn days often find the new-born mother experiencing a whole spectrum of new emotions engendered by her experience of childbirth (Eagan 1985). Sometimes relief, triumph, and joy combine with bewilderment and sorrow. Suffused with emotional rainbows, these first days are passed in partial seclusion in a hospital or at home, while to the rainbow are added whatever emotions the new baby arouses in the mother, along with the flowers, the gifts, and the ritual congratulations of friends. Even after their return home, most new mothers remain in partial seclusion[7] with their babes for some length of time, sometimes glowing, sometimes trembling, as they absorb the impact of their experiences and try to integrate the new sets of meanings associated with them.

Many of the women in my study stressed the importance of having someone with them at all times for the first week or two after the birth. Those who were left alone reported that feelings of bewilderment, confusion, isolation, and exhaustion often came to define this period far more strongly than the special magic felt by those women who did have the supportive and reassuring presence of a companion—mother, significant other, or friend.

INTEGRATION: "SWIMMING UP ON THE OTHER SIDE"

One day when my baby was almost three months
old, I had the strangest sensation that I swam up on
the other side, lifted my head out of the water, and
looked back at a whole year during which I seemed to
have been underwater.

—Elise Pearsall

The final integrative phase of this rite of passage begins and ends gradually during the newborn's first few months of life. This phase is sometimes experienced as "postpartum depression." For some women, this depression begins when the everyday demands of the structural outside world start to invade and dispel the special magic circle surrounding mother and child. Some women say the birth was such a high that when its energy faded and dispersed, they plummeted to an all-time low. For others, "PPD" is primarily a result of their perception of their birth experience as negative; when this is the case, the depression will usually be deeper and longer-lasting, as it forms part of an important grieving process during which the woman must attempt to work through and reinterpret her birth experience in order to make some kind of structural sense out of it. Entwisle and Doering (1981) find a positive correlation between PPD and the administration of anesthesia during labor, whereas Oakley (1980) finds a positive correlation between PPD and high technology birth. She notes that depression often stems, not from the technology itself, but from the implications of its use and the manner of its application. In other words, the woman who enters the hospital seeing herself as Earth Mother, and comes out with a Cesarean scar, is likely to have a hard time reconciling those images. She may go through a lengthy process of cognitive restructuring (discussed in Chapter 6) in order to reach some form of accommodation between who she was when she entered the hospital, and who she is when she comes out.

Richard Seel (1986a), writing about childbirth in Great Britain, makes the relevant point that the lack of effective rituals of reintegration in the West may be a major cause of postpartum depression among new parents. Explaining that an incomplete ritual process can lead to feelings of alienation and distress, Seel points out that after discharge from the hospital or the last visit from the midwife, the new mother often feels "utterly lost and alone." He recommends that a representative of society, such as a health care visitor or social worker, should go to the new mother's home to present her with a bouquet of flowers and a congratulations card, or that her religious institution collaborate with the clinic to provide her with some sort of reintegrative ceremony.

Harriet Rosenberg (1987:181–196) points out that in kin-based communities women who adhere to customary postpartum rituals do not experience postpartum depression—a phenomenon that she identifies as a structural problem of industrial society. Rosenberg shows that the twenty-four-hour-a-day job of mothering a newborn is not culturally acknowledged as "work" but is viewed as part of the "role" of mothering. There is little relief—no paid vacations, no time off—for its incessant demands. "Motherwork" in American society, performed within the narrow confines of the nuclear family, is often accompanied by financial dependence on mates, intellectual dependence on "experts," physical limitations on the mother's activities, which she must structure to accommodate the needs of the newborn, and emotional isolation.

The need for postpartum rituals is filled among Jewish families, if a son is born, by the traditional bris, and among many Christian families by the christening ceremony followed by a party. But for the many who do not practice such religious rituals, friends and/or family could provide effective rituals of reintegration. There could be tremendous benefit for new mothers if a postpartum baby-welcoming party were to become as standard as the prepartum baby shower.

In any case, on the most mundane level integration generally comes through an escalating series of successful minor encounters with the outside world—like the first trip to the supermarket, to church, to class, or to a restaurant with baby in arm or stroller, back- or frontpack. At some point all the new mothers I interviewed realized that they no longer felt trembly or potential, but mundane—their sense of special separateness was gone and they were "mainstreaming it" again. Some go back to work. Others stay home. In either case, their change in state is complete—whatever else they might be, they are finally and completely mothers:

> Some of the pride I had was having felt that I'd crossed a barrier, that I had joined the rest of the mothers in the world, and that I had joined my mother, in a sense. And that that was an experience that nobody could ever take away from me. (Constance O'Riley)

CHAPTER 2

The Technocratic Model

Past and Present

> Then God said, "Let us make man in our image, after our likeness; and let them have dominion over the fish of the sea, and over the birds of the air, and over the cattle, and over all the earth.
>
> —*Genesis 1:26*

> In all societies, technology is the ritual replication of origin myths.
>
> —Peter C. Reynolds, *Stealing Fire: The Atomic Bomb as Symbolic Body*

The rituals of initiatory rites of passage convey symbolic messages that speak of a culture's most deeply held values and beliefs. Many of American society's most deeply held values and beliefs derive from the model of reality we inherited from the Scientific Revolution in Europe. As Carolyn Merchant demonstrates in *The Death of Nature* (1983), it was during the seventeenth-century period of the rapid commercial expansion of Western society that the machine replaced the organism as the underlying metaphor for the organization of man's universe. (Prior to this time, the dominant European folk view held that the earth was a living organism infused with a female "world-soul.") Descartes, Bacon, Hobbes, and others developed and widely disseminated a philosophy that assumed that the universe is mechanistic, following predictable laws that those enlightened enough to free themselves from the limitations of medieval superstition could discover through science and manipulate through technology. These ideas fit in so well with our already ancient cultural belief in our right to dominate nature (chartered in *Genesis*) that by the end of the seventeenth century they had become the philosophical cornerstones on which rested the belief system of Western society.

As a result of this switch in base metaphors, nature, society, and the human body soon came to be viewed as composed of "interchangeable atomized parts" that could be repaired or replaced from the outside. Merchant says:

[These philosophers] transformed the body of the world and its female soul . . . into a mechanical system of dead corpuscles, set in motion by the creator. . . . Because nature was now viewed as a system of dead, inert particles moved by external, rather than inherent forces, the mechanical framework itself could legitimate the manipulation of nature. (1983:193)

Under this model, God set in motion a chain of events. Man could discover the laws by which these events proceeded and could intervene in them for his own benefit. Power was to be "derived from active and immediate intervention in a secularized world" (Merchant 1983:193).

MEDICINE AS A MICROCOSM OF AMERICAN SOCIETY

Obstretrics is the branch of medicine that deals with parturition, its antecedents, and its sequels (*Oxford English Dictionary* 1933). It is concerned principally, therefore, with the phenomena and management of pregnancy, labor, and the puerperium, in both normal and abnormal circumstances. In a broader sense, obstetrics is concerned with the reproduction of a society.

—Cunningham, MacDonald, and Gant,
Williams Obstetrics

The widespread cultural acceptance of the mechanical model in the seventeenth century was accompanied by the fragmentation of the system of organized religion which had unified the conceptual framework of European society. As the mechanical model itself became the conceptual factor "unifying cosmos, society, and self" (Merchant 1983:192), the primary responsibility for the human body, a responsibility that had once belonged to religion, was assigned to the medical profession. This developing science had taken the mechanical model as its philosophical foundation and so was much better equipped than religion to take on the challenging conceptual task of transforming the organic human body into a machine—a transformation that was crucial to the development of Western society.

The elaboration of an intelligible conceptual universe is an essential step in the formation and continuation of any society. Social cohesion and continuity are enhanced when a society's founding metaphors for cosmos, culture, and individual self are consistent with each other—when each element becomes a scaled-down version of the other. Such consistency requires that the body—the basic vehicle of human, and thus social, existence—officially reflects society's vision of itself. For example, if a society chooses to see itself and the universe it inhabits as mechanistic, then it will need to see as equally mechanistic the human bodies that comprise it. The problem here, of course, is that bodies are not machines, and therefore the human body represented a great conceptual challenge to the mechanical model. And so it became both the cultural mission and the vested interest of Western medicine to prove the ultimate truth and viability of this model by making the body *appear to be* as mechanistic as possible. Medicine's eventual success in this mission—a success that was not at all guaranteed until the introduction of the germ theory of disease in the late 1800s (Duffy 1979:236; Ehrenreich and English 1973*b*:30)—played a major role in the permeation of the machine metaphor into every aspect of American life.

Along with responsibility for maintaining the consistency of our dominant belief system, doctors hold another social duty that had previously been the responsibility of the priest—namely, that of inculcating individual members of society with the basic tenets of this belief system. It is no cultural accident that doctors themselves must undergo an eight-year-long initiatory rite of passage, a process of socialization so lengthy and thorough that at its end they will become not only physicians but the representatives of American society (see Chapter 7). For our medical system encapsulates the core value system our society has based on its technocratic model of life and thus is well-qualified to pass this system on. American biomedicine's cures are based on science, effected by technology, and carried out in institutions founded on principles of patriarchy and the supremacy of the institution over the individual.

The simplest way to conceptualize these medically enacted core cultural values is in terms of an oppositional paradigm (i.e., a model of reality based on an inherent tension between two sets of categories) in which the interests of science, technology, patriarchy, and institutions are held as superior to—and are often imposed on—those of nature, individuals, families, and most especially (because of their devaluation under the technocratic model) women, as in the following illustration.

Of course, a high valuation of technology does not *necessarily* entail a low valuation of those on the other side of the paradigm: technology itself is increasingly of service to individuals, families, women, and nature in countless empowering ways. But the technology of a society is embedded in and created out of its dominant belief system and, as we saw in the Introduction, core cultural rituals generally serve to aug-

SCIENCE

TECHNOLOGY

PATRIARCHY

INSTITUTIONS

NATURE

INDIVIDUALS

FAMILIES

WOMEN

American core values: An oppositional paradigm
(original drawing by Janice van Mechelen)

ment the given power system. Our society is no exception to these
rules. Our technological artifacts are both embedded in and formative
of our worldview, and their primary uses will reflect and perpetuate
the paradigm underlying that worldview. I label that paradigm the
technocratic model, because it is removed by a century of astonish-
ingly sophisticated technological developments from its predecessor, the
mechanistic model, and because these technologies have developed in
a hierarchical social context that supervalues them and the individuals
who control them.

The term *technocracy* implies use of an ideology of technological
progress as a source of political power (Reynolds 1991). It thus expresses not only the technological but also the hierarchical, bureau-
cratic, and autocratic dimensions of this culturally dominant reality
model—dimensions that are immediately visible in many realms of post-
industrial American life. Stories of the ravaging of nature by technology
serving institutional interests fill the nightly news. Women striving for
equality with men still earn about sixty-nine cents for every male-earned
dollar. And as many students of American medicine have attested, in
our major medical institutions science, technology, and patriarchal patterns reign supreme while individuals must often subsume their very
selves to institutional convenience and routine (Beuf 1979; Goffman
1961; Hahn 1987; Illich 1976; Klein 1979; Konner 1987; LeBaron

1981; Mendelsohn 1979, 1981; Nolen 1979; Parsons 1951; Stein 1967; Tao-Kim-Hai 1979; Taylor 1970). These technocratic medical institutions are especially effective as mechanisms through which society's core values can be perpetuated because the hierarchical principles on which they are organized allow responsibility to be so generalized and diffused that few individuals have enough power to fundamentally alter how things are done. Individual physicians and nurses who try to alter "the system" often find themselves thwarted and stymied by other physicians, by hospital administrators, and ultimately by the combined forces of the legal and business systems of our society.

In very recent times, the threat of lawsuits and the rising cost of malpractice insurance have become major social deterrents against the efforts of individual physicians to humanize and personalize American medicine (see Chapter 7). These legal and financial deterrents to radical change powerfully constrain our medical system, in effect forcing that system to precisely reflect and to actively perpetuate the core belief and value system of American society as a whole. Thus, this medical system can most productively be understood as American society's microcosm—the condensed world in which our society's deepest beliefs, greatest triumphs, and grossest inadequacies stand out in high relief against their cultural background. For this reason, the anthropological study of this system can be particularly revealing. And for the same reason, our medical system is in a unique position to respond to conceptual challenges to the core beliefs of American society which center around that basic social unit for which medicine is responsible—the human body.

THE BODY AS MACHINE

Oh, don't worry about him! Just think of it this
way—he's like an old Cadillac that has broken down
and needs to be repaired. He's in the shop now, and
we'll have him just as good as new in no time. We're
the best Cadillac dealers in town!
    —San Antonio heart specialist to me, while my
        stepfather was in the hospital

The human body presents a profound conceptual paradox to our society, for it is simultaneously a creation of nature and the focal point of culture. How can we be separate from nature when we are of it? Western philosophers such as Descartes and Bacon neatly resolved this problem for us in the 1600s when they established the conceptual separation of mind and body upon which the metaphor of the body-as-machine depends. This idea meant that the superior cultural essence of man—his mind—could remain unaffected while the body, as a mere part of mechanical nature, could be taken apart, studied, and repaired:

> The Cartesian model of the body-as-machine operates to make the physician a technician, or mechanic. The body breaks down and needs repair; it can be repaired in the hospital as a car is in the shop; once fixed, a person can be returned to the community. The earliest models in medicine were largely mechanical; later models worked more with chemistry, and newer, more sophisticated medical writing describes computer-like programming, but the basic point remains the same. Problems in the body are technical problems requiring technical solutions, whether it is a mechanical repair, a chemical rebalancing, or a "debugging" of the system. (Rothman 1982:34)

That this paradigm is still strongly with us, despite changing times and technical capabilities, is clearly illustrated in the February 1989 issue of *Life*: "If we think of the human body as a kind of machine, doctors of the future will be like mechanics, simply replacing those parts that can't be fixed." Anthropologist Emily Martin argues that obstetricians are more like supervisors than mechanics, given that their primary role in hospital birth is, increasingly, the "active management" of labor and birth (1987:57). Certainly obstetricians are also highly skilled, hands-on technicians: their training stresses the acquisition of the most sophisticated technical knowledge and expertise that can be brought to bear on the birthing body-machine.

In the seventeenth century, the practical utility of the application of this mechanical metaphor to the human body lay in its removal of the body from the purviews of religion and philosophy, as well as superstition and ignorance. To conceive of the body as a machine was to open it up to scientific investigation and get on with the research, leaving all bothersome questions of spirituality and the integrity of the individual to the priests and philosophers (Sheper-Hughes and Lock 1987). (The same questions, by the way, kept many other societies from attempting any type of surgical intervention into the body's integrity.)

The philosophical links between the seventeenth-century metaphor of the body-as-machine and the core value system current in the United States today are to be found in the Greek Aristotelian tradition that formed a developmental stimulus for both modern science and modern religion. Returned to Europe through renewed trade with the Arab world in the twelfth and thirteenth centuries, Aristotelian precepts were thoroughly studied and eagerly incorporated by religious thinkers such as Thomas Aquinas, and by early scientists like Galileo, creating a hegemony of opinion about the superiority of the male in both the scientific and religious thought of post-medieval Europe. From this hegemony we moderns have inherited a pervasive legacy of symbolic thinking—a legacy of which we are largely unaware. In *De Generatione Animalium* (II, 3) Aristotle wrote:

> When [semen] has entered the uterus it puts into form the corresponding secretion of the female and moves it with the same movement wherewith it is moved itself. For the female's contribution also is a secretion, and has all the parts in it potentially though none of them actually; it has in it potentially even those parts which differentiate the female from the male, for just as the young of mutilated parents are sometimes born mutilated and sometimes not, so also the young born of a female are sometimes female and sometimes male instead. For the female is, as it were, a mutilated male, and the catamenia [female secretions] are semen, only not pure; for there is only one thing they have not in them, the principle of soul. (Aristotle, in Ross 1955:194–195)

This definition of women as mutilated males permeates Aristotle's biological and philosophical work (see M. C. Horowitz in Lerner 1986: 207). Its wide dissemination by the late 1400s is amply evidenced in the following excerpt from the *Malleus Maleficarum* (*The Hammer of Witches*), a witchhunting manual so influential that it was used in witch trials throughout Europe for nearly three centuries after its publication in 1486:

> All wickedness is but little to the wickedness of a woman. . . . [S]ince they are feebler both in mind and body, it is not surprising that they should come more under the spell of witchcraft. . . . But the natural reason is that she is more carnal than a man, as should be clear from her many carnal abominations. And it should be noted that there was a defect in the formation of the first woman, since she was formed from a bent rib, that is, a rib of the breast, which is bent as it were in a contrary direction to a man. And since through this defect she is an imperfect animal, she always deceives. (Kramer and Sprenger 1972:120–121)

In theory, the mechanistic model that provided the philosophical basis for the Scientific and Industrial Revolutions could have been inherently egalitarian—human bodies could have been metaphorized as equal in their mechanicity. But both the Protestant Reformation and the Scientific and Industrial Revolutions, which transformed so much of European society, left generally untouched this fundamental assumption of the superiority of the male—an assumption whose conceptual hegemony in fact intensified as the Industrial Revolution progressed.[1]

One way to re-metaphorize reality in mechanistic terms while still perpetuating the established male/female power relationship was simply to declare one normal and the other deviant in terms of the new model, thus undermining its potential for equalizing the sexes at the very beginning. So the men who established the idea of the body as a machine also firmly established the male body as the prototype of this machine. Insofar as it deviated from the male standard, the female body was regarded as abnormal, inherently defective, and dangerously under the influence of nature, which due to its unpredictability and its occasional monstrosities, was itself regarded as inherently defective and in need of constant manipulation by man (Merchant 1983:2; Reynolds 1991).

Thus, despite the acceptance of birth as mechanical like all other bodily processes, it was still viewed as inherently imperfect and untrustworthy. The demise of the midwife and the rise of the male-attended, mechanically manipulated birth followed close on the heels of the wide cultural acceptance of the metaphor of the body-as-machine in the West and the accompanying acceptance of the metaphor of the female body as a defective machine—a metaphor that eventually formed the philosophical foundation of modern obstetrics. Obstetrics was thereby enjoined from its beginnings to develop tools and technologies for the manipulation and improvement of the inherently defective and therefore anomalous and dangerous process of birth.

THE TECHNOCRATIC MODEL OF BIRTH

"But is the hospital necessary at all?" demanded a young woman of her obstetrician friend. "Why not bring the baby at home?"

"What would you do if your automobile broke down on a country road?" the doctor countered with another question.

"Try and fix it," said the modern chaffeuse.

"And if you couldn't?"

"Have it hauled to the nearest garage."

"Exactly. Where the trained mechanics and their necessary tools are," agreed the doctor. "It's the same

with the hospital. I can do my best work—and the best
we must have in medicine all the time—not in some
cramped little apartment or private home, but where I
have the proper facilities and trained helpers. If anything goes wrong, I have all known aids to meet your
emergency."
                              —*The Century Illustrated Magazine,*
                                February 1926

Birth. This is the complete expulsion or extraction
from the mother of a fetus irrespective of whether the
umbilical cord has been cut or the placenta is attached.
                              —Cunningham, MacDonald, and Gant,
                                Williams Obstetrics

According to the technocratic model of birth,[2] the human body is a
machine. The male body is metaphorized as a better machine than the
female body, because in form and function it is more machine-like—
more consistent and predictable, less subject to the vagaries of nature
(i.e., more cultural and therefore "better"), and consequently less likely
to break down. It is also straighter-lined. Technocratic reality is constructed on the premise of the straight line as inherently "good to think
with"; the high cultural value attached to the straight line entails a concomitant devaluation of nonlinear reality (Lee 1980). The curves, dips,
caves, and hollows of the female figure, in contrast to the more linear
male figure, seem rather more evocative of nature's rivers, hills, and
valleys than of culture's dams, bridges, and highways. Males, because
they are the most machine-like, not only set the standard for the properly functioning body-machine, but also are thought best-equipped to
handle its maintenance and repair.

Because of their extreme deviation from the male prototype, uniquely
female anatomical features such as the uterus, ovaries, and breasts,
and uniquely female biological processes such as menstruation, pregnancy, birth, and menopause are inherently subject to malfunction. In
The Woman in the Body, Martin (1987:47–49) notes that the medical
language used to describe ovarian egg production, menstruation, and
menopause often speaks of "degeneration," "decay," and "failed production," whereas that used to describe male sperm production speaks
glowingly of its "remarkable," "amazing" nature and its "sheer mag-
nitude." It is thus understandable that the woman in whose body such

degenerative processes take place is often seen, under the technocratic model, as better off without them.

As a number of physicians and medical anthropologists and sociologists have pointed out, our medical system has done a thorough job of convincing women of the defectiveness and dangers inherent in their specifically female functions (Corea 1985a; Ehrenreich and English 1973a; Leavitt 1986; Mendelsohn 1981; Oakley 1984; Wertz and Wertz 1989). The hysterectomy is the most commonly performed unnecessary operation in the United States (one out of every three American women has a hysterectomy by the time she reaches menopause [Corea 1985a:287]), with the radical mastectomy in second place (Mendelsohn 1981). A common surgical expression states, "If ovaries were testicles, there'd be a lot fewer of them removed" (Nolen 1979:202). It has been a recurrent theme in American medicine that to remove a woman's sexual organs is to restore her body to full health and greater potential for productive life. Paralleling this theme, most standard medical diagrams of various body systems—nervous, lymphatic, musculoskeletal, and so forth—depict the male body to illustrate the proper functioning of that system, whereas dysfunctional conditions like obesity are usually depicted with female bodies. In short, under the technocratic model the female body is viewed as an abnormal, unpredictable, and inherently defective machine:

> Women are known to suffer at least some inconvenience during certain phases of the reproductive cycle, and often with considerable mental and physical distress. Woman's awareness of her inherent disabilities is thought to create added mental and in turn physical changes in the total body response, and there result problems that concern the physician who must deal with them. (Abramson and Torghele 1961:223)

During pregnancy and birth, the unusual demands placed on the female body-machine render it constantly at risk of serious malfunction or total breakdown. This belief, the foundation of modern obstetrics, can be found behind the lines of much early obstetrical literature:

> In order to acquire a more perfect idea of the art, [the male midwife] ought to perform with his own hands upon proper machines, contrived to convey a just notion of all the difficulties to be met within every kind of labor; by which means he will learn how to use the forceps and crotchets with more dexterity, be accustomed to the turning of children, and consequently, be more capable of acquitting himself in troublesome cases. (Smellie 1756:44)

> It is a common experience among obstetrical practitioners that there is an increasing gestational pathology and a more frequent call for art, in supple-

menting inefficient forces of nature in her effort to accomplish normal delivery. (Ritter 1919:531)

More recently, the 1985 issue of the prestigious *New England Journal of Medicine* includes an editorial on the potential advantages of universal prophylactic Cesarean section. The authors question whether, since birth is such a dangerous and traumatic process for both woman and child, the best obstetric care should perhaps come to include complete removal of the risks of "normal" labor and delivery. A still more recent article in *Female Patient* asserts that natural childbirth is associated with "maternal death, infant death, and maternal tissue destruction. . . . Some practitioners are asking whether an even higher Cesarean rate may be appropriate. Should we not offer the ultimate in pelvic and birth-canal protection to the mothers?" (Beecham 1989).

Dr. Beecham's words are eerily reminiscent of those of one of the most famous founding fathers of modern obstetrics, Joseph B. DeLee, whose well-known pitchfork analogy is still occasionally heard in contemporary medical training (O'Banion 1987:41):

> Labor has been called, and still is believed by many to be, a normal function. It always strikes physicians as well as laymen as bizarre, to call labor an abnormal function, a disease, and yet it is decidedly a pathologic process. Everything, of course, depends on what we define as normal. If a woman falls on a pitchfork, and drives the handle through her perineum, we call that pathologic—abnormal, but if a large baby is driven through the pelvic floor, we say that is natural, and therefore normal. If a baby were to have his head caught in a door very lightly, but enough to cause cerebral hemorrhage, we would say that is decidedly pathologic, but when a baby's head is crushed against a tight pelvic floor, and a hemorrhage in the brain kills it, we call this normal, at least we say that the function is natural, not pathogenic. (DeLee 1920:39–40)

Although most modern obstetrical texts do give lip service to pregnancy as a natural and intrinsically healthy process, this is usually done in a paragraph or two. For example, the eighteenth edition of *Williams Obstetrics*, the preeminent text in the field, states:

> The expectant mother has been commonly treated as if she were seriously ill, even when she was quite healthy. All too often she has been forced to conform to a common pathway of care that stripped her of most of her individuality and much of her dignity. . . . Too often the expectant mother has felt that her fate and the fate of her baby were dependent not so much on skilled personnel but upon an electronic cabinet that appeared to possess some great power that prevailed above all others. (Cunningham et al. 1989:6)

Meanwhile, most of the next nine hundred pages are devoted to a detailed discussion of everything that can possibly go wrong and of how to use the "electronic cabinet" to solve these problems. (For a detailed cultural analysis of *Williams Obstetrics*, see Hahn 1987.) For the vast majority of modern obstetricians, technology and birth are inseparable:

> I'm totally dependent on fetal monitors, 'cause they're great! They free you to do a lot of other things. I couldn't practice modern obstetrics without them. I couldn't sit over there with a woman in labor with my hand on her belly, and be in here seeing twenty to thirty patients a day. You couldn't see the volume of people, you couldn't treat people. I'd say that in the twenty years that I've been in practice, what we do today is 90 percent different than what we did. We have laparascopes, we have ultrasound. We couldn't stop labor in those days—we stop labor with tocolytic drugs today. At least 90 percent of the things I do now weren't part of my training. (male obstetrician, age 53)

A younger colleague emphasizes that "anybody in obstetrics who shows a human interest in patients is not respected. What *is* respected is interest in machines."

The rising science of obstetrics ultimately reached this position by adopting early on the model of the assembly-line production of goods—the template by which most of the technological wonders of modern society were being produced, as its base metaphor for hospital birth. In accordance with this metaphor (and in response to a variety of related economic incentives), in the hospital a woman's reproductive tract is treated like a birthing machine by skilled technicians working under semi-flexible timetables to meet production and quality-control demands:

> We shave 'em, we prep 'em, we hook 'em up to the IV and administer sedation. We deliver the baby, it goes to the nursery and the mother goes to her room. There's no room for niceties around here. We just move 'em right on through. It's hard not to see it like an assembly line. (fourth-year resident)

The hospital is a highly sophisticated technocratic factory; the more technology the hospital has to offer, the better it is considered to be. As an institution, it constitutes a more significant social unit than the individual or the family, so the birth process should conform more to institutional than personal needs. As one physician put it, "There was a set, established routine for doing things, and the laboring woman was someone you worked around, rather than with."

This tenet of the technocratic model—that the institution is a more significant social unit than the mother—will not be found in obstetrical texts, yet is taught by example after example of the interactional patterns of hospital births (Jordan 1983; Scully 1980; Shaw 1974). For example, Jordan describes how pitocin (a synthetic hormone used to speed labor) is often administered in the hospital when the medical delivery-room team shows up gowned and gloved and ready for action, yet the woman's labor slows down. The team members stand around awkwardly until someone finally says, "Let's get this show on the road!" (1983:44). (Over 80 percent of the hospital-birthers in my study had their labors augmented with pitocin.)

Of course, the question of individuality and variability among physicians arises throughout this delineation of the hegemonic technocratic paradigm. Whereas Lock (1985), Hahn (1985), Helman (1985) and others have shown that individual physicians do develop individual working models for female processes during the course of their clinical experience, I suggest that at least in the case of obstetrics, such individual models are subject to the pervasive philosophical devaluation of the female body-machine. Although the twelve obstetricians I interviewed for Chapter 7 of this book certainly exhibited individual variations in their beliefs and practices, a strong technocratic orientation was easily detectable in all but three.

According to the technocratic model, the uterus is an involuntary muscle that starts labor in response to mechanical hormonal signals:

> The final event in initiating a uterine contraction is an increase in the intracellular concentration of ionic calcium ($Ca2^+$) in myometrial smooth muscle cells in response to the actions of a uterotonin. The ATP-energy-dependent translocation of calcium to a stored form in the sarcoplasmic reticulum is associated with uterine relaxation. . . . Uterine contractions are involuntary and . . . independent of extra-uterine control [except that labor-slowing can be caused by administration of epidural anesthesia too early in labor]. (Cunningham et al. 1989:210–214)[3]

Given the involuntary nature of contractions, the mother's personal participation in the birth process is not necessary, but is to be welcomed to the extent that she complies with institutional needs and facilitates the necessary interventions. States *Williams,* "The proper psychological management of the pregnant woman throughout pregnancy and labor is a valuable basic tranquilizer" (Cunningham et al. 1989:328). Should "proper psychological management" prove insufficient for the naturally caused pain of labor, a variety of pain-relieving drugs, all of which reach the baby within minutes of administration, will (usually) be readily proffered. But when the pain the woman feels is caused by obstetrical procedures, she is told she must bear it "for the baby's sake."

Another basic tenet of the technocratic model of birth holds that some degree of intervention is necessary in *all* births. (For example, episiotomies—a surgical incision of the vagina at the moment of birth—are performed on over 90 percent of all first-time mothers who birth in U.S. hospitals [Inch 1984:126]). Birth is thus a technocratic service that obstetrics supplies to society; the doctor delivers the baby to society. (Traditionally, he hands the baby to the nurse immediately after birth, not to the mother.) If the product is perfect, the responsibility and the credit are his; if flawed, the responsibility will transfer to another technical specialist up or down the assembly line; any blame will be categorically assigned to the inherent defectiveness of the mother's birthing machine:

> Yesterday on rounds I saw a baby with a cut on its face and the mother said, "My uterus was so thinned that when they cut into it for the section, the baby's face got cut." The patient is always blamed in medicine. The doctors don't make mistakes. "Your uterus is too thin," not "We cut too deeply." "We had to take the baby," (meaning forceps or Cesarean), instead of "the medicine we gave you interfered with your ability to give birth." (Harrison 1982:174)

The most desirable end product of the birth process is the new social member, the baby; the new mother is a secondary by-product:

> It was what we were all trained to always go after—the perfect baby. That's what we were trained to produce. The quality of the mother's experience—we rarely thought about that. Everything we did was to get that perfect baby. (male obstetrician, age 38)

This focus on the production of the "perfect baby" is a fairly recent development, a direct result of the combination of the technocratic emphasis on the baby-as-product with the new technologies available to assess fetal quality. Amniocentesis, ultrasonography, "antepartum fetal heart 'stress' and 'non-stress' tests . . . and intrapartum surveillance of fetal heart action, uterine contractions, and physiochemical properties of fetal blood" (Pritchard and MacDonald 1980:329) are but a few of these new technologies:

> The number of tools the obstetrician can employ to address the needs of the fetus increases each year. We are of the view that this is the most exciting of times to be an obstetrician. Who would have dreamed, even a few years ago, that we could serve the fetus as physician? (Pritchard and MacDonald, 1980:vii)

This statement from the sixteenth edition of *Williams* reflects an increasing insistence in obstetrics that, from conception on, the fetus is a being separate from its mother and can grow and develop without the mother's will or involvement—"its" best interests are often antagonistic to hers. Thus the labor process necessarily entails close monitoring of the mother by procedures that enact the underlying view that the female body-machine is inherently defective and generally incapable of producing perfect babies without technological assistance from professionals, even when such monitoring causes the mother considerable stress and increased pain. (This technocratic premise of maternal-fetal antagonism reaches full expression in several recent cases of Cesareans performed by court order against the mother's will [Jordan and Irwin 1989] and in the escalating national political debate on maternal versus fetal rights.)

Such profound conceptual separation of mother and child both mirrors and extends the fundamental Cartesian doctrine of mind-body separation. This separation is given tangible expression after birth as well, when the baby is placed in the nursery for four hours of "observation" before being returned to the mother; in this way, society symbolically demonstrates ownership of its product. The mother's womb is replaced, not by her arms but by the plastic womb of culture. As Shaw points out, this separation is intensified after birth by the assignment of a separate doctor, the pediatrician, to the child (1974:94). This idea of the baby as separate, as the product of a mechanical process, is a very important metaphor for women, because it implies that men can ultimately become the producers of that product—and indeed it is in that direction that reproductive technologies are headed (see Chapter 8).

Although the early Cartesian model of reality offered man unprecedented power to control his environment, there were restrictions on this power, as under this model humans were limited by the divinely imposed—albeit strictly mechanical—limitations of the natural and cosmic worlds. In today's world, these restrictions have been conceptually—and significantly—removed. Modern technology has "progressed" far beyond what was imaginable to the seventeenth-century philosophers who originated the mechanical model. There is an unprecedented promise inherent in today's technology—a recent development peculiar to this century and formative of the next. To the earlier philosophers, the phenomenon of death was the inevitable fate of every human body-machine, and although the birth process came to be seen as mechanical, the phenomenon of conception remained a mystery beyond human manipulation or control. But for our generation, modern technology holds the twin promises of our actual creation of life and our actual transcendence of both death and the planetary bounds of nature. Cryogenic suspension, test-tube conception, and space travel are physiological realities today, whispering the promise of ultimate transcendence through technology tomorrow.

Our increasing cultural faith in this promise holds special significance for birth. As the process that perpetuates society through generating new members and transmitting key cultural values, birth must intensively reflect those values. Thus, as this technocratic model continues to evolve, the technocratic treatment of birth will continue to intensify. The very real and ongoing discrepancies between the technocratic paradigm and objective reality will increasingly necessitate obstetrical resolution of certain conceptual anomalies inherent in our growing dependence on the promises of technology.

THE ROLE OF AMERICAN OBSTETRICS IN THE RESOLUTION OF CULTURAL ANOMALY

> The solidity of everyday reality stems from the
> shoring up and replastering we constantly give it as we
> talk about the world and inspect it for the materials
> that talk requires. Beneath our busy scaffolding there
> may be nothing at all.
> —Michael Moerman, *Talking Culture*

As noted earlier, most viable human cultures depend on a high degree of cohesiveness and consistency in the cognitive categories through which their members are socialized to make sense of the world around them. Yet any such conceptual system, no matter how carefully worked out, is bound to confront experiences in nature and in the supernatural that do not comfortably fit its categories nor support its premises (Douglas 1966, 1973). Cultures like that of the United States, whose conceptual systems are founded on principles of man's superiority to nature, are especially challenged to develop successful ways of dealing with powerful natural and supernatural experiences that demonstrate the inadequacy of their belief systems. Birth is one such experience. The unique constraints on reality inherent in our system of core values and beliefs ensure that the natural process of birth will confront our society with a thorny set of philosophical problems concerning its relationship to the individuals who comprise it, and to the natural and cosmic worlds that sustain and encompass it.

I have been able to identify at least eight major conceptual and procedural dilemmas with which the natural birth process confronts American society. I choose to emphasize the label "dilemmas" (in the sense of "a problem seemingly incapable of a satisfactory solution" [*Webster's* 1979:317]), instead of "oppositions" or "anomalies"; I present these dilemmas below in "how-to" terms in order to emphasize that they are conceptual problems whose successful resolution depends on concrete, operational, "how-to-proceed" plans for action in the face of a potentially paralyzing paradox. These dilemmas may be summarized as follows:

1. Our society is conceptually grounded in the technocratic model of reality and thus has a vested interest in maintaining the conceptual validity of that model. Yet the natural process of birth appears to refute the technocratic model because the birth process confronts us with graphic evidence that babies come from women and nature, not from technology and culture. This dilemma can be stated as follows: how to make the natural process of birth appear to confirm, instead of refute, the technocratic model?

2. Our culture has a strong need to feel that it is in control of nature and its own future, and yet the birth process, on which the future of our society (still) depends, in many fundamental ways cannot be predicted or controlled. So the dilemma becomes, how to create a sense of cultural control over birth, a natural process resistant to such control?

3. The birthing of a child constitutes one of the most profoundly transformative and uniquely *individual* experiences a woman will go through in her life. Across cultures, people seek ways to generalize such experiences—that is, to turn them into cultural rites of passage in order to make it appear that the transformation is effected, not by nature, but by the culture itself, and to utilize the transformative period to inculcate the individual with basic cultural beliefs and values through ritual. So the dilemma is, how to generalize an individual transformation—that is, how to turn the natural birth experience which, left unshaped by ritual, would remain a purely individual transformation, into a cultural rite of passage?

4. Rites of passage entail a period of liminality (Turner 1979) in which the initiate is considered dangerous to society, because he or she

is living in a transitional realm between social categories which is officially not supposed to exist; the fact that it does exist threatens the entire category system of the culture. Yet this danger, if properly handled,
can be culturally revitalizing, as it carries the tantalizing possibility of
cultural change. Although too much contact with this danger can be
culturally disruptive, some is essential for combating the constant dangers of entropy which threaten to undermine those societies who never
flirt with the unknown. So the problem becomes, how to "fence in"
the dangers associated with the liminal period in birth, while at the
same time allowing controlled access to their revitalizing power?

5. Babies are natural beings, born essentially culture-less. Yet people
universally seem to insist that being culture-full is what makes us human. How to enculturate a noncultural baby?

6. The majority of human cultures are strongly patriarchal, ours included. Yet birth, upon which men must totally depend for their own
and their children's existence, is a purely female phenomenon. As such,
birth poses a major conceptual threat to male dominance, as male dependence upon females for birth would seem to demand that women
be honored and worshipped as the goddesses of their society's perpetuation. The dilemma here: how to make birth, a powerfully female phenomenon, appear to sanction patriarchy?

7. The technology and the institutions in which we place our faith
for the perpetuation of our culture are inherently asexual and impersonal. The birth process, upon which the perpetuation of our culture
depends, is inherently sexual and intimate. Thus its intimacy and sexuality constitute yet another arena in which birth threatens to undermine
the conceptual hegemony of the technocratic model. So those responsible for the cultural management of birth in the United States have had
to devise culturally appropriate ways to remove the sexuality from the
sexual process of birth.

8. Our society remains strongly patriarchal, yet pays increasing lip
service to the ideal of equality. Since growing numbers of women espouse this ideal, our culture will not survive in its present form unless
these women can also be made to internalize the basic tenets of the
technocratic model of reality. This dilemma is one of the most intrigu-
ing: how to get women, in a culture that purports to hold gender equality as an ideal, to accept a belief system that inherently denigrates them?

Some of the above dilemmas are universal problems presented by the
birth process to all human societies; others are specific to American cul-

ture. Each contains within it a fundamental paradox, an opposition that must be culturally reconciled lest the anomaly of its existence undermine the fragile conceptual framework in terms of which our society understands itself in relation to the universe. That conceptual anomalies do in fact have such power is abundantly illustrated throughout history: every new religion has promoted itself by daring to spotlight the conceptual discrepancies in the belief system that went before it (Feeley-Harnik 1981). Irreconcilable oppositions may be tolerable as long as no one points the finger at them, but once they are put in front of the public eye, they can and often do topple governments.

Thus any society's ability to perpetuate its belief system depends greatly upon offering its members a variety of ways to mediate those conceptual oppositions that constantly threaten to tear it apart. As we have seen, the cultural responsibility for mediating these eight dilemmas in which birth and American culture are fundamentally opposed lies with our obstetrical profession. The response of the science of obstetrics to this cultural challenge has been: (1) to work out carefully a strong and consistent philosophical rationale for the management of birth which interprets birth specifically and exclusively in terms of the technocratic model; and (2) to develop a set of ritual procedures that could be uniformly applied to the natural process of human reproduction in order to transform it conceptually into a cultural process of human production, similar to the production of any other technocratic artifact. We will now turn to specific consideration of each dilemma and of how it is successfully (more or less) resolved by the rituals developed by American obstetrics.

THE CONCEPTUAL AND PROCEDURAL DILEMMAS PRESENTED TO AMERICAN SOCIETY BY THE NATURAL PROCESS OF BIRTH AND RESOLVED BY OBSTETRICAL RITUALS

> In all cases, the immediate attempt of the human organism in the face of an unknown stimulus is to organize it within a known framework.
>> —Eugene d'Aquili, "The Neurobiology of Myth and Ritual"

First Dilemma—Natural versus Technocratic Reality: How to Make the Natural Process of Birth Appear to Confirm the Technocratic Model In developing its belief system, every culture must make the basic conceptual move of separating itself from the natural world that spawned it, of deciding and then delineating where one ends and the other begins. Yet because it is only through nature that new members can enter culture, childbirth calls into question any conceptual boundaries a culture tries to establish between itself and nature. Such a visible and constant reminder that we can never really separate ourselves from the natural world presents an especially serious challenge to our culture, for it threatens to undermine the promise of ultimate transcendence inherent in our technocratic model.

A common cultural response to this type of conceptual threat is to wall it off from the mainstream of social life by creating special categories of "tabu," which are often reflected in actual social spaces specifically constructed to contain the conceptual danger (Douglas 1966). Another common cultural coping technique is to then defuse the conceptual bomb through the careful and consistent performance of rituals designed to mold the inconsistent phenomenon into apparent compliance with society's official belief system (Vogt 1976).

Our culture, like many others, has availed itself of both of these techniques in its struggle to cope with the conceptual threat presented by natural birth. We have tabued birth, removing it from everyday life by walling it off in hospitals (institutions specifically designed to isolate most of the boundary-threatening reminders of our subordination to nature presented to our culture by the human body, including disease and death, as well as birth [Kearl 1989; Miner 1975]). Finally, we have defused birth's explosive potential for conceptual upset by processing it through rituals specifically designed to eliminate the inconsistency between the birth process and our technocratic belief system by making birth appear to confirm, instead of challenge, that belief system, as Chapter 3 will investigate in detail.

Second Dilemma: How to Create a Sense of Cultural Control over Birth, a Natural Process Resistant to Such Control   Underneath our stubborn insistence on the mechanistic nature of birth hide the truths of its natural unpredictability and spiritual unknowability. Because ritual mediates between cognition and chaos by appearing to restructure reality, humans in all cultures have chosen it as the most effective means of overcoming their fear of the mystery and unpredictability of the natural and cosmic realms. As discussed in the Introduction, to precisely perform a series of rituals is to feel oneself locked onto a set of cognitive gears which, once set in motion, will inevitably carry one all the way through the perceived danger to a safe and predictable end. Just so do obstetrical rituals serve physicians and nurses. These routines psychologically enable medical personnel to attend births; without their routines, birth attendants would feel powerless in front of the power of nature, conceptually adrift in a category-less sea of uncontrollable and uninterpretable experience (see Chapter 7). (Said one obstetrician, "I could never attend a home birth. I wouldn't know what to do.") But *with* their routines, medical personnel are empowered, physically and psychologically, to (1) define and categorize the events of labor and birth that confront them, and (2) act confidently in terms of those definitions to impose cultural order on inchoate nature, as is indicated in the following quote from *Williams*:

> Except for cutting the umbilical cord, the episiotomy is the most common operation in obstetrics. The reasons for its popularity among obstetricians are clear. It substitutes a straight, neat surgical incision for the ragged laceration that otherwise frequently results. It is easier to repair and heals better than a tear. It spares the fetal head the necessity of serving as a battering ram against perineal obstruction . . . [which] may cause intracranial injury. Episiotomy shortens the second stage of labor. (Pritchard and MacDonald 1980:430)

As obstetricians began to take on the cultural responsibility for birth, their own belief in birth's inherent danger made essential the development of rituals they could rely on to give them the courage to face daily the challenge nature presents. Thus the performance of obstetrical rituals themselves had to take on the predictable pattern of a mechanical process. From the prep to the episiotomy, these procedures had to serve for birth attendants as the cranking gears that would mechanically and inevitably carry the birth process right on through the perceived danger to a safe and predictable end.

The same kind of psychological reassurance is sought by many birthing women who must individually face the same unknowns. Whether these women are traumatized or empowered by obstetrical rituals (see Chapter 5), these rituals usually provide at least a sense of certainty and security to the women that their babies will get born, and that neither they nor their babies will die. But they are also, most reassuringly, shown in most cases that a natural process perceived as terrifying and uncontrollable can be controlled and rendered conceptually safe when its course is mechanistically channeled into predictable pathways:

> I've never been able to understand women who want to watch the birthing process in a mirror—I'd rather see the finished product than the manufactur-

ing process. [I had a friend who delivered at home, everything was fine, but] I am too practical and too pragmatic. I want to be near somebody who can fix it if something's wrong. I don't want to bleed to death being a hero. (Joanne Moorehouse)

Third Dilemma: How to Generalize an Individual Transformation
This third conceptual dilemma presented by the naturally transformative birth process is one faced by all human cultures at various points in the human life cycle: how to generalize an individual transformation. Such generalization is necessary to ensure conformity with the official social belief system; otherwise, unchanneled individual transformative experiences might (and often do) challenge the dominant belief system. Of course, most societies resolve this dilemma by routing individual transformations through an established cultural channel—the generalized process known as a rite of passage.

More elaborate than any heretofore known in the "primitive" world, the obstetrical procedures through which American birth is channeled carry and communicate cultural meaning far beyond their ostensibly instrumental ends. In so doing, they not only transform individual birth transitions into cultural rites of passage, but also resolve another potentially worrisome dilemma peculiar to a society that insists on appearing as rational, scientific, and nonritualistic as possible: how to make birth into a rite of passage that does what it is supposed to do (transform the initiates through inculcating them with core social values and beliefs) without *looking* ritualistic at all.

Moore and Myerhoff point out that unusually extensive elaboration of ritual is most likely to occur when the ideological system enacted by a series of rituals is not explicit, "precisely because more presentation and persuasion, more communication of information is needed when ideology is scanty or fragmentary" (1977:11). Unlike religious doctrines that are explicitly spelled out, the technocratic core value system of our culture, although it pervades our experience in countless ways, is below the level of consciousness for most of us. The enormous variety of more explicit religious, philosophical, and ethnic core value and belief systems in this country necessitates special efforts on the part of the representatives of society-at-large to preserve and to perpetuate its dominant core value system. Thus the largest social institutions founded on the principles of that system, which can be counted on to touch the lives of the vast majority of American citizens, become primary socializing agents for the inculcation of mainstream American beliefs and values into young citizens, beginning with their birth in hospitals and continuing throughout their requisite years in schools. Even more profound indoctrination of society's core values can be accomplished with adults in special, intensely ritualized situations (which again, don't look to us like the rites of passage they really are) such as college football (Fiske 1975), Army basic training (Cafferata 1975; Eisenhart 1983), medical school and residency (Carver 1981; Davis-Floyd 1987a; Konner 1987; LeBaron 1981), and hospital birth.

Moreover, most becoming mothers, who are undergoing quite powerful and psychologically compelling physiological and cognitive transformations, feel a very real need for social acknowledgment and cultural alignment to give meaning and order to this often chaotic and bewildering experience (see Chapter 5). It is precisely these needs, of course, which officially conducted rites of passage are specifically designed to fulfill. In spite of the uniqueness of each birth and each woman who gives birth, standardized obstetrical procedures give this, the ultimately transformational process, the reassuring appearance of sameness and conformity to the socially dominant reality model.

Fourth Dilemma: How to "Fence In" the Dangers Associated with the Liminal Period in Birth, while at the Same Time Allowing Controlled Access to Their Revitalizing Power A fundamental paradox presented by most initiatory rites of passage to the cultures that design them lies in their official recognition and indeed, publicizing, of officially nonexistent transitional stages of being. The category systems of most cultures allow individuals to be either "here" or "there," but not in-between, for the existence of in-between calls into question the absoluteness of "here" and "there" (Douglas 1966). It is a well-documented feature of rites of passage that those in the liminal phase must be conceptually, as well as physically, isolated from the rest of society (Chapple and Coon 1942; Turner 1969), as their existence poses a threat to the entire category system of that society. Yet it is also well documented that this very threat can be of tremendous benefit to society, for in the process of the symbolic inversion of a culture's category system lies the potential for the expansion, growth, and change of that category system, and thus of the culture itself. This brings us to the fourth conceptual dilemma presented to American society by birth: how to "fence in" the dangers associated with the liminal period in birth, while at the same time allowing controlled access to their revitalizing power.

Roger Abrahams (1973) points out that a tremendous amount of energy is generated in the profound symbolic inversion of a culture's deepest beliefs that is characteristic of the liminal period in initiation rites. He states that although this energy may remain unfocused for the initiates, who often do not know exactly where they are or exactly what is happening to them, it is focused and thus usable by the elders conducting the rite. Therefore, Abrahams suggests, initiatory rites of passage may be carried out as much for the benefit of these elders as for the initiates (1973:12, 39*b*). Brigitte Jordan illustrates the symbolic process through which the focusing of the energy generated by the birth process away from the mother and toward the medical personnel who attend her takes place:

> In hospital deliveries, responsibility and credit are clearly the physician's. This becomes visible in the handshake and "thank-you" that resident and intern (or intern and medical student) exchange after birth. "Good work" is a compliment to a physician by somebody qualified to judge, namely another physician. Typically, nobody thanks the woman. In the common view, she has been delivered rather than given birth. (1983:50)

This interactional pattern of focusing the creative energy of birth onto the physician works to revitalize and perpetuate the medical system in its present form, and thus our core value system is perpetuated as well. Many women attempt to reclaim this revitalizing birth energy through subsequent, self-empowering births in the hospital and at home:

> I sat there . . . and then I realized—Hey, I did it! I wanted to have the baby at home and I read the books to figure out how and then I really did it! It worked! I didn't have to go to the hospital at all; the doctors didn't touch me! Then I realized that if I could do that great thing, perhaps I could do other things as well. (Ashford 1984:80)

The cultural significance of such efforts at refocusing this revitalizing birth energy onto women themselves will be discussed in Chapter 9.

Fifth Dilemma: How to Enculturate a Noncultural Baby Although birth is certainly a passage for the baby from the womb to the world, it is not a *rite* of passage for the baby unless, as for the mother, specific cultural actions are taken to make it so. A fifth conceptual problem with which the birth process confronts our culture, and indeed every culture, is how to find an effective means of removing new members from the noncultural realm of the womb and placing them in the cultural realm of society; in other words, how to enculturate a noncultural baby.

In the past, before the mechanistic model of the universe had diminished the hegemony of religion, the symbolic (in the eyes of the older members of society) enculturation of new members of society was accomplished through the ritual of baptism. Today, we do it through the rituals of hospital birth. American babies are baptized by inspection, testing, bathing, weighing, and wrapping in a technocratic process that extends even to the alteration of their internal physiology through the administration of a Vitamin K shot and antibiotic eye drops.

Of course, we have chosen to develop medical instead of religious rituals to fulfill the universal social need for symbolic enculturation of the newborn because we have taken ultimate responsibility for the human body, for the perpetuation of society, and for the performance of any necessary mediation between society and the supernatural which concerns the body, away from the churches and given it to our medical system. So medical procedures replace religious ones, fulfilling many of the same purposes and satisfying many of the same cultural and psychological needs. Moreover, whereas most cultures seem content to use their baptismal rituals simply to make the baby "human," we in our arrogance—or fear—use our entire set of birth rituals to actually make it appear that our babies are cultural products.

Sixth Dilemma: How to Make Birth, a Powerfully Female Phenomenon, Appear to Sanction Patriarchy   In Renaissance Europe, birth was an exclusively female phenomenon, but the baby was considered impure and unable to go to heaven until baptized by a male priest. Moreover, birth was considered so impure that afterward the mother was required to be ritually cleansed in a church—a practice known as "churching" (Arx 1978; Reynolds 1983).[4] Thus the powerfully female phenomenon of birth was channeled, albeit after the fact, into sanctioning patriarchy after all. Such religious rituals clearly delineated the high cultural value placed on the male realm and the fundamental cultural devaluation of the female realm characteristic of Renaissance Europe.

If, as I and others argue (Arditti et al. 1985; Corea 1985b; Hertz 1960; Rothman 1982, 1989), the basic thrust of our technology still is toward the right hand of maleness, then the birth process confronts American society with the same conceptual challenge faced by Renaissance society: how to make birth, a powerfully female phenomenon, appear to sanction patriarchy. For in spite of its technology and its cleavage to a patriarchal system of social life, our society's perpetuation still depends on women. The conceptual tension inherent in this paradox is also neatly dissolved by the rituals of hospital birth, as these procedures not only make birth appear to be a mechanistic process by which a baby is produced, but also make the (mostly male) "managers" of that process appear to be the producers.[5]

Seventh Dilemma: How to Remove the Sexuality from the Sexual Process of Birth   Of course, if babies are to be technologically instead of naturally produced, and if their production is going to sanction patriarchy instead of equality, then sexuality is going to become an anomaly in relation to birth, which brings us to our seventh dilemma: how to remove the sexuality from the sexual process of birth.

Women's sexuality, thought in the Renaissance period to be a devil-inspired temptation to righteous males (Kramer and Sprenger 1972), has long been a problematic issue for Western society (e.g., Freud 1938; Jones 1985). Today, sexuality remains a potent conceptual threat to the creative powers of technology, and female sexuality remains the chief reminder of that threat.

Our society has developed no more effective response to this conceptual dilemma than obstetrical rituals. As Sheila Kitzinger (1972) and Niles Newton (1973, 1977) stress, birth is a normal female sexual function (the fact that I feel the need to reference authorities on this point itself speaks eloquently for the desexualization of birth in our times), as is evident in Lynda Coleman's description of her labor:

> Labor for me was a total turn-on. Yes, there was pain—a lot of pain, and the most effective relief for it was stimulation of my clitoris. Larry rubbed my breasts and my clitoris and kissed me deeply and passionately for hours until the baby came. And when he had to go out of the room, I masturbated myself until he came back. I had lots of orgasms. They seemed to flow with the contractions. Even when I was pushing I wanted clitoral stimulation. It was the sexiest birth ever! And I loved every minute of it. I was completely alive and alove—turned on in every cell of my body. I felt that the totality of Larry and me—the fullness of everything we were individually and together—was giving birth to our child.

Yet it is precisely female sexual functions that the technocratic model finds threatening and labels both "defective" and "tabu." So effective are hospital routines at masking the intense sexuality of birth that most women today are not even aware of birth's sexual nature. For example, stimulation of the laboring woman's breasts and clitoris has been proven to be extremely effective in strengthening labor (Field 1985), yet is utterly tabu in most hospitals, where the synthetic hormone pitocin is administered intravenously instead. The routine performance of the episiotomy is another excellent example of the desexualization of birth in the hospital: an effective alternative recommended by many midwives is perineal massage with warm olive oil, far too overtly sexual a procedure for most obstetricians. Through pitocin and episiotomies, sterile gowns and sheets, enemas and pubic shaves, anesthesia and orange antiseptic, the intense and potentially ecstatic sexuality of birth is consistently and effectively masked.

That this masking was no historical accident is revealed in Mary Poovey's (1986) article on the introduction of anesthesia in obstetrics, in which she graphically describes the emergent medical profession's fear of female sexuality in childbirth. For example, Poovey quotes W. Tyler Smith, an eminent British obstetrician of the mid-nineteenth century, as he discusses the use of ether to remove the pain of labor:

> In one of the cases observed by Baron Dubois, the woman drew an attendant toward her to kiss, as she was lapsing into insensibility, and this woman afterwards confessed to dreaming of coitus with her husband while she lay etherized. . . . In ungravid women, rendered insensible for the performance of surgical operations, erotic gesticulations have occasionally been observed, and in one case, in which enlarged nymphae were removed, the woman went unconsciously through the movements attendant on the sexual orgasm, in the presence of numerous bystanders. (Smith 1847:377, quoted in Poovey 1986:142)

Commenting on Poovey's article, Laura O'Banion notes the horror that the idea of childbirth as a primal sexual experience induced for the early obstetrician—"since it was supposed that only the penis (or an analogue thereof) was capable of providing sexual satisfaction, the penis-analogue in childbirth must be—the child itself!" (1987:34). The nineteenth-century Dr. Smith, unable to imagine that women would wish to expose themselves to this possibility, wonders if the natural and "proper" function of pain might be to obliterate the underlying ecstasy that would be released if the pain were eliminated, and he therefore argues *against* the use of ether in labor:

> May it not be, that in woman the physical pain neutralizes the sexual emotions, which would otherwise probably be present, but which would tend very much to alter our estimation of the modesty and retiredness proper to the sex. . . . Chastity of feeling, and above all, emotional self-control, at a time when women are receiving such assistance as the accoucheur can render, are of far more importance than insensibility to pain. They would scarcely submit to the possibility of a sexual act in which their unborn offspring would take the part of excitor. (Smith 1847, quoted in Poovey 1986)

"Oh yes they would!" is the response, in 1988, of midwife Jeannine Parvati-Baker. Her description of her own experience reveals just how intense the sexuality of birth can be:

I feel the baby come down. The sensation is ecstatic. I had prepared some-what for this being as painful as my last delivery had been. Yet this time the pulse of birth feels wonderful! I am building up to the birth climax after nine months of pleasurable foreplay. With one push the babe is in the canal. The next push brings him down, down into that space just before orgasm when we women know how God must have felt creating this planet.

The water supports my birth outlet. I feel connected to the mainland, to my source. These midwife hands know just what to do to support the now crowning head, coming so fast. How glad I am for all those years of orgasms! Slow orgasms, fast ones, those which build and subside and peak again and again. That practice aids my baby's gentle emergence so that he doesn't spurt out too quickly. He comes, as do I.

Eighth Dilemma: How to Get Women, in a Culture that Pays Increasing Lip Service to the Ideal of Equality, to Accept a Belief System that Denigrates Them The eighth and final conceptual dilemma with which birth confronts American society constitutes a potential cultural bomb-shell: how to get women, in a culture that pays increasing lip service to the ideal of equality, to accept a belief system that denigrates them. As noted folklorist Richard Bauman once said, "Folklore is about the politics of culture." For me personally, the decoding of the symbolic messages hidden behind the scientific guise of hospital routines has led to a chilling reminder of the twin political threats presented to women by our technocratic model of reality. On the one hand, this model de-prives women of their innate uniqueness and power as birth-givers. On the other, it perpetuates our cultural belief in women's innate physio-logical inferiority. And yet, because of the potential for egalitarianism inherent in technology, this model does contain certain conceptual ad-vantages for women which, in the early part of this century, proved alluring enough for many women themselves to actively work for the cultural adoption of this model of birth, and which today offer to women the freedom from biological constraints which many increas-ingly desire.

The birth process in American culture is and always has been a ma-trix of gender differentiation. In the 1800s, when most women gave birth at home, motherhood was the central defining feature of woman-hood, and women's appropriate domain was the home. Early feminists eagerly sought technological hospital birth, in the hope that it would constitute a positive step toward true equality of the sexes through removing the cultural stereotypes of women as weak and dependent slaves to nature. Many of these early feminists went to great lengths to achieve anesthetized births (Wertz and Wertz 1977:150–154; Leavitt 1986:171–195).

However, of course, instead of leading to equality, in its blanket categorization of the female body as an inherently defective machine, the technocratic model reflects and perpetuates our profound cultural belief in the innate inferiority of women to the men who more perfectly mirror our cultural image of the properly functioning machine. Thus our society is presented with the dilemma of how to get women to accept a belief system based on the machine, as this system entails the principle of the male as the physically and intellectually more perfect member of the species no less profoundly than did the Aristotelian philosophy that watered its roots. The following chapter will demonstrate exactly how this socialization is accomplished in American society by the rituals of hospital birth, as through these rituals, the full force of the belief and value system on which our society is based is brought to bear on American women.

CHAPTER 3

Birth Messages

... symbolic acts operate through their capacity to map
changed or adjusted perceptions of the possibilities inherent
in a situation onto the actor's orientation to it.
    —Nancy Munn, "Symbolism in a Ritual Context"

This chapter decodes the messages conveyed by hospital birth rituals, otherwise known as "standard procedures for normal birth." These ritual procedures, common in many American hospitals, make birth appear to conform to the technocratic model and babies appear to have been produced by society. Each procedure is explained in detail in the body of the chapter; here I will provide the reader with a brief overview of these "standard procedures" in order to provide a basis for the symbolic analysis that follows.

"STANDARD PROCEDURES FOR NORMAL BIRTH"

Upon entering the hospital, the laboring woman is taken in a wheelchair to a "prep" room. There she is separated from her partner,[1] her clothes are removed, she is asked to put on a hospital gown, her pubic hair is shaved, a vaginal exam is performed, and she is given an enema. She is then reunited with her partner, if he chooses to be present, and put to bed. Her access to food is limited or prohibited, and an intravenous needle is inserted in her hand or arm. Some type of analgesia is administered. A pitocin drip may be started through the IV. The external fetal monitor is attached to the woman by means of a large belt strapped around her waist to monitor the strength of her contractions and the baby's heartbeat. The internal monitor may also be attached through electrodes inserted into the baby's scalp, prior to which the amniotic sac, or membranes, must be ruptured. Periodic vaginal exams are performed at least once every two hours, and more often in later labor, to check the degree of the baby's descent. Epidural analgesia is often administered. The preceding procedures may be performed at varying intervals over a variable time period and in differing order, depending on the length of the woman's labor and the degree to which it conforms to hospital standards.

As the moment of birth approaches, there is an intensification of actions performed on the woman, as she is transferred to a delivery room, placed in the lithotomy position, covered with sterile sheets and doused with antiseptic, and an episiotomy is performed. As her baby is being born, the mother may be slightly raised and allowed to watch in a mirror. After the birth, she is handed the baby for a certain amount of time, her placenta is extracted if it does not come out quickly on its own, her episiotomy is sewn up, her uterus is palpated, more pitocin is administered to assist her uterus to contract, and finally, she is cleaned up and transferred to a hospital bed.

The baby too receives a good deal of procedural attention during her hospital birth. While still in the womb she may be viewed with ultrasound; her heart tones are monitored; sometimes an electrode is inserted under the skin of her scalp. As the baby emerges from the birth canal, her head is supported and turned, her shoulders may be slightly twisted, and the mucus is sucked from her mouth and nostrils with a suction device. Immediately after her birth, the newborn's umbilical cord will be cut. She will be rated with an Apgar chart at two different times, washed, weighed, and wrapped; silver nitrate or an antibiotic substitute will be put into her eyes, and she will be given a Vitamin K injection. She may then be handed to her mother and/or father for a brief period of time, after which she will be transferred to the nursery and placed in a plastic bassinet or a radiant warmer for about four hours, for assessment and observation.

Of course, there are many variations on this theme in hospitals around the United States. Some procedures that used to be standard in the 1940s, 1950s, and 1960s such as handstrapping, the exclusion of fathers, and the use of "twilight sleep" for labor seem part of the Dark Ages now. Other major changes since then have involved the incorporation of increasingly sophisticated machines and drugs and of the ideas that it is good for the father to be present and for women to be conscious during birth. In recent years many younger doctors have begun to drop shaves and enemas from their standard orders (although several complained to me that the nurses, also strongly socialized into the technocratic model, frequently administer them anyway). Increasing numbers of women opt for delivery in a birthing suite or LDR (labor-delivery-recovery room), where they can wear their own clothes, do without the IV, walk around during labor, and where the options of side-lying, squatting, or even standing for birth are increasingly available. (The fact that many standard procedures can be instrumentally omitted underscores my point that they are rituals.) Yet in spite of these concessions to consumer demand for more "natural" birth, a basic pattern of high-technological intervention remains: most hospitals now *require* at least periodic electronic monitoring of all laboring women; analgesics, pitocin, and epidurals are widely administered; and one woman in four is delivered by Cesarean section. Thus, although some medical procedures drop away, the use of the most powerful signifiers of the woman's dependence on science and technology intensifies.

Moreover, in spite of the increasing availability of various options, and of nearly three decades of effort by childbirth activists to change them, the procedures analyzed below are all still standard in many American hospitals; they were all experienced by the majority of the women in my study. Together they paint a composite picture of American core values and beliefs. I argue that these procedures serve as rituals and are so widely used in hospital birth because they successfully fulfill several important needs: (1) the individual psychological needs of the hospital personnel officially responsible for birth for constant confirmation of the rightness of the technocratic model, and for reassuring ways to cope with birth's constant threat to upset that model; (2) the individual needs of birthing women for psychological reassurance in the face of these same unknowns, for official recognition by society of their personal transformations, and for official confirmation of the rightness and validity of their belief systems; and (3) the need of the wider culture to ensure the effective socialization of its citizens and thus its own perpetuation.

A SYMBOLIC ANALYSIS OF STANDARD OBSTETRICAL PROCEDURES

Each procedure will be discussed in four sections. The first section will briefly describe the procedure and will present a summary of the official rationale for its use as explained in medical textbooks or taught in medical schools and training hospitals. These rationales are often complex; I have tried here to select their most salient features for presentation. The second section will summarize evidence about the physiological and psychological effects these procedures have on laboring women. Often this evidence directly contradicts or refutes the medical rationale. Sometimes this refutation is compelling. Cases where available evidence indicates that obstetrical procedures either fail to accomplish their stated purpose, or actually cause harm, lead to the obvious conclusion that the only possible reasons for the continued performance of such procedures are ritual and symbolic. Indeed, one of the values of this research for me personally has been to be able to answer a question I have frequently heard from childbirth educators and birth activists: "Since so many of these procedures are so bad for women and babies, why do they keep on doing them?"

Here I must add a brief caveat: these first two sections, on "Official Rationale" and "Physiological Effects," do not pretend to be exhaustive and may seem oversimplified. Space considerations do not allow me to present all of the medical rationale for each procedure, nor all of the evidence for or against their physiological efficacy. The relevant literature includes hundreds of medical studies and a number of easily accessible books that sum up the scientific evidence for the lay reader (see, for example, Brackbill, McManus, and Woodward 1988; Brackbill, Rice, and Young 1984; Inch 1984; Stewart and Stewart 1976, 1977, 1979, 1981; Wertz and Wertz 1989).

The third section presents verbal reactions of the women in the study to these procedures in order to enliven and humanize my scholarly analysis, to remind the reader that these procedures are experienced by thousands of women across the country every day, and to indicate the range of women's responses to these hospital birth routines. (Chapter 5 presents an in-depth look at these responses.) The last section will present each routine as a transformative ritual that, through the careful and precise manipulation of powerful symbols, transmits a specific set of messages to the birthing woman, her partner, her new baby, and the hospital staff.

WHEELCHAIR

Description and Official Rationale   When a laboring woman walks into a hospital, one of the first things that happens to her is that she will be asked or told to sit in a wheelchair, in which she will then be wheeled to the "prep" room, instead of walking. The rationale behind this procedure is that the woman might faint or stumble, and fall, hurting either herself or her baby, and making the hospital vulnerable to lawsuits.

Physiological Effects   The primary effects of a brief ride in a wheelchair will be cognitive, not physiological.

Women's Responses   Most laboring women feel that they are perfectly capable of walking and are no more likely to fall during labor than before it began. Some report enjoying the ride, whereas others dislike being made to feel silly and weak. Some women accept the message sent to them by the wheelchair, whereas others invert its symbolism, and so avoid internalizing its message:

> I can remember just almost being in tears by the way they would wheel you in. I would come to the delivery or into the hospital on top of this, breathing, you know, all in control. And they slap you in this wheelchair! It made me suddenly feel like maybe I wasn't in control anymore. (Suzanne Sampson)

> The maternity room sent somebody down with a wheelchair. I didn't have any need for a wheelchair so we piled all of the luggage up in the wheelchair and wheeled it up to the floor. (Patricia Hellman)

Ritual Purposes   As we have seen, under the technocratic model labor is viewed as a mechanical process taking place inside a machine inherently predisposed to malfunction. It is thus incumbent upon the hospital to assume in its treatment of birth that malfunction may occur at any time and to be constantly prepared for its occurrence—an assumption that has led to what Suzanne Arms has called "just-in-case obstetrics" (Ettner 1976:38). It is also incumbent upon the hospital to make the premises of the technocratic model appear to be true and to map the reality contained within this model onto the birthing woman's perceptions of her situation so skillfully that she will be able to perceive her experience in these terms *only*.

The wheelchair is an interesting first step in this process. To place a healthy woman in a wheelchair instead of allowing her to walk on her own is to tell her that at the very least the hospital thinks of her as disabled and weak. Although she may reject this message on a conscious intellectual level, its passage through her body and into the right hemisphere of her brain will guarantee that, on an unconscious level, she will receive the message, "you are disabled"; in other words, she will receive what one psychologist has called a "felt sense" (Gendlin 1980) of her body as suddenly weak and dependent, as in Suzanne Sampson's response above.

The cognitive ramifications of the wheelchair do not end with its effect on the laboring woman's perceptions of herself. Seeing his wife being pushed along in a wheelchair transforms her as well in the eyes of her partner, who may suddenly perceive her as weaker, more passive, and more fragile than before. Moreover, the first impression she makes on her hospital attendants will include the images of fragility, passivity, and disability, images on which their further assessments of her will be based. Her lowered position has the effect of making hospital personnel talk *to* the partner standing, while talking *down to* the laboring woman in the wheelchair. The image of disability will most especially include the image of inability to walk; from the moment of her entry into the labor and delivery unit, the laboring woman is marked as someone who should not or cannot walk (a significant message, since walking is one of the most beneficial things a woman in labor can do—as is discussed later in this chapter). As in any initiatory rite of passage, this estranging or "strange-making" device is employed at the very beginning; the effect is to start the breakdown of the initiate's category system necessary to ensure her openness to new learning.

THE "PREP"

This friend of mine and I had spent a lot of time
talking . . . about IVs for example. So when the nurse
said, "I'm going to put an IV in your arm," and she
left the room to go get it, I said, "Laura, why are you
letting her do this? You said you weren't going to have
one." She looked at me with this real confused expression on her face and she said "I don't know." The
nurse stuck her with an IV. She was given an enema.
She was shaved and everything, and she just sat there
and let it be done to her.
                                        —Kim Lozenski

The "prep" is a multistep procedure that usually includes: (1) separation of the woman from her partner, as he is asked to go fill out papers while she is ushered into the "prep" room; (2) replacement of the woman's clothes with a hospital gown; (3) shaving the pubic hair of the woman in labor; and (4) the administration of an enema. These procedures all take place in the "prep room" or the labor room, one right after the other, but for the sake of clarity I will discuss each one separately.

PRESENCE OF PARTNER/SEPARATION FROM PARTNER

Description and Official Rationale The partners (husbands, friends, significant others) of laboring women are nowadays widely admitted to the labor and delivery rooms from which they were excluded until the 1970s. Their admission did not occur easily in the United States; it was the result of a long and hard-fought campaign by parents, childbirth educators, and obstetricians such as Robert Bradley, originator of the Bradley Method of "husband-coached" childbirth. Hospital tolerance of the fathers' presence increased as it was discovered that when fathers are educated and prepared for birth, the support they provide the laboring woman enables her to cope with her labor in more socially acceptable ways (breathing instead of screaming, for example), thus both helping her and making it easier for hospital personnel to cope with her. (Some of the obstetricians I interviewed expressed the belief that the couple is less likely to sue in case of problematic birth outcome if the father is present during labor and birth and "can see how hard the doctor is working to take care of his wife and child.")

Although 91 percent of the women in my study who gave birth in the hospital expected to be with their partners throughout labor, all of these women were separated from their partners during the "prep," even those who had been promised by their obstetricians that they would be able to remain together at all times—an experience they share with the vast majority of American women who try to birth in the hospital with their partners present. I have been unable to find any scientific justification for this separation period in the obstetrical literature—indeed, the wheelchair and the separation of the laboring couple are not even mentioned in the obstetrical texts I examined (Benson 1980; Cunningham, MacDonald, and Gant 1989; Oxorn and Foote 1975; Pritchard and MacDonald 1980; Pritchard, MacDonald, and Gant 1985; Wynn 1975). The reasons given by medical personnel for this separation were that the husband would not want to see his wife given an enema nor to watch her pubic hair being shaved. Some nurses also felt that they could get their routine diagnostic and examination work done more efficiently while they had the patient all to themselves.

Physiological Effects Positive effects of the presence of the partner generally include decreased anxiety and fear, increased concentration on breathing techniques with his help, enhanced self-confidence, and decreased emotional stress. Negative effects of separation from the partner during the prep are generally minimal if the woman is not in much pain, although some of the women in my study, for example, reported that their labors slowed down until they were reunited with their partners. Those women who were "prepped" during heavy labor reported that the pain of their contractions increased during the separation period, whereas their ability to maintain "control" decreased.

Women's Responses Many of the women, in response to the official rationale presented to them for the separation period, noted that their partners were with them through vomiting, using the bathroom, and giving birth, all of which made their exclusion at the beginning rather absurd. Yet all those who asked not to be separated found tremendous resistance on the part of the hospital staff to the idea, and *none* were successful at remaining together. July Sanders and her husband experienced this resistance as follows:

> They get you and whisk you away from your husband, and he has got to fill out these papers. We went every time [she has four children] and registered and paid. We even paid a $500 deposit the first two times so he wouldn't have to spend one second away from me. And you know, he barely got there for the second one, and we had done all that stuff! I kept saying "Where's my husband? This baby's crowned!" And he was down there filling out unnecessary—we're not going to skip town . . . You know? We were going to be there for several days, and they just treat you—I really feel like they need a lot of education for um, for making it a lot easier.

Susan Betts also found this procedure discouraging:

> By the time my husband was allowed in the labor room so many things had happened and so many people had tried to help as his substitute that I was confused and losing control.

Ritual Purposes In the separation of husband and wife during the "prep," we see the continuance of the conceptual demarcation of ritual boundaries begun with the wheelchair, as the woman's body is claimed for the institution by its representative, the nurse.

In "Is There a Family? New Anthropological Views," Collier, Rosaldo, and Yanagisako state:

> The family is seen as representing not only the antithesis of the market relations of capitalism; it is also sacralized in our minds as the last stronghold against the State, as the symbolic refuge from the intrusions of a public domain that constantly threatens our sense of privacy and self-determination. (1982:25)

In the hospital, the father stands as witness to and participant in not only the birth of his child, but also his wife's birth into her new identity as mother, his own birth as father, and the birth of his family as a new social unit. Thus his presence represents a strong conceptual victory for the family in relation to the core values of American society, insofar as it constitutes: (1) acknowledgment on the part of society of the ritual significance of the father's own individual passage into parenthood; and (2) a powerful symbolic recognition of the family's integrity and importance in relation to society.

However, in other, equally significant ways, the father's inclusion at birth constitutes a victory for *society*. By including the father at birth, society stands to: (1) strengthen and reinforce the stability of the nuclear family as its basic organizational unit in an era when the integrity of that unit seems threatened by the high divorce rate and by growing rates of "unpartnered" pregnancy and birth; and (2) ensure that the father too will receive the messages sent by the rituals of hospital birth. As Coleman Romalis points out in "Taking Care of the Little Woman" (1981), including the father at birth often enables the hospital to co-opt him in favor of the technocratic model and then to utilize his influence to further the alignment of his wife's perceptions with that model. Moreover, including the father enables society to "have its cake and eat it too": by ritually separating husband and wife during the "prep," the hospital can make the very clear symbolic statement that, although the family is indeed important in American society, the institution is more so.

This "standard hospital policy" sends two powerful messages: "the hospital has the *right* to separate husband and wife, and thus holds an authority higher and greater than the family," and "the laboring woman, soon to deliver to society its new member, now conceptually belongs to the institution, and must be marked as such." This marking is accomplished by the prep itself.

REPLACEMENT OF CLOTHES WITH HOSPITAL GOWN

Description and Official Rationale   The official rationale for requiring women in labor to wear a standard hospital gown, which ties at the neck and is open in the back, has to do with the idea that hospital gowns are cleaner than a woman's own nightgown and more practical as well, allowing as they do easy access to her genital area for cervical exams and for delivery of the baby, and to her back for the administration of epidural or caudal anesthesia. Should they become soiled, they are also very easy to change.

Women's Responses   None of the women in my study liked the way they *felt* in the gown. However, some saw it as entirely practical and appropriate, whereas others found the degree of exposure of their private areas which "those ugly gowns" entailed to be decidedly distasteful.

Ritual Purposes   A woman's clothes are her markers of individual identity; removing them effectively communicates the message that she is no longer autonomous, but dependent on the institution. Like the identical uniforms of Marine basic trainees, the hospital gown indicates the woman's liminal status:

> Liminal entities, such as neophytes in initiation or puberty rites, may be represented as possessing nothing. They may . . . wear only a strip of clothing, or even go naked, to demonstrate that as liminal beings they have no status, property, insignia, secular clothing indicating rank or role. . . . Their behavior is normally passive or humble; they must obey their instructors implicitly, and accept arbitrary punishment without complaint. It is as though they are being reduced or ground down to a uniform condition to be fashioned anew. (Turner 1969:95)

The gown begins a powerful process of the symbolic inversion of the most private region of the woman's body to the most public. Its openness intensifies the message of the woman's loss of autonomy: not only does it expose intimate body parts to institutional handling and control, it also prevents her from simply walking out the door anytime she chooses. Like a prison inmate, she is now marked in society's eyes as belonging to a total institution—the hospital (Goffman 1961).

SHAVING THE PUBIC HAIR

Description and Official Rationale   *Williams* provides no rationale at all for shaving the pubic hair, simply stating that it is done in many hospitals (Cunningham et al. 1989:309). Physicians interviewed stated that shaving the perineal area both provides clearer visibility for them and reduces the danger of infection, since hair cannot be sterilized. (It is worth mentioning here that the usual response by the Marine sergeant to the question of why the heads of his trainees must be shaved is "to prevent lice.")

Physiological Effects   "No scientific study has shown that shaving reduces rate of infection" (Brackbill et al. 1984:4). Shaving in fact *increases* the risk of infection in the open abrasions and small lacerations often left by the razor, which can serve as excellent breeding grounds for bacteria (Cruse 1977). In a study of wound infection in 406 preoperative patients, Seropian and Reynolds (1971) reported an infection rate of 5.6 percent after shaving and 0.6 percent after no preparation. Most significantly for predelivery shaving, "the infection rate was 3.1% if the shaving was done just before surgery, 7.1% if done 24 hours before surgery, and a striking 20% if done more than 24 hours before surgery" (Mahan and McKay 1983:243.) Other physiological effects of shaving include bothersome itching and burning sensations as the hair grows back.

Women's Responses   The women in my study often questioned why the visibility issue couldn't simply be resolved by clipping the pubic hair short instead of shaving it off completely, complaining that the shaving causes them a good deal of unnecessary and easily avoidable itching and discomfort as the hair is growing back, and that it makes them feel "dehumanized" and "unfeminine." (Clipping has indeed replaced shaving in a growing number of hospitals.) *No one* liked the shave or felt it was necessary, not even those who *wanted* a technocratic birth—a report consistent with a British hospital study that found that 98 percent of mothers, when asked, objected to shaving (Tew 1982).

Ritual Purposes   The ritual shaving of her pubic hair further intensifies the institutional marking of the laboring woman as hospital property. States Hallpike, "Cutting hair equals social control" (1979:105). Just as the head-shaving of the Marine basic trainee functions as a "strange-making device" that both alienates the young man from his former conceptions of self and ritually marks him as being in a liminal state and belonging to "a particular disciplinary regime within society" (Hallpike 1979:103), the Marines, so pubic shaving separates the laboring woman from her former conceptions of her body, and, like the gown, further marks her as being in a liminal state and as belonging to the hospital. It also (1) ritually establishes a boundary separation between the upper and lower portions of a woman's body; and (2) strips the lower portion of her body of its sexuality, returning the woman to a conceptual state of childishness and its accompanying characteristics of dependency and lack of personal responsibility (it is significant here to note that the hospital gown, although exposing the woman's genitals, thoroughly covers her breasts, which retain their sexual connotations); and (3) continues the powerful process of symbolic inversion begun with the hospital gown.

THE ENEMA

Description and Official Rationale As part of the prep, an enema is usually administered by a nurse. Medical personnel maintain that enemas reduce the chance that fecal material will be pushed out during birth, thus decreasing the chance of infection. A few whom I interviewed also frankly admitted that they do not like to clean up feces and so give enemas to all their patients in the hopes of avoiding this unpleasantness. Others reasons include "preventing hard fecal matter in the rectum from compressing the birth canal, stimulating labor progress, and avoiding the embarrassment for the woman" that might result if she expels stool during labor—especially likely during pushing (Mahan and McKay 1983:244).

Physiological Effects *Williams* recommends a simple Fleet enema. In a short diatribe against the all-too-common misuse of the enema, the seventeenth edition of *Williams* states that the "infamous 3H enema (High, Hot, and a Hell of a Lot) has no place in obstetrics!" (Pritchard, MacDonald, and Gant 1985:333). (This felicitous statement has been removed from the eighteenth edition [Cunningham et al. 1989:309]). Unfortunately, this hot water and soapsuds enema is still most commonly used in many hospitals. Soap often causes rectal irritation and other complications, and its use in enemas is medically contraindicated (Barker 1945; Benditt 1945; Lewis 1965; Pike 1971; Smith 1964).

"A substantial portion of women in labor will have bowel movements, whether or not enemas are given," especially during both early labor and pushing (Mahan and McKay 1983:247). Available evidence indicates that enemas do not in fact decrease the chances of elimination during birth nor the incidence of fecal contamination during labor, whereas they do often cause considerable pain and distress to the laboring mother (Romney and Gordon 1981; Whitley and Mack 1980). Moreover, the expulsion of feces during labor does not seem to increase infection rates: in a study of 274 birthing women randomly assigned to enema or no enema groups, no difference in infection rates was found (Romney and Gordon 1981), and the risk of neonatal infection was very remote (seven babies from each group showed signs of infection that may or may not have had to do with bowel organisms). Another finding of this study was that the two groups had similar durations of labor, contradicting the notion that enemas shorten labor.

Women's Responses   Toni Kyle: "The enema was the single most painful part of Johnathan's birth." Melinda Simpson: "I simply refused to have an enema. I wasn't going to let anybody humiliate me like that." Jacqueline Barrett: "I asked for the enema; I felt it would be just too embarrassing to push without it. But when the time came, I pushed out some feces anyway." Betsy Yellin: "I didn't want to . . . um . . . inconvenience the nurses like that." And Patricia Hellman:

> I did want an enema. I had talked with other people and I was convinced that it would help. In fact, I had to insist. [My obstetrician, who was very accommodating] said, "You can if you want to." But I had to insist on it during labor. I don't know why—I guess because I was in the alternative birth center—I had to ask for it three or four times, but it did help. It relieved a lot of the pressure and I felt better. But I didn't get the rest of the prep at all. It didn't seem to give anybody any problems.

The consensus on the enema among the women in my study seemed to be that it should be strictly a matter of personal choice. Some also felt that doctors should let women know that the self-administration of Fleet enemas at home is a viable option.

Ritual Purposes   The enema is readily recognizable as the obligatory ritual cleansing of the initiate traditional in many rites of passage. But because it is the lower region of the body that is cleansed, the enema also constitutes an intensification of the symbolic inversion accomplished by the shaving and the gown—from most private to institutional property. Accompanying this process (especially when the enema is high, hot, and soapy) is the clear message that the laboring woman's most private parts were internally dirty while they were private, and that it is the institution—as society's representative—which made them clean. Underlying this message is the deeper message that individuals are impure, whereas society (like Ivory soap) is pure.

(As is indicated in Patricia's response above, when an individual herself requests or administers the enema, it loses many of its symbolic connotations in terms of the technocratic model—a phenomenon that will be investigated in detail in Chapter 5.)

BED

Description and Official Rationale   One hardly needs a description of or a rationale for going to bed in a hospital, for in a hospital, bed is simply where one is usually supposed to be. Under the technocratic model women in labor are conceived of as weak and in danger of falling or tiring themselves unduly if they get out of bed too much to walk the halls during labor. A common complaint of nurses is that they can't keep track of the whereabouts of "ambulating" women. Furthermore, staying in bed is necessary when electronic monitors are attached and is much more practical when fluids are being intravenously administered than trying to ambulate towing an IV stand.

Although side-lying in bed is a safe position for labor, "dorsal recumbency" (lying flat on one's back) is still the most common position in many hospitals. This supine position facilitates both vaginal exams and the woman's connection to the monitoring equipment. Shifts in position after the monitors have been hooked up can result in wild swings on the monitor printouts, leading to potential misdiagnoses of fetal distress, and can necessitate readjustment of IV lines.

Physiological Effects   The evidence is unequivocal: nonmoving, back-lying positions during labor are dangerous! In both sitting and reclining positions in bed, the mother's cardiac output is reduced (Ueland and Hansen 1979), and the inferior vena cava and the lower aorta are compressed, resulting in reduced blood circulation in the mother and reduced blood supply to the baby (Abitol 1985; Eckstein and Marx 1974), which can lead to fetal distress and necessitate a rapid Cesarean section. Moreover, contractions in supine and sitting positions are much less efficient than in side-lying and standing positions (Roberts et al. 1983), which are by far the most efficacious for labor (Mendez-Bauer et al. 1975; Roberts et al. 1984):

> It was established in 1976 that an increase of 30 to 40 mmHg pressure is exerted by the fetal head on the cervix as a result of the effects of gravity, that is, standing instead of lying down. This means that, although the frequency of the contractions is the same, [their] effectiveness is much greater, and hence the efficiency and rate of the dilatation of the cervix is improved. (Inch 1984:30)

A number of studies indicate that first-time mothers who stood and/or walked for most of their labors had significantly shorter labors (Caldeyro-Barcia et al. 1978, 1979; Diaz et al. 1980; Flynn et al. 1978; Liu 1974; Mitre 1974; Stewart and Calder 1983), and tended to require less pain medication (Flynn et al. 1978). No adverse effects from standing or walking (far more common cross-culturally than lying in bed) during labor have been reported in any clinical trials. In contrast, the increased pain resulting from lying down throughout labor seems to play a role in women's demands for analgesia, and the slowness of labor in supine positions often results in a medical decision to administer pitocin.

In the medical studies that take maternal preference into account, most of those mothers who preferred standing or walking in early labor reported that after they had entered the most active phase of labor (defined as beginning at 5–6 centimeters dilation), they preferred side-lying in bed (Calvert et al. 1982; Stewart and Calder 1983; Williams et al. 1980).

Women's Responses

> It's funny—it seems so normal to lie down in labor—just to be in the hospital seems to mean "to lie down." But as soon as I did, I felt that I had lost something. I felt defeated. And it seems to me now that my lying down tacitly permitted the Demerol, or maybe entailed it. And the Demerol entailed the pitocin, and the pitocin entailed the Cesarean. It was as if, in laying down my body as I was told to, I also laid down my autonomy and my right to self-direction. (Elizabeth Fisher)

> I walked the halls for most of my labor. It just hurt more when I laid down. I felt strong and in control when I walked, even though it still hurt, so I kept on walking, because that was a lot better than being in bed and feeling like a little sick kid. (Paula Cooley)

I was in labor for a long time. I was stuck in transition at least 8 centimeters I guess for about six hours and finally wound up having to have [pitocin and] an epidural to shake the kid out of there. I just laid on my back in that stupid hospital bed. You know, if I had known to get up and walk, or turn on my side, or do something, I might could have handled it better. (Georgia Adams)

Well, where else would you be when you are in labor besides in bed? (Betsy Yellin)

Ritual Purposes   Many a laboring woman wearing a hospital gown at this moment would perhaps tell us that she believes herself to be healthy and strong. But this conviction, which the hospital staff may verbally reinforce, is steadily being undermined by the messages with which the woman's environment bombards her. Being put to bed, as nearly all laboring women sooner or later are, intensifies messages already communicated by the wheelchair and the gown: that she is a patient, that she is sick. Or, more precisely, it tells her that the hospital conceptualizes her as sick—a message that, as time passes and labor becomes more intense, becomes more and more likely to be internalized as "I am sick." Moreover, going to bed, like sitting in a wheelchair, is a lower structural positioning of the laboring woman that carries heavy symbolic weight (Goffman 1961). Level eye contact in American society is a significant indicator of interactional equality. The fact that the laboring woman in bed must constantly be talked down to puts her at a significant conceptual and interactional disadvantage.

Standing and walking during labor have contrasting symbolic ramifications: the woman who moves and positions herself flexibly, according to her own comfort and needs, appears powerful, healthy, and in charge of her own labor and birth, and is the interactional equal of those attending her. Although today women may often choose to walk around during labor, the periodic monitoring required in most hospitals necessitates regular returns to their conceptual locus—the bed and its messages. Although monitors that work by telemetry have been around for a decade (they require no wires and can be attached unobtrusively to the laboring woman's thigh), we need not wonder why there has been no rush to incorporate them in most hospitals (McKay and Roberts 1989).

FASTING

Description and Official Rationale   Food and most drinks are routinely withheld from laboring women in most hospitals. Food digestion sometimes slows a little during unmedicated labor; narcotic analgesics cause considerable slowing of digestion. The rationale behind the practice of not permitting women in labor to eat is that, should they need a general anesthetic, the danger of inhaling undigested stomach contents if they vomit while anesthetized is greatly reduced. Aspiration of solid food can cause choking, and aspiration of acidic gastric juices can lead to a number of complications, including pulmonary edema and partial lung collapse, part of a rare and potentially lethal complication known as Mendelson's syndrome. According to *Williams,* "Vomiting with aspiration of gastric contents is a constant threat and often a major cause of serious maternal morbidity and mortality [in obstetric anesthesia]" (Cunningham et al. 1989:327). Stating that such dangers were "described by Mendelson in 1946" (1989:331), they cite as evidence a 1972 survey by Crawford that identified inhalation of gastric contents as associated with at least half of all maternal deaths.

Physiological Effects   The commonly held belief in the dangers of gastric aspiration is not based on fact but on anecdote and "hype" (McKay and Mahan 1988b:224). This medical myth continues to deprive hundreds of thousands of laboring women in this country of the nourishment their bodies need. The truth is that aspiration itself is extremely rare, and most women who aspirate do not die. Mendelson's original 1946 article reported several cases of aspiration and the subsequent development of aspiration pneumonia, but *no* deaths. The cumulative results of more recent studies show that aspiration, far from being the *leading* cause of maternal death, is a minor and rare cause, accounting at the most for 2 percent of maternal deaths (Baggish and Hooper 1974), or 1 in every 200,000 laboring women (Scott 1978). And, as Moir (1979) pointed out, even this small risk of gastric inhalation under general anesthesia can be avoided, under all but the most dramatic of circumstances, by the use of regional anesthesia.

Ironically, insisting that women fast during labor may actually, should they inhale their vomitus, increase their risk of pulmonary edema, because the gastric juices left in the stomach after hours of fasting are far more acidic than usual; highly acidic fluids in the lungs are more toxic to lung tissue.[2] Moreover, the supine position necessitated by the administration of anesthesia increases the risk of gastric inhalation and likelihood of aspiration (Pedersen and Finster 1979). The risk of aspiration increases further when medical personnel apply yet another fairly common intervention: pushing on the abdomen (fundal pressure) to speed up the birth (Kruse and Gibbs 1978).

Starving laboring women may also result in ketosis—a condition of weakened muscle cells and alterations in the blood chemistry which results from too-rapid depletion of the laboring woman's stores of glycogen, which then causes her to start using her fat stores as a form of energy; ketones are the by-products of this process; their unchecked buildup in the bloodstream causes the uterus to contract less efficiently and labor to slow down. When this happens, the usual hospital response is to speed up labor with the synthetic hormone pitocin, which entails its own set of risks, as we will see below.

Would an athlete run a twenty-four-hour marathon without food or drink? Both the athlete and the laboring woman need quick energy from food to maintain their increased cardiac output. Both take more time than usual to digest solid foods but can use oral fluids to keep blood glucose levels up. Hazle has suggested that women in early labor should be encouraged to eat meals similar to the pregame meals of athletic competitors: "high in carbohydrates for quick energy, and fluids for hydration, and low in fats for digestive ease" (1986:174). Such foods, as well as electrolyte-replenishing fruit juices and fluids (such as Recharge, Third Wind,[3] and Gatorade) can be used during active labor (Hazle recommends at least four ounces per hour) as long as narcotic analgesia (which slows digestion dramatically) is avoided.[4]

Such evidence and suggestions seem to confront laboring women with a choice: to eat and drink during labor to keep up their strength but stay away from digestion-slowing analgesics, or to utilize pain-relievers, accept the lessening of endurance that comes with fasting during extreme physical exertion, and rely on synthetic labor stimulation should a resultant slowing of labor occur. Such a choice, however, is in practice not usually the woman's to make, as standard policies in most hospitals prohibit her from eating or drinking anything more sustaining than ice chips, tea, or lollipops.

Pointing out that "studies of the nutritional needs of laboring women are virtually nonexistent," McKay and Mahan suggest:

> Labor is very hard work—perhaps the most prolonged and intense physical exertion that many women ever undertake. We would do well to pay attention to the rapidly emerging field of exercise physiology for new ideas about oral nutrients we might use to maximize the natural progress of labor. Improvement of the mother's nutrition and strength, if done correctly, may have salutory effects on fetal outcome. (1988a:219)

After reviewing all recorded cases of actual maternal deaths from aspiration, these authors suggest that the standard NPO policy actually serves to displace preventive efforts onto the *mother* and to distract clinicians from focusing on the true causes of the few cases of maternal aspiration that do occur: inadequate equipment, faulty practitioner training or technique, and hospital understaffing.

Women's Responses

> I went into labor just after dawn. I called my OB, and he said not to eat, so I skipped breakfast and went on in to the hospital. By that evening, when things were getting really intense, I was so weak from hunger I thought I would die . . . it wasn't till I had the epidural that I started to feel like I could make it. (Charla Lovett)

In the responses of individual women to the obstetrical procedures thus far analyzed, we can begin to detect the gradual process of the conceptual fusion of the laboring woman's beliefs with the technocratic model. This process, from beginning to end, will be analyzed in detail for a number of individual women in Chapter 5. Here I will only pause occasionally to point out this process of cognitive transformation as it occurs or is subverted by the women whose responses are included here.

Suzanne Sampson's response to the wheelchair, for example, was that she suddenly began to feel that maybe she was not "in control anymore"; Susan Smith's response to being separated from her husband was to become "confused" and to begin to "lose control." In these responses we can detect the beginnings of the cognitive disorientation that is a prerequisite for the reconstruction of their individual belief systems in conformity with the technocratic model.

Further examples of this process at work are provided by Charla Lovett's response to fasting (above) and by Elizabeth Fisher's response to lying down ("I felt defeated. And it seems to me now that my lying down tacitly permitted the Demerol, or maybe entailed it. And the Demerol entailed the pitocin, and the pitocin entailed the Cesarean . . ."). As these two women indicate, birth rituals often function like "cranking gears": as they work to map the technocratic model onto the laboring woman's perceptions of her birth experience, they also set in motion a physiological chain of events that will make this model *appear* to be true and their intensified performance to be both appropriate and necessary. By the time I interviewed Elizabeth and Charla some months after their births, they had become consciously aware of this cranking gear process and pointed out how one procedure had inevitably led to another in their labor and birth experiences.

Ritual Purposes According to Feeley-Harnik, "persons undergoing rites of passage are usually prohibited from eating those highly valued foods that would identify them as full members of society" (1981:4). In rites of pregnancy and birth across cultures, food tabus serve the purpose of marking and intensifying the liminal status of the pregnant woman. The pseudo-foods (ice chips and lollipops have no nutritional value) allowed in the hospital are often fed to the laboring woman by her partner as if she herself were a baby, a symbolic process that can heighten her own sense of weakness and dependence.[5]

In a recent article in *Birth,* Broach and Newton (1988) address the question of why laboring women are still prohibited from eating and drinking in labor in spite of mounting evidence that such prohibitions are medically contraindicated. Pointing out that this custom started in the 1940s when general anesthesia was widely used for childbirth and the danger from aspiration was therefore high, they posit that its continuance is the result of "culture lag"—that is, of "culturally patterned behavior [that] continues to be practiced long after the reasons for doing so have disappeared" (1988:84).

On the contrary, I would suggest that this custom forms an integral part of the technocratic tapestry of birth in the United States, continuing as routine procedure not because of culture lag but because it serves so well to legitimate and further necessitate the technocratic interventions we investigate here as transformative rituals. To deny a laboring woman access to her own choice of food and drink in the hospital is to confirm her initiatory status and consequent loss of autonomy, to increase the chances that she will require interventions, and to tell her that only the institution can provide the nourishment she needs—a message that is most forcefully conveyed through the "IV."

INTRAVENOUS FEEDING (IV)

Description and Official Rationale The fluid administered from a glass bottle on a high stand through a tube inserted into the laboring woman's arm is supposed to compensate for the food and drink she is denied during her four- to thirty-hour labor, to correct or prevent the occurrence of ketosis, to facilitate the administration of analgesics and pitocin, and to prepare for epidural anesthesia. Keeping the IV line open is also viewed as important "just in case" blood is suddenly needed or other emergencies arise. (This need, however, could be easily satisfied by the use of a heparin lock, which also keeps the vein immediately available.)

Physiological Effects   The sugar and water solution administered through the IV presents potential hazards to both mother and child, especially when, as is common, dextrose is used in place of glucose (found naturally in the body). Dextrose is a refined sugar with deleterious physiological effects: it rapidly elevates blood sugar content, causing a temporary energy rise, but this too-high elevation causes the pancreas to secrete more insulin, resulting in a rapid drop in blood sugar and a sudden energy slump. When dextrose is administered intravenously for many hours, the result can be internal physiological havoc, which the patient will experience as exhaustion (Abrahamson and Pezet 1977).

Even IV solutions containing glucose can cause problems. Studies comparing laboring women allowed to drink oral fluids with those intravenously fed have found that the latter often suffered from fluid overload (Cotton et al. 1984; Gonik and Cotton 1984). Researchers consistently noticed that the amount of IV fluids received was more than double what was ordered during labor, and four times more than was ordered during delivery. As IV fluid levels are increased, a drop in colloidal osmotic pressure occurs—that is, too much fluid begins moving in and out of the woman's body tissues, a situation that can lead to electrolyte imbalance, cardiac arrhythmia, and pulmonary endema (fluid in the lungs).

Indication of still another potentially significant risk of glucose administration during labor comes from another field. In a series of studies comparing pain tolerance of both diabetics and healthy subjects after glucose infusions, Morley et al. found that "a 50 g glucose infusion resulted in a significant decrease in both the threshold level of pain and the maximal level of pain tolerated, as measured by responses to electrical pain induced by Gass stimulator" (1984:79). Although the diabetic experimental subjects had a lower pain tolerance than the healthy subjects, both groups demonstrated marked decreases in their ability to tolerate pain after glucose infusions. These results suggest that the glucose administered through the IV during labor may actually reduce the birthing woman's ability to tolerate pain.

Risks for the infant include severe hypoglycemia after birth, which can result from the excessive insulin production generated by the baby's pancreas in response to the high blood sugar levels developed in its circulatory system by the large amounts of dextrose and/or glucose which rapidly cross the placenta from the IV bottle (Grylack et al. 1984; Jawalekar and Marx 1980; Kennepp et al. 1980; Lucas et al. 1980; Mendiola et al. 1982; Rutter et al. 1980). In addition, both 5 percent and 10 percent glucose or dextrose infusions have been implicated as possible causes of neonatal jaundice (Kennepp et al. 1982; Rosengren and De Vault 1963a; Singhi et al. 1982). In the above studies, women who drank oral fluids only maintained their colloidal osmotic pressure levels better than women with IVs, and their babies had fewer problems with hypoglycemia, jaundice, and weight loss.

Moreover, because the IV solution usually contains no protein, it does not replace the protein expended during labor, and so throws the woman's system into "negative nitrogen balance—a condition of starvation" (Birnbaum 1977:107). In addition, puncturing the skin's protective layers increases the chance of a hospital-induced infection. Maintaining the sterility of IV devices is not easy; in one study, when 411 IV devices were cultured, 47 (11.4%) were colonized with bacteria (Larson et al. 1984). Hospital-induced infections

> are particularly dangerous for two reasons. First, they involve organisms that can survive in a hospital environment and that have become immune to standard treatment. Second, mother and child have never been exposed to this danger before and therefore have no established defense to the infection. The result is a greater chance of infection in the hospital that is more difficult to eradicate. (Birnbaum 1977:106)

According to Birnbaum, himself a physician, "the conservative estimate of iatrogenic disease developing after hospital admission is 25%" (1977:105).

Other types of risk are also imposed by the IV. The awkwardness of walking around pushing an unwieldy metal stand while trying not to get the cord tangled up is often a major factor in a laboring woman's decision to remain in bed. When IV use is prolonged, the patient can develop phlebitis, the pain of which can linger for weeks (Jones and Koldjeski 1984; Newton et al. 1988).

Women's Responses

> Well I was determined to walk around in spite of that IV, and when I needed to go to the bathroom I swore I would do it myself, in the john like a human being. So there I go down the hall in my slippers, pushing this huge heavy thing. I managed to get it inside the bathroom by holding the door open with my foot, but there was this little ridge or curb thing in front of

the stall and I couldn't get the IV stand over it. So I had to leave it with the door open, but the cord (sic) wouldn't reach all the way to the toilet, so there I am, trying to position my bottom over the toilet, leaning as far forward as I can with my arm out in front of me as far as it will go, not to mention having a contraction at the same time—and all I could think was, "If only Robbie could see me now!" (Charla Lovett)

I explained to the labor nurses that I wanted to have a natural delivery. . . . One of them wanted to give me the IV right away and that was the one that panicked and lost the heartbeat when I changed position and gave me the oxygen and wanted to insert the fetal head monitor and all that, and the other one let me delay as long as possible on the IV. And so she was willing to work with me and understood what I wanted to do. The other nurse did not, because she came in and said, "Why isn't your IV hooked up? I'm going to hook it up right away." And I said, "No, no, the other nurse is going to do it, and she said we're going to wait," and she said "Oh, no, you shouldn't wait." She really wanted to put it in because she said I had really nice veins. . . . [Several hours later when it did get inserted] I didn't like it one bit. . . . I wanted to be able to get up and go to the bathroom, and with the IV somebody had to walk you there and walk you back. I thought I was perfectly capable. (Margaret Boone)

Ritual Purposes   The intravenous drips so commonly attached to the hands and arms of birthing women make a very powerful symbolic statement: they are umbilical cords to the hospital. The long cord connecting her body to the fluid-filled bottle places the woman in the same relation to the hospital as the baby in her womb is to her. She is now dependent on the institution for her life and is receiving one of the most profound messages of her initiation experience: we are all dependent on institutions for our lives. But this message is all the more compelling in her case, for she is the real giver of life. Society and its institutions cannot exist unless women give birth; yet the birthing woman in the hospital is shown not that she gives life, but rather that the *institution* does.

THE "PIT DRIP"

Description and Official Rationale   Pitocin is a synthetic form of oxytocin, which is the hormone that stimulates uterine contractions. It can be utilized either to induce or to augment labor. According to the authors of *Williams Obstetrics,* labor augmentation with pitocin is officially indicated when the clinical practitioner diagnoses "hypotonic uterine dysfunction"—a condition in which the contractions of labor become ineffective at producing cervical dilation (Cunningham et al. 1989:344). Following this rationale, pitocin should be contraindicated in normal labors, and therefore should not even be included in my analysis. Yet, although *Williams Obstetrics* warns against its dangers (1989:345), it is commonly used in hospitals throughout the country to augment normal labors. Eighty-one percent of the women in my study who gave birth in the hospital received pitocin during their labors. Harrison reports a statement by one of her professors in medical school: "If they were to put a dye in the pitocin, you'd see it in the IV of almost every woman in this country who is in labor" (1982:116).

Under the technocratic model, this near-universal use of pitocin for labor augmentation makes sense, as that model holds that labors do not stop and start again, so that any slowing of labor (as was quite common among the women in my study) is interpreted as abnormal or dysfunctional, necessitating intervention (Rothman 1982:260).

The technocratic model also interprets as dysfunctional labors that have not started by a maximum of two weeks past the official medical "due date," as well as labors that have not started after the waters have broken. In most hospitals, the rule is that once the membranes have ruptured, birth must take place within twenty-four hours, because the danger of infection (mostly from hospital interventions) rises dramatically after that. Under either of these circumstances, the physician will recommend induction of labor with pitocin.[6] The woman and baby are then subject to all the dangers discussed below throughout the entire labor. If the due date is inaccurate (as frequently happens), such induction may result in the birth of a premature baby.

Physiological Effects   In a matched-sample comparison of home and hospital labors (Mehl et al. 1977*a*), the hospital labors were shown to be considerably shorter, most probably as a result of the combination of interventions designed to speed labor, including amniotomy, pitocin, fundal pressure, forced pushing, and forceps and Cesarean deliveries. Pitocin augmentation certainly plays a major role in shortening labor, the greatest risk from which is to the fetus: the increased pressure of the contractions can, and often does, compress the umbilical cord and cut down the baby's oxygen supply:

> Dr. Roberto Caldeyro-Barcia has demonstrated that uterine contractions stimulated with pitocin reach over 40 mm Hg pressure on the fetal head. The quality and quantity of uterine contractions are greatly affected when oxytocin is infused. The contractions tend to be longer, stronger, and with

shorter relaxation periods between. . . . With each uterine contraction, blood supply to the uterus is temporarily shut off. If deprived of blood supply, a fetal bradycardia (decreased fetal heart-rate deceleration) follows with oxygen deprivation and cerebral ischemia causing the grave possibility of neurological sequellae. Truly the fetus has been challenged, and the EFM dutifully records the stressed fetal heart rate. With suspicions confirmed, a diagnosis of fetal distress is noted and elective Cesarean section is the treatment of choice. (Ettner 1977:153)

To this warning, the authors of the eighteenth edition of *Williams* add their voices: "Oxytocin is a powerful drug, and it has killed or maimed mothers through rupture of the uterus and even more babies through hypoxia from markedly hypertonic uterine contractions" (Cunningham et al. 1989:345). These authors go on to urge careful administration of the lowest possible amount of pitocin in order to avoid the tetanic contractions that can cause uterine rupture, and to insist that once the drip is started, the mother should never be left alone. Obviously the potential for abuse here is high: twelve of the women in my study reported that they were left alone for extended periods after a pitocin infusion had been started. (Three of them did experience long "tetanic" contractions, usually resulting from too much pitocin suddenly flowing into their vein when the nurse jiggled the bottle or straightened out the plastic tube.)

Aside from their risks of uterine rupture and decreased oxygen supply to the baby, the increased pain for the mother of the pitocin-induced contractions, which are often double-peaked and back-to-back with little or no rest time in between (a function of the amount of the pitocin being administered), is likely to increase her stress and anxiety levels as well, and to cause her to repeatedly request increased pain medication. Moreover, pitocin is a strong antidiuretic, even at low doses; its combination with the IV fluids administered to fasting women can result in water intoxication, which itself heightens the woman's risk of pulmonary edema in those rare instances of gastric aspiration (Cunningham et al. 1989:344; McKay and Mahan 1988b:214).

Women's Responses   All the women in my study who were given pitocin reported increased pain from the pitocin-induced contractions. Some were able to keep on with their Lamaze breathing techniques (discussed as mediating rituals in Chapter 4) without any pain medication, whereas others called for analgesia soon after the administration of the pitocin. Some felt grateful that their labors had been shortened; others would have preferred less stress and a slower pace:

I was glad to have the pitocin—anything to get the whole thing over with as fast as possible. (Laura Parker)

Once they put me on the pitocin, it was all over for me. The pain was unbearable. I couldn't wait to have the Cesarean—at least it would get me out of that misery. (Lisa Thomason)

I needed the pit drip. My uterus just wasn't doing anything. I might have lain there forever with nothing happening, and then they would have cut me, because my waters had already broken. Given that the hospital was only going to give me twenty-four hours to dilate, I was glad for the chance the pitocin gave me to have a vaginal birth. (Donna Chapman)

Ritual Purposes   Under the technocratic model, time—mechanical and linear—is viewed as being measurable in discrete, almost weighable units, so we say that something should take place within a specific "amount" of time (Lee 1980; Ornstein 1972). As the process that reproduces society, birth must set the standard for the general cultural handling of time: birth must be culturally shaped to occur within a specific amount of time, just as must the production of any factory good. When a woman's labor fails to conform to production timetables (labor time charts), it will be speeded up with pitocin:

> At Doctor's Hospital we use [Friedman's] chart of labor, a curve developed by Dr. [Emmanuel E. Friedman] which defined on a graph how a labor should progress. Each woman's chart has a blank graph of hours and of centimeters of cervical dilation which we must record approximately hourly in order to evaluate the shape of her labor curve. When a woman's labor is off the "proper" curve, she is subjected to intervention in several possible forms. (Harrison 1982:121)

Moreover, the tendency of pitocin to set in motion the chain of events described above by Ettner is entirely in keeping with the structuring and ordering characteristics of ritual described in the Introduction, and with the sense of inevitability—the "conceptual cranking gears"—that ritual's consistent performance can invoke.

The administration of pitocin through the umbilical IV sends several messages to a laboring woman: (1) that our cultural concept of time as linear, measurable, and a valuable commodity is right and true; (2) that her body is a machine; (3) that her machine is defective because it is not producing on schedule; (4) that the institution's schedule is much more important than her body's internal rhythms and her individual experience of labor. Moreover, the increased pain during contractions that results from the administration of pitocin serves the ritual purpose of hazing—that is, of speeding up the breakdown of the initiate's category system through the intensification of physical stress.

Description and Official Rationale

With cervical dilation and uterine contractions that cause discomfort, medication for pain relief with a narcotic such as meperidine [Demerol], plus one of the tranquilizer drugs such as promethazine, usually is indicated. The mother should rest quietly between contractions with a successful program of anesthesia and sedation. In this circumstance, discomfort usually is felt at the acme of an effective uterine contraction, but the pain is not unbearable. Finally, she should not recall labor as a horrifying experience. Appropriate drug selection and administration should accomplish these objectives for the great majority of women in labor, without risk to them or their infants. (Cunningham et al. 1989:328)

Physiological Effects Nearly all American women delivering in the hospital receive some type of drug (Woodward et al. 1982). One study reports an average administration of seven different drugs during vaginal delivery and fifteen during Cesarean delivery (Doering and Stewart 1978). Many of these drugs are documented teratogens or toxins (Brackbill et al. 1984). A study by Woodward et al. (1982) found that 86 percent of women delivering in hospitals receive at least one teratogenic drug, and 64 percent receive at least two, whereas women giving birth by Cesarean receive even more. "Virtually all drugs given during labor tend to cross the placenta rapidly and alter the fetal environment as they enter the circulatory system of the unborn infant within minutes or seconds of being administered to the mother" (Inch 1984:84). When a baby is born with drugs in her bloodstream, her own liver, which is one of the last of her systems to mature, must detoxify those drugs; a drug like Demerol, for example, can remain in the baby's system for several days (Inch 1984). Studies of babies whose mothers have received obstetrical drugs during labor

have repeatedly and consistently demonstrated the sort of adverse effects that are associated with central nervous system damage: impaired sensory and motor responses; reduced ability to process incoming stimuli and control responding to them; interference with feeding, sucking, and rooting responses; lower scores on tests of infant development, and increased irritability. Bonding may also be impaired. . . . The most frequent . . . physiological changes include respiratory depression, general sluggishness and fatigue, extremes of muscular tone (limpness or rigidity), skin discoloration (blue instead of pink) . . . jaundice, abnormal EEG and sleep/alertness patterns, and increased tremulousness. (Brackbill et al. 1984:17–18)

There are few studies of the long-term effects of pain-relieving drugs on babies; most of those conducted have not tested babies beyond six weeks of age, and very few have tested beyond the first year. (One very recent study finds evidence of a statistically significant correlation between the use of analgesics during labor [primarily pethidine—aka Demerol], the administration of drugs [primarily Vitamin K] in the week after birth, and the development of childhood cancer before age ten [Golding et al. 1990].) But a paucity of studies does not mean a lack of lasting effects. Available evidence indicates that when early drug-related damage occurs, it may be compensated to some extent. However, as Brackbill et al. (1988:23) point out, organisms that have to compensate for such damage do not perform as well under stress as nondamaged organisms. Ucko (1965) found that children who had suffered oxygen deprivation at birth functioned as well as normal children in everyday situations but exhibited more behavioral disturbances in stressful situations. Relevant animal studies show impaired learning resulting from exposure to analgesics at birth (Iseroff 1980). Perhaps obstetrical drugs are generally safe for mothers and babies; perhaps they are not. The truth is that no one knows for sure, one way or the other.[7]

For many laboring women, analgesics do provide welcome relief from pain and tension, and can make the difference between a positive and a traumatic labor experience. But there is no guarantee that such drugs will accomplish that purpose—a common source of confusion and disappointment for women who are expecting complete relief with the first shot of Demerol. It has been suggested that analgesics may result in a slowing of labor (which will then entail the administration of pitocin, if the woman has not already received it, or in an increased dosage, if she has); too few studies have been done on this subject for any definitive conclusions to be reached. As with the long-term effects of analgesics on babies, little is known about the effects of such drugs on the woman and her labor.

Women's Responses   Some of the women in my study reported effective pain relief from the Demerol or Nisentil they were given:

I requested medication one time—I requested some Nisentil [which I had been told] was a good safe drug. . . . I was doing pretty well, but then going into transition, it was just getting real hard. . . . [the Nisentil] made all the difference. . . . It didn't really help the pain as much as it—it was like when the dentist gives you gas, it makes you not care that much. And what it really did was help me relax in-between, you know, it just kind of took the edge off so that I could really relax in-between contractions, which was nice. (Constance O'Riley)

Others reported that the drugs had no effect on the pain, but only made them drowsy and less able to deal with their contractions. The women who felt that pain medication was forced upon them resented the interference in their experiences of labor and the lack of support for their desire to avoid medication:

> I asked for pain medication, but I didn't really want it. What I really wanted was for someone to tell me that I could do it—to remind me that I was just in transition and tell me I was terrific, doing *great*. But they were only too eager to get me to take it. For just a few minutes I thought I couldn't do it, and so I lost it and took the drugs, and then it was all over for my natural childbirth experience—I got too woozy after that to do my breathing right. I know I asked for the medication myself, and that my reaction is irrational, but I am so angry that it was given so quickly. I didn't really want medication—I really wanted support. (Georgia Adams)

In contrast, the women who requested pain medication and meant it expressed *firm* beliefs in their right not to have to be in pain. Potential depressive effects of analgesia on the baby were not an issue for most of these women, as they assumed that their obstetrician would regulate their dosages appropriately. They strongly felt that the choice to use analgesia was relevant only to themselves and their labor experiences:

> I read all this stuff that told me that I would be a complete asshole to have drugs, because "it's so much better for the baby" and "it's a natural experience," and there was just all this pressure, and I revolted. I mean, my attitude was that I had quit smoking, had been eating meat and drinking milk for months and months, had been such a good girl. A couple of hours of whatever the drugs were going to do to me, tough. You can put up with it, kid. (Lina Oppenheimer)

Ritual Purposes   States physician Michelle Harrison (personal correspondence):

> I've always maintained that what hospitals needed were soundproof labor rooms. A lot of medication is given because of crying or screaming and its effects on other laboring women. Women, always taking care of everyone else, will be persuaded to take medication to alleviate the pain on the faces of their partners, or to appease nurses, or because they've been told they are making too much noise.

It seems to be a fundamental assumption of Western culture that pain is bad. As our society's microcosm, the condensed world in which our cultural values stand out in high relief, our medical system is constantly engaged in demonstrating the high negative value we place on pain. Perhaps we devalue pain so much because it, like birth, reminds us of our human weaknesses—our naturalness, our dependence on nature. Machines don't feel pain, so if we are going to be like them, neither should we. The physical—and conceptual—experience of pain, like the physical and conceptual experience of birth, grounds us in our natural selves. The experiential and conceptual combination of pain *and* birth presents a double-whammy threat to the technocratic model; to birth without pain removes half of that threat, bringing us one step closer to our long-term goal of technological transcendence.

The analgesia that most laboring women receive intensifies the message that their bodies are machines by adding to it the clear statement that their machines can function without them. The sending of such a message would not have been possible without our cultural notion of the separation of mind and body—a basic tenet of the technocratic model. At the same time, this procedure teaches and reinforces that concept.

This ritual, of course, also serves the purpose of intensifying the strange-making process and its accompanying breakdown of the initiate's category system. What the woman feels and what her body does become separate, disconnected. Sensory experience and bodily knowing can serve her no longer as guides; now she must rely totally on machines and medical attendants for guidance and direction. A clue to the service that analgesia for laboring women provides for hospital staff members may be found in their nickname for Nisentil—"nice n'still."

ARTIFICIAL RUPTURE OF THE MEMBRANES (AMNIOTOMY)

Description and Official Rationale Amniotomy is frequently performed on women who labor in hospitals for the purpose of speeding up their labors, or for insertion of the internal electronic fetal monitor; occasionally it is performed so that the physician can take fetal blood samples, and/or ascertain whether or not there is evidence of meconium staining (fetal bowel movement), which under the technocratic model is considered to be indicative of fetal distress. The procedure is simple:

a hospital attendant inserts an instrument like a crochet hook through the cervix, and snags and breaks the amniotic sac.

Physiological Effects   In a review of the literature, McKay and Mahan find that, if amniotomy is not performed and membranes are allowed to rupture spontaneously, most women will have intact membranes until they are either in very active labor or reach complete cervical dilation (1983:173). Although amniotomy does indeed often result in speedier labors (if performed once active labor is well-established), it also increases the danger of fetal infection from vaginal exams and/or inserted instruments. (Such infections can of course be cured with antibiotics, but that process can mean considerable discomfort and many extra days in the hospital, as several of the women in my study discovered.) Should false labor be mistaken for real labor, and amniotomy be performed too early, the 24-hour rule will be invoked, and pitocin induction with all its attendant hazards will be required (this particular complication can be avoided if anmiotomy is performed only after 5–6 centimeter dilation is reached).

A further hazard of amniotomy is that without the protective cushion of the amniotic fluid the baby's head is subject to greater pressure during contractions, and the umbilical cord is more likely to become compressed, resulting in oxygen deprivation and consequent respiratory distress. Cord prolapse is also more common after amniotomy (Pritchard, MacDonald, and Gant 1985:289). Moreover, unruptured membranes often cushion not only the fetal head but also the mother's perineum, allowing for more gentle stretching and reducing the likelihood of tears. The combination of rupture of the cushioning bag with pitocin-augmented contractions often leads to more rapid and forced stretching of the perineum and so to more tears (Brigitte Jordan, personal communication).

Women's Responses

> The doctor came in and examined me, and said that if he broke my waters the baby would come in no time. So I said okay. And he was right! Three contractions later, I felt like pushing. (Darlene Abney)

> Some guy came in, broke my waters with a long hook, you know. Apparently they said that would help. Well, that for me was one of the worst moments of the whole experience. It was like all of my hopes and dreams of how it was going to be just sort of floated out with the waters. I'll never

forget that. It was just an awful feeling. Warm and sad, it was like tears flowing out, you know? (Elise Pearsall)

Ritual Purposes   Amniotomy was one of the first things the early male midwives of the 1700s figured out that they could do to intervene in the process of labor. Then as now, breaking the waters of a laboring woman was an effective means of making it appear that she could not have the baby without a physician's assistance (Wertz and Wertz 1989).

When performed for the purpose of speeding up labor, rupturing the membranes of a laboring woman reinforces and intensifies the urgency of the institution's message about the necessity of condensing the woman's experience of labor and birth into a discrete, measurable unit of time. When performed so that an internal fetal monitor can be inserted, artificial rupture of the membranes further intensifies the message of the birth machine. In both cases, the underlying message is clear: culture, not nature, knows best.

EXTERNAL ELECTRONIC FETAL MONITOR

Description and Official Rationale   The pattern of the baby's heartbeat during labor often reflects the baby's condition. During contractions, the normal pattern is for the fetal heart rate to slow, picking up again as the contraction ends. The heart rate must be monitored during labor, because certain fluctuations in this pattern, such as precipitous drops in the heart rate at the end of a contraction, can constitute a true life or death situation requiring immediate emergency delivery of the baby. Before the invention of the electronic fetal monitor in the 1950s, nurses and doctors periodically monitored the baby's heartbeat themselves by placing a stethoscope on the mother's adbomen. Electronic monitors, attached to the mother by large belts strapped around her abdomen, continuously print out a record of both the fetal heartbeat and the strength, duration, and frequency of the uterine contractions, so that deviations from normal patterns can be identified. New attachments, not yet commonly used, may enable them also to monitor the mother's temperature, blood pressure, blood oxygen, heart rate, and cervical dilation (Arney 1982:146–148).

Physiological Effects   Part of what makes the use of the electronic fetal monitor so questionable is that acceptable degrees of variation in the fetal heart rate have never been firmly established. Not uncommonly, even extreme fluctuations result in perfectly normal babies born without technological intervention. Several studies have established that continuous external electronic monitoring is no more effective at identifying those fluctuations that do in fact indicate fetal distress than periodic manual auscultation (Chalmers 1978; Haverkamp and Orleans 1983).

The physician-inventor of the electronic fetal monitor, Dr. Edward H. Hon, identified several factors that could have an adverse effect on the fetal heart rate, and so made such monitoring seem most desirable: (1) intrinsic fetal disease; (2) placental disease; (3) cord compression; (4) maternal disease; (5) drugs administered for analgesia and anesthesia; and (6) maternal hypotension from the supine position, from conduction anesthesia, or from both (Hon 1974). Many of these factors are either directly generated by or made more dangerous in the hospital, where fetal infections commonly result from too many vaginal exams; where cord compression often results from improper maternal positioning and/or the administration of pitocin; and where drugs are often pressed on laboring women who otherwise might choose to do without (further examples of the "cranking gear" effect). At a conference on "Crisis of Obstetrics, The Management of Labor," held in New York City in March 1987, Hon himself emphatically stated, "If you mess around with a process that works well 98% of the time, there is much potential for harm. . . . [Most women in labor may be] much better off at home [than in the hospital with the electronic fetal monitor]" (Young and Shearer 1987).

According to Brackbill et al., in "the only four methodologically sound studies" carried out to evaluate the effects of electronic monitoring (Banta and Thacker 1979; Haverkamp and Orleans 1983), women in labor were randomly assigned to manually monitored and electronically monitored groups that were comparable in other respects:

> Results were the same in all four studies: more electronically monitored women ended up . . . with Cesarean deliveries. Cesarean section rates ranged between 63% and 314% higher for electronically monitored women than manually monitored women. There was no improvement in perinatal outcome for the babies delivered by Cesarean section. The principal "reasons" alleged for these surgical deliveries—fetal distress and cephalopelvic disproportion (disproportion of head to pelvis)—cannot be proved or disproved. The real reasons, according to these studies, are attending physicians' impatience and nervousness. (Brackbill et al. 1984:10)

A subsequent and much larger study comparing the results of universal versus selective monitoring of 34,995 parturients found *no* significant differences in stillbirths or fetal health between the universally monitored and selectively monitored groups; these researchers did find a slight but significant incidence in the incidence of Cesarean section for fetal distress in the universally monitored low-risk group (Leveno et al. 1986). Even in the high-risk case of prematurity, no benefits result from using electronic fetal monitors instead of periodic manual auscultation (Shy et al. 1990). (For an excellent summation of all available studies on EFM published before 1987, see Prentice and Lind, "Fetal heart rate monitoring during labor—too frequent intervention, too little benefit" [1987:2:1375–1377].)

About the heightened risk of Cesarean resulting from EFM use, its inventor Dr. Hon had this to say, "Most obstetricians don't understand the monitor. They're dropping the knife with each drop in the fetal heart rate. The Cesarean section is considered as a rescue mission of the baby by the white knight, but actually you've assaulted the mother" (Young and Shearer 1987).

Besides the risk of unnecessary Cesarean section, other risks posed to the mother by the EFM include her immobilization in bed, which, as we have seen, can decrease her own blood supply and hence the oxygen supply to the fetus, leading to heart rate abnormalities, and "therefore, electronic monitoring tends to produce the very abnormalities it is supposed to measure" (Young and Shearer 1987:10–11).

The authors of *Williams Obstetrics* (Pritchard, MacDonald, and Gant 1985; Cunningham, MacDonald, and Gant 1989), far from advocating universal monitoring, judiciously assess its limited benefits and considerable risks. At their hospital (Parkland Memorial in Dallas) in 1985, the monitors were used on about one-third of all laboring women under such circumstances as pitocin induction or augmentation, manually detected variations in fetal heart rate, and for conditions medically defined as high-risk, such as meconium staining, abnormal fetal presentation, maternal diabetes, or previous Cesarean delivery (Pritchard et al. 1985:291). By 1989, with the publication of the eighteenth edition of *Williams*, the number of women electronically monitored had risen to 40 percent. Somewhat caustically, the authors of both editions state:

> Although the application of continuous electronic monitoring cannot by itself be credited for any remarkable reduction in intrapartum or neonatal mortality at Parkland Memorial hospital, it has provided an elegant means of demonstrating to physicians in training, medical students, nurses, physi-

cians' assistants, and others the normal and abnormal forces of labor and the cardiac responses of the fetus during this important event. (Pritchard et al. 1985:290; Cunningham et al. 1989:302)

Supporters of electronic fetal monitors attribute the 1970s fall in the infant and perinatal death rate to their use. Critics point out that the decrease is attributable to other factors, such as a decrease in the number of unwanted pregnancies, improved prenatal care and maternal nutrition, and increased intervals between births (Brackbill et al. 1984:10).

Women's Responses

As soon as I got hooked up to the monitor, all everyone did was stare at it. The nurses didn't even look at me anymore when they came into the room—they went straight to the monitor. I got the weirdest feeling that *it* was having the baby, not me. (Diana Crosse)

[They put me in bed and] put on the fetal monitor. I didn't want fetal monitoring either. That was something else they agreed to. But they put it on "just to check." . . . That was kind of fun. I could watch [and my husband could help with the breathing better because he could tell when a contraction was starting sooner than I could, so he could help me get ready]. . . . Then around seven . . . I got real uncomfortable. I said "Get this thing off of me"—the fetal monitor—because I needed to rub—you know, do that Lamaze rub on my stomach. Well, if the fetal monitor is on, you can't rub. That's where I wanted to rub, so I said "Get it off of me." They said "Fine, we'll get it off." (Patricia Hellman)

Being hooked up to the monitor may seem a bit overly technological, but if it's going to make it easier for the doctor and the nurses, I'll do it. (Alana Colson)

In Diana's response to the electronic fetal monitor, we can observe the successful progression of conceptual fusion between Diana's perceptions of her birth experience and the technocratic model. So thoroughly has this model been "mapped on" to Diana's birth that she has begun to *feel* that the machine itself is having her baby, whereas she is reduced to a mere onlooker.

In contrast, in Pat's response to the fetal monitor, as well as in her demand for the enema and her earlier conversion of the wheelchair to a luggage cart, we can observe that by maintaining conceptual distance from the technocratic model, Pat is able to avoid conceptual fusion with the messages sent by obstetrical procedures. Conceptual distance can be maintained, as Pat demonstrates, when the woman places technology and the institution at *her* service, instead of the other way around.

Ritual Purposes   A common feature of rites of passage across cultures is the ritual adornment of the initiates with the visible physical trappings of their transformation. In "primitive" (i.e., low technology) societies, these adornments usually consist of objects representing the most deeply held values and beliefs of the society, such as "relics of deities, heroes, or ancestors . . . sacred drums or other musical instruments" (Turner 1979:239). In Marine basic training, the rifle, backpack, and ammunition belt constitute the sacred symbols with which the initiate is adorned. This perspective provides a fascinating insight into the symbolic significance of the "EFM," a machine that has itself become *the* symbol of high technology hospital birth. Observers and participants alike report that the monitor, once attached, becomes the focal point of the labor, as nurses, physicians, husbands, and even laboring women themselves become visually and conceptually glued to the machine, which then shapes their perceptions and interpretations of the birth process—as in Diana's response above.

Under the technocratic model, the information produced by machines is considered more authoritative than the information produced by people. (Jordan and Irwin define "authoritative knowledge" as "legitimate, consequential, official, worthy of discussion, and useful for justifying actions by people engaged in accomplishing a certain task or objective" [1989:13].) Initially in medicine, the physician was totally dependent on the patient's verbal report and on his own senses of touch and observation for knowledge about an ailment or condition. With the invention of tests and procedures, medical practitioners have become increasingly removed from the need to physically interact with their patients. The recent shift in birth from a focus on the woman herself to a focus on diagnosis by machine parallels the same move in medicine as a whole (see Chapter 7), and both reflects and perpetuates our higher cultural valuation of objective knowledge over subjective experience. Brigitte Jordan (personal communication) reports repeated observations in hospitals of women still writhing in pain from an ongoing contraction while the nurse stood by insisting that, since the monitor was not recording it, the contraction must be over. Such indeed was the experience of several women in my study, one of whom added, "I even found myself apologizing to the nurse, who was waiting for the contraction to be over to do a cervical check, for the pain I was still feeling, because clearly I shouldn't have been feeling it." Such reliance on machines assures that the question of who knows what is really going on, as well as what is best for the woman and her baby, will be neatly resolved in favor of those who have access to the more valued technologically obtained information.

A further ritual and symbolic function provided by the electronic fetal monitor involves the role of rhythmic auditory stimuli in synchronizing the central nervous systems of ritual participants with the redundant symbolic messages presented in the ritual (as discussed in the Introduction):

> The amplified fetal heartbeat sounds like galloping horses, so with two or three monitors going in a room, the sound is one of a galloping herd. In the hall, the sounds of different monitors in different rooms fuse into a roar of childbirth. Frequently, there are also the intermittent commands to the women—"Push! Push!"—reminiscent of stampedes and posse chases in the old Westerns. Both the sound of the galloping and the vision of the needle traveling across the paper, making a blip with each heartbeat, are hypnotic, often giving one the illusion that the machines are keeping the baby's heart beating. (Harrison 1982:90)

If we stop a moment now, to see in our mind's eye the visual and kinesthetic images that a laboring woman will be experiencing—herself in bed, in a hospital gown, staring up at an IV pole, bag, and cord on one side, and a big whirring machine on the other, and down at a steel bed and a huge belt encircling her waist—we can see that her entire visual field is conveying one overwhelming perceptual message about our culture's deepest values and beliefs: technology is supreme, and you are utterly dependent upon it and the institutions that control and dispense it.

INTERNAL ELECTRONIC FETAL MONITOR

Description and Official Rationale   Because it uses ultrasound waves to penetrate into the woman's uterus and record the baby's heartbeat, external fetal monitoring is subject to various forms of inaccuracy, which include the confusion of the mother's heartbeat with the baby's, and the possibility "that the fetal heart rate may double at low rates and can be halved at high rates" (Cetrulo and Freeman 1975). Therefore, when the medical staff desires increased accuracy in the recording of the fetal heart rate, they will insert an electrode (a needle) up through the birth canal and directly into the baby's scalp.

Physiological Effects   The physiological risks of internal monitoring to both mother and infant are severe, extending far beyond the contraindicated supine position that this procedure necessitates. The insertion of the electrode requires the rupture of the protective membranes, whereas the electrode itself provides a convenient route for the entry of bacteria and viruses into the amniotic fluid and the fetal scalp (Cunningham et al. 1989:301). Consequently, the fetal infection rate in internally monitored women is double that in those who are externally monitored only:

> When monitoring continues more than 4.5 hours, the risk of infection is 50%. If it were not for antibiotics, the death rate for monitor-produced infections would be staggering. . . . The baby is also at risk of infection from the scalp-implanted electrodes. . . . Of all internally monitored babies, 4–5% suffer scalp abscesses, lacerations, hematomas, and hemorrhages. (Brackbill et al. 1984:11)

Possibly the greatest risk to the infant comes from the sharp increase in the risk of prolapsed cord (a condition in which the cord delivers before the baby is born) which is often the direct result of the amniotomy that must be performed (if the bag of waters is intact) so that the electrode can be inserted (Cunningham et al. 1989:301):

> Many mothers leave the hospital firmly convinced that electronic monitoring saved their babies from otherwise certain death caused by cord prolapse when in fact it was the monitoring (and prerequisite amniotomy) that caused the prolapse in the first place. (Brackbill et al. 1984:11)

Women's Responses

> Anything that they said would be good for the safety of the baby was okay with me. (Debbie Lawson)

> We let them put it on, and they had to do it twice before they got it in. And then he had these little scabs on his head—I really wish I hadn't let them do that. I really don't see how they could possibly think that it didn't hurt him. (Clara Riley)

Ritual Purposes   To the profound message of the external monitor, the internal fetal monitor adds an equally profound footnote: your baby is a technocratic artifact too. And as such, it is the institution's product, not yours. In fact, *your* machine is so defective that society's product may be in danger from its potential malfunction, so it is necessary to apply a special machine to more exactly monitor the product's progress in order to protect it from potential harm caused by *you*.

Here we can see clearly how conceptually essential is this metaphorizing of the baby as a mechanical product—to stick an electrode into an infant's scalp must be an easier job if one holds a belief that, being an object, the not-yet-born does not feel any pain:

> At Doctor's Hospital I learned to screw a monitor lead into the scalp of a baby not yet born. . . . Was the baby frightened? Is this baby curious anymore? Does this baby still want to be with us? What have we taught this new person about what life is like? At Doctor's Hospital I attached the woman to the monitor, and no one looked at her any more. Held in place by the leads around her abdomen and coming out of her vagina, the woman looked over at the TV-like screen displaying the heartbeat tracings. No one held the woman's hand. Childbirth had become a science. (Harrison 1982:91)

CERVICAL CHECKS

Description and Official Rationale   Both nurses and physicians insert gloved hands into laboring women's vaginas to find out how many centimeters the cervix has dilated, how far it has effaced (thinned out), and whether or not the membranes are intact, as well as to check on the insertion of the internal monitor and to measure fetal descent during second stage. Under the technocratic model, cervical checks are very important and must be performed at regular intervals, as a woman has only so many hours available to her for labor; if her progress along Friedman's curve is not steady, interventions must be instituted.

Physiological Effects   Cervical exams are often quite painful. The pain they cause is increased when the exam is performed during the height of a contraction—as is often the case because more information can thus be obtained. These exams are most likely to be performed by the attending nurses or physician, but, in teaching hospitals, any resident in need of practice is likely to pop in without introduction. Each exam performed increases the possibility of infection of the mother, especially if her membranes have been ruptured. Heightened maternal tension and anxiety can result from the disruption of her breathing exercises and of the natural rhythmicity of her labor, as well as from the psychological stress produced when the mother is told that she is not progressing well—as in Patricia's following response.

Women's Responses

> They would do exams every once in a while. I got some real conflicting reports on them. . . . They really didn't bother me. It was exciting to find out

how far along I was. But the strange thing is, the doctor and the nurse were doing them at different times. It was going along—I was 8 and then I was 9 and then I was 7—you know, that began to disturb me and that was kind of a problem. . . . Supposedly you don't go backwards. That would get discouraging when I was finding out I was 9. I thought I was really close and then to go back and I was 7, and it was still going to be a long time. (Patricia Hellman)

[After taking the Demerol] I would [doze between contractions and] wake up to this blinding, overwhelming pain. But then Stan would grab me and we'd look at each other, and I'd do the breathing, and you know, we were maintaining well. But then every hour they would come and do a cervical exam, you know? God, that was painful. That was the worst part of all of it, when they stuck their fingers up in there. After I had the baby, about six weeks later when I went back for my checkup the doctor said, "You know, it's a wonder you didn't get an infection with all those people sticking their hands up inside of you." (Lisa Smith)

The routine cervical checks they did every hour really bothered me, because they threw off my breathing. (Terry Lutzer)

Ritual Purposes   Any strategies, from ambulation to breathing to taking showers, that the mother has developed for coping with her labor in her own way can be disrupted by the frequent performance of vaginal exams "for her own good." Brigitte Jordan (personal communication) points out that such exams are only necessary under the technocratic model that so drastically attempts to minimize production time. In no other culture have such invasive, disruptive, and painful procedures been performed with such frequency and regularity as in the American hospital. In Holland, a country whose infant mortality and Cesarean rates are considerably lower than our own, such exams are considered necessary much less often than in the United States—women are encouraged to push when they experience the urge to push, not when and only when their cervix has reached the arbitrary standard of 10 centimeters dilation. These frequent production control checks are necessitated by the standardization of American birth, not by the physiological needs of the birthing woman and her child.

Frequent cervical checks drive home to the laboring woman the physical significance of the messages about time, about the suspected defectiveness of her own body, and about her lack of status and power relative to the hospital staff (the institution's representatives) and the institution (society's representative). When they are painful, cervical checks also function as part of the impersonal hazing of the initiate, the ritual process she must undergo to ensure the complete breakdown of her category system so that she will be as psychologically open to the reception of the messages imparted by her birth experience as possible. Cervical checks powerfully intensify the process of symbolic inversion begun with the "prep"—to have a series of strangers sticking their hands through her vagina and deep into her cervix approaches the extreme of opposition to a woman's usual ideas of appropriate relations between herself and society—an extreme that will ultimately be reached on the delivery table with the lithotomy position.

EPIDURAL/CAUDAL ANALGESIA/ANESTHESIA[8]

Description and Official Rationale Epidurals and caudals are two similar types of regional anesthesia that free a laboring woman from pain without dulling her mental faculties. They are commonly used during Cesarean section when the woman wishes to be "awake and aware," and also, in lower doses, during normal labor and delivery for complete or near-complete pain relief. The administration process is complex. Briefly, a local anesthetic is injected into the lumbar region of the woman's back, and then a long needle is inserted into the epidural space "outside the last of the three membranes that cover the spinal cord, just inside the bone and ligament of the vertebral column" (Inch 1984:93). This needle makes a hole into the epidural space, and through it a soft catheter is threaded. The needle is then removed, the point of entry sealed, and the catheter is taped to the skin. At its end a small filter and stopper are attached, through which doses of anesthetic can periodically be administered. The whole process, during which the mother must hold herself as still as possible, takes about twenty minutes to complete.

Physiological Effects It is important to note the high degree of variation in the effects epidurals have on the mother's experience of birth: skillfully given, epidurals can eliminate the pain of contractions while reducing neither the urge to push nor the mother's ability to do so; applied with a heavy hand, epidurals can completely deaden the woman's sensations, severely reducing her ability to push and increasing the likelihood of forceps application (Pritchard et al. 1985:364) and Cesarean section (Thorp et al. 1989). At the same time, there is wide variation in the effect the epidural will actually have on the individual woman. Her body may not respond to the epidural as the anesthesiologist intends—some women find that they still experience pain in spite of their expectation that the pain will be gone, whereas others who may have wanted to feel some sensations so that they could push may find themselves completely deadened and unable to do so. Crawford (1979) finds that in the best of circumstances, about 85 percent of parturient women are free of pain, 12 percent experience partial relief, and 3 percent feel no relief. A 1985 study by Crawford and his colleagues of lumbar epidural analgesia given during labor to 26,490 women at Birmingham Maternity Hospital in England between 1968 and 1985 found no maternal deaths. The relatively rare dangers for the mother included loss of consciousness (1 in 3,000); cardiac arrest (1 in 3,000); severe hypertension and headache (1 in 2,000); and numbness and weakness (1 in 2,000).

There are several other potential disadvantages of epidural anesthesia to the mother. These include lowering of the blood pressure and paralysis of the breathing muscles if there is an accidental lumbar puncture (Inch 1984:95–98; Pritchard et al. 1985:363), as well as long-term backache (MacArthur et al. 1990). Dangers to the baby include oxygen deprivation, slowing of the heart rate, an increase in the acidity of its blood, and poor muscle tone, which affects the baby's ability to suck (Inch 1984:97–99). If an epidural is administered before the woman enters active labor (defined as beginning around 5–6 centimeter dilation), marked slowing of labor can result. During second stage labor, epidurals are likely to decrease a mother's ability to push, leading to delay of the birth, to "failure of descent," and/or to spontaneous rotation to the proper position—all of which can lead to an increased incidence of midforceps deliveries and forceps rotations (Chestnut et al. 1987; Cox et al. 1987; Kaminski et al. 1987).

Women's Responses

If you're doing so well, why do they have to slap you with an epidural? . . . I was ready to push, and they gave me an epidural [and it slowed my labor] and I had the baby *eight hours later*. And on my next birth, I was determined to stay home so that they couldn't do that. I left home at 4:30, had the baby by 6:00. They gave me an epidural and it didn't take effect until after the baby came. Because I was only there a few minutes before—they got me all set up and prepped and ready to go and then gave me an epidural and I wasn't numb until after the baby started coming. Why do they feel like they've got to give you an epidural? Is it something within them? (Louellen Jones)

While I was trying to do it naturally, I was nervous, tense, uptight, and scared. As soon as I had the epidural, I relaxed! The baby popped right out soon after that, and I was able to really relax and enjoy the birth. (Caroline Freeman)

I definitely think that the epidural is the *only* way to go. Why would anyone want to go through all of that when there is a better way? (Gretchen Lauderman)

Ritual Purposes   So common is the use of epidurals today that many childbirth professionals are calling the 1990s the age of the "epidural epidemic." Sixty percent of the women in my study, and 80 percent of the women in a recent study by Sargent and Stark (1987) received epidurals or their equivalent. To numb a woman about to give birth is to intensify the message that her body is a machine by adding to it the message that this machine can function without *her*. In particular, epidural anesthesia puts the final seal on this message, dramatically illustrating to the woman the "truth" of one of Western society's fundamental principles—the Cartesian maxim that mind and body are separate. (See Chapter 5 for a discussion of the many women who *demand* epidural anesthesia during labor and birth because they desire this separation.)

Yet to fully understand the symbolic significance of the epidural in hospital birth, we need to consider the meaning of its replacement of *scopolamine* and *general anesthesia* as routine procedures in most hospitals. Although "scope" did serve to reinforce the technocratic model of birth in that it told women that their machines did not need them to produce a baby, it did not make women act like machines but like wild animals—an uncomfortable metaphor because it undermined society's attempts to make birth appear to be mechanical enough to conform to the reality created by the technocratic model:

When I was in medical school, the ward patients in labor received little or no pain relief, while the private patients were given scopolamine, a drug that wiped out the memory of the labor and birth. Many women loved it and would say, "My doctor was wonderful. He gave me a shot to put me out as soon as I came to the hospital. I never felt a thing." Those women weren't put out, but they didn't remember what had happened to them—at least not consciously. When these women thought they were "out" they were awake and screaming. Made crazy from the drug, they fought; they growled like animals. They had to be restrained, tied by hands and feet to the corners of the bed (with straps padded with lamb's wool so there would be no injury, no telltale marks), or they would run screaming down the halls. Screaming obscenities, they bit, they wept, behaving in ways that would have produced shame and humiliation had they been aware. Doctors and nurses, looking at such behavior induced by the drug they had administered, felt justified in treating the women as crazy wild animals to be tied, ordered, slapped, yelled at, gagged. (Harrison 1982:87)

Furthermore, any type of general anesthesia meant that the woman would miss many of the important messages she could have been receiving. The "awake and aware" Lamaze patient with the epidural fits the picture of birthing reality painted by the technocratic model much better than the "scoped out" and "gassed out" mother, as the epidural makes a physical reality out of the conceptual separation of mind and body, a reality that the woman will grasp precisely because of her awareness. (See Chapter 4 for a discussion of the conceptual mesh between the philosophy on which the Lamaze method was originally based and the technocratic model of birth.)

"YOU'RE 10 CENTIMETERS—NOW PUSH!" / "DON'T PUSH!"

Description and Official Rationale It is thought that the baby's head cannot pass through the mother's cervix until it reaches full dilation to 10 centimeters, and that if the woman begins to push before complete dilation, the baby's head will become "a battering ram," as it will be unnecessarily and harmfully smashed against the pelvic floor and the cervix may rip. Too early pushing can also cause the cervix to become swollen from the pressure of the baby's head, thus making complete dilation take longer and be more painful to achieve. Correspondingly, once the woman is fully dilated ("complete"), the baby can and therefore should be pushed through her cervix as quickly as possible, as the pushing stage is held to be hard on both mother and baby and should be expedited. Most hospital guidelines allow no more than a maximum of two hours for completion of the second (or pushing) stage of labor.

Thus, as soon as completion is announced, hospital personnel often immediately begin to exhort the laboring woman to push, whether she actually feels the urge to push, or not. But when the baby is near to being born, the woman must be transported to the delivery room. So that the baby will not be born *en route,* the laboring woman in transit will be exhorted *not* to push with as much vigor as she was previously commanded *to* push.

Physiological Effects Physician Michelle Harrison (personal correspondence) states that the physician's basing of judgment concerning readiness to push on the arbitrary standard of full cervical dilation eliminates the more physiologically efficacious possibility of basing such judgment on the woman's urge to push. Harrison notes that she often allowed her home birth mothers to begin to push gently whenever they felt the urge, even if they were not completely dilated, and that this gentle pushing would serve to help, rather than hinder, the woman to achieve full cervical dilation (1982:98). Although it is sometimes true that hard and prolonged pushing before 10 centimeters dilation can have harmful effects, it is also true that pushing after dilation is complete, but before one has the actual urge to push, can be harmful as well. Many of the women in my study described long, discouraging, and exhausting pushing phases in which they were repeatedly yelled at to push because they had dilated to 10 centimeters, but their efforts seemed to be to no avail. Susan McKay reports that nurses, when asked why the two-hour rule exists, commonly responded that

> it was learned as part of institutional norms, and that if the nurse doesn't urge and cajole the woman to push harder and faster in order to meet specified time limits, more intrusive intervention, such as forceps or vacuum extraction, may be used. The message can be imparted even more strongly as the birth attendant conducts frequent sterile vaginal exams to ascertain even the slightest evidence of progress of the descending fetus. This occurs despite no evidence that two hours of second stage is any safer than any other length of time providing the mother and the baby are in good health. Urging the mother to push harder and longer may, in fact, make things worse as the baby's head and umbilical cord are compressed through the mother's intensive effort, leading to [heart-rate] decelerations and fetal hypoxia [oxygen deprivation]. (McKay 1990*a*)

In *Spiritual Midwifery,* internationally renowned midwife Ina May Gaskin reports that home birth women, after reaching complete dilation, often experience a slowing or lessening of contractions, sometimes to the point where they can even rest for a while before actually feeling a pushing urge (1990:358). Midwife Jerianne Fairman explains that forcing the mother to push before she feels the urge to push usually accomplishes little more than to drain her energy:

> Once the cervix is completely dilated and the baby's head has passed into the birth canal, the uterus, which had been tightly stretched around the baby, now fits flaccidly around the rest of its body. Because of this, uterine contractions do not yield sufficient pressure against the baby's bottom to assist the

abdominal muscles in moving the baby down through the birth canal. As the uterus continues to contract during the resting phase, muscle fibers in the uterus gradually retract, reducing the uterus in size until it again fits snugly around its contents. Once the uterus has contracted sufficiently, contractions once again become effective; the baby's head descends lower into the birth canal and a bearing down reflex is simulated. The resting phase has ended. It may take anywhere from a few minutes to two or three hours. (Fairman 1990)

Midwives, after making sure that the mother's bladder is empty, and that her psychological condition and the position and heartrate of the baby are favorable, will encourage her to simply rest, sometimes even sleep, during this latent period of second stage labor, which Sheila Kitzinger has labeled the "rest and be thankful stage" (quoted in Fairman 1990:10). But this stage, although common, is largely unknown in the hospital, where it is rarely given time to occur naturally.

Women's Responses

I became aware that I was indeed in the throes of transition. Contractions were inordinately forceful, were periodically back-to-back, and often appeared to have two peaks of intensity. I was extremely uncomfortable during contractions, experiencing considerable backache and intermittent urges to forcefully push near the end of the fifty-minute transition phase. In light of this, the obstetrician reported that the cervix was fully dilated, and I should begin voluntary pushing with subsequent contractions. Shortly thereafter, though, I didn't perceive the contractions to be as intense as before, nor at the same rate, all of which was confirmed on the monitor. Having finally arrived at the second stage, it seemed as though my uterus had suddenly tired! When the nurses in attendance noted a contraction building on the recorder, they instructed me to begin pushing, not waiting for the *urge* to push, so that by the time the urge pervaded, I invariably had no strength remaining but was left gasping, dizzy, and diaphoretic. The vertigo so alarmed me that I became reluctant to push firmly for any length of time, for fear that I would pass out. I felt suddenly depressed by the fact that labor, which had progressed so uneventfully up to this point, had now become unproductive. (Merry Simpson, from her Lamaze story-report)

With the head crowning, it was decided to take me into delivery. I was feeling the urge to push. Blow, blow, blow. Anne asked me to move onto the delivery table, but as hard as I tried to summon all my muscles, I couldn't budge. They had to pick me up. Blow, blow, blow. I was becoming frantic and felt as though I was losing control. Where was the doctor, any doctor? You have to blow, Lee. . . . I felt as though my whole pelvic area would explode if I didn't push. But I heard Anne (whose hand was my lifeline at that point) saying, "You can't push yet, Lee!" (Lee Heit, from her Lamaze story-report)

In Merry's response, we can observe her internalization of the message that her machine was defective. She does not say "the nurses had me pushing too soon," but "my uterus had suddenly tired," and labor "had now become unproductive." And Lee, who according to a witness had been ready to push her baby out for half an hour before she was allowed to, gives us a fair idea of both the depth of her conviction that institutional orders are to be obeyed above bodily imperatives, and of the physical agony which her following those orders entailed.

Ritual Purposes   Although babies' heads come in many different circumferences, standardization of production necessitates reliance on the arbitrary standard of 10 centimeters for every cervix, regardless of the size of the baby that must pass through it. If the birthing woman's body is a machine producing a product, then it makes perfect sense that once the production opening reaches the standard, the product should be immediately produced, given that time is of the essence if production schedules are to be maintained. And, given the constant danger of damage to the product from maternal mechanical malfunction, it seems in the product's best interests as well to get it out as soon as possible.

To have a number of people continually exhorting and commanding her either to push or not to push constitutes a complete denial of the validity of the natural rhythmic imperatives of the laboring woman's body and intensifies the messages of the mechanicity of her labor and of her subordination to the institution's expectations and schedule.

TRANSFER TO THE DELIVERY ROOM

Description and Official Rationale   Delivery of the infant in a "delivery room" seems necessary to obstetrical personnel, especially those in tertiary care centers, for a variety of reasons. These include the sterility of the environment, not achievable in the labor room, and the availability of bright lights and the full array of instruments. So when delivery is imminent, the laboring woman is wheeled down the hall from her labor room to the delivery room, where she is positioned on a high, flat table in the center of the room.

Physiological Effects   As is indicated in the women's responses below, the physiological effects of being moved when one is ready to push include increased stress and pain, not to mention the sheer physical effort of climbing on and off of tables with a baby about to emerge from one's body. Various animal studies have indicated that environmental disturbances have strongly detrimental effects on labor (Bleicher 1962; Freak 1962; Hafetz 1962; Newton et al. 1968; Newton 1973), including inhibition of maternal oxytocin production and subsequent labor slowing.

Women's Responses

> Another thing that bugged the heck out of me is they would come in and here you were—and I was really in control. I had done all these things and was in control. And they'd say, all right, get over here on this bed. We want to take you to the delivery room. Jack would say, well, wait until she finishes this contraction. *"Get over here on this bed!"* Now here I am in the middle of a contraction. Leave me alone! And you know, they'd start moving you, and moving the IV. They didn't even stand there and wait until it's over. . . . Well, heavens. To crawl over on that metal table and wheel you down the hall and they'd get the IV, you know, and they'd take it and say "Get over here" and then you'd have to crawl over this cord. You know, why didn't they say . . . just hop on over here! (July Sanders)

> Then I got in the delivery room and they said okay, get on the delivery table. Well, there was nobody there to—nobody offered to kind of help me get off the guerney onto the delivery table and I was having contractions, and quite a bit of discomfort, and I just thought gee, I would expect someone to kind of lift me up or something. I felt like I got on that table with my grit and fingernails. It was a real awkward kind of thing. And I realized too in that transition [to the delivery room] that with nobody to push and breathe with me during the contractions, that it was really hard. [My husband] was there, but I guess he may have been getting on his mask . . . or something like that. (Constance O'Riley)

Ritual Purposes   In Western biomedicine, the operating room constitutes the inner *sanctum sanctorum*—the technocratic equivalent of the Ndembu sacred shrine (a place where all the categories must be carefully kept, and where the presence of the other world is palpable). In the "O.R." the surgeon demonstrates his skill at manipulation of the human body-machine. From its inception, the obstetrical profession was constrained to justify itself as of equal medical value to other branches of medicine in which the inherent pathology of the disease or accident treated was perhaps clearer than is the "pathology" of normal birth (Wertz and Wertz 1989:145). Therefore, obstetrics' procedures had to parallel those of other, more immediately respected areas of medicine as closely as possible. Thus, although the normal deliveries performed in the delivery room hardly compare in terms of pathology to the climactic surgical emergencies handled in the operating room, because the birth of the baby was *the* climactic event of the labor process, conceptually speaking, it *had* to be performed in the delivery room—the obstetrical equivalent of the surgical O.R.

As such, and as the place where the laboring woman knows that, one way or another, her baby will finally be born, the delivery room carries for her a high emotional charge. Transportation to the delivery room thus increases the affectivity of the birth event for both mother and staff, an affectivity that is further increased by the strong element of drama established by the rapid intensification in the number of ritual actions performed upon the laboring woman's body immediately before and after she enters the holy of holies. In July's and Constance's descriptions above, we can observe how the woman herself, so carefully ushered up to the labor room in a wheelchair at the beginning when she could have walked, now has become fundamentally irrelevant to this process, as she is ordered about and ignored as the moment of birth approaches. While Constance was climbing onto the delivery table with her "grit and fingernails," all of the medical personnel in the room were busy getting ready for the birth. They each had a function, a specific job to do, but those functions did not include recognizing, celebrating, or honoring the woman as birth-giver.

Once established on the delivery table, and appropriately cleansed and draped, the birthing woman's genital region becomes the stage upon which the doctor—supported by his cast and crew—directs, produces, and stars in the play of the baby's birth (Shaw 1974:84). And, in the manner of all dramatic rituals, every successful performance works to ensure that the play will continue to be produced.

LITHOTOMY POSITION

Description and Official Rationale   The majority of hospitals and obstetricians in this country (still) insist on a birthing position that quite literally makes the baby, following the curve of the birth canal, be born heading upwards. States *Williams*: "The most widely used and often the most satisfactory [position for delivery] is the dorsal lithotomy position on a delivery table with leg supports" (Cunningham et al. 1989: 315). No reasons why this position is "the most satisfactory" are given, but a strong clue is provided in an earlier text:

> The lithotomy position is the best. Here the patient lies with her legs in stirrups and her buttocks close to the lower edge of the table. The patient is in

the ideal position for the attendant to deal with any complications which may arise. (Oxorn and Foote 1975:110)

This position, in other words, is the easiest for performing obstetric interventions, including maintaining sterility, monitoring fetal heart rate, administering anesthetics, and performing and repairing episiotomies (McKay and Mahan 1984:111).

Physiological Effects   Roberto Caldeyro-Barcia, past president of the International Federation of Obstetricians and Gynecologists, states unequivocally, "Except for being hanged by the feet, the supine position is the worst conceivable position for labor and delivery" (1975:11). There are a number of problems generated by this position: (1) it focuses most of the woman's body weight squarely on her tailbone, forcing it forward and thereby narrowing the pelvic outlet, which both increases the length of labor and makes delivery more difficult (Balaskas and Balaskas 1983:8); (2) it compresses major blood vessels, interfering with circulation and decreasing blood pressure, which in turn lowers oxygen supply to the fetus (for example, several studies have reported that in the majority of women delivering in the lithotomy position, there was a 91 percent decrease in fetal transcutaneous oxygen saturation (Humphrey et al. 1973, 1974; Johnstone et al. 1987; Kurz et al. 1982); (3) contractions tend to be weaker, less frequent, and more irregular in this position, and pushing is harder to do because increased force is needed to work against gravity (Hugo 1977), making forceps extraction more likely and increasing the potential for physical injury to the baby; (4) placing the legs wide apart in stirrups can result in venous thrombosis or nerve compression from the pressure of the leg supports, while increasing both the need for episiotomy and the likelihood of tears because of excessive stretching of the perineal tissue and tension on the pelvic floor (McKay and Mahan 1984).

Studies comparing women's preferences for supine versus upright positions for delivery reported, without exception, more positive responses from women using the upright position. These women tended to experience more ease in pushing, less pain during pushing, fewer backaches, shorter second stages, fewer forceps deliveries, and fewer perineal tears (Gardosi et al. 1989; Liddell and Fisher 1985; Stewart et al. 1983; van Lier 1985). Advantages for the baby included higher levels of oxygen in the umbilical cord and higher Apgar scores than babies whose mothers delivered them in the lithotomy position. There were no adverse effects from delivering in the upright position, "although a few birth attendants reported that this position was inconvenient for them" (McKay and Roberts 1989:23). In one study, by far the most popular upright position among women given the option was the supported squat, in which the woman gives birth on a bed supported in a squatting position by a special "birth cushion," which allows most of the woman's weight to rest on her thighs instead of her feet. Ninety-five percent of the subjects in this study wanted to use this position in subsequent births; the researchers found that if women not originally assigned to the study heard about the birth cushion from others, they would often request it for themselves (Gardosi et al. 1989).

Women's Responses   Most of the hospital-birthers in my study *expected* to be in the lithotomy position for birth; the idea of an alternative occurred only to those who delivered in birthing suites or utilized the services of a nurse-midwife who would let them give birth in the labor room in almost any position they wanted. As a result of this expectation, the comments made to me about the lithotomy position had more to do with how women worked to adapt to that position than with the position itself:

> I just simply felt like I had to be sitting up to push, so I refused to push until Lenny got behind me and held me up, pushed my shoulders up off the delivery table so I could push every time I had a contraction, because I mean, there was nothing at all to lean on besides him. (Constance O'Riley)

> My arms were not tied or anything. It was hospital policy to do it, but I told them I wouldn't go to the hospital if they tied my arms. I didn't mind if they tied my legs down because I knew I would still be able to push with my ankles. (Terry Lutzer)

Ritual Purposes   This lithotomy position completes the process of symbolic inversion that has been in motion since the woman was put into that "backwards" hospital gown. Now we have her normal bodily patterns of relating to the world quite literally turned upside down: her buttocks at the table's edge, her legs widespread in the air, her vagina totally exposed. As the ultimate symbolic inversion, it is ritually appropriate that this position be reserved for the peak transformational moments of the initiation experience: the birth itself. The official representative of society, its institutions, and its core values of science, technology, and patriarchy stands not at the mother's head nor at her side, but at her bottom, where the baby's head is beginning to emerge.

Structurally speaking, this position puts the woman's vagina in the relationship to society (through its representative, the obstetrician) that her head normally occupies—a total inversion perfectly appropriate from a societal perspective, as the technocratic model promises us that we can have babies with our cultural heads instead of our natural bottoms. The cultural value here is clearly on the baby, who is emerging at the "top." As Lakoff and Johnson (1980) point out, in this culture, "up is good; down is bad," so the babes born of science and technology must be born "up" toward the positively valued cultural world of men, in *opposition* to the natural force of gravity, instead of "down" toward the negatively valued natural world of women. As we perpetuate our society, we also symbolically enact the driving thrust upward, in defiance of earthly gravity, that has characterized it since its inception.

Conceptually speaking, the overthrow of the initiate's category system is now complete: this position expresses and reinforces her now-total openness to the new messages she is about to receive and itself constitutes one of those messages, as it speaks so eloquently to her of her powerlessness and of the power of society at the supreme moment of her own individual transformation.

In spite of the strength of these covert symbolic messages, the technocratic model of birth is overtly predicated on scientific fact. When the discrepancy between scientific fact and actual practice becomes as obvious as it is with the lithotomy position, that model must either be abandoned altogether (as have many such paradigms of the past) or be expanded to accommodate at least the most compelling pieces of scientific evidence that challenge its standard operating procedures. For example, as research showing the benefits of walking during labor gains more acceptance, it is to be hoped that monitoring by telemetry will gradually replace the kind that physically ties women down—but the fundamental values and beliefs that necessitate electronic monitoring in the first place will not have to change.

So it shall be with birth position. So much evidence has been gathered that demonstrates the advantages of an upright position for pushing that science has responded with the development of electronic birthing chairs, in which the woman sits in a physiologically efficacious position for pushing with perineum exposed (or covered by a sheet) and legs spread apart on plastic supports. The symbolic ramifications of this chair are considerable, as it places the woman higher than the obstetrician as she delivers the baby, looking almost like a queen on a throne surrounded by her servants. Yet, because the chair is incorporated into many hospitals without any fundamental accompanying shift in core values and beliefs, its potentials for empowerment of the birthing woman are often co-opted.

Placing the woman alone on her technocratic throne can become almost as much a symbolic expression of depersonalization and objectification as the lithotomy position itself. Although women can easily reach the controls on the chairs to alter their position, medical personnel rarely provide this information, usually preferring to retain such control. Because the chair is elevated so high, women cannot get out of it to shift position between contractions. Several studies show that some women who stayed in the chairs to push for more than thirty minutes at a time developed hemorrhoids and perineal swelling. Others complained that the chairs are uncomfortable and prevented them from rocking their pelvis or otherwise moving during second stage (McKay and Mahan 1984:113), or that their partners were now too far away to touch them very much. (Early, low-tech birthing chairs and hammocks in this country and others were designed to have someone sitting behind the laboring woman, intimately embracing and supporting her [Ashford 1988b; Jordan 1983].)

Thus it would appear that, in spite of the obvious physiological advantages of the high-tech birth chair over the delivery table, being forcibly locked into *any* position during labor is less preferable than being able to freely change position as desired. Women who birth without technocratic control on double beds, on stools, on beanbag chairs, on the floor, or in water frequently change positions, perhaps resting on their sides between contractions, perhaps sitting or squatting to push (Ashford 1988b; Engelmann 1977; Jordan 1983; McKay and Mahan 1984; Odent 1984). But this very unmechanical behavior is too incompatible with the technocratic model to be a viable delivery option in most hospitals. Moreover, women themselves have been so conditioned to labor and give birth lying down that the idea of such alternatives never occurs to many (McKay and Mahan 1984:118). Therefore, though challenged, the dominance of the lithotomy position continues.[9]

STERILE SHEETS, DISINFECTANT, AND HAND-STRAPPING

Description and Official Rationale

No one should be permitted in the delivery room without a scrub suit, a mask covering both nose and mouth, and a cap that completely covers the hair. Preparation for actual delivery entails thorough vulvar and perineal

scrubbing and covering with sterile drapes in such a way that only the immediate area about the vulva is exposed. (Cunningham et al. 1989:315)

I could find no rationale for such sepsis in obstetrical texts, merely
the flat statement that it was necessary. Attention to sterility is generally
necessary in the hospital because of the enormous number of germs concentrated there. Historically speaking, of course, sterile techniques for
birth were developed to prevent the spread of childbed fever, a major
killer of postpartal women in hospitals until the germ theory of disease
became widely accepted.[10] According to one of the obstetricians I interviewed, sterility at delivery is necessary because the routine episiotomy
makes birth a surgical procedure with a high chance of infection for
the mother. Moreover, he continued, the manual extraction of the placenta common in hospital birth also carries with it a high chance of
infection for the laboring woman. This particular obstetrician insisted
that the need for sterility had nothing to do with the *baby*.

If he is correct, then I am hard-pressed to find an official rationale
for the practice of strapping women's hands and forbidding them to
touch their babies. (To some extent, it may have been a carry-over
from the days of heavy scopolamine use, but it continued for many
years after scopolamine was replaced by the epidural.) Although this
practice, common fifteen years ago, has nowadays been phased out in
most American hospitals, it seems to have reflected a basic tenet of the
technocratic model—the deep belief that the mother is (conceptually)
dirty whereas the baby is clean. Only the recognition of this underlying
belief can make sense of the convoluted reasoning that allowed a baby
to be placed on the mother's abdomen while she was forbidden to touch
it with her hands, because if she were to do so *she* would contaminate
the sterile field, whereas the baby itself would not. That this belief is
still extant in modern, enlightened hospitals that no longer require the
strapping of hands is indicated by the fact that those women in my
study who delivered in alternative birthing centers in the hospital without such sterile techniques were not allowed to put their babies in the
nursery, as these babies were considered to be "contaminated."

Women's Responses

Well, they poured this bucket of stuff over my crotch and splashed me
with colored disinfectant—that was weird. And I had my hands—they said
they wouldn't have to cuff my hands or anything if I'd just keep them under
the sheets and at one point I said "Lenny, get my glasses," I sure wanted

my glasses on so I could see because I couldn't wear my contacts in labor. And at one point I instinctively tried to adjust my glasses, and about three people yelled at me—get my hands back under the sheets, because I would kind of mess up their sterile conditions. [I knew] that was dumb, [but] I was so afraid that I was going to break one of the rules and that they weren't going to let me touch my baby or something. (Constance O'Riley)

They strapped my hands down with all three of my births. I thought it was awful. The second two they did loosely so—I mean the first one it was like I was in prison or something. And so I said, "You know, that really hurts, can . . ." "You might touch something sterile." Here it is *your* baby and they don't want you to even—but the second two they still tied them down after I'd had such good success. You would think—and here I was doing the same thing the second and third time. You'd think that they would show a little respect for you and treat you—if I wasn't the type personality I was, that sort of stayed on top of things, all those combinations could really tend to throw you into depression. You know, treating you like you're not very bright, like you don't really know what's going on with your own body. (July Sanders)

Ritual Purposes   The sterile sheets with which the birthing woman is draped from neck to foot reinforce the symbolic inversion that was completed with the lithotomy position, as the one part that is always covered in public is now the one part left uncovered. The sterility of the sheets itself carries a profound series of messages. Besides intensifying both society's purification of the initiate begun during the prep and the message of her fundamental irrelevance to the birth, the emphasis on sterilizing the area around the vagina graphically illustrates to the woman that she and her sexuality are intrinsically dirty, whereas her baby—society's product—is pure and clean. The profound invisible message behind this more obvious one is that our culture's categories are real and are to be believed in and practiced in behavior.

EPISIOTOMY (AND SOME NOTES ON FORCEPS
AND THE CESAREAN SECTION)

Description and Official Rationale   During labor, when the baby's head is exposed to a diameter of 3 to 4 centimeters, the attending physician will pick up a pair of sterile scissors and snip the stretching skin of the perineum downward toward the anus (median episiotomy) or downward and sideways (mediolateral episiotomy) to enlarge the vaginal opening and make it easier for the head to emerge. Most physicians sincerely believe that episiotomy shortens the pushing phase and thus reduces the chance the baby will suffer from oxygen deprivation, that it protects the fetal skull and brain from damage as it is "thrust against" the pelvic floor like a "battering ram," and prevents ragged perineal tears and "permanent relaxation of the pelvic floor with its possible sequelae of cystocoele, rectocele, and uterine prolapse" (Pritchard et al. 1985:339). Another reason given by many doctors in support of episiotomy is to maintain vaginal tightness for the enhanced pleasure of a sexual partner. According to several physicians I interviewed, so strong is the medical community's belief in the value of episiotomy that many obstetrical residents are not trained to deliver babies without performing one.

Physiological Effects   That episiotomy protects the fetus from damage is an unproven assumption revealing physicians' deep-seated belief that the fetus, their product, is in danger from malfunction of the mother's birthing machine. That birth without episiotomy will result in prolapse of the uterus, or in weakened support for the bladder from excessively stretched muscles has also never been proven (Cunningham et al. 1989: 323; Harrison 1982:98; Thacker and Banta 1983). Moreover, should the woman desire enhanced sexual pleasure for herself or her partner from increased vaginal tightness, she can achieve the desired results by exercising the pelvic floor muscles after birth. States Harrison:

> Think of the episiotomy this way: if you hold a piece of cloth at two corners and attempt to tear it by pulling at the two ends, it will rarely rip. However, if a small cut is made in the center, then pulling at the ends easily rips the cloth. Doing an episiotomy is analogous, and sometimes results in tears that extend into the rectum. Physicians argue that this "clean" tear is more easily repaired than the ragged one that occurs when a woman tears without the cut. My experience has been that the small tears that sometimes occur without episiotomy are easy to stitch and less bothersome to the woman. Episiotomies, once repaired, are often debilitating and are the source of much pain in the postpartum period. (Harrison 1982:97)

One obstetrician I interviewed stated flatly, "I have never had a third or fourth degree extension [tear] through the sphincter or rectum unless I did an episiotomy." His observation is confirmed in a comparative study of home and hospital births (discussed in detail in Chapter 4), in which nine times more episiotomies were performed in the hospital births, accompanied by nine times as many severe (third and fourth degree) perineal tears. Another study of 241 first-time hospital-birthers showed that "the proportion of deep perineal lacerations was lowest (0.9%) in women without episiotomy who were not confined to the lithotomy position; it was greatest (27.9%) in women delivered in stirrups with an episiotomy.... There was more than a twenty-fold increase in the rate of deep laceration when episiotomy was used," as well as a fourteen-fold increase in the rate of deep perineal lacerations when stirrups were used (Borgatta et al. 1989:295). In other words, the combination of episiotomy with the lithotomy position and stirrups works to offer women the highest possible chance that they will have deep perineal lacerations as they give birth.

Women's Responses This was one of the single most-hated procedures by nearly all of the women in my study who experienced it, primarily because it took so long to heal, and thus made their first newborn month of motherhood far more painful and awkward than they felt it needed to be:

> I hated having an episiotomy. I didn't think I needed it. It was three weeks before I could get around comfortably afterward, and I was miserable with it for all that time. (Melinda Simpson)

> My sister tore, so I didn't mind having an episiotomy, if it made the doctor feel better. I figured that a nice smooth cut was not going to be any worse than whatever else might happen, and if it made him happy, I didn't really care all that much. But it was very uncomfortable for a long time after—really messed up those special newborn days. (Madeleine Oppenheimer)

Ritual Purposes Episiotomies are performed on over 90 percent of first-time mothers delivering in major U.S. hospitals (Thacker and Banta 1983). (In the Netherlands, by way of contrast, they are performed in only 8 percent of births [Thacker and Banta 1983:165].) Besides its obvious function of hazing and ritual mutilation of the initiate, this procedure conveys to the initiate the value and importance of one of the most fundamental markers of our separation from nature—the straight line. The vagina constitutes the cross-cultural symbol *par excellence* of the natural, powerfully sexual, creative, and male-threatening aspects of women (long honored in myth as the *vagina dentata*, the vagina with teeth which threatens to consume or castrate the impotent male). Through episiotomies, physicians, as society's representatives, can deconstruct the vagina (and, by extension, its representations), then reconstruct it in accord with our cultural belief and value system. Episiotomies are performed in part because doctors are taught that straight cuts heal faster than jagged tears—a teaching that is in accord with our Western belief in the superiority of culture over nature. The straight line does not exist in nature, and is therefore most useful in aiding us in our constant conceptual efforts to separate ourselves from nature.

The episiotomy is also conceptually useful to obstetrics. Since surgery constitutes *the* central core of Western medicine, the ultimate form of manipulation of the human body-machine, the legitimization of obstetrics necessitated the transformation of childbirth into a surgical procedure. Routinizing the episiotomy has proven to be an effective means of accomplishing this transformation—even "natural" births in the modern LDR or birthing suite can be transformed into surgical procedures by routine episiotomy.

On top of all that, the episiotomy reinforces and intensifies the messages of the other procedures about the importance of on-time production, the inherent defectiveness of the female birth machine, and the supremacy of the male over the female both in society and in the social production of the baby.

All of these messages are reinforced if the baby is pulled out with forceps. The application of forceps shows the mother beyond all doubt that her machine is indeed defective, and brings home the message that the lives of the mother and her baby are truly dependent on the institution and its technology. However, the use of forceps is no longer routine in many hospitals, as this procedure is rapidly being replaced by the *Cesarean section,* the operation that is increasingly moving childbirth into the real O.R. The possibility of the routinization of delivery "from above" is the most extreme manifestation of the cultural attempt to use birth to demonstrate the superiority and control of Male over Female, Technology over Nature:

> I found myself last night thinking about the day and the Cesarean I had done. Performing a Cesarean is the one time that truly gives you the feeling of delivering the baby. I remember having my hand in the uterus. Pressure was being applied by Dr. Joseph at the top of the uterus while my hand grasped the head of the baby and assisted it out through the incision. I felt a sense of excitement and of power and of personal accomplishment that is not present in a vaginal birth. This is the time the *obstetrician* truly delivers the baby; in a vaginal birth, it is the mother. (Harrison 1982:125)

Technically speaking, the Cesarean section should not even be considered here, as it is supposed to be a life-saving procedure, resorted to only when it becomes clear that vaginal birth is not an option. By this criterion, the Cesarean rate nationwide should be no more than 5 per-

cent, as indeed it was before 1970. However, the Cesarean rate nationwide as of 1988 stood at 24.7 percent (National Bureau of Vital Statistics). In many large teaching hospitals, it reaches 50 percent; in 1991
in a non-teaching private hospital in Anycity it was 58 percent. A 1987
report from the National Center for Health Statistics concluded that at
least half of the 934,000 Cesareans performed in the United States in
1987 were unnecessary, costing the public an extra $1 billion and un-
calculated increases in maternal morbidity, with no discernible benefit
to neonatal outcome. Private, for profit hospitals, and patients with the
best-paying insurance plans had the highest rates, whereas state, local,
and federal hospitals had the lowest.

An alarming example of just how far this trend could continue is
provided by Brazil. A Brazilian childbirth educator residing in Rio de
Janeiro recently informed me that the Cesarean rate in public teaching hospitals in Rio and Sao Paulo hovers around 65 percent and in
many private hospitals stands at 95 percent. Latin women in general
are more strongly socialized to passively obey men than American
women; further, middle- and upper-class Latin women are often concerned with demonstrating their cultural distance from Indian and peas-
ant women through highly cultural births and bottle- instead of breastfeeding. Additionally, as Carole Browner (personal communication)
points out, Brazilian women place high value on scientific knowledge
and control. Whatever the factors behind them, such Cesarean rates
graphically demonstrate the potential inherent in the technocratic model
for the complete technocratization of birth.

But in the American public mind, the ominously rising Cesarean
rate—which obviously has the potential to keep on going upward—
uncomfortably highlights the discontinuities between the technocratic
model and true physiological necessity, and obstetricians have been
under increasing public pressure to lower it. According to 1989 figures
(the most recent available), public outcry, combined with medical acceptance of new research on the technocratic viability of the VBAC (vaginal
birth after Cesarean) option, has apparently resulted in the stabilizing of the Cesarean rate:

> The 25 years of rising Cesarean delivery rates in the U.S. may have finally
> run their course. In 1989 the rate of 23.8 Cesareans per 100 deliveries was
> not significantly different from 24.7 in 1988, 24.4 in 1987, or 24.1 in
> 1986. . . . The percentage of vaginal births after Cesarean section per 100
> deliveries showed a remarkable rise between 1988 and 1989—from 12.6%
> in 1988 to 18.5% in 1989. Data are from the National Hospital Discharge

Survey conducted by the National Center for Health Statistics, Centers for Disease Control. (Taffel et al. 1991:1)

In ongoing interviews for a new study (Davis-Floyd 1992), I have recently become aware of what may be the development of another counteractive trend besides the VBAC. It seems that some obstetricians, in an effort to lower their Cesarean rates, are revitalizing the epidural/episiotomy/forceps delivery (previously in decline). Three of my new interviewees who gave birth this summer (1991) in this manner proudly reported to me, "He cut a *big* episiotomy, and pulled the baby out with forceps, but I didn't have to have a Cesarean!"

MIRROR

"Imagine mankind as dwelling in an underground
cave . . . in this they have been from childhood, with
necks and legs fettered . . . they cannot move their
heads round because of the fetters, and they can only
look forward, but light comes to them from a fire
burning behind them higher up at a distance . . ."
"Now consider," said I, "what their release would
be like . . . What do you think they would say, if someone told [them] that what they saw before was foolery,
but now [they] saw more rightly, being a bit nearer
reality . . . Don't you think [they] would be puzzled,
and believe what [they] saw before was more true than
what was shown to [them] now?"
"Far more," said he.
                                    —Plato, *The Republic*, Book VII

I hope that my readers will grant me a brief escape from the analytical confines of my own "standard procedures" and allow me here the literary luxury of a freer flow. Many of the women in my study group were offered mirrors, held by doctor or nurse, so that they could, if they wished, visually as well as physically experience their baby's entrance into independent life and their own transformations. Aware that mirrors often symbolize reflexivity, I have pondered for a long time the possible interpretations of the meaning of the mirror in hospital birth. To look in a mirror can entail a certain degree of self-consciousness, but it seems to me that who holds the mirror, and the situational context in which it is held, can have a profound effect on the cognitive content of what one sees.

Myerhoff and Ruby have provided me with some helpful insights into the nature of reflexivity:

> "Reflexive" . . . describes the capacity of any system of signification to turn back upon itself, to make itself its own object by referring to itself: subject and object fuse. . . . Within the self, detachment occurs between self and experience, self and other, witness and actor, hero and hero's story. We become at once both subject and object. Reflexive knowledge, then, contains not only messages but also information as to . . . the process by which [this knowledge] was obtained. It demonstrates the human capacity to generate second order symbols or metalevels—significations about signification. (1982)

As Babcock says of Narcissus, his tragedy

> is that he . . . does not reflect long enough to effect a transformation. He is reflective, but he is not reflexive—that is, he is conscious of himself as an other, but he is not conscious of being self-conscious of himself as an other, and hence not able to detach himself from, understand, survive, or even laugh at this initial experience of alienation. (1980:2)

From the mother's point of view, birth becomes reflexive when she becomes aware not only of the Other, the baby, but of herself giving birth to the Other. This can be at once an experience, not of alienation, but of some degree of distance from the physical sensations of birth and of the integration of consciousness and body in the act of giving birth:

> Pain. Grinding, blinding, absorbing intensity. Only pain, and pushing in spite of the pain. Only pain, and pushing. Then a voice, summoning forth my consciousness from its burial in the depths of sensation. I emerge, suddenly aware that *I* am here, that there is still a Me that can be called forth from this primordial absorption. The voice says Look! Look in the mirror. I look, and there is hair. Blonde, white blonde hair, starkly and miraculously framed by the curly dark locks on the sides of my distending vagina. I am stunned. There is *not* only this pain, this grinding, bone-crunching agony of raw sensation. There is Another! A baby! A not-me. My hair is dark. But in the mirror, I see blonde hair framed in my vagina. Oh yes. That is what I am doing. I am giving birth to a baby. There is a baby. I am birthing it. My pushes are working! My pain is for something! I push again, and watch transfixed as the oval of hair grows larger. It's working! *I* am working. I am doing this; it is me, this is Me, doing this, giving birth.
>
> I fall back, exhausted, and rest until the next contraction seizes me in its bony grip, and I galvanize every fiber in my body and PUSH. I know what I am doing now.

A sudden sharp burn. I gasp in surprise, lost in the sensation once more. And then the voice says, reach down. Reach your hand down. And I reach down—what am I reaching for? What am I? And my hand encounters a head—warm, wet, enormous. I will never forget that sensation—it is imprinted in my hand's palm and my heart's memories. And I rest between contractions, cradling my baby's head in my hand, perfectly sure now that there is Another. I am giving him birth. (Elizabeth Davey, from a story she wrote about her birth)

For many birthing women, there is no such self-awareness. Many wave the mirror away, too immersed in the imperatives of their bodies to desire the dissociation of consciousness from experience that looking entails:

You know before it happened, I thought that maybe I'd have this mystical sense of connecting with womankind and all this kind of stuff, and somehow that I was crossing some kind of barrier, you know—but at the time I was so preoccupied with physical sensations that you don't have time for all those mystical kinds of thoughts. I didn't even look in the mirror to see her come. It's just such an animal kind of feeling that takes you over that you just instinctively grunt and moan and push and puff and just want that big thing, that is very uncomfortably lodged in your birth canal, you just want to get it out. (Constance O'Riley)

Others, like Elizabeth, gaze in awe, their pain suddenly secondary to the overwhelming realization of the reality on the other side of Plato's fire. When the process by which her reflexive knowledge was obtained is *her own* process, for the mother who watches herself push the Other into his Otherness, whether in the hospital or at home, her birth will forever stand as a symbol of her ability to give birth, and as a metasymbol for her significance in life.

But what of the woman who is technocratically removed from her birth process? To watch one's body give birth to a baby without one's participation is also to internalize "information as to the process by which [reflexive knowledge] is obtained" (Myerhoff and Ruby 1982). In this case, as we have seen, the information internalized will reflect the woman's conscious awareness that not she, but It, gives birth to the Other; she takes the role of Witness to a process clearly demarcated as separate from the boundaries of her Self. Society, through its medical representative, holds up the mirror so that she can see how its product is born. In that act, society itself stands Witness to its self-regeneration.

But when the mirror is held for the woman who births the baby herself, society stands witness to its dependence on *women* for its regeneration; then birth for society becomes a metasymbol of that dependence. Perhaps that one reason alone is enough to explain the careful and ordered sequence of the procedures of hospital birth. Through these procedures, each necessitating the other, society creates the illusion that the shadows on the wall are indeed all there is to life.

What would happen if all the birthing women in the cave were suddenly released from their chains? Would they, as Plato thought, be blinded by the fire and turn back to the comforting familiarity of the shadows on the wall? Or would they put out the fire—and leave the cave?

APGAR SCORE

Description and Official Rationale The Apgar scoring system provides a standardized means by which birth attendants can assess the baby's condition at birth. Signs rated at two points each on a preprinted chart are skin color, muscle tone, breathing attempts, heartbeat, and response to stimulus, such as a touch or a pin-prick. Babies are rated twice, immediately after birth and five minutes later, because many babies, especially anesthetized ones, take some time to turn pink and to begin full breathing on their own. Ten is the highest obtainable score.

Women's Responses Mothers whose babies receive high Apgar scores reported feeling proud and pleased that their babies were so healthy; mothers whose babies received low Apgar scores at birth reported feeling tremendous anxiety until the second, higher score was reported.

Ritual Purposes Just as meat for the supermarket must be inspected, stamped "USDA APPROVED," and placed in a plastic wrapper that makes it look like it did not come from a cow, so must society's new product, the baby, be inspected and rated (and wrapped and placed in a plastic box). If the rating is high, the institution, and through it, society, can then claim the credit for a job well done. If there are defects, they can be used as reinforcers of the standard cultural view of nature as dangerous, untrustworthy, and inferior to culture, and of the inherent defectiveness of the female birth machine. The Apgar score is but the first in a long series of ratings that society will give its new member; scoring the baby at birth sets up the mother to respect and rely on society's rating system to judge her baby by for the rest of "its" life.

WASHING THE BABY

Description and Official Rationale   The baby emerges from the birth canal covered with vernix, a white, waxy substance, and blood, and sometimes meconium (fetal bowel movement). In other words, under the technocratic model, it is born dirty and needs to be cleaned. As soon after birth as possible, the baby will be whisked away from the delivery table by a nurse and washed.

Physiological Effects   Vernix is a protective coating that prevents the baby's skin from getting too dry. Many health care practitioners believe that it is good for the baby's skin and so should be massaged into the skin instead of being washed off.

Women's Responses   In conversation, July Sanders said:

> They didn't even clean him off—I mean just wiped him off with a little gauze and stuff or a blanket, and they didn't take him off me and bathe him or clean him off until 1:30. I was sitting up in the rocking chair rocking him when they came in. You know, he was still sitcky and had dried blood on him which was beautiful.

Responded Elsie Drew:

> I know. That's really—I really wanted to see Kristin like that and they washed her off before they gave her to me. I wanted to see her all covered with vernix—I wanted to see her and know her just exactly as she was when she came out of me.

Ritual Purposes   Blood and vernix are natural substances that must immediately be removed from society's product because their presence threatens the fragile conceptual framework (so painstakingly established and guarded through hospital birth rituals) within which the birth takes place—the framework that claims that the institution produces the baby. To wash the baby before giving it to the mother is in part to conceptually remove it from its natural origins and to begin immediately the process of enculturation. As I wrote in my journal some years ago:

> The baby I saw born today was inchoate against the green crisp shapes of the sterile sheets—blotchily, frighteningly white and red, leaking at the edges, formed and formless—a true anomaly, totally out of place in that over-formed green world of clean edges and sharp boundaries. No wonder the baby is so quickly cleaned, and wrapped, and whisked away.

PROPHYLACTIC EYE TREATMENT

Description and Official Rationale   Silver nitrate or an antibiotic substitute is placed in the eyes of almost every hospital-born baby in this country to prevent the development of blindness in case the mother should have gonorrhea, as required under state law in most states, on the theory that it is impossible to know which babies really need it and which ones do not.

Physiological Effects   Silver nitrate binds with the membranes of the baby's eyes, causing redness, irritation, swelling, and blurred vision in the first few days of her life, thus interfering with her visual learning and adjustment to her new environment. Antibiotic ointments do not seem to have these irritating effects and are increasingly utilized in place of silver nitrate. The authors of *Williams* state that at Parkland Memorial, penicillin is routinely injected into newborns "soon after delivery" instead of the ointment, which does not have a 100 percent success rate at preventing blindness (1985:384). These physicians do not question the wisdom of injecting antibiotics into minutes-old babies, as do many in the wholistic health movement who object to the routine administration of antibiotics even to adults (e.g., Odent 1986:71; Weil 1988).

Women's Responses

> All my baby's eyes poofed out. . . . It was almost like they were having a reaction—they were red and yucky, and I feel like as far as the bonding is concerned, that just wiped it out for the first two or three days. Paul has never had relations except for with me, and I have never had relations except for with Paul. We know we don't have VD, so why punish us? (Beverly Childress)

> I demanded as soon as she was born that they not put any silver nitrate in her eyes. I got a lot of static about that. You know, the traditional, "Oh, honey, you don't really mean that. You don't know what you are talking about." I was really thankful that Dr. Dorson walked in right at the height of that discussion with the nurses there. . . . He stepped in and [defended our right to refuse the procedure, as he had promised us that he would]. (Marla Bronstein)

Ritual Purposes   Prophylactic eye treatment of the newborn once again tells the mother that she—and the father—are impure in society's eyes and that they have potentially polluted society's product, which science and technology must now restore to purity—a purity that *only* society can bestow. The force of this message is increased by the fact that no individual distinctions are made in this universal process of ritual purification.[11]

VITAMIN K INJECTION

Description and Official Rationale   This practice was instituted in hospitals during the era of routine mother-infant separation. According to *Williams,* "although controversial in other countries," injection of the newborn with Vitamin K right after birth is almost universal in the United States (Cunningham et al. 1989:611). The rationale for this is that newborns are born with a "deficiency" of Vitamin K, which they also do not receive in breast milk. This leads to a decrease in Vitamin K-dependent blood coagulation factors, making newborns more susceptible to hemorrhage in the first several days of life until Vitamin K is manufactured in their systems (Cunningham et al. 1989:611). The risk is small—about 1 in 200—but real.

Physiological Effects   Injection of newborns with Vitamin K in large doses has been implicated as a cause of neonatal jaundice (Allison 1955; Cunningham et al. 1989:611). A small dose of 1 milligram seems to have no ill effects on the baby beyond the pain caused by the injection itself. If newborns are allowed to suckle soon after birth, the injection of Vitamin K is less necessary, since the colostrum that comes immediately from the mother's breast before her milk lets down is usually rich in Vitamin K (Trevathan 1987:213). In about 1 out of 200 babies, even in those that are breastfed, however, there is significant danger of hemorrhage. For this reason, even midwives attending home births sometimes give injections of Vitamin K. One Anycity midwife, for example, feels that the risk of cerebral hemorrhage is heightened in very fast or very long labors, when the baby has a strongly cone-shaped head, or when the baby demonstrates significant heart-rate decelerations during late labor. Because she believes in their value, she gives Vitamin K injections to around 40 percent of the babies she catches. But she feels strongly that breastfed babies born with "easy births" do not need Vitamin K and that it should not be administered routinely to all babies.

Ritual Purposes   If the pain that the individual newborn feels from a shot with a needle were up for consideration under the technocratic model, then the decision as to whether or not to inflict that pain on a newborn would be made on an individual basis according to specific need. But instead, the medical response to the danger of hemorrhage, as to the danger of blindness from VD, has been to standardize the Vitamin K injection for all newborns. In *The Technological Society*, Jacques Ellul has written:

> Standardization means resolving *in advance* all the problems that might possibly impede the functioning of an organization. It is not a matter of leaving it to inspiration, ingenuity, or even intelligence to find a solution [to a problem]; it is rather in some way to anticipate both the difficulty and the resolution. From then on, standardization creates impersonality, in the sense that the organization relies more on methods and techniques than on individuals. We thus have all the marks of a technique. Organization is thus a technique. (Ellul 1965:11–12)

Symbolically speaking, the standardization of the Vitamin K injection and indeed *all* the routine procedures performed on the newborn baby reinforce the messages to both baby and mother that nature is inadequate, that they are now dependent on organizations—that is, on *techniques*—for their lives and health. This message seems a fair and accurate reflection of the realities of technocratic life. In effect, these postpartum procedures form the modern structural equivalent of baptism: they symbolically enculturate the newborn, removing her step-by-step from the natural realm through restructuring her very physiology in accordance with technocratic standardization.

BONDING PERIOD

Description and Official Rationale   There is no mention of bonding in the 984 pages of *Williams Obstetrics*, and only one short paragraph about "rooming-in" (1989:243). Nevertheless, most of the women in my study were handed their babies in the delivery room so that they could experience a short "bonding period," usually after the babies had been washed, weighed, wrapped, and given their shots and their eye drops, but sometimes immediately after the birth.

Bonding became part of normal birth routine in many hospitals due to the combined efforts of La Leche League and other childbirth activists, and to the concerted pleas of two pediatricians, Marshall Klaus and John Kennell. In *Parent-Infant Bonding*, first published in 1976, Klaus and Kennell point out the existence of a "sensitive period" immediately after birth during which maternal-infant attachment seems to occur much more readily than if mother and child are separated after the birth, as used to be standard hospital practice: "We believe that there is strong evidence that at least 30–60 minutes of early contact in privacy should be provided for every parent and infant to enhance the bonding experience" (Klaus and Kennell 1982:56).

Physiological Effects   Some researchers believe that there are no physiological effects of early bonding, that it is in fact a "scientific fiction" (Eyer 1992). However, proponents of bonding suggest that the physiological benefits of early "bonding" may be numerous.

These potential benefits are eloquently summarized by Wenda Trevathan, who provides an exhaustive analysis of bonding research in *Human Birth: An Evolutionary Perspective* (1987:193–220):

> Touching and massaging the infant stimulates breathing, provides warmth, and serves to rub the fatty vernix caseosa into the skin, which may prevent dehydration. If she holds it over her heart, on the left side of her body, the mother may be quieting the infant with the rhythmic beat that was an important part of its intrauterine environment. Holding it on the left may also facilitate eye contact, in that most infants prefer to turn their heads and look to the right. . . . The infant may lick, nuzzle, or even suckle the mother's breast in the immediate postpartum period. Nipple contact stimulates release of oxytocin into her bloodstream, which results in uterine contractions, expulsion of the placenta, and inhibition of postpartum bleeding. The colostrum that the infant ingests provides immunological protection and is the only natural source of Vitamin K, a substance essential for normal clotting of blood, necessary, for example, for preventing hemorrhage at the site of the umbilical cord. In addition, this early suckling may enhance later breast-feeding success. (1987:213)

Other benefits may possibly include growth of healthy maternal bacteria in the infant's system, instead of the hospital bacteria she would have absorbed in the nursery (where strep and other bacterial epidemics are frequent occurrences), and "entrainment" of the bodily rhythms of mother and baby:

> Detailed studies (Condon and Sander 1974) of the amazing behavioral capacities of the normal neonate have shown that the infant sees, hears and moves in rhythm to his mother's voice in the first minutes and hours of life, resulting in a beautiful linking of the reactions of the two and a synchronized "dance" between the mother and the infant. (Klaus and Kennell 1982:63)

Klaus and Kennell also stress that fathers who were observed interacting with their newborn infants went through the same sort of exploratory and synchronizing process as the mothers. Benefits to the infant of early bonding with parents involve taking advantage of the "quiet-alert state," relatively rare in the first few days of life, which most normal newborns remain in for about forty-three minutes immediately after birth, and in which rapid learning takes place. (Marshall Klaus postulates an evolutionary advantage to mothers and babies utilizing this period to get to know each other immediately after birth [personal communication].)

Over the longer term, and more controversially, Klaus and Kennell postulate the value of uninterrupted bonding for the mother's integration of her "mental picture" of the baby with the real child; they hypothesize an increased incidence of child abuse if such integration does not take place (1982:66–67). (The mental images held by mothers who batter their infants are often radically different in appearance and behavior from the actual child.) Long-term psychological benefits may include increased ease of parent-child relationships (O'Connor et al. 1978, 1980; Siegel 1982). There is some evidence to indicate that child abuse is statistically slightly more likely to occur when no opportunity for early bonding is provided, although good data are very difficult to procure. A well-controlled study of 301 mothers and babies (O'Connor et al. 1980) found a significantly decreased incidence of child abuse and neglect and parenting disorders among mothers who received twelve extra hours of contact with their newborns during the first two days after delivery. But it is important to note that other researchers have taken great issue with the research methods used in such studies (Amighi 1990; Eyer 1992; Lamb et al. 1985; Tronick et al. 1985, 1987). In fact, serious methodological problems with most of the bonding studies done to date have rendered them inconclusive in their attempts to demonstrate any long-term results of early bonding or of early maternal-infant separation (Laughlin 1990:43; Trevathan 1987:212).

Addressing earlier research on mammalian bonding behavior that seemed to indicate the biological necessity of immediate attachment, Trevathan concludes that

> extremely rapid bond formation, such as has been described for goats and sheep, is "unnecessary" unless there is a good chance that the young will be mixed with others in the first few minutes or hours after birth. This is . . . certainly not the case for higher primates and human beings who live in groups too small for synchronous deliveries to be common and who have a level of awareness that would preclude great confusion over individual identity during the postpartum period. Thus it is untenable to argue for a rapidly forming bond in most mammalian species including our own. . . . [But] a strong and specific bond must ultimately form so that the mother is

motivated to provide the high level of care needed by the helpless infant. Such attachment and motivation can develop in an adoptive mother as well, so neither the experience of parturition nor close biological relatedness is necessary for a strong mother-infant bond in human beings. (Trevathan 1987:202)

Trevathan also notes that there are unusually high levels of endorphins present in mothers and infants during and immediately after delivery (1987:204); Odent (1984) suggests that these natural opiates contribute to maternal-infant bonding. Other researchers have also suggested that various hormones play roles in the maternal-infant attachment process, but, as Trevathan again points out, "thousands of cesarean-delivered, bottle-feeding, and/or adoptive mothers offer proof of the ability of maternal solicitude to develop in the absence of hormonal precursors" (1987:205).

Women's Responses

Jack helped cut the cord, and they gave the baby to me right away and never took him away from me. They wrapped him up and put him on my stomach and—they did not put the drops in his eyes immediately. He looked at me . . . I do feel that this baby has good eye contact with me. And I wonder if it's because we looked into each other's eyes for several minutes before the drops were put into his eyes. You know, before they get all blurry. I think that does make a difference. (July Sanders)

I had herpes, and they whisked the baby away to intensive care for obser-´ vation and wouldn't even let me touch him for three whole days. I grieved. I felt that he had died. Finally on the third day I went to the nursery and demanded him. But I felt very little when I got him. I know it's nonsensical, but my emotional feeling was that he had died, and this was someone else. I wanted desperately to love him, and I knew that nursing would be the fastest way to make up for the bonding I had missed, so I made myself nurse him and I hated it for a long time. When I would sit down to nurse him I would feel so impatient I could scream. It took *months* for me to feel that I was really his mother, and he was really my baby. Finally it did happen, but it was awful for a long time. (Jean Jordan)

The miracle of the birth was so fantastic that I think I was in awe of the whole experience. It was beautiful and I'll *never* forget it or lose the powerful emotion of it. The fact that my husband was there made it even more wonderful and he feels closer to me and his son because he helped and shared in the whole event, and we held our baby together. I don't think any couple should have to be apart during labor and delivery if they have an alternative. I think that because we were together my postpartum depression has always been instead postpartum ecstasy and all my tears those of joy. (Carmen Fogell, from her Lamaze story-report)

They put the baby on my tummy but they told me *not* to touch it. They didn't want my hands down anywhere near there. . . . Then they took it away, and I just turned off like a clam. It was awful. . . . I didn't want to have anything to do with it. . . . I finally told my mother—she was the only one I felt I could admit it to—I just came out and told her that I just wanted to give it away. It sounds terrible but it was an honest feeling. It was six weeks before I felt like I really loved him. . . . And now I wouldn't part with him—he's great.

Well and the next time—it was really weird. I put my hand down on him and I didn't expect to feel that way, I thought well it won't be as bad as last time but you know it might take some time to get to love him. But the second he came out, they put him on my skin and I reached down and I felt him and it was something about having that sticky stuff on my fingers. . . . It was like gosh, it's almost like part of him or something—I don't know what it was but it was really important to feel that waxy stuff . . . and they covered him up and he was crying and I made soothing sounds to him. . . . And he started calming down and somehow that makes you feel—like he already knows you, he knows who you are—like animals or something, perhaps the smell of each other . . . but it was marvelous to hold him and I just touched him for a really long time and then they took him over but something had already happened. But it was much more than I ever felt or thought I would feel. Just instant love. And I can remember when they would bring him into the room afterwards—it didn't diminish at all. It just always seemed to be there—I was crazy about him right from the beginning. (Anne Mallone)

Ritual Purposes   Throughout most of human history, mothers and babies have stayed together after birth.[12] It would seem that today's "bonding period" might simply represent a commonsensical return to a formerly universal human practice, but few customs in our technocratic society are that straightforward. Although birthing women are no longer routinely put to sleep, institutional interests are still better served when mothers and babies are separated (see below), so general acceptance of the importance of a bonding period has been far from automatic.

Since the original research on bonding in the 1970s, a great deal of controversy has erupted over the long-term effects of this simple practice. Many medical personnel, and many mothers, felt that Klaus and Kennell were "way off base" to suggest that when mothers missed this "sensitive period," their relationships with their babies had somehow been impaired. Yet proponents of bonding theory have consistently stressed that, even if the initial contact is not experienced, long-term attachment can and usually does occur. A primary goal of the publications by these two pediatricians was to eliminate (1) the practice of denying new parents of premature babies access to intensive care units;

(2) the whisking away of all babies to the nursery immediately after birth; (3) the practice of keeping parents and even healthy newborns separated for hours after birth. All these were standard procedure in most American hospitals before the research of Klaus and Kennell on the attachment process—and that of many others—gained such wide recognition. Their point has been that this initial contact in the sensitive period *facilitates,* but is not essential to, the development of a strong maternal-infant attachment:

> Some misinterpretations of studies of parent-to-infant attachment may have resulted from a too literal acceptance of the word bonding and so have suggested that the speed of this reaction resembles that of epoxy materials. . . . The human is highly adaptable, and there are many fail-safe routes to attachment. Sadly, some parents who missed the bonding experience have felt that all was lost for their future relationship. This was (and is) completely incorrect. (Kennell and Klaus 1984:281)

Social scientists Arney and Martin present interpretations of bonding that deplore its ideological underpinnings. Arney feels that bonding, "like so many other ideologies that pose as social theories, turns social issues into individuals' problems" because it "lends legitimacy to the notion that women are the only appropriate attendants for children" and so justifies keeping women at home (1982:171). Martin suggests that the focus on bonding

> diverts our attention from how the whole process of birth has been sundered by the application of the production metaphor. To put it baldly, if a worker feels lack of involvement with a product when she does not feel she made it and when her work is regimented and controlled, think how a woman would feel if in her view her baby's birth was taken away from her by the exertion of control over her body? Surely restoring contact between mothers and babies immediately after birth could not restore automatically a sense of engrossment with the baby when the process of birth has been so deeply interrupted. (1987:86)

Yet the statements of the women in my study indicate that it can and often does restore such a sense—perhaps in part because that sense is not new. Birthing mothers—and fathers—have been "bonding" with their babies for months before birth in myriad ways. The strength of this prenatal bond is indicated by the devastation both parents can experience when they miscarry or choose to abort:

> For two weeks, Mike and I breathed as one person. His distress, loss and concern were never one whit less than my own. But we were sometimes upset and angered by unconscious cultural attitudes which precluded acknowledg-

ment of his loss. He was expected to "cope," while I was nurtured through my "need." We've struggled for male responsibility in birth control, sexual mutuality, childbirth and childrearing, and I think we need to acknowledge that those men who do engage in such transformed practices have mourning rights during a pregnancy loss as well. And yet, having spent fifteen years arguing against biological determinism in my intellectual and political life, I'm compelled to recognize the material reality of this experience. Because it happened in my body, a woman's body, I recovered much more slowly than Mike did. By whatever mysterious process, he was able to damp back the pain and throw himself back into work after several weeks. For me, it took months. As long as I had the 14 pounds of pregnancy weight to lose, as long as my aching breasts, filled with milk, couldn't squeeze into bras, as long as my tummy muscles protruded, I was confronted with the physical reality of being post-pregnant, without a child. Mike's support seemed inadequate. I was in deep mourning while he seemed distant and cured. (Rapp 1984:323)

The intensity of grief Rapp experienced—biological, psychological, and social—is mirrored by the intensity of joy—biological, psychological, and social—that parents experience when they hold their newborn babies.

Marshall Klaus reports that in the early work on bonding that he and others carried out:

We put the mother, when *she* was ready, in a private room after the birth with plenty of heat provided. There she spent uninterrupted time alone with the baby. We found from studying the videotapes we made that the mother's behavior when alone with the baby differed radically from her behavior when handed the baby in a crowded and busy delivery room for "bonding." For example, on the videos we saw lots of mothers gazing at their babies and saying, "Look into my eyes," which we did not observe them doing in the delivery room. The 10-minute bonding period was the result of an AMA meeting in the 1970s to which we were not invited. It was never our intention to institutionalize 10 minutes—the whole thing very quickly got taken out of our hands. (personal communication)

As Klaus indicates, the routinization of "here's your baby—now bond!" demonstrates the rapid ideological co-option of attachment theory by institutional interests: it directly conveys the message that society gives the baby (produced by its technology) to the mother. At the same time, the handing of the baby to the mother constitutes a powerful ritual acknowledgment on the part of society that she *is* now a mother, that her transformation is complete: that the child she carried, nurtured, and loved inside her for so long is now in physical union with her in a new and thrilling way. As the statements of the women in my study and

Rapp's eloquent testimony make clear, there are emotions involved in the "bonding" process that are simply not co-optable. Even if bonding as ideology serves patriarchy (Arney 1982) or the economic interests of the hospital (Eyer 1992), or fails to redress the wounds of the baby's technological production (Martin 1987), bonding as experience offers profound joy and meaning to mothers, fathers, and babies.

Immediately after birth, the mother is still physically and psychologically at her most open. Her baby constitutes for her a powerful symbol of her motherhood, her individuality, her new family, the beauty and wonder of nature, and the perfection of her own body and her procreative powers. To hold, touch, gaze at her newborn unhindered is to internalize these messages, to incorporate her newborn through all her sensory channels into the transformed identity with which the mother will emerge from her initiation experience. Often this bonding experience is powerful and positive enough to entirely override, in the mother's conscious perception of her birth experience, any negative feelings of powerlessness, humiliation, or pain she may have been experiencing before her baby's birth.

The presence of the father at these very special moments of highest affectivity ensures that he too will be incorporated into the mother's new sense of her identity, and she and the baby into his. True bonding, when it is allowed to occur in the hospital, conveys an extremely potent message of the integrity and worth of the family in relation to science, technology, patriarchy, and institutions—a message so powerful that it will often override all others in both parents' memories of their birth. Given the perceived threats to the American family as the fundamental social unit posed by the high divorce rate, it would seem to be in society's interest to foster this process, send this message. As with the routinization of father's presence in the delivery room, routine bonding, insofar as it strengthens the beleaguered American family, strengthens society as well.

Nevertheless, some recent research that denies anything special about the period immediately after birth (Lamb 1982; Lamb and Hwang 1982; Myers 1984) is now being used to undo the work of the 1970s, so that in some hospitals that routinely used to provide such a period of togetherness, the baby is once again whisked away. The readiness of such institutions to do away with the bonding period seems to reflect an acknowledgment of its symbolic and psychological mystique and power. As I stated above, the symbolic ramifications of bonding are profound for both the mother and the father: all the efforts at con-

ceptual separation of mother-machine from child-product made in hospital birth rituals can be completely undone in the mother's psyche at
that integrating contact. Time and again I heard women describe highly
technocratic labor experiences that were alienating up until the moment
of birth as "positive" and "wonderful" because of the intensity of the
joy they experienced upon touching and gazing at their newborn babes.

FOUR- TO TWELVE-HOUR SEPARATION

Description and Official Rationale   The routine separation of mother
and infant after birth accompanied the movement of birth into the hospital. The baby was immediately removed to the nursery; the mother,
after a recovery period, was placed in a hospital room. Epidemics were
common, and the nursery was regarded as a fortress against the germs
brought into the hospital by the mother and her visitors. According to
one obstetrician I interviewed, this policy also meshed well with the
routine use of scopolamine for labor and birth, as the mother was quite
literally unable to care for her baby for some time after its delivery. Its
continuance today, often after a brief "bonding period," reflects both
past precedent and current events—many mothers are still too anesthetized after their births to be able to care well for their babies, visitors
still bring germs into the hospital, and it is a fact of institutional life
that the nurses have to do a good deal of paperwork concerning the
baby, which they feel best-equipped to take care of in the nursery.

Physiological Effects   Aside from whatever may or may not be the
physiological effects of separating babies from their mothers, there are
some clear physiological effects of putting babies in hospital nurseries:
infectious strains of bacteria and viruses often run rampant in spite of
all precautions, resulting in epidemics among the babies; bottle-feeding
newborns with sugar water is common procedure even for those babies
whose mothers wish to breastfeed them (sugar can lower immunity
to disease); and bright lights burn constantly, disrupting the babies'
womb-developed sleeping patterns.

Women's Responses

They let me nurse Joseph immediately—my second one. And they put him
up on the delivery table with me. And I nursed him for thirteen minutes.
And then when they took him away, the nurse had to help me break the

suction on him. And he cried his heart out when they took him away. Supposedly they have to take him to the nursery to check him. Supposedly. They *want* to—the nurses feel like it's *their* baby instead of your baby, and they want to get them warm. They feel like they'll lose their body temperature, and they want to check them. I didn't see him for eight hours. (July Sanders)

Ritual Purposes   What society gives, society can take away. The four- to twelve-hour ritual separation of mother and child after birth and bonding, still common in many hospitals, powerfully reminds the mother that her baby belongs to society first. By sending the mother this message now, this procedure interrupts the powerful feelings that holding her newborn baby generates in her, working to ensure that she will be willing to give her baby over to society's institutions (hospitals for its medical care, schools for its socialization) for the rest of its life.

BASSINET/WARMER

Description and Official Rationale   The baby must be kept warm and must be observed, so she or he will be wrapped up in a blanket and placed in the nursery in a plastic bassinet. Should she get too cold, or develop respiratory difficulty, she will be transferred to a radiant warmer.

Physiological Effects and Ritual Purposes   Placing the infant in a separate room to sleep is characteristic only of technocratic society. In the vast majority of human societies, and among other primate species, the infant sleeps in a social environment with direct, skin-to-skin contact between infant and caretaker (Laughlin 1990:43). James McKenna and his colleagues have demonstrated through sleep research that the breathing patterns of mothers and babies who sleep together synchronize, and have found evidence to suggest that nocturnal separation may contribute to the problems of Sudden Infant Death Syndrome (SIDS) (McKenna 1987, 1988; McKenna et al. 1990).

Stephen Thayer calls North America a "noncontact culture" with low rates of touch as compared to "contact cultures" such as those around the Mediterranean. For example, a cross-cultural study of touch between adults and children two to five years old found that although touch rates for retrieving or punishing were the same in all cultures studied (Greece, the USSR, and the U.S.), touch rates for soothing, holding, and play were significantly lower in the United States (Thayer

1988). Concomitantly, although Trevathan points out that "most of us who were born between 1935 and 1975 can attest to our health and that of our mothers, despite the fact that we were separated from each other for several hours or even days after birth," (1987:212) she allows herself the luxury, in a footnote, of the following speculation:

> It is intriguing that this is the age group that has experienced spiralling divorce rates, increased incidence of child abuse, and greater exent of familial alienation than that seen in previous generations, and the temptation to associate this with U.S. birth practices is hard to resist. (Trevathan 1987:212)

Whether or not there is an actual connection between divorce, child abuse, and American birth practices, the symbolic association is quite clear. The routine separation of mothers and babies at birth, and the placement of the baby in a bassinet in another room, mirror and perhaps work to reinforce the patterns of separation that characterize both our society and our social treatment of children. Commented Marcia McCoy:

> The other day I saw a friend with her new baby for the first time. She never puts that child down—that baby is always in her arms. I don't know how she does it, but she is so graceful about it that the baby never seems to have any trouble sleeping, even when her mother is moving around or talking. It made me realize that I had never seen a mother constantly connected to her child like that. It looked so strange to me that I found myself wanting to rush out and buy her a stroller or an infant seat.

From the viewpoint of the hospital staff, I think that placing a baby in a clear plastic box is like telling a story about an experience you had for the very first time: it is to give form, order, and definition—a beginning, middle, and end—to a creature now defined as human because she is suddenly in her proper cultural space. The hospital bassinet, with its clean straight lines, its see-through plastic walls, and its soft blankets gives a special message, not only to the hospital staff, but also to the newborn baby. A symbol of society itself, the bassinet tells the baby[13] that he or she belongs to society more than to her mother and that the only sure comfort, peace, and warmth in life will come ultimately not from people but from society and its products. The warmer, when used, intensifies this message by adding to it the additional message that machines are more reliable than mothers. The mother's womb is replaced by the womb of culture, which, comfortably or uncomfortably, cradles us all.[14]

WHEELCHAIR

Just as the woman in labor, in transition from one social identity to another, undergoing one of the most profound transformations she may ever experience in her cultural life, enters the place of her initiation, so will she leave it:

> It's almost like programming you. You get to the hospital. They put you in this wheelchair. They whisk you off from your husband. And I mean just start in on you. Then they put you in another wheelchair, and send you home. And then they say, well, we need to give her something for the depression. [Laughs] Get away from me! That will help my depression! (July Sanders)

No matter what kind of birth the new mother has experienced in the hospital, no matter how healthy and strong she may or may not feel, institutional insurance requirements usually necessitate that she be carried out in a wheelchair. So the message going out of the hospital becomes the message coming in, as she is once again symbolically reminded that she cannot stand on her own, that she is still—even as she begins her new life as a mother—dis-abled and dependent on society and the institutions that control and disseminate its technological representations.

FROM NATURE TO CULTURE: THE OBSTETRICAL RE-STRUCTURING OF ACCIDENTAL OUT-OF-HOSPITAL BIRTHS

Two of the women in my study accidentally gave birth outside the hospital. The treatment these women received upon entry into the hospital provides a very clear example of the tremendous force of the hidden cultural process at work in obstetrical rituals.

Virginia Larsen gave birth to her second child in the car on the way to the hospital. She wrapped the baby in her husband's jacket and held him in her arms and nursed him as they continued on. Upon arrival, the hospital staff "acted horrified." The baby was whisked away to the nursery and the mother to a room; she was required to stay in the hospital for three days, and was not allowed to see the baby for a full twenty-four hours—a period much longer than normal in that hospital.

Genevieve Cummins gave birth to her first child, accidentally, at home. She had planned to deliver in the hospital labor room with a certified nurse-midwife; but her labor was very quick—she was starting toward the stairs to get in the car and head for the hospital when the head crowned. She made it back to her bed, and her mother called the midwife, who lived only a few minutes away. The midwife arrived, expecting to check her and take her on to the hospital, but ended up calling a paramedic team and catching the baby a few minutes later. The birth was completely successful; Genevieve felt thrilled. But the midwife, who had officially committed herself to do only hospital deliveries, felt that her job and reputation were in danger, so she requested that Genevieve go to the hospital to be checked and to explain the circumstances of her accidental home birth:

GENEVIEVE: After she was born, I got a surge of energy and was feeling really high in spirits. . . . I got dressed and was heading to the hospital to get checked out. I was just so fired up. I just remember being exhilarated.

ROBBIE: [looking at a photograph]: You *look* exhilarated. You combed your hair and put a dress on. You put your necklace on. I can't believe it. You put your gold necklace on and everything. You walked into the hospital like a different person [from the way she looked in the preceding photographs].

GENEVIEVE: Then they put me down in a wheelchair. As I started paying attention, I realized I was pretty sore. One of the doctors that [the nurse-midwife] works with just absolutely insisted that I should have stitches. I didn't need them. I really was mad about that because I was proud that I had not torn badly. [My midwife] said that it was just a very superficial little tear and would have healed on its own, but the doctor insisted I be stitched. That was really the most uncomfortable thing about the whole birth. Normally when they give you the shot for your episiotomy in the hospital, the baby is pressing down on some nerve and you don't feel it. But she was already born, and I felt everything. I felt the shot—they did it all the way around—and even when she started stitching, I was still feeling some of it. They gave me about three stitches. It was just negligible. It made me so mad. But after I realized that it was what I was going to have to put up with, I didn't fuss anymore because I didn't want to make it any more difficult on [the midwife] than it already was. She had a tough time explaining why we had it at home. "Why didn't we get to the hospital?" I made it a point to tell all of the doctors when I saw them that it was an emergency, that she and I did not plan this—I was really fearful that I was going to make difficulties for her.

          After she was born, I just stared at her for a while. They wanted to take me to the hospital and I just wanted to lay there and look at her. After the discomfort was gone, I was just so into what was happening right now. I kept thinking, why do we have to go to the hospital? But [the midwife] kept saying, "Come on now. We really need to get to the hospital and make sure you both are all right." I thought that was kind of silly. I kind of rebelled at that idea. I wanted to stay right there where I was. I thought, I've done it all here now. Why do I have to have anything to do with the medical establishment?

ROBBIE: What did she say that convinced you to go?

GENEVIEVE: Probably making sure that the baby was all right. That probably just snapped me out of it and I thought, Hey, yeah, I really should make sure.

The hospitals missed their chance to socialize Genevieve and Virginia into our society's core value and belief system during their births, but they did not fail to do their best to achieve that socialization after the fact. The experiences of these two women indicate that the process of birth—the manner in which a baby is born—is as important to the hospital as that it is born: it is not just *that* a baby is produced, but *how* it is produced that matters.

SUMMARY: BIRTH RITUALS AND SOCIETY

Although not all of the above procedures are performed on all mothers and babies, most of them are performed on most women most of the time. They fully satisfy the criteria for ritual listed in the Introduction: they are patterned and repetitive; they are profoundly symbolic, communicating messages through the body and the emotions concerning our culture's deepest beliefs about the necessity for cultural control of natural processes, the untrustworthiness of nature and the associated weakness and inferiority of the female body, the validity of patriarchy, the superiority of science and technology, and the importance of institutions and machines. Hospital procedures provide an ordered structure to the chaotic flow of the birth process; in doing so they both enhance the affectivity of that process and create a sense of inevitability about their performance. Obstetrical interventions are also transformative in intent. At the same time that they attempt to contain and control the inherently transformative process of birth, they also transform the birthing woman into a mother in the full social sense of the word—that is, into a woman who has internalized the core values of American society: one who believes in science, relies on technology, recognizes her inferiority (either consciously or unconsciously), and so at some level accepts the principles of patriarchy. Such a woman will tend to conform to society's dictates and meet the demands of its institutions.

These birth rituals also transform the obstetrical resident who is taught to do birth in no other way into the unwitting ritual elder who performs the procedures as a matter of course (see Chapter 7):

> No, they were never questioned. Preps, shaves, enemas, episiotomies—we just did all that; no one ever questioned it. . . . And I'd say that about 80% of the doctors in this town still do all that, all the time. That's just the way it's done. (male obstetrician, age 42)

This transformative process is neither inherently negative nor inherently positive: every society in the world has the need to thoroughly socialize its members into conformity with its norms. Reliance on policemen for ensuring the conformity of every individual would be impractical; there would not be enough to go around. It is much more practical for societies to find ways to socialize their members from the inside, by making them *want* to conform to societal needs. And every culture has developed rituals to do just that. Yet human beings are not automatons, and the extent to which this type of ritual succeeds in such thorough socialization depends a great deal on the individual involved, as we will investigate in the following chapters.

Through hospital ritual procedures, obstetrics deconstructs birth, then inverts and reconstructs it as a technocratic process.[15] But unlike most transformations effected by ritual, birth does *not* depend upon the performance of ritual to make it happen. The physiological process of labor itself transports the birthing woman into a naturally liminal situation that carries its own affectivity. Hospital procedures take advantage of that affectivity to transmit the core values of American society to birthing women. From society's perspective, the birth process will not be successful unless the woman and child are properly socialized during the experience, transformed as much by the rituals as by the physiology of birth.

CHAPTER 4

Belief Systems About Birth

The Technocratic, Wholistic, and Natural Models

A belief is an assumption made about the world that may
or may not be conscious, has a great deal of emotion connected with it, and determines the interpretation of sensory
perceptions.
　　—Lewis Mehl, "The Influence of Belief in Childbirth"

THE SIGNIFICANCE OF BELIEF

As most writers in symbolic anthropology will acknowledge, it is one
thing to decode the messages that a particular society sends in its rituals,
and quite another to discover exactly how those messages are received.
Clearly, the passive absorption of core beliefs and values during rites
of passage cannot be taken for granted.

How successful are hospital birth rituals at accomplishing their
didactic and socializing goals? What is the relationship between the
number and type of ritual procedures performed on a birthing woman
and her overall psychological perception of her birth experience? Can
ritual fail? Can a woman give birth in the hospital without absorbing the
basic tenets of the technocratic model? When can hospital rituals be
said to be completely successful? How can one determine their degree
of success? Do these procedures make women feel victimized, raped,
helpless, betrayed? Or do they make women feel nurtured, cared for,
protected, safe? What makes the difference in how they are perceived?

These questions are crucial to an understanding of the meaning of
birth as a rite of passage in contemporary American society. From the
point of view of the wider society, hospital birth rituals are successful
when socialization is achieved: when there is conceptual fusion between
the model of reality the rituals are designed to convey and reality as
perceived by the birthing woman. Obviously, this fusion will be facilitated, even ensured, if the deep underlying belief system that the birth-

154

ing woman holds before entering the hospital is already either similar to or the same as that which hospital rituals are designed to teach. In this case, any deeper degree of fusion between her belief system and that of the hospital achieved by obstetrical procedures is unlikely to cause her psychological distress. Likewise, such fusion can be rendered far more difficult to achieve, or prevented entirely, if the woman enters the hospital with a belief system radically different from the technocratic model.

It should be noted here, however, that the simple fact that a woman enters the hospital at all to have her baby clearly indicates that, to some degree, she already holds categories in her mind which correspond to some of those categories that form our dominant technocratic model. These categories already mutually held will provide a point of linkage at which the fusion of realities can begin. The more of these mutually held categories, the greater are the chances that hospital rituals will be successful from a sociocultural perspective. The fewer of these mutually held categories, the more psychologically traumatic will be the result if obstetrical rituals do succeed in melding their version of reality with the birthing woman's. For these reasons, *the single factor that most influences the conceptual outcome of a woman's birth is the degree of correspondence between the technocratic model of reality dominant in the hospital and the belief system she herself holds when she enters the hospital.*

At present in our society, the culturally recognized spectrum of possible beliefs about pregnancy and birth is encompassed by two basic opposing models, or paradigms, which are available to pregnant women for the perception and interpretation of their pregnancy and birth experiences—the technocratic and wholistic models.[1] A third—the "natural childbirth" model—attempts, often unsuccessfully, to mediate the oppositions of the first two. The responses of individual women to the rituals of hospital birth to be described in Chapter 5 are best understood in the context of these three models. The technocratic model of birth was described in Chapter 2. The wholistic and "natural" models of birth will be described in the following sections.

THE WHOLISTIC MODEL OF BIRTH[2]

We value:
    The oneness of the pregnant mother and her unborn child;
    an inseparable and interdependent whole.

The essential mystery of birth.
Pregnancy and birth as natural processes that science will
never supplant.
The integrity of life's experiences; the physical, emotional,
mental, psychological and spiritual components of a process are
inseparable.
Pregnancy and birth as intimate, internal, sexual and private
events to be shared in the environment and with the attendants
a woman chooses.
A mother's intuitive knowledge of herself and her baby before
and after birth.
A woman's innate ability to nurture her pregnancy and birth her
baby; the power and beauty of her body as it grows and the
awesome strength summoned in labor.
Our relationship to a process larger than ourselves,
recognizing that birth is something we can seek to learn from
and know, but never control.
The concept of self-responsibility and the right of individuals
to make choices regarding what they deem best for themselves.
                           —Excerpts from a working draft of the
                             Midwives Alliance of North America
                             Statement of Values and Ethics

From the point of view of the women in my study who espouse the
wholistic paradigm of birth, the family is the significant social unit.[3]
Within this paradigm, birth rituals should affirm and reaffirm the unity
and integrity of the family and the individuals that comprise it, instead
of sending patriarchal messages about the primacy of science, technology, and institutions. Each of these has its place, but that place is to be
of service to—rather than to exploit—nature, individuals, families, and
most especially birthing women.

Under this wholistic model, the human body is a living organism
with its own innate wisdom, an energy field constantly responding to
all other energy fields. Health or illness is the reflection, the mirror, the
manifestation of the health or illness of one's self, one's daily life, one's
family, one's past, one's society—one's whole world. The female body
is normal in its own right and should not be judged in terms of the male.
Female physiological processes, including birth, are healthy and safe:

> Well this one customer, I guess she's maybe 28, she said "Sandra, are you
> still thinking about having this baby at home?" She said, "I'm not going to
> say anything but I think you're absolutely insane. What if something hap-

pened?" I said, "Are you not going to drive your car because you could have a wreck? You've got a higher risk doing that than having a baby at home." My friends think I'm crazy. But I think they are. I mean really, *they* are— they're the ones that have missed the whole birth experience, not me. (Sandra Keiler)

Whereas under the technocratic model of birth it is quite possible for the baby to require a Cesarean delivery although the mother desires a vaginal birth, under this wholistic model, the needs of mother and baby are complementary: there will be no conflict, for example, between the emotional need of the mother for a self-empowering home birth, and the safety of the child, as the baby and the mother choose each other and form one energy field, so that *what is good for one is good for the other*. Moreover, communication and understanding are possible on many levels and often occur between mother and child before birth:

When I was about two months pregnant I was lying on my waterbed one night in the dark, not sleeping, but also not really thinking, just drifting along, when suddenly, from somewhere inside of the front of my head I heard these words, "I'm here, I'm a girl, and my name is Joy Elizabeth." . . . One night [much later on], I had a Braxton Hicks contraction and I heard a voice inside say "I'm scared." I told her I was scared too and that everything would be okay because we were partners and we would do this thing together. (Kristin Smithson)

The mother's body knows how to grow a baby and how to give birth; she can trust the "knowing," for it belongs to her. The uterus, much more than an involuntary muscle, is a responsive part of the whole; the mother's mental and emotional attitudes affect its performance during labor, as do the beliefs and actions of the father. The birthing woman's needs and feelings, and the flow of her experience are important, and should supersede an institution's schedule. The institution itself, and science and technology, are there to serve the *mother,* not the other way around, and she accepts the responsibility for her choices. The birth attendant's role is to nurture and empower the mother and father. Her technical knowledge and skills will supplement and support the mother's actions, intuitions, and desires. Birthing is an activity that only a woman can do; *she* delivers the baby to its family and to its new life:

Pushing can be a very delicate process of balancing the energy with your body when the baby's head starts coming out. . . . That is when a woman may tear from pushing too hard and not being relaxed. Marimikel, the midwife, was very helpful in her support at this time. She would gently say, "That's good, that's good, now rest," guiding me carefully. Finally the top of Mela's head was out and I could reach down and touch her. This was such a blessing to feel her, to realize the complete circle of contact. She was outside of me, yet still in. I was aware of my energy becoming even more focused. I felt her whole head come out. Imagine something thirteen and a half inches in circumference coming out of you! I knew my body was made to do this and it was: I didn't tear.

It was another minute until another expansion came, I pushed down again, and she was completely born. What a miracle! This complete being came right out of my body: toes, fingers, hands, spirit, body, energy, and beauty. (Rima Star 1986:54)

THE TECHNOCRATIC AND WHOLISTIC MODELS OF BIRTH COMPARED

The uterus is a muscular organ that is covered, partially, by peritoneum, or serosa. The cavity is lined by
the endometrium. During pregnancy, the uterus serves
for reception, implantation, retention, and nutrition of
the conceptus, which it then expels during labor.
—Cunningham, MacDonald, and Gant,
Williams Obstetrics

You can't take a woman and tear her apart—that's
what the doctors do.

—Midwife

Here polarized in their extreme forms for the sake of clarity in table 1, these models represent opposite ends of our culturally recognized spectrum of possible ways of thinking about pregnancy and childbirth. The wholistic model is fundamentally different from the technocratic model—to fully believe one is to fully disbelieve the other. A clear example of this fundamental difference is provided by the contrasting approaches of a Centertown obstetrician and an Anycity midwife to a woman's labor completely stopping after several hours of regular contractions: the obstetrician said, "It was obvious that she needed some pitocin"; the midwife said, "So she went to sleep, and we went home."

It has been my experience that few individuals, including physicians and midwives, espouse one of these models to the complete exclusion of the other. Most *lean* more toward one or the other while espousing some elements of both. Modern midwives who attend home births tend to be highly skilled in techniques of objective evaluation, and many physicians, midwives, and nurses try to minimize interventions in the hospital. However, because the institutional management of birth is clearly based on the technocratic model, even those medical attendants who lean more toward the wholistic approach often have as much difficulty as pregnant women when they attempt within the hospital to redefine an individual birth experience as "natural." (Some of their difficulties will be examined in Chapter 7.) Hospital birth as experienced by both laboring women and their caretakers, then, can turn into a tug-of-war between the two conceptual models of birthing reality outlined in table 1.

Because the technocratic model is dominant in the hospital, women who choose to birth there and medical specialists who train and work there place themselves on the technocratic side of the spectrum; for these individuals, the wholistic model may exist either as an unattainable ideal, or as a set of ideas too far-fetched for any rational person to actually espouse. And yet, for many of these individuals, the technocratic model itself is also too extreme. When that model held complete conceptual hegemony over birth in the United States (from the 1920s to the 1960s), birthing women were often tied to their beds and rendered totally unconscious throughout their entire labor and delivery experiences. Because the new paradigms of Dick-Read and Lamaze seemed to offer the possibility of returning birth to women, in the early 1950s[4] a long and continuing challenge to the conceptual hegemony of the technocratic paradigm of birth was presented by many individuals across the nation, as a groundswell of consumer activism began to center around the ideal of "natural childbirth" in the hospital.

"NATURAL" MODELS OF BIRTH

NATURAL CHILDBIRTH VERSUS PREPARED CHILDBIRTH: DICK-READ VERSUS LAMAZE

My daughter's birth was the greatest "high" of my life. I felt absolutely lifted up by the incredible power and the absolute beauty of it all.

—Karen Sloan, a proponent of the Dick-Read method

As a team, we were all working together to bring our baby calmly, coolly into the world.

—Ellen Cauly, a proponent of the Lamaze method

TABLE 1. THE TECHNOCRATIC AND WHOLISTIC MODELS OF BIRTH COMPARED*

The Technocratic Model of Birth	The Wholistic Model of Birth
male perspective	female perspective
male-centered	female-centered
woman = object	woman = subject
male body = norm	female body = norm
female = defective male	female normal in own terms
classifying, separating approach	wholistic, integrating approach
mind is above, separate from body	mind and body are one
body = machine	body = organism
female body = defective machine	female body = healthy organism
female reproductive processes dysfunctional	female reproductive processes normal, healthy
pregnancy and birth inherently pathological	pregnancy and birth inherently healthy
doctor = technician	midwife = nurturer
hospital = factory	home = nurturing environment
baby = product	mother/baby inseparable unit
baby grows itself through mechanical process	intimate connection between growth of baby and state of mother
fetus is separate from mother	baby and mother are one
safety of fetus pitted against emotional needs of mother	safey and emotional needs of mother and baby are the same
best interests of mother and fetus antagonistic	good for mother = good for child
supremacy of technology	sufficiency of nature
importance of science, things	importance of people
institution = significant social unit	family = essential social unit
action based on facts, measurements	action based on body knowledge and intuition
only technical knowledge is valued	experiential and emotional knowledge valued as highly as or more than technical knowledge
appropriate prenatal care is objective, scientific	best prenatal care stresses subjective empathy, caring
health of baby during pregnancy insured through drugs, tests, techniques	health of baby insured through physical and emotional health of mother, attunement to baby
labor = a mechanical process	labor = a flow of experience
uterus = an involuntary muscle	uterus = responsive part of whole
time is important; adherence to time charts during labor is essential for safety	time is irrelevant; the flow of a woman's experience is important

TABLE 1. THE TECHNOCRATIC AND WHOLISTIC MODELS
OF BIRTH COMPARED* (CONTINUED)

The Technocratic Model of Birth	The Wholistic Model of Birth
birth must happen within 26 hours	labors can be short or can take several days
once labor begins, it should progress steadily; if it doesn't, intervention necessary	labor can stop and start, follow its own rhythms of speeding up and slowing down
some medical intervention necessary in all births	facilitation (proper food, effective positioning, support) is appropriate, medical intervention usually inappropriate
environmental ambience is not relevant	environmental ambience is the key to safe birth
woman in bed hooked up to machines with frequent exams by staff is appropriate	woman doing what she feels like— movement, sexual play, eating, sleeping—is appropriate
labor pain is problematic, unacceptable	labor pain is acceptable, normal
analgesia and anesthesia for pain during labor	mind/body integration, labor support for pain
iatrogenic pain is acceptable	practitioner must strive not to cause pain to the woman
once a Cesarean, always a Cesarean for many women; VBAC high risk	vaginal birth after Cesarean (VBAC) low risk, normal
unusual presentations, such as breech, require severe intervention, usually Cesarean	midwifery techniques for unusual presentations—e.g., external version or delivery on hands and knees for breech
birth = a service medicine owns and supplies to society	birth = an activity a woman does that brings new life
obstetrician = supervisor/manager/ skilled technician	midwife = skillful guide
the doctor controls	the midwife supports, assists
responsibility is the doctor's	responsibility is the mother's
the doctor delivers the baby	the mother births the baby

* These outlines are based in part on Rothman's (1982:134–140) explication of the medical and midwifery models of birth, and in part on the understanding of these two models that I have gained from interviews with birthing women, midwives, and medical personnel; and from my reading of obstetrical texts (Benson 1980; Cunningham et al. 1989; Oxorn and Foote 1975; Pritchard and Macdonald 1980; Pritchard et al. 1985; Wynn 1975) and home birth literature (Davis 1983; Edwards and Waldorf 1984; Gaskin 1990; Kitzinger 1979; Peterson and Mehl 1984; Sousa 1976; Star 1986; Stewart and Stewart 1976, 1977, 1979, 1981; Sullivan and Weitz 1988).

From the 1960s through the 1980s, the natural model of birth became for thousands of women the preferred image, or ideal, of what
birth *should* be like. The core of this "natural childbirth" model has to
do not with the presence or absence of obstetrical procedures but with
the conscious participation of the mother in her own birthing process,
in other words, with (1) her being "awake and aware" as she labors
and gives birth; (2) her *feeling* the sensations of labor and birth; and
(3) her active efforts to push the baby out. I reached this conclusion
after countless occasions on which I heard new mothers who ended
up with epidural/forceps vaginal deliveries or Cesarean sections say,
"Well, I had planned to 'go natural,' but I didn't make it"; and the
not-so-countless times I heard women whose births included shaves,
enemas, IVs, pitocin, frequent cervical checks, external and internal electronic monitoring, sterile sheets and antiseptic, and the lithotomy position say, "I went completely natural" when asked about their births.
For most mothers, only analgesia/anesthesia or its absence seems to be
the defining factor in whether a birth is "natural" or not; for many,
even light analgesia during labor does not deprive them of the right to
say they had "natural childbirth," as long as they were able to feel much
of their labor and to push by themselves.

This phenomenon results from the notion introduced by Grantly
Dick-Read and Ferdinand Lamaze that properly prepared women can
choose to labor without pain-killers, and the resultant association of
the term "natural childbirth" with that idea. Dick-Read's book *Childbirth Without Fear: The Principles and Practices of Natural Childbirth*,
first published in England in 1933, and in the United States in 1944,
constituted the first widely known attempt to counteract the increasing
medicalization of childbirth. This book introduced the term "natural
childbirth" into popular usage; by that term, Dick-Read meant unmedi-
ated and uninterfered-with labor and birth, in which the major function
of the birth attendant was to support the woman to relax and to have
"faith in the normal and natural outcome of childbirth" (1959:165).
Dick-Read attended both hospital and home births; his philosophy of
childbirth arose out of his experience with home birth, and in many
ways mirrors the wholistic model as I have outlined it above. As Rothman points out in "Awake and Aware, or False Consciousness: The Co-
option of Childbirth Reform in America," Dick-Read's approach

> failed in the United States because it did not prepare women for the social
> situation they would have to face in labor. . . . He said that women needed

continual comforting and emotional support throughout labor. While that may have been possible for his patients in the hospital, and was certainly possible for his home birth patients, it was not provided for the American women who "failed" at natural childbirth. The majority of women who attempted to follow Dick-Read's advice did so under hostile conditions. They shared labor rooms with women who were "scoped" and whose screams, combined with the repeated offering of pain relief medication by hospital staff, reinforced the fear of birth Dick-Read set out to remove. The results were generally perceived as failures of the method, or failures of the individual woman, rather than the result of systematic interference by the institution. (1981:166)

The "failure" of this approach to become widely adopted in American hospital birth is hardly surprising, as it constitutes far too radical a philosophical departure from the technocratic model to be in any way conceptually tenable within the hospital. The Lamaze method, in contrast, was successful in American hospitals precisely because it presents no threat to the hegemony of the technocratic model, working instead to aid in its transmission and perpetuation.

At its inception, the childbirth education organization created to encourage the use of the Lamaze method, ASPO (American Society for Psychoprophylaxis in Obstetrics) was geared to the American hospital and the American way of birth. The only challenge ASPO initially offered to the technocratic model was over the use of analgesia and anesthesia: ASPO advocated "the substitution of psychological for pharmacological control of pain" (Rothman 1981:167). (*Today's ASPO-trained childbirth educators adopt a wide spectrum of approaches to childbirth; many of them are wholistically oriented. This discussion addresses only the philosophical origins of the Lamaze method.*)

Table 2 is a comparison of the principal elements of the models of birthing reality held by Dick-Read and Lamaze. Structurally, these two models may be viewed as fitting in between the technocratic and wholistic paradigms that define the two ends of the broad spectrum of culturally acknowledged beliefs about childbirth in the United States.

Although the model of birthing reality established by Lamaze does offer the possibility of consciousness and dignity to the laboring woman, it does not threaten in any fundamental way the basic tenets of the technocratic model; from a rite of passage perspective, as we have seen, it does actually facilitate the woman's reception of the messages birth rituals send to her about the accuracy and validity of that model and the values and beliefs on which it is based. For these reasons, the wide-

TABLE 2. "PREPARED" VERSUS "NATURAL" CHILDBIRTH:
A COMPARISON OF THE PHILOSOPHIES OF LAMAZE AND DICK-READ*

"Prepared Childbirth"	"Natural Childbirth"
birth is normal, natural, and inherently dangerous	birth is normal, natural, and inherently trustworthy
pain and trauma not necessary	pain and trauma not necessary
analgesia/anesthesia should be available, in case the woman "can't take it"	analgesia/anesthesia not necessary if environment is sufficiently supportive
birth is a physician-controlled event	birth can be a woman-controlled event
birth is physician's work	birth is mother's work
woman owns her behavior	woman owns her birth
social support is helpful	social support is essential
technique coaching by husband	emotional support from attendant
mothers can witness birth	mothers *do* birth
baby is physician's reward for his work	baby is mother's prize for her work
birth can be an emotionally satisfying experience for a woman, as long as the emotional needs of the mother don't interfere with fetal safety	birth should be an emotionally and spiritually satisfying experience for a woman—a high point of her life
birth is a mechanical process	birth is a natural process
businesslike, matter-of-fact approach to birth	emphasis on orgasmic, spiritual qualities of birth
birth is part of institutional context of reproduction	birth is part of social context of mothering
role of mothering in a woman's life not relevant to birth	motherhood is the defining central feature of womanhood

*These distillations are taken both from Rothman's "Awake and Aware" article (1981) and from my own reading of the works of these innovators and their proponents (Bing 1967; Dick-Read 1959; Karmel 1965; Lamaze 1956).

spread cultural and medical acceptance of the Lamaze method is as unsurprising as was the "failure" of Dick-Read's philosophy. As Rothman says,

the Lamaze method became so popular in the 1960s and 70s not because it met the desire for control over their bodies, or autonomy, of middle-class educated women, but because it was the only practical method designed to deal with the hospital situation. . . . In essence, the method keeps the woman quiet by giving her a task to do [the breathing techniques], making being a "good"—non-complaining, obedient, cooperative—patient the woman's primary goal. . . . The husbands are co-opted into doing the staff's work, moving the patients through the medical routines as smoothly as possible. Mother, coached by father, behaves herself, while Doctor delivers the baby. (1981:169)

The Lamaze model of birth gained wider acceptance than Dick-Read's for another crucial reason. Dick-Read insisted on the central place of motherhood in a woman's life:

If there is one characteristic more desirable to be maintained in communal life, it is the dignity of motherhood. Those of us who have known it from personal experience . . . visualize it in those calm, competent and companionable women who live to a great age, acutely sensitive to, but unshakeable by, the cruelties and the rewards of having lived. . . . Five hundred million Roman Catholics revere the Madonna and Child and all that their divinity and dignity imply. . . . Politicians have long recognized the power of the woman in the home. (Dick-Read 1959:21–22)

In his insistence on the spiritual attributes of motherhood, Dick-Read seems to have been seeking to restore to women the sense of their wider cosmic significance which is a central feature of cross-cultural female initiation rites (Lincoln 1981:107). But a corollary of this wider cosmic significance is the woman's day-to-day restriction to "the traditional place of a woman within a given culture" (Lincoln 1981). In Dick-Read's surely well-intentioned effort to restore the cosmic spiritual dimension to birth, he was also narrowing women's social spheres back to the limitations of the domestic realm from which they had been trying to escape since the early 1900s.

According to Wertz and Wertz in *Lying-In: A History of Childbirth in America* (1989), in the 1800s in the United States, motherhood was indeed the central defining feature of a woman's life. *Lying-In* documents the historical process by which women, especially middle-class women who did not have household help, eagerly sought out the hospital as their preferred birthplace because of the relief it provided from their daily chores. More profoundly, to give birth outside the home was to conceptually redraw the boundaries of women's appropriate spheres and hence to achieve a greater possibility of earlier escape from the enforced "confinement" of motherhood:

Colonial women, most of whom lived and worked on farms, could not remove themselves from view because their labor was essential to farm life, but leisured women of the nineteenth century embroidered the niceties of female conduct by withdrawing from social life. The word "confinement" pointed to the complex symbolism associated with their withdrawal, for the word also described the social separation of the dangerous criminal and the insane. "Confinement" never meant simply punishment or bland custody, however, even when applied to criminals or the insane; rather, it betokened society's hope to regenerate a self in institutions modeled upon the regularity, duty, and piety of the home. Thus, confinement for childbirth was withdrawal to the supreme source of a woman's identity and purpose, the home. There, in her domain, a woman relearned who she was and, in maternity, performed her essential duty. Thereafter she might return, richly renewed, to society. (Wertz and Wertz 1989:80)

By the early 1900s, the Wertzes continue, women were rejecting both the rituals of confinement and the accompanying exclusive definition of their lives by maternity. The first maternity clothes appeared in 1904; hospital birth was on the rise, and the next step in women's liberation from the home was the appearance and spread of bottle-feeding. As one mother put it to her daughter in a novel written in 1936, "The bottle was the war cry of my generation" (1989:150). Moreover, women themselves campaigned for the acceptance in America of scopolamine-induced "twilight sleep," as a further means of freeing themselves from what they were increasingly beginning to perceive as enslavement to their biological processes (Leavitt 1986).

It is hardly surprising, then, that when women in the early 1960s began to wish to claim back the right to their birth experiences which their mothers had so eagerly abdicated, *these* modern women should choose the paradigm of natural childbirth presented by Lamaze over that of Dick-Read. The Lamaze model, unlike that proposed by Dick-Read, offered women the right to participation, dignity and self-control in their birthing processes, without also entailing a return to the "motherhood as central feature" paradigm that they had so recently left behind.

According to a current ASPO member, "Other childbirth education organizations have worked to shake the medical tree from the outside. We made a decision at the very beginning to work within the system to shake it up from the inside" (personal communication). The two major innovations sought by early Lamaze instructors in order to achieve the desired transformation of unconscious to conscious birth were the elimination of requisite general anesthesia and the admission of fathers to the labor and delivery rooms to provide labor support, in the form of "coaching" in the breathing techniques, for their wives. At first these pioneers encountered tremendous resistance on the part of medical personnel to their innovative efforts. But they eventually prevailed because of their culturally wise decision to work "within the system"—that is, to leave the most fundamental precepts of the technocratic model unchallenged. And they were successful. Once the initial resistance to anything new had been overcome, obstetrics proved quite receptive to husband-coached breathing instead of screaming, epidurals instead of scopolamine, self-control instead of hand-strapping, because (as we saw in Chapter 3) an awake and aware female mind, divorced from its mechanical body, fit the technocratic model far better than the "wild animal" of yesteryear, and the presence of the husband meant that he would get the messages too.

But there was a certain conceptual price that obstetrics had to pay for this newly available receptivity of husband and wife. The model of reality behind this emerging phenomenon *did* represent to some extent a departure from a purely patriarchal and institutional system of birth. The introduction of the concept of natural childbirth in the hospital, although in other ways supporting it, did threaten to undermine the conceptual hegemony of the technocratic model: modern women, previously not educated for the technocratic surprises of childbirth, *were* newly empowered by the knowledge they received from childbirth educators. Many natural childbirth candidates, whose labors were too short or too "textbook" for pathology to be imputed or inferred, did achieve labor and birth experiences in the hospital which were relatively unmarked by obstetrical procedures. The presence of fathers, combined with the introduction of bonding, served symbolically to enhance and strengthen the importance and integrity of the family in American society. Many women went away from their hospital birth experiences feeling that they gave birth all by themselves, that the hospital was fundamentally irrelevant to the process. (We will examine some of their stories in Chapter 5.) These developments, disturbing from a sociocultural perspective because they threatened the hegemony of the dominant technocratic model, did not go unnoticed by its defenders. As the "awake and aware" Lamaze birth gained increasing popularity during the years 1971–1976, so did the "awake and aware" Cesarean section, which had a 95 percent increase in performance during those same years. This fascinating phenomenon, which I interpret as a tightening of ritual boundaries in response to conceptual threat (Douglas 1966; Vogt 1976) will be further discussed in Chapter 8.

LAMAZE BREATHING TECHNIQUES AS
STABILIZING RITUALS OF SELF-CONTROL

> When my husband didn't rub my back in just the
> right place, I didn't say no dear, that's not right. I said
> NO! OVER HERE! and I did feel guilty about it a lit-
> tle bit.
>
> —Becky James

> I never lost control.
> —Jennifer Stanley

In the original training course for ASPO, founders Elizabeth Bing and Marjorie Karmel state: "In all cases the woman should be encouraged to respect her own doctor's word as final. . . . It is most important to stress that his job and hers are completely separate. He is responsible for her physical well-being and that of her baby. She is responsible for controlling herself and her behavior" (1965:7).

This self-control is to be achieved during labor through the practiced use of a number of complex and precisely sequenced breathing techniques; these techniques are supposed to be practiced so frequently during the six weeks of Lamaze "training" prior to birth that their utilization during labor will be the result of reflex. It is the husband's job to practice these techniques along with his wife, so that he can coach her during labor whenever she starts to "lose control":

> By 12:30 P.M., after shifting into shallow chest breathing, Stephanie decided that the breathing exercises were simply not helping the pain. I guess it was much easier for me to say it, but I knew that they did work; after all, she had squeezed my shoulder in a practice session while I tried the exercises. Anyway, I suggested that on the next contraction, she attempt going through it without breathing. It soon came, and about a second after it started, she was suddenly enlightened to the fact that breathing correctly really *did* work. I guess neither of us had ever considered that the pain doesn't go away when one uses the Lamaze method of breathing; the whole thing just becomes tolerable. But then, that's a whole lot. (from the Lamaze story-report written by Stephanie's husband)

As was discussed in the Introduction, high stress levels can reduce individuals from high cognitive complexity (stage four—ability to view the world from a broad and abstract perspective, consider many options, judge each situation on its own merits) to a much simpler level of cognitive complexity (stage one—conceptual grounding in a specific cognitive matrix, ability to consider only concrete either-or options, to see the world as black or white). If the stress continues, the individual can be reduced even further, to "substage," a condition of cognitive disorientation and disintegration.

The physiological process of labor is itself a stressful state to which the noise, bustle, and continual interference from the hospital environment often add stress upon stress. The more pain, fear, and stressful interference that laboring women experience, the more likely they are to go into substage—to scream and writhe in pain and terror, to beg for anesthesia, to act in interactionally disruptive ways. Ritual "stands as a barrier" between stage one and substage; its repetitive familiarity provides its performers and recipients with a sense of safety, securely orienting them to the stage one worldview upon which the rituals themselves are based:

> In shielding the cognitive system, the practice of ritual itself can place the broad choice of executable behaviors into a subset under automatic control and out of the realm of cognitive choice and thereby reduce the decision universe. This coordination and the accompanying affective states themselves aid internal equilibration for the individual. (McManus 1979b:226)

Lamaze breathing techniques are rituals based on a cognitive matrix that insists that labor is not a terrifying unknown but a fully understandable mechanical process, with specific stages that have certain characteristics; women socialized into this matrix are able to utilize these breathing rituals to prevent themselves from going into substage, and to utilize the belief system behind these rituals as a reliable cognitive framework within which they can conceptually ground themselves, to keep from "losing their minds" during labor:

> The nurse said I was at 4 centimeters at the last checking. Soon the contractions were coming so quickly and with such force that I began to use pant-blow. . . . I was perspiring, my feet were cold, and I got the hiccups which threw my breathing off. . . . The contractions were extremely strong with no rest periods, multipeaked and I began to lose control. . . . I did breathing for rectal pressure continuously now and looked right at Bill's eyes for a focal point. I can truly say this was unending pain, and I asked for something to take at least the edge off. The nurse checked me and said I was at 8 centimeters. Then I realized I was in transition [the last stage of labor before pushing, during which the cervix dilates from 7 or 8 centimeters to the 10 centimeters it must reach before, under the technocratic model, pushing can be allowed] and that it would be over soon, so I said to forget the medication (Lorraine Sampson, from her Lamaze story-report)

> By taking Lamaze classes, I knew what to expect and was not frightened by the experience. I felt so removed from the ladies down the hall who were screaming and thrashing around, totally out of it. (Christine Biesele)

Moreover, as we saw in Chapter 3, the grounding and stabilizing ritual presence of the "labor coach" (be he/she father, friend, relative, or significant other), whose presence is integral to the Lamaze method, also works to connect the woman to the known and familiar during the chaotic and sometimes frightening labor process:

> Some time between 7:30–8:00 P.M. the doctor came in and examined me. I was fully effaced and between 5–6 centimeters dilated. He broke the membranes and went to prepare for delivery. Almost immediately my contractions became stronger and ran together, no time in-between to relax. With about the second or third contraction I began to feel the need to push. At this point Michael had to coach me continually to blow and not lose control. With the next several contractions I was fully dilated.
>
> They took me to the delivery room. As the doctors and nurses got me ready to deliver, the urge to push brought me near to panic and I couldn't see Michael anywhere. I finally felt him take my hand; I was all right then, though I was blowing like the house was on fire! (Gloria Lewis, from her Lamaze story-report)

As is evident in Gloria Lewis's description of her experience, "ritual is behavior generated by the central organic or cognitive structure, and its effect is to stabilize that structure" (McManus 1979a:213).

The conceptual stability offered by the Lamaze method is not only salient in the birth experiences of its proponents but also in ASPO's highly successful thirty-one-year history, during which this organization has trained and certified over 10,000 childbirth educators (current total ASPO membership is around 4,000). Most childbirth professionals interviewed estimated that as many as 25,000 childbirth educators nationwide use some variation of the Lamaze method in their classes. A national staff member confirms that current ASPO training courses are still very much in accord with the methods, philosophy, and goals of the organization's founders. And ASPO has purposefully deepened its integration with our dominant social institutions in recent years: nationwide, all ASPO certification courses are now offered only through colleges and universities (Mary Brucker, personal communication).

THE BRADLEY METHOD AND ICEA:
TENSION AND DILEMMA IN THE PARADIGMS
OF POSTMODERN CHILDBIRTH EDUCATION

Doris Haire, President of the American Foundation
for Maternal and Child Health, said there are only two
kinds of childbirth classes in America today, "obedi-

ence classes" and "Bradley classes." I fear that, all too
often, obedience-type childbirth classes merely teach
parents to be unquestioning, uninformed "meat" on
their obstetrician's table . . . grist for the mill, as it
were. These classes sometimes do, in fact, teach you to
lie down and roll over, just like Rover.

> —Jay Hathaway, Executive Director,
> The Bradley Method, from a letter
> dated 21 October 1991

A precept of modern childbirth education is that
childbirth is a natural biologic process. It stresses positioning the woman in a comfortable upright position.
It recognizes the benefits of changing the woman's position, emptying her bladder often, walking, relaxation,
distraction, touch, and massage, and breathing and
concentration techniques. Epidural anesthesia and
its required safety protocols prohibit most of these
practices.

> —Margery Simchak, "Has Epidural Anesthesia
> Made Childbirth Education Obsolete?"

In partial response to Hathaway's assertion and Simchak's question,
I want to stress that in this age of disconnection from the extended
family and traditional women's culture, women are finding childbirth
education of *all* types to be indispensable. As we saw in the preceding
section, postmodern childbirth educators, whether teaching eclectically
or within the framework of a particular paradigm, provide the invaluable service of giving women across the nation a cognitive matrix for
the interpretation of their childbirth experiences. The essentiality of
such a matrix is highlighted by the women in my study who birthed
without one, who experienced labor and delivery as chaotic, bewildering, and terrifying (see Chapter 5).

Although there are many philosophies of childbirth education in the
United States (most of which I do not have the space to discuss), the
only one to achieve nationwide surname recognition besides Lamaze
and Dick-Read is the Bradley Method of "husband-coached childbirth"
(an unfortunate label which has resulted in much criticism for its paternalistic overtones [Romalis 1981:102]). Robert Bradley, M.D., developed this method during the 1940s from watching animals labor and
give birth (Bradley 1984). Noting that animals sought quiet and safe

places and then went into a state of total relaxation, and stressing our shared mammalian genes, Bradley sought to make the hospital soothing and safe and to teach women to relax fully in labor. He was instrumental in getting fathers allowed in delivery rooms across the country, and yet his pioneering efforts in that area have gone largely unacknowledged—popular thinking attributes the arrival of fathers in the delivery room to Lamaze:

> The Bradley Method® was preceded only by the late Dr. Grantly Dick-Read's *Childbirth Without Fear* in 1944. I met Dr. Read in Chicago in 1948, and he accepted my invitation to visit with me later in Denver. . . . From the very first I had included husbands in the birth team as coaches and minimized the role of the physician to resemble that of a lifeguard who, when watching swimmers, did nothing as long as everything was going along all right. I put the husband where Dr. Read sat, at the head of the bed, to capitalize on the lover relationship, and found it worked marvelously. . . . Inevitable conflicts arose between advocates of The Bradley Method® and the Lamaze method. . . . I was ridiculed for my no-drugs approach, as they continued to claim "a little medication wouldn't hurt anything." Also, I was mocked with the label "Barnyard Bradley" for my insistence on imitating animals and for the term "natural childbirth," which I still prefer to "psychoprophylaxis." Recent new research on the effects of maternal medication on the fetus and infant verifies the assumptions I first made in 1947: drugs are all bad during pregnancy. Also, the meddlesome interference with nature's instinctual conduct and plans (induction of labor, silly "due dates," routine IVs, monitoring, etc.) [is harmful]. . . . Regardless of where you have your baby, or whom you choose to have in attendance, do not deviate from nature's great principles. (Bradley, in McCutcheon-Rosegg 1984)

In nearly three decades of practice during which he attended the births of over 14,000 babies, 94 percent of Bradley's patients had intervention-free, unmedicated births. Three percent utilized medication, and another 3 percent gave birth by Cesarean (Bradley 1981:15). Although Bradley was practicing in the United States before Lamaze was known, the Bradley method as taught by the American Academy of Husband-Coached Childbirth or AAHCC (founded in 1970 by Marjie and Jay Hathaway of Sherman Oaks, California) has achieved only a small portion of the culture-wide acceptance enjoyed by the Lamaze method, as the Bradley philosophy comes very close to the wholistic model and thus is conceptually unacceptable in many hospitals:

> In the Bradley Method®, when we say successful outcome, we mean a totally unmedicated, drug-free natural childbirth without routine medical intervention that enables the woman to exercise all her choices in birthing and give her baby the best possible start in life. And we expect this over ninety percent of the time. (McCutcheon-Rosegg 1984:8)

According to Jay and Marjie Hathaway, this expectation—a standard set by the now-retired Dr. Bradley—has been fulfilled in more than 90 percent of the birth experiences of over 4,000 low- and high-risk couples taught the Bradley Method® in their own personal classes. Its uncompromising stance is tempered by Laurie Fowler, Teacher Relations Coordinator for AAHCC, who explains that "for many of us, a successful birth is one in which the woman thoroughly understands her options and makes her own choices. Our goal is for her to feel good about her birthing experience."

In contrast to Lamaze instructors, Bradley teachers do not teach or recommend the use of sequenced breathing techniques. This difference stems from the fundamental philosophical grounding of the Lamaze method in the technocratic model and the Bradley method in the wholistic model: Lamaze breathing techniques tend to enhance mind/body separation by helping the woman "stay on top of " the contractions, whereas Bradley techniques stress mind-body integration:

> The laboring woman needs to keep her breathing simple and normal since her primary aim is complete, skillful relaxation. . . . Therapists in various fields use calm, abdominal breathing to relax excited patients, from asthmatics to the emotionally upset. . . . Think of putting your breath low in the abdomen with an extremely relaxed abdominal wall. The abdomen will naturally expand outward with low abdominal breathing, so you do not need to push the abdomen out or try to hold it there. If you are listening within your body to the calm, quiet, steady rhythm of your breathing, it is impossible to breathe too quickly. . . . Think of your uterus as that big bag of muscle that is opening the door for your baby . . . the more it flexes the more you relax with it . . . let go and open, *and open.* (McCutcheon-Rosegg 1984:91–95)

Bradley instructors, who work "determinedly and assertively for unmedicated, natural childbirth without routine interventions" (McCutcheon-Rosegg 1984:8) are often barely tolerated or harassed outright by the obstetrical establishments in their areas, whereas Lamaze instructors are frequently hired by the hospitals themselves. The only Bradley instructor in Centertown, for example, was usually thrown out of the hospital when she attempted to provide on-going labor support for her clients—a not-uncommon experience for Bradley instructors. Nationwide, there are today over 1,000 certified Bradley instructors. Although their numbers are small, in their ideological cleavage to the wholistic model, Bradley teachers offer a strong conceptual alternative for thousands of women.

An important and influential childbirth organization is the International Childbirth Education Association (around 9,000 members in thirty countries). ICEA, established in 1960, "unites people who support family-centered maternity care and believe in freedom of choice based on knowledge of alternatives" (Keller 1990:4). Respected for its excellent research and publications, as well as its well-informed, effective, and woman-centered efforts to shape health policies in many countries, ICEA began to offer an intensive certification program in 1982 and has as of this writing certified 1,000 childbirth educators (Dungey 1991). Its methods do not come under consideration here because its members, out of an expressed desire not to become identified with any one particular method, have been consciously eclectic in their approach. Current president Jeanne Rose explains that ICEA "affords its educators the right to choose the approach that best meets their needs and those of their clients" (personal communication).

Fortuitously for the many thousands of women served by its members, ICEA's motto, "freedom of choice based on knowledge of alternatives," and its emphasis on "family-centered maternity care" have proven sufficiently broad to encompass both the natural childbirth movement of earlier decades and the more recent intensification of high-tech birth, for even Cesareans can be family-centered and freely chosen, as we will see in Chapter 5.

In the 1960s and 1970s, modern childbirth educators of all types struggled with the dilemma of "how to teach natural childbirth to couples without getting ostracized by the medical community." Now well-integrated into that community, the mainstream postmodern childbirth educator's dilemma might be stated as "how to retain some connection with the conceptual origins of the natural childbirth movement while serving a technocratic clientele." The essence of that dilemma is highlighted in a brief literary exchange between AAHCC cofounder Jay Hathaway and Margery Simchak, an ICEA consultant. In 1990, Simchak published an article on "Medications for Labor Pains" in ICEA's *International Journal of Childbirth Education* which presented a thoughtful approach to the pros and cons of various types of medications commonly used during labor (Simchak 1989). In a subsequent letter to the editor, Hathaway decried Simchak's seeming endorsement of the use of drugs in labor:

> As Dr. Bradley (one of the founders of ICEA) has said for decades, ALL KNOWN CHILDBIRTH ANALGESICS AND ANESTHETICS REACH THE UNBORN BABY WITHIN SECONDS OF ADMINISTRATION. . . . Setting aside the fact [that Simchak] neglected to mention the numerous

maternal and fetal DEATHS from obstetric anesthesia . . . ANY medication reaching the baby may be too much. ALL these procedures ALWAYS expose the baby to narcotics. In this era when major national forces are said to be conducting a "war on drugs," the place to begin is at birth, not as teenagers. JUST SAY NO TO DRUGS. (Hathaway 1990)

To Hathaway's effort to get childbirth educators to hold the conceptual line on "natural childbirth," Simchak responded:

I appreciate Mr. Hathaway's strong feelings. Perhaps I should have stated more clearly that no medication is best during labor. . . . But the truth is, this is 1990 and a very high percentage of our students have decided definitely before they enter our childbirth preparation class that they *will* take medication during labor. The decision they have to make during our class is *which* medication they will choose. Nothing we say will convince them to have that totally natural birth that was popular in the 70s. (Simchak 1990:3)

THE NATURAL IDEAL

Natural birth is difficult, but a woman's body is designed for this function. When a woman births without drugs, anesthesia, or medical intervention, she learns that she is strong and powerful. She learns self-confidence. She learns to trust herself, even in the face of powerful authority figures. Once she realizes her own strength and power, she will have a different attitude, for the rest of her life, about pain, illness, disease, fatigue, and difficult situations.

　—Paulina (Polly) Perez, RN, monitrice,
　　and author of *Special Women*

"Natural childbirth" kept us going all through the seventies and eighties, but it's dead now, I'm sorry to say. The times have really changed. All everyone (except home birthers) wants is that epidural.

　　　—Susan Broyles, midwife

In spite of the efforts of ASPO-trained educators to replace Dick-Read's "natural childbirth" with the more realistic "prepared childbirth" as the popular term for their approach, Dick-Read's original label came into widespread lay usage during the early 1970s as the generic term for the kind of birth people thought the Lamaze method would facilitate, namely: an ideal hospital experience, belonging primarily to the couple, in which the woman conducts herself in culturally appropriate ways (no screaming, no embarrassing loss of self-control) and consciously gives birth with a minimum of obstetrical intervention.

The term "natural childbirth" explicitly connected birth with the whole away-from-technology and back-to-nature movement of the past three decades. Natural childbirth's co-option in the hospital by the technocratic model mirrors in microcosm that model's attempts at co-option of the entire back-to-nature movement (e.g., the same cultural logic that calls hospital birth "natural" also labels as "natural" many artificial foods). This phenomenon reflects a fascinating conceptual split in American society: on one level, we believe that "natural" is better for us, but our deepest belief is in the superiority of technocratic culture. So we start to think of certain technocratic phenomena as natural, hoping that now we have the best of both worlds.

Because it was fashionable to do so, or because they thought "natural is better," many pregnant women whom I interviewed during the 1980s professed to believe in, and strove to achieve, that popular ideal: to quote Becky, "you know when you go through those Lamaze classes you think 'oh I'm going to be one of those ones that has it in two hours and no pain and just totally relaxed.'" Yet this "natural" ideal was subject to the same situational problem as Dick-Read's original method; trying to achieve it in the very cultural hospital easily set them up for "failure." Women who tried for the natural ideal and "failed," if they internalized the technocratic model during that "failure," tended to blame it on their own individual weaknesses, when in fact (if their labors did not conform closely enough to the hospital standard to fend off intervention), by virtue of being in the hospital in the first place they never stood a chance of achieving "natural" birth.

Now, in the 1990s, many childbirth educators and midwives are finding that fewer and fewer women give even lip service to the natural childbirth ideal. The co-option of natural childbirth is nearly complete—its philosophy and applications have been so subsumed under the technocratic paradigm that many women have discarded the label "natural" as too discontinuous with the realities both of their expectations and of hospital birth (see Chapter 5). This trend seems to be resulting, at least for the present, in an ideological polarization: the "natural childbirth" ideal that used to define the middle of the paradigmatic spectrum of beliefs about birth seems to be disappearing from that middle and moving more and more to the wholistic side. In other words, generally speaking, women who give birth in hospitals are seeking to be prepared but not to be "natural," and women who aspire to truly natural childbirth are choosing to give birth in freestanding birthing centers (see below, this chapter) or at home.[5]

THE IDEOLOGY OF SAFETY[6]

> A baby's birth can be wonderful, no matter how
> you deliver. You can't control whether you deliver
> vaginally or by Cesarean, but you can have some con-
> trol over your emotional response to the birth. If you
> focus on having the safest delivery possible, you're
> more likely to have a satisfying experience.
> —*The Birth Book: Your Guide to Vaginal,
>   Cesarean, and VBAC Deliveries* (a
>   booklet distributed free of charge in
>   obstetricians' offices)

> I think women who have their babies at home are
> self-indulgent. They are only thinking about what they
> want, and not at all about what will keep their babies
> safe.
> —Suzanne Samuels

Although the quality of the process through which a baby is born is of tremendous psychological and emotional importance to many pregnant women, the ultimate goal of every pregnant woman is to have a healthy baby. And, as stated in *Williams Obstetrics*, "the transcendent objective of obstetrics is that every pregnancy . . . culminate in a healthy mother and a healthy baby" (Pritchard and MacDonald 1980:2). Our fundamental technocratic belief that birth is inherently unsafe, coupled with the equally fundamental belief that technology can make it safe, provides a point of linkage between the philosophical base of obstetrics and the desires of every woman's heart so strong that the vast majority (99 percent) of American women—including even most of those who would prefer to stay at home—will go to the hospital to give birth, "just in case something should go wrong." As Becky puts it:

> I read everything I could get my hands on the first time around and I just had leaned toward the more progressive style rather than traditional delivery. I had read the book that the people that live on that commune farm over in Summertown—they have a book about midwifery and I had read that and there was a lot of psychic stuff, you know, mystical relaxation, which sounded good, a little bit way out you know but I still thought it

sounded good if you could really be that into it and make it that positive
an experience, that seemed like the thing to do if at all possible, and how
about the fact that they had their babies at home? They made a big case for
that. And I agree with that too although I wouldn't want to do that myself . . . and I wouldn't go to any hospital other than City because that's
where the intensive care thing is if something should go wrong. I just want
to have everything right there, you know, to save that baby if at all possible
because they are precious. (Becky Bonne)

The cultural force of this ideological notion that birth is "safer" in
the hospital is indicated by the story of one of the women I interviewed,
who reported traveling to the hospital in early labor during a severe
blizzard, with road visibility almost zero. When their car slid off the
road several blocks from the hospital, she and her husband had to
clamber over walls and piles of ice and snow to make it the rest of the
way. She especially remembered slipping and sliding during contractions on the ice in the parking lot as she neared the hospital doors.
When I asked her if she and her husband had considered staying home
to have the baby, she looked at me in horror and replied, "Oh no, it
would have been too dangerous!"

Would it? One must be careful in any comparison of the safety of
home versus hospital birth, as the statistics are often skewed on both
sides. On the one hand, home birth statistics will give a false picture
when they do not include those births that begin at home but end up
in the hospital. On the other hand, medical statistical studies seeking
to prove the dangers of home birth are often wildly skewed in favor of
the safety of hospital birth when they lump together in the same category all out-of-hospital births. For example, a 1974 North Carolina
medical study of out-of-hospital births showed a 21 per 1,000 neonatal death rate, as compared to 16 per 1,000 in the hospital. However,
when other researchers went back and separated the planned, midwife-
attended home births from the unplanned, accidental out-of-hospital
births (which usually involve rapid, precipitous labors and premature
babies), they found a 4 per 1,000 neonatal death rate in the first category, and a 101 per 1,000 neonatal death rate in the second (Burnett et al. 1977). Likewise, a British survey of 1979 home birth outcomes in England and Wales found that the perinatal mortality rate for
planned home deliveries was 4.1 per 1,000, while that for unplanned
home deliveries jumped to 67.5 per 1,000 (Campbell et al. 1984). A
1982 study of 1,597 planned, midwife-attended out-of-hospital births

in Oregon found only 5 neonatal deaths (in other words, about 3 per 1,000) (Clark and Bennets 1982).

The best comparative study of which I am aware is a matched-sample comparison between planned home and hospital births conducted in 1977 by Lewis Mehl, M.D., and his associates (and revised in 1980). The study matched 1,046 planned home-birth women with 1,046 planned hospital-birth women for maternal age, parity, socio-economic status, and risk factors. All home-birth women who transferred to the hospital during or after labor remained in the home-birth group for analysis. After the births were analyzed for length of labor, complications of labor, neonatal outcomes, and procedures utilized, home births were found to be *safer* than hospital births for both mothers and babies:

> The hospital births had a five times higher incidence of maternal high blood pressure, which may be indicative of the greater physical and emotional stress for mothers in the hospital, as may be the three-and-a-half times more meconium staining (fetal bowel movement expelled into the amniotic fluid, [sometimes] indicative of fetal distress). The hospital births had eight times the shoulder dystocia (the shoulder getting caught after the head is born). Mehl and his associates state that this may be caused by the flat-on-the-back position, in which the fetus must rise upwards to be born, with a greater chance of the shoulder's catching on the mother's pelvic bone. Several mid-wives told them that they move the mother to a hands-and-knees position [which widens the pelvic outlet] for shoulder dystocia . . . a procedure not used in American hospitals. Hospital births also had three times the rate of postpartum hemorrhage. Cutting the cord too early, or pulling on the cord to extract the placenta, or reaching in and manually removing the placenta, are practices found in hospital and not in home births which may contribute to postpartum hemorrhage. Medication during labor and delivery may also be a factor.
>
> The infant death rates, both perinatal (during birth) and neonatal (after birth) were essentially the same for the two groups. . . . Three and seven-tenths times as many hospital babies required resuscitation, and four times as many hospital babies became infected. Thirty times as many hospital babies suffered birth injuries, a difference attributable to the use of forceps, which were twenty-two times more common in labors planned to be in the hospital. The birth injuries consisted of severe cephalhematoma (a collection of blood beneath the scalp, sufficient to cause anemia and to require photo-therapy and/or exchange transfusion), fractured skull, fractured clavicle, fa-cial-nerve paralysis, brachial nerve injury, eye injury and the like. Fewer than five percent of the home birth mothers received analgesia or anesthesia, while such drugs were administered to over seventy-five percent of the women in the hospital group (even though almost all of the women in both

groups had attended childbirth preparation classes). Cesarean sections were three times more frequent in the hospital [8.2%] than in the planned-home-birth group [2.7%]. Finally, there were nine times as many episiotomies (which are supposed to prevent tearing) in the hospital group, and nine times as many severe (third- and fourth-degree) tears in the hospital group. Although as many mothers and babies survived the hospital births as the home births, the home-birth group had appreciably better outcome. (Rothman 1982:44)[7]

Marimikel Penn, a midwife and director of New Life Birth Services, Inc., in Austin, Texas, has been in practice since 1974 and has attended over 1,000 deliveries. She recently compiled statistics spanning eight and a half years of her practice (1980–1989). Out of 476 women served by herself and/or her associates, 92 percent delivered successfully either at home (440) or in the New Life Birth Center (36), and 8.19 percent (39) were transferred to the hospital. Of the transfers, who continued to receive midwifery support in the hospital, 21 had Cesarean sections, giving for this midwifery practice an overall Cesarean rate of 4.41 percent. No mothers or babies died. States Penn, "The last few years of my practice show a dramatic drop in the rate of hospital transfers and Cesareans—in the last two years, out of 120 births there has been only one Cesarean. We are finding that as we grow more experienced, we trust birth more, and that the more we trust birth, the better the process works" (personal communication).

Penn's statistics are supported by data from eight years of reactivated licensed midwifery in Arizona (Sullivan and Weitz 1988:117–126), where licensed midwives attended 3,666 labors, resulting in 3,255 out-of-hospital births (most in homes, some in private clinics). Eleven percent of those women attended in labor were transported to a hospital during labor, and 2 percent entered the hospital postpartum. There were 4 fetal deaths and 5 neonatal deaths (3 due to congenital anomalies, 1 to severe prematurity, and 1 to unknown causes), resulting in an overall perinatal death rate of 2.2 per 1,000 with a neonatal death rate of 1.1 per 1,000 (as compared to the 1989 U.S. hospital perinatal death rate of 10 per 1,000). (It is important to note that these midwives screen their clients carefully for risk factors. Those who do not qualify are referred to physicians, which is why direct comparisons between home and hospital birth are skewed in favor of home birth—hence the significance of Mehl's matched-sample study, which corrects for this discrepancy.)

Additional midwifery data that complement the above findings come from Canada. In an effort to provide information to the Task Force on the Implementation of Midwifery in Ontario, the Association of Ontario Midwives (AOM) requested that member midwives submit data on the births they had attended in the period 1983–1985. Twenty-five midwives from the province of Ontario responded. These results were incorporated into a computerized database by Kenneth C. Johnson (personal correspondence, 1990). Out of the 627 deliveries that were intended to take place at home (and screened for risk by the midwives), 568 (90.6 percent) actually did, while 59 (9.4%) were transferred to the hospital during labor. Primipara women were transferred in 20 percent of home births, whereas multiparas were transferred only 5 percent of the time. Twenty-five, or about 4 percent of the home birth sample of 627, had Cesarean sections (most of these were primiparas). There were no maternal deaths, and only one fetal death. The data also indicate that postpartum hemorrhage[8] occurred twice as often in hospital deliveries originally classified as low-risk (7.7 percent) as in low-risk home deliveries (3.3 percent).

A study of home births attended by midwives in Toronto between 1983 and 1988 was reported in the journal *Birth* (Tyson 1991). Out of the 1,001 deliveries that were intended by the parents to take place at home (and screened for risk by the midwives), 836 (90.6 percent) actually did, whereas 165 women (9.4%) were transferred to the hospital during labor. (One hundred sixteen of the transfers were primiparas; 49 were multiparas). Thirty-five, or about 3.5 percent of the sample of 1,001, had Cesarean sections. There were two neonatal deaths, one each after birth at home and in the hospital. No mothers died.

Internationally-recognized midwife Ina May Gaskin reports the following outcomes for 1,786 births attended by the Farm Midwives in Summertown, Tennessee, between 8 November 1970 and 31 October 1991. Of these, 1,707 (95.6 percent) delivered successfully at home; 79 (4.4 percent) were transferred to the hospital. Cesareans were performed for 29 of these women (1.6 percent of the total sample); 31 (1.7 percent) used anesthesia; 9 (0.9 percent) were delivered with forceps. Fifty-five births were breech; of these, 38 (69 percent) gave birth at home, and 17 were transferred to the hospital (4 had Cesareans). No mothers died. Eight babies died in the neonatal period (3 from lethal congenital defects, 3 from severe prematurity, 1 from respiratory failure, 1 from unknown causes) giving an overall neonatal mortality rate of 4 per 1,000 (Gaskin, personal correspondence).

Perhaps the most broadly significant home birth data comes from the

Netherlands, a country in which fully one-third of all births take place at home attended by midwives. In 1986, perinatal mortality in Dutch hospitals was 13.9 per 1,000, whereas for home births it was a very low 2.2 per 1,000 (Tew 1990:266). Analyzing unpublished data from Holland collected in 1986 on far larger numbers of births than any other study I have so far cited, Tew and a Dutch colleague found striking differences between midwife- and physician-attended home and hospital births, in a pattern that repeated at every level of risk on account of parity and maternal age:

> The PNMR [perinatal mortality rate] was higher for doctors in hospital (18.9/1,000 [83,351 births]) than for doctors at home (4.5/1,000 [21,653 births]), which was in turn higher than for midwives in hospital (2.1/1,000 [34,874 births]) than for midwives at home (1.0/1,000 [44,676 births]). . . . [The authors suggest] that care by obstetricians is not only incapable, save in exceptional cases, of reducing predicted risk, but even that it actually provokes and adds to the dangers. . . . [They suggest] that midwives, practicing their skills in human relations and without sophisticated technological aids, are the most effective guardians of childbirth and that the emotional security of a familiar setting, the home, makes a greater contribution to safety than does the equipment in hospital to facilitate obstetric interventions in cases of emergency. (Tew 1990:267)[9]

At the very least, these data do indicate that there is *no* case to be made for the greater safety of hospital birth over planned, midwife-attended home birth. Intensified technocratization does *not* equal intensified safety. In birth, risk can never be completely eliminated as a factor, no matter where one births—it can only be either minimized or increased. Contrary to our cultural ideology, hospital birth does not minimize risk as much as most people think it does, and can increase it; planned home birth does not increase risk, although most people think it does, and can minimize it. Yet so pervasive is our cultural belief in the superiority of modern medicine that the very real risk-enhancing dangers of hospital birth are simply not culturally acknowledged, whereas mothers who choose to birth at home are often accused of selfishness and irresponsibility.[10]

Carolyn Sargent (1989) describes a mirror image of this phenomenon in the African nation of Benin, where hospital birth has but recently become firmly established as the norm for city dwellers in conjunction with a long government campaign to move birth out of the home. Hospitals in Benin are understaffed, undercleaned, and underequipped with the technology upon which personnel schooled in Europe were trained to rely, and are inarguably no safer than homes for giving birth. Yet "they will save you if you suffer" is a primary motivation for the women who choose hospitals, whereas women who still choose to birth at home are scorned as "ignorant" and "uncivilized."

In *Where To Be Born? The Debate and the Evidence* (1987), researchers Rona Campbell and Alison Macfarlane report that the British Maternity Services Advisory Services Committee made the following policy statement: "As unforeseen complications can occur in any birth, every mother should be encouraged to have her baby in a maternity unit where emergency facilities are readily available." At the conclusion of their very thorough review of the evidence for Great Britain, Campbell and Macfarlane remark:

> Today, as in the past, it is unclear to what extent these statements from ministers and official committees . . . simply reflect a consensus of views about practice. Perhaps the most persistent and striking feature of the debate about where to be born, however, is the way policy has been formed with very little reference to the evidence. (1987:59)

In their Introduction to *Secular Ritual,* Moore and Myerhoff draw a distinction, pertinent to these issues of ideological safety and policy formation, between the "doctrinal efficacy" of ritual and its "operational efficacy." The *doctrinal efficacy* of religious ritual "is provided by the explanations a religion itself gives of how and why ritual works. The explanation is within the religious system and is part of its internal logic. The religion postulates by what causal means a ritual, if properly performed, should bring about the desired results" (1977:13). *Operational efficacy,* however, refers to observable results—successes and failures—in which there is great variation. Healing rituals, for example, may or may not make a patient feel better; political rituals may or may not sway popular opinion. As Moore and Myerhoff go on to demonstrate, "analyses of ritual can never be exhaustive and definitive because participants themselves cannot explain some of the effects of ritual upon them" (1977:13).

In the cultural arena of childbirth, the hospital is the institution that embodies and enforces belief through ritual. From within the belief system out of which hospital rituals have developed, the rituals of hospital birth can be said to have "succeeded" when visible birth outcomes are successful—that is, when a "healthy mother and a healthy baby" are the final results. Yet I would call this an example of doctrinal, and not operational, efficacy. Like the home birth data cited above, data from

earlier historical periods before modern obstetrics also indicate that
95 percent of all births were successful without obstetrical procedures
(Wertz and Wertz 1989:19–24). Successful and safe birth outcomes can
be interpreted only as the operational results of hospital procedures
from within the conceptual confines of the technocratic model of birth.

Birth is an amazingly resilient natural process. It can be technocratically de- and reconstructed in the hospital, or protected and nurtured
at home, and it will still turn out well almost all of the time. "Safety"
is the disguise worn by technocratic ideology. The real issue in the home
versus hospital debate is not safety but the conflict between radically
opposed systems of value and belief.

THE ALTERNATIVE BIRTH CENTER:
A MIDDLE GROUND?

> In fact, I wanted a home birth but it made Brad
> nervous. He didn't want it. He was afraid that if any-
> thing did go wrong, that it would be just so risky. In
> that 5 percent of the cases where the baby has compli-
> cations—if I started hemorrhaging or something—if
> there would be some kind of problem like that. So, the
> birthing room was actually a compromise for us be-
> cause we had come to the best of both. We had gotten
> to do exactly as we wanted. The staff was oriented
> that we could do anything we wanted to do, and we
> really did. Yet, if anything had happened, there was
> the delivery room right down the hall, you know
> where all the modern, whatever, is needed. So it was a
> compromise. I like the idea of it very much. It is kind
> of what I wanted. . . . I like to control what happens
> to me.
>
> —Patricia Hellman

This issue of "control," so important to Patricia Hellman, has led
to a great deal of confusion: many couples who take hospital-sponsored
childbirth education classes enter the hospital when labor begins expecting to retain control over the *birth,* although the method they are
taught generally promises only that the laboring woman can retain control over her *behavior.* The expectation of the couple that they will be
able to control the management of the birth often clashes with (1) the
hidden cultural forces for socialization behind the application of obstet-

rical procedures; (2) the nature of the passive patient role that accompanies the definition of birth as a techno-medical event; (3) the fact that the couple is on hospital territory and is thereby placed at a tremendous interactional disadvantage; and (4) the fact that the couple would not *be* on hospital territory in the first place if they did not also share in the overall cultural definition of birth as a techno-medical event. Thus, even if they are in a space that appears to be designed for natural childbirth, the couple is placed, interactionally and psychologically, under the sway of the technocratic model—sometimes to their liking, sometimes to their great surprise.

In pursuit of the perfect balance between safety and the ardently stated desires of many women for "control" and "natural childbirth," hospitals across the nation began during the late 1970s and 1980s to provide "alternative birth centers" and "birthing suites." These birthing centers were the medical profession's answer to the consumer demands of women scarred by their experiences in regular labor and delivery, and to the many sympathetic nurses and doctors who sincerely sought to provide something better. With their attractive decor, privacy, kitchenette, big double bed, and open door to family and friends, they seemed to represent the perfect mediation of the wholistic/technocratic dichotomy for many couples.

Yet, as Jordan points out, the birthing center is still hospital territory, where the woman "still gives birth . . . attended by unfamiliar people [who retain] the real decision-making power. A guest on somebody else's turf with few rights and fewer resources, [she] still does not own the birth" (1983:35). Moreover, these centers only accept "low-risk" women, so that many couples are ineligible to use them. And "low-risk" can quickly become "high-risk" if the laboring woman should, for example, fail to dilate in the appropriate amount of time. Kip Kozlowski, a certified nurse-midwife and childbirth educator who fought successfully for the introduction of in-hospital birthing centers in her hometown, says of the results of that battle: "It looks like you're getting something, and what you get is a lot of family-centered Cesarean sections." Correspondingly, during her OB/GYN residency physician Michelle Harrison was told by a resident that "ABC"—alternative birthing center—actually stood for "a beautiful Cesarean" (personal correspondence). Robert Mendelsohn, also an M.D., explains why:

> Don't kid yourself into thinking that birthing rooms made up to look just like a real (motel) bedroom are going to make any big difference. Once you allow yourself to be lured onto Modern Medicine's turf, they've got you. I

have the recurring dream of a nice young couple going into the birthing room, like the one at Illinois Masonic hospital—complete with brass bed and color TV set. The doctor smiles and acts just like a friendly uncle. But once the mother is strapped into the brass bed, the doctor pushes a button on a secret panel and the papered walls slide away, the furniture disappears, and they're suddenly in an operating room under the glare of the operating light with a surgeon standing there scalpel in hand, ready to slice her belly from one end to the other. That fantasy isn't so unreal. Birthing rooms are not so isolated from the operating rooms that the brass bed can't be rolled into action before the young mother and father know what's going on. If you're on the doctor's turf, you play by the doctor's rules. (1979:139)

However, a very viable mediation of the technocratic/wholistic, hospital/home opposition is provided by free-standing alternative birth centers growing in number across the nation. In a recent study of 11,814 births in such centers (Rooks et al. 1989), the results showed clearly that the physical lack of connection to a hospital is accompanied by a conceptual lack of connection to the technocratic model. Births in such centers tended to be intervention-free, and the outcomes were outstanding: the overall Cesarean rate was 4.4 percent and the perinatal death rate was 1.3 per 1,000 (as compared to a national average of 10 per 1,000). The rate of transfer to a hospital was 15.8 percent; only 2.4 percent of these transfers were emergency situations (37.1 percent of those transferred had Cesarean sections).

In dramatic contrast, at the major hospital in Anycity, according to the nurse in charge, only 15 out of every 40 (about 40 percent) of first-time mothers who attempt to birth in the attractively decorated "ABC" (alternative birth center) actually do; the rest end up going down the hall through the big double doors into the standard labor and delivery unit. In Centertown, the success rate for first-time mothers in the three hospital birthing centers there ranged from 30 to 45 percent. Some of the women in my study who started out in these centers stayed there; others who began there ended up in labor and delivery with Cesarean sections. Their stories will be told and the factors affecting their responses will be considered in the following chapter.

CHAPTER 5

How the Messages Are Received

The Spectrum of Response

I've never felt so powerful in all my life.
—Diana Chapin

I've never felt so helpless in all my life.
—Elise Pearsall

In order to understand the broad spectrum of individual response to the rituals of hospital birth, we will focus on the relationship between three factors: the technocratic model of reality dominant in the hospital, the belief system with which a birthing woman enters the hospital, and the ultimate *conceptual outcome* of her birth experience. By "conceptual outcome," I mean the woman's ultimate psychological interpretation of her birth experience as positive or negative, empowering or victimizing, joyful or traumatizing—in other words, whether that experience tends to affirm or to destroy the self-image she wishes to hold. As stated previously, the single factor that most influences the conceptual outcome of a woman's birth experience is the degree of correspondence between the technocratic model of reality dominant in the hospital and the belief system the individual woman holds when she enters the hospital. This belief system may be upheld, or overthrown, by the rituals of hospital birth. When it is upheld, her birth experience will generally be perceived as positive and joyful (although not necessarily also as self-empowering, as we will see in the following discussion). When it is overthrown, her birth experience will be perceived as negative and traumatic and as personally disempowering or degrading.

What makes this whole issue so delicate and complex is the tension inherent in the natural ideal, and thus, within the belief systems of the women who hold that ideal, between the wholistic and the technocratic paradigms of birth: many pregnant women consciously espouse one

187

while at the same time unconsciously believing in the other. When this is the case, a woman may only find out what she *really* believes in the act of giving birth.

If her conscious belief in the wholistic ideal is very strong, a pregnant woman will choose to give birth at home (or in a free-standing birth center). Yet if her deep, unconscious beliefs revolve around the technocratic model, she may well find that her labor does not progress until she finally "gives up" and goes to the hospital. Lewis Mehl expresses the experience of many home birth attendants when he says, "What we believe is what can come true for us. . . . If a woman believes on the deepest emotional level that the hospital is the only safe place to birth, then if she tries to deliver at home she won't be successful" (1981:313). A corollary of this statement, expressed to me by several nurse-midwives, is that if a woman believes on the deepest emotional level that home is the only safe place to birth, yet goes to the hospital because, for example, she can find no one to attend a home birth, or because her husband insists, she may experience a stressful labor with little progress, and end up with a forceps delivery or a Cesarean section. I do not mean to oversimplify here—the relationship between belief, behavior, and birth outcome is surely complex—but simply to call attention to the importance of this relationship.

In the following section, we will attempt to arrive at an understanding of the spectrum of response to hospital birth rituals through the birth narratives of those women in my study whose responses are most representative of the categories of response which I have been able to identify. Because of the close relationship between these responses and the belief systems held by the women prior to birth, I have chosen to name these categories in terms of those belief systems. Thus the three basic divisions that I will consider are: (1) women who consciously espouse the technocratic model of birth; (2) women who consciously espouse the wholistic paradigm; (3) women in-between. I base my assignments to one or another category primarily on the women's responses to my queries about their beliefs and expectations about pregnancy and birth.

Most of the women in my study had more than one child, so that all together, after interviewing 100 women, I had data on 194 births. Sometimes all of the births experienced by one mother would follow roughly the same pattern; for example, Beryl had five children, all by Cesarean section. But more often, there were radical differences in the multiple birthing experiences of individual women: the same woman might have had her first birth under the technocratic model, her second in accord with the "natural" ideal, and her last birth at home, whereas another might have had "natural childbirth" the first time, and a Cesarean the next. For the sake of clarity and simplicity, in this chapter I will present and categorize only responses to the first birth experienced by each woman in my study. (These categorizations will be summarized later in this chapter.) Responses to subsequent birth experiences will be discussed in Chapter 6.

FULL ACCEPTANCE OF THE TECHNOCRATIC MODEL OF BIRTH

> Birth is just something you have to go through in
> order to get your baby.
> —Gladys Meyers

Eighteen percent of the first-time births of the women in my study occurred in full accord with the extreme form of the technocratic model, which holds that birth is done not by mothers but by physicians. For half of these women, such full participation in the technocratic model took the form of complete and unquestioning acceptance of physicians' authority and hospital routine, with little or no sense of themselves as active agents in the process. For the other half, it took the form of active self-removal from the biological realm.

EXPECTING THAT "THE DOCTOR WILL TAKE CARE OF EVERYTHING" (9%)

Most of the nine women to be discussed in this particular category had their babies during the 1960s and early 1970s (most of those who espoused the "natural" ideal or the wholistic model gave birth after 1975). The two exceptions were women who gave birth in the eighties who were both medical technicians and thus had been thoroughly socialized into the technocratic model through the medical educational system.

From these women's point of view, "full espousal" of the technocractic model did not usually constitute a conscious belief in the mechanicity of their bodies or of the labor process, but rather took the form of unquestioning acceptance of the value and validity of the medical definition and management of their births. In fact, women who expect the doctor to take care of everything will feel ignored and slighted if their births are *not* acknowledged as important by the wider society through the performance of hospital birth rituals:

> My husband and I got to the hospital, and we thought they would take care of everything. I kept sending my husband out to ask them to give me something for the pain, to check me—anything—but they were short-staffed and they just ignored me until the shift changed in the morning. (Sarah Kendall)

For these women, none of whom received any formal childbirth education, the conceptual tension in hospital birth is not between a "natural ideal" and the technocratic model, but between their own technocratically oriented belief systems and the natural aspects of the birth process. They often perceive the processes of labor and birth as bewildering and frightening and wish for their labors to be made as reassuringly mechanical as possible. Hospital birth rituals help to alleviate their fears when these rituals work to bring the threateningly natural labor process into conformity with their visions of the appropriate technocratic birth:

> My husband was in Vietnam when my daughter was born. I was scared to death of the whole thing. I didn't want to have anything to do with it, didn't want to know about it. I just wanted the doctor to take care of it and give me my baby. And when I got to the hospital they put me out, and when I woke up they showed me my baby girl, and that was just fine with me. (Toni James)

> I was terrified when my daughter was born, because I had had a section and I had been told, you know, that once you have a section you can't have a baby via vaginal delivery because you will burst or something and I was kind of scared. I just knew I was going to split open and bleed to death right there on the table, but she was coming so fast they didn't have time to do anything to me. . . . I would rather have had a section like my other births. . . . I like sections, because you don't have to be afraid. (LeAnn Kellogg)

When you come from within a belief system, its rituals will comfort and calm you. For these women, the rituals of hospital birth serve the same function as the Lamaze breathing rituals do for those women who espouse the "natural" ideal. The technocratic model is their cognitive matrix, and the monitors, drugs, and authoritative uniforms of the nurses reassure them that (1) their individual transformations are significant to the wider society; and (2) their culture will pull them safely through this terrifying and threatening natural event. And when they are indeed safely "pulled through," the technocratic model will confirm the necessity of their technological births, thereby reinforcing and reaffirming its basic tenets in their minds:

[My doctor] told me the minute that he examined me to see if I was pregnant that I may not be able to deliver naturally because my pelvic bones were so small, so close together, or whatever. So they just kept real close tabs on me. . . . Later, the pediatrician joked and laughed and said that it would have killed both of us. He said there was no way. He said, "I have never seen such a big baby" and Lacy was only 7 lbs. 6 oz. I mean, back then, it was bigger than it is now. But he said "for such a small space, you were really lucky that they did a C-section." (Elaine Goodrich)

Well, it's a good thing I didn't listen to my crazy home-birth friends. I hemorrhaged really badly after the birth, and my doctor told me I would have died if I hadn't been in the hospital. (Suzanne Sampson)

However, hospital procedures are not specifically designed to serve as vehicles of concern and reassurance to birthing women, and often they do not. Women who fully believe in the technocratic model, expecting that "the doctor will take care of everything," often experience feelings of shock, upset, and abandonment if he doesn't. Since these women do not take childbirth preparation classes, they usually have no cognitive matrix in terms of which they can interpret their experiences, no breathing rituals, no "labor support person," to mediate for them between cognition and chaos. They expect that hospital procedures will serve that function for them, will reassure them and make them feel safe. But the technocratic model on which these procedures are based, especially in its extreme traditional form, does not acknowledge the mother's cognitive need for an intelligible framework within which to interpret her experience, nor the psychological devastation that can result from living through such an intense experience in the total absence of such a framework, as is poignantly illustrated in the following letter, which I received from a student after guest-lecturing in her anthropology class at the University of Houston.

Mary: "I Was Terrified the Entire Time"

Dear Robbie,

I want to tell you how glad I am that you are doing research into the birthing practices here in the United States. I hope that you guest lecture at as many colleges as you can possibly lecture. It is too late for the information which you presented to do me, personally, any good, but I hope that maybe I will be able to use this information to help others.

I am including a summary of my own personal child-bearing experiences. I hope that these experiences will help you in your research. My experiences began as a young teenager when I would listen to the tales that my grandmother would tell about how horrible natural childbirth was. She said that it was so painful that she never forgot the pain. My mother who had her babies under analgesia did not tell me anything at all.

I went into pregnancy not even knowing what an epidural was. I was twenty-seven years old when my first child was born, but I might as well have been twelve for all I knew about having babies. I read all that I could get my hands on on being a good parent, but it did not even occur to me to read up on having a baby. I read the information that the doctor provided me with and that was the extent of it.

My pregnancy did not go well. I was sick almost the entire nine months. I also had terrible problems with swelling. The doctor took me off of salt but the problems got worse. He would fuss at me and tell me that I was eating too much salt. I was gaining a lot of weight, but most of it was fluids. I tried to tell the doctor that I was not eating any salt, but he refused to listen. This refusal nearly cost both my baby and me our lives. I awoke one morning and the bed was getting wetter and wetter, and I thought to myself that I had never wet the bed before. Then it dawned on me that my water had broken. I got to the hospital as fast as I could go (considering that I did not know how to drive and had to find someone to take me to the doctor). When I got there I had to wait in the hall because they did not have a labor room available. I was caught up in the once a year last minute rush to deliver before midnight on December 31, 1974. By the time they finally got me on a table I began to hemorrhage and the really bad part was that I was not even in labor. According to the information I had been given by the doctor, I should not be due for another four weeks. They waited for the doctor to get there and he ordered them to induce labor and to also prep me for a C-section. I was younger and vainer then and I really did not want a C-section; I made it real clear to the doctor that I did not want one.

I labored all day and they induced labor as hard as they could possibly induce it. I was terrified the entire time. It looked like to me that I might bleed to death. I remember them making me sit up and push real hard. I did that several times. Then I was informed that the doctor was caught in traffic and I would have to wait for him. Then when the doctor was finally there, the nurse whispered something to the doctor. He replied by telling them to gas the hell out of her. The last time that I looked at the clock it was 6:15 and the baby was born at 6:36. I can only tell you what happened next from what my husband told me. He could hear the baby crying and it would stop, then it would cry again, and then stop. He said that they worked on the baby an eternity. I only know that I woke up about 10:30 P.M. Someone wished me Happy New Years and told me that I had a baby boy. I asked for my husband and they said that he had been sent home. I also was informed that I could not see my baby until the next morning. I have no idea what happened to the four hours that passed from the time I went to sleep until I woke up. I do know that two nurses came to my room to check on me. They told me that my blood pressure had dropped to zero and they were real worried about me. I was not worried about myself.

The next morning I got out of bed and walked about ten feet before I collapsed and bled on their carpet. The nurses were very angry with me. I had not been told to stay in bed. I thought it was natural to get up. I was going to the bathroom.

Babies were delivered to the mothers in the morning, but my baby was not one of them. It was explained to me that there was a minor problem and they wanted the doctor to check him over before he was brought to me. About 2:00 I finally got my baby for ten minutes. I also got him at suppertime.

My husband got to hold him first since he had been there when I got him the first time. When it came my turn to hold the baby I was supposed to nurse him. I asked my husband to raise up my bed and when he did I screamed out in pain. I had not been aware up until then how bad off I was.

When I screamed the baby began to look ill. They snatched him from me and scolded me for screaming. (Later I realized I had a broken tail bone.)

The doctor informed me that they were not sure what was wrong with Anthony, but that they were doing all they could for him. I was also told that I was not given any blood to make up for what I had lost because I could get diseases from the blood.

I was dismissed from the hospital and had to leave empty-handed. In the first three days of my son's life I had seen him three times. I could not come back to the hospital and visit him because I was in such terrible condition. They finally discovered that my son had a calcium deficiency and they attributed this to the fact that there is diabetes in my family. They did not tell me that a difficult delivery could cause the same problem. I had nearly starved myself to death because I was sick all the time.

It is clear from her letter that Mary had a woefully inadequate cognitive matrix for the interpretation of her birthing experience. Her grandmother gave her a scary view of "natural childbirth," whereas her mother gave her nothing at all. She accumulated no knowledge through books or anywhere else that could have provided her with a more coherent matrix. Early on in her pregnancy she was conceptually plugged into the metaphor of her body as defective because of her toxemia (swelling of the hands and feet, high blood pressure); in this case, it was the technocratic model of pregnancy that *caused* her trouble: under that model, the treatment for toxemia is (still) to stop eating salt, although research has been available since the early 1960s indicating that going off of salt causes toxemia, that in fact, increased salt intake is necessary during pregnancy for adequate blood circulation (Brewer 1966; Brewer and Brewer 1977).

The doctor's belief that it was Mary's consumption of salt which was causing her problem illustrates a tenet of the technocratic model frequently reflected in the narratives to follow: when something goes wrong during pregnancy or birth, it is the woman's fault, due either to her refusal to follow doctor's orders, to the inherent defectiveness of her body, or to her own inadequacy as a person. This principle is also reflected in the nurses' reaction to Mary's screaming out in pain when her husband raised the bed: they "snatched the baby" away and blamed his condition on her screaming. It is entirely possible that the increased illness that resulted from Mary's going off of salt also resulted in her being unable to eat an adequate diet, which resulted in her son's calcium deficiency, which, in accord with this principle, the hospital attributed to the fact that "there is diabetes in my family."

Just before the birth, "the nurse whispered something to the doctor." Mary was not told why she was gassed, nor what was wrong with her baby, nor what was wrong with her. Under the extreme form of the technocratic model, the assumption is that the woman simply does not need to know, but should passively accept whatever treatment the staff sees fit to dole out. In her literal and conceptual "absence" from any kind of cognitive grasp of or control over her pregnancy and birth experience, Mary constitutes a prototypical example of the woman seen as "passive victim" in feminist theory (Dubois et al. 1985:48).

Sometimes women who espouse the technocratic model agree in advance with the messages of hospital birth rituals but change these beliefs during labor. To their astonishment, several of the women in this group who entered the hospital expecting labor to be one long horror, who couldn't wait to be drugged, found during the actual labor process that they were enjoying it—enjoying the excitement, the anticipation, the rhythm and flow of their contractions. Contrary to their expectations, the sudden imposition of hospital routines deprived them of an experience they hadn't even known they wanted to have:

> I was pretty scared beforehand about it all, but I was never in all that much pain. I didn't mind the labor really at all, and I couldn't wait to see the baby. I kind of got into the rhythm of the contractions, and I was really proud of myself for doing so well. I was so thrilled to be having my baby, and to find out that it wasn't so bad after all. I wanted to see my baby be born—I really wanted to watch her come out. I wasn't afraid anymore—I knew I could do it. But then, when they were wheeling me down the hall, I saw a nurse come at me with a gas mask. I said, "Oh, please, don't gas me" and then the mask came down on my face and that was it. I cried for hours when I woke up, and I've never gotten over it. (Barbara Sandowski)

For most of the women in this group, the rituals of hospital birth can be said to have succeeded in their didactic and socializing purposes. Like Mary, these women did, by and large, receive the messages sent from society to them through birth rituals. Occasionally, if hospital personnel were especially thoughtful and attentive to them, they would come away from their birth experiences with enhanced notions of the importance of science, technology, patriarchy, and institutions, *and* with enhanced notions of their own importance in relation to these things. But most often, the women in this group internalized messages about their own helplessness and insignificance in relation to our society's core value system.

REJECTING BIOLOGY IN FAVOR OF
TECHNOLOGY: "SCHEDULE MY CESAREAN
FOR 5:30" (9%)

Another 9 percent of the women in my study fully espoused the technocratic model in a very different way. They believed that their bodies were not suited for giving birth naturally, and they liked it like that. Birth to these women (all of whom were high-ranking professionals) was not something to be afraid of, but something to control, to plan, to manage as actively as they managed their careers. Said Joanne,

> Even though I'm a woman, I'm unsuited for delivering. . . . and I couldn't nurse. . . . I've told my mother—I just look like a woman, but none of the other parts function like a mother. I don't have the need or the desire to be biological.

Control was an overriding concern of these nine women in all aspects of their lives. They plainly feel that as long as they are in control, they are happy, everything is fine. They achieve control over their lives through careful planning and organization of their time and activities; they achieve control over their bodies through regular exercise; and they achieve control over others and their own destinies through reaching positions of independence and importance in the wider society. They seem to judge most situations by the degree of control they feel they can maintain. Even their pregnancies were carefully controlled— planned to occur at just the chosen times in their careers. But once those processes were set into motion, they became uncontrollable and thus presented these women with a division within their most treasured notions of self, between the cultural parts within their control, and the physical processes outside of it.

Predictably, then, most of the women in this group did not derive any great joy from their pregnancies. They tended to find the changes in their bodies "normal" at best and "frustrating" and "irritating" at worst. I found no traces in this group of the "Earth Mother" who glories in her physical creativity. One woman, in fact, took pains to distinguish her own experience of pregnancy from that of her "Earth Mother" sister:

[Question: You don't think pregnancy is beautiful?]
No, I don't. I don't. To me, I think there are a lot of women who love being pregnant and they would say that. My sister, the Earth Mother, did. Especially before I got pregnant, I thought, "Maybe I'll get into it." But I didn't get into it. I felt bad and large and awkward and nauseated. And oh, I love having the baby but I wish there were an easier way. . . . No, I didn't find it to be the most beautiful time of my life, even though John was very supportive, and very encouraging, but I just felt huge and humongous. (Betsy Jenkins)

Lina Eckstein shared her feelings:

[Question: How did you feel about your body while you were pregnant?]
I didn't like it. It just overwhelmed me, the kinds and the variety of sensations, and the things that happen to your body because of the pregnancy. I didn't like it at all. I felt totally alienated from my body. . . . I can't relate to my son as being that monstrous little tumor I was carrying around for nine months. To me it's day and night having him inside and outside.

Joanne Moorehouse also voiced some of her concerns:

I was real apprehensive going into labor; it kind of terrified me, mostly because I like to be in control . . . and you don't have any control when that happens. I used to have nightmares about standing in front of the president making a presentation and having my water break.

In line with not being thrilled with pregnancy, none of these women seemed to desire or expect any great glory or special magic from birth. As one of them put it, "If my husband could do it the next time instead of me, that would be just fine." Far from demanding natural childbirth, they have a great deal in common with their 1920s sisters who ardently campaigned to get American doctors to start using scopolamine to blot out women's consciousness of the pain of labor. These crusaders felt that they were not and should not be slaves to their biological processes, which seem to be exactly the sentiments held by the women in this category. None of them hesitated to ask for technological interventions when they felt the need, nor expressed any major dissatisfaction with their highly technological hospital births, except to mention that they really went on too long (the longest labor among them was twenty-one hours). In fact, the only true dissatisfaction I heard expressed resulted not from the administration of anesthesia, but from its withholding. Kay said:

They finally did admit me at 9:30 and she was born at 11:00, so I had a pretty quick time of it, the second time. I actually asked for an epidural at one point, but they said they didn't have time to do it.

[Question: Was that okay with you?]
Not really! I was awfully uncomfortable and I had remembered how wonderful it was [to have an epidural during my first birth] and that I had instantly felt terrific. I did feel the victim of a plot and it made me mad this time. . . . I was mad that I was in so much pain, and then they would tell me something like, we don't have time—you know?—that just drove me wild. I didn't like that at all—I wanted to have it when *I* wanted to have it.

Lina expressed outrage that a friend of hers in advanced labor had been denied anesthesia for the same reason as Kay, saying earnestly, "No one has the right to tell you that you have to go through that kind of pain."

Far from passively accepting whatever the system doled out, these women expected and usually received attentive personal care from their obstetricians, who were sometimes personal friends. They usually took hospital-sponsored childbirth education classes, not to prepare for natural childbirth but for the same intellectual empowerment they desired from any kind of education. If their physician recommended a Cesarean, they expressed no sense that they were missing anything. Those whose obstetricians recommended scheduled Cesareans expressed relief at being able to plan in advance for the birth. They relied on their physicians as they would on any professional in his or her area of expertise, expecting them to make reasoned decisions about their own needs and those of the baby during labor and birth, and they expected to be fully informed about the reasoning. As long as the lines of communication stayed open and their wishes were respected, these women tended to feel fully satisfied with their hospital treatment.

Accordingly, Joanne appreciated her Cesarean birth not only because she could plan her business needs around the scheduled time, but also because the anesthesiologist explained what was happening to her step-by-step, enhancing her feelings of being in control, and because, since she felt no pain, she was able to be so *intellectually* present to the birth that she could watch the time to see which of her many friends who had placed bets on the time of birth would win the $18 in the pot. She stated:

I liked that because I didn't feel like I had dropped into a biological being. Which is something that's real hard for me. I don't like doctors, I'm not real fond of things that remind me I'm a biological creature, because I am—I prefer to think and be an intellectual and emotional person, so you know, it was sort of my giving in to biology to go through all of this.

[Question: What did you want out of the birth experience?]
Out of the birth experience itself I wanted no pain. I wanted it to be as simple and uncomplicated and easy as most everything else has been for me.

Unlike the prior group of women who fully espoused the technocratic model, the women in this category would abhor giving birth under general anesthesia or without the supportive presence of their husbands. While they welcome the distance from their biological sensations that the epidural provides, at the same time they insist upon bearing witness to birth with their conscious and highly valued minds and upon the mental attentiveness of their husbands as well. But they expressed no desire for natural childbirth, no feeling of need to actively give birth themselves. They seemed to find their personal fulfillment in their professional identities, in mothering their children, and in their relationships with their husbands (which all of these women reported to be extraordinarily egalitarian). Their bodies are vehicles of achievement in these realms and carry no particular meaning in the body's own physical and biological realm. Biology to them is a means to an end; said Joanne, "I'd rather see the finished product than [experience] the manufacturing process."

Because the women in this category are all in the sort of important management positions that many middle-class women increasingly seek, I wonder to what extent their desires and beliefs may represent the wave of the future for American birthways; these form for me the subject of a new and ongoing investigation of the relationships between career, pregnancy, and parenting among modern professional women (Davis-Floyd 1992).

Comparative Analysis For the women in the two preceding categories the value of the technocratic model as a cognitive matrix for birth was unquestioned. The first group of women did not see themselves as active participants in the technocratic process of birth and internalized messages about their own insignificance in relation to American society's core value system. Those in the second group saw themselves as partners in a process of production best carried out by personnel with the appropriate training and expertise. Their birth experiences tended to enhance their appreciation for the knowledge and skill of the experts and for the technology that they perceived as essential to successful outcome. At the same time, they internalized pictures of themselves as powerful active agents in the production process, not because of what they *did* as much as because of who and what they perceived themselves to be—women in control, comfortable in and empowered by the technological reality in which they live, and which they help to shape.

FULL ACCEPTANCE OF THE
WHOLISTIC MODEL OF BIRTH

> I did not react to labor as is taught in some child-birth books, where they suggest doing a very fast breathing that will keep you above the pain. This creates a sensation of separation. . . . What I did was to go deeper into my body and the sensation. My whole training in rebirthing taught me to go into the body. For me the ideal way to labor was not to avoid the pain but to go into it. I would take a deep breath, let go, and relax into my body.
>
> —Rima Star, *The Healing Power of Birth*

Pregnant women who fully accept all the premises of the wholistic model of birth will generally choose to give birth at home, as under this model hospital birth is a contradiction in terms. (In the late 1970s the home-birth rate stabilized at about 1 percent of all deliveries [McClain 1987*a*; National Center for Health Statistics 1982; Pearse 1982].) This can be a position arrived at after one or more actual experiences of hospital birth leads these women to make a conscious shift in their dominant belief system (a phenomenon discussed in Chapter 9), or a choice made for a woman's first birth, as is the case with the two women whose birth narratives I will present in this section.

BIRTH IS A NATURAL ASPECT
OF WOMANHOOD (3%)

Three of the home-birthers in my study consider themselves to be ideologically mainstream in many aspects of their lives, but are all politically very liberal. They tend to see birth as a natural aspect of their womanhood, which they cherish and wish to allow to unfold without technological interference. They are professionals like the women discussed in the previous section, but seem to desire no concomitant distance from their female biological processes, as Tara Oakes's story will illustrate.

Tara: "It Seemed Just Right and Real Natural"

TARA: Fifty percent of who I am is my body, just in terms of the way I interpret my physical being and try to project that to my family and to the people around me. . . . I never felt any conflicts between the needs of the baby and my own needs. . . .

Hunter's birth was about thirteen and a half hours and it was real hard. My water broke first, and of course we were real excited. It was about midnight. And I always had it in my mind that morning sickness was psychological and that I could control all these things. If I did things right, ate the right things and treated my body the right way . . . that I could have a quick easy labor. I exercised a lot, you know, I paid attention to my diet and everything, and I realized finally, after nine months and a birth, that there are a lot of things in that situation that you don't have control over. You just can't control it. But it took me that long to admit it. . . .

Anyway, I went into labor about midnight, and I was convinced that by three or four in the morning this baby would be here. And I progressed very quickly for a while and then I stopped. And part of it was that I was tired. The nurse-midwife encouraged me to lay down and rest. And later they gave me some herbal stuff that works sort of like pitocin—blue cohosh, I think. And I could tell that that herbal tea did make the contractions more intense.

Later on I could tell that they were discussing whether or not I needed to go to the hospital and I was adamant about not going. I mean we did not talk about it, but I really did not want to go. But I would have, but finally he was born about 1:15 or 1:30 in the afternoon. We tried the birthing stool and the birthing platform and we walked around and I did every position and I was willing to do anything, which I think was the positive part. She would say, "Do you feel like trying this?" and it was just a matter of whatever I could do to make this happen. And it really wasn't that long in the scheme of things when I talk to other people, but it seemed like forever to me. It was just hard. . . . And when he was born, he was fine . . . and all of it seemed just natural to me. . . . I delivered in a semireclining position. I pushed for what I thought was a long time—about two and a half hours.

ROBBIE: How do you feel about having given birth at home?

TARA: Great! It just seemed right and real natural. It was so nice after it was over—we were there; we didn't have to go anywhere. And we didn't have to worry about strangers or interventions. And the midwives were wonderful, and they did home visits afterward, which was just grand. I didn't have to get up and go. It seemed like the way things ought to be. I don't preach about it to people because I know it makes them uncomfortable, but for the right people, I think it's a wonderful option.

ROBBIE: Would you say that your birth experience was consistent with the way that you think about yourself in general?

TARA: Yes, I think that had I gone to the hospital, that would have been inconsistent. I already saw myself as a different kind of person because so many of the things I do [in politics] are not mainstream. I am the kind of person that a lot of people think is mainstream, but then they find out some of the other things that I have been involved in, and they are just incredulous. And birth is one of them. I felt very proud that I was able to pull everything off at home and not at a hospital. I mean, it's just such a miraculous accomplishment and to think that people do it all the time. I just kept thinking what a miracle this is. . . . People would say, you're so brave, and it didn't seem brave to me at all . . . the bottom line was that I felt safer at home. . . . That's why it didn't seem unusual to me. It seems strange to me that people feel safer with the drugs and that type of thing, because I'm just not that way.

ROBBIE: Did it mean anything to you to go through the pain?

TARA: Oh yes. I would never have done it differently. I think that's part of the whole experience. I mean, I have a general feeling about pain in our society. We try not to experience pain—drugs, lots of drugs. I feel that's why a lot of people get into other forms of drug abuse. I've never been a person to take much medicine at all. Most of the pain that I've experienced is not unbearable, and even though I remember feeling that the pain of labor was sometimes almost unbearable, it never entered my mind to wish for something to take it away, never. . . . I wanted it to stop, but I didn't want it to stop by somebody giving me something. I guess part of it is that there is such a change from that heavy intense pain to this wonderful physical and emotional stuff going on along with the pain, to this wonderful thing when the pain is gone. And then you have this wonderful product of all that pain. You know, it's like the reward for all your hard work. And what a reward! When she laid the baby on my stomach—it's indescribable. I can't find the words to tell you. I mean, anybody who hasn't been through that—there are no words to describe it. And every time I watch the film of Justin's birth, I feel the same way—just like it's happening again, you know—this miracle! You know, it still seems just like a miracle to me.

BIRTH IS A SPIRITUAL PROCESS OF GROWTH (3%)

Three of the home-birthers in my study explicitly identify themselves with New Age ideology—in other words, with a wholistic, systems-oriented vision of reality in which the individual creates or attracts to herself the life experiences she most needs to further her spiritual growth. Under such a model, high value is placed on experience and individual responsibility. Intellectual knowledge, although important, is secondary in value to intuitive bodily knowing. The body, instead of a vehicle that carries the mind, is the supreme expression of self, as in one's body are stored the memories of all one's life (and past-life) experiences. Taking responsibility for birth thus includes not only nutrition and exercise, but active participation in a healing process of releasing past negative feelings from the body so that those old patterns will not reenact themselves during birth, as is illustrated in the birth story Kristin wrote down for me after our interview time was cut short.

Kristin: "Motherhood Is Trusting Myself"

I had no interest in becoming a mother when I found myself pregnant with Joy. I was single and committed to having a career. Discovering that I was pregnant was horrifying news. I gathered my support network around me and within a very short time decided that I would have the baby. That decision was based primarily on my belief that although I was not conscious of choosing to have a child, I was responsible for my pregnancy, and on some unconscious level, had chosen it.

With this choice in mind I began to prepare myself for childbirth and motherhood. I was primarily guided by my intuition, my friends, and books that came to me through friends. I began to be rebirthed, which is a breathing process that supports clearing negative emotions and in many cases helps the person to remember their own birth. My rebirther was Rima Star, a wonderful woman who had given birth to a daughter at home several years prior to this time.

I began seeing a homeopath and using homeopathic remedies. He supported me to cleanse and strengthen my system, and he gave me isometric exercises to strengthen the muscles used in childbearing. I also had ten rolfing sessions.

All this occurred during my first trimester. It was a very turbulent time in my life. Finally, I married the baby's father and began to settle into my pregnancy and new life circumstances. I thought a great deal about childbirth itself, and often I would cry as I saw pictures of women having babies. It looked so painful, and I was always very careful to avoid pain at all costs. However, as I learned more and more about birth, I began to see the possibility that what showed on the face of the laboring woman was not only pain, but also concentrated effort and determination. I talked to women about their pregnancies and births, and the women who had delivered their children at home rarely emphasized the pain. They spoke more often about the wonder of childbearing and the ecstasy of delivering their children consciously.

When I was about two months pregnant I was lying on my waterbed one evening in the dark, not sleeping, but also not really thinking, just drifting along, rocking myself a little, when suddenly, from somewhere inside the front of my head I heard these words "I'm here, I'm a girl, and my name is Joy Elizabeth." I pondered this experience for the entire duration of my pregnancy. I thought perhaps I made it up, but Joy Elizabeth was not a name I would have chosen for my child. Yet I told people about the experience and I called the baby Joy from then on. I decided that when the baby was born I would know whether or not I made the whole thing up and if the baby was a boy, well, having called him Joy during my pregnancy couldn't hurt.

After my third prenatal visit my obstetrician wanted to do an ultrasound test. The date of the baby's conception was not clear and he wanted to measure the baby to get a better idea of how old it was. I had read somewhere that ultrasound was very traumatic for the baby. Apparently the sound waves, while undiscernible to us, are discernible to the baby, at least in the opinion of the author of the article I read. I was unwilling to take the chance, and declined the opportunity. He was very unhappy about this and described the possible alternatives should I go past my due date with stress tests and other unpleasant notions. I felt that he was threatening me. That was my last visit. . . . I chose homebirth.

Somewhere during this time I remembered my birth during a rebirthing session with Rima's husband Steven. I didn't want to come out of my mother and finally the obstetrician had to deliver me with forceps. I remembered being inside trying not to come out of my mother, setting it up so that someone else did it for me and forced me to be born. I have had to deal with issues of helplessness and force my whole life. I had a powerful emotional release and cried for a very long time. Steven held me and provided safety to experience the tremendous trauma that surrounded that incident.

I enrolled in the childbirth education classes held at the office of a group of midwives. I learned the details of labor and delivery, how the baby would engage and come through the cervix and through the birth canal and be born. I talked to the baby a great deal about how it worked and what she should do when. I remember one night I had a Braxton-Hicks contraction and I heard a voice inside say, "I'm scared." I told her I was scared too and that everything would be okay because we were partners and we would do this thing together.

We had been to approximately half the classes and my baby was due in four more weeks when suddenly, one night about midnight, I had a contraction. I didn't think too much about it, but they persisted through the night, although they were mild and I easily slept between them. Finally, about 7 A.M. I woke my husband up and told him I was having contractions and had been having them all night. I was upset because I was afraid I was having the baby prematurely and I was afraid that I might have to have her in the hospital after all. I called the midwives and they said to come over and they would check me. Sure enough, I was dilated 3 centimeters. The baby was coming.

They took some measurements and decided that the baby would be about six pounds and they felt that was big enough for me to stay at home for the delivery. I hadn't done any of the things to prepare a birth kit thinking I had plenty of time. We didn't even have a diaper in the house, and the baby shower was still in planning stages. But my friends took care of everything, and it was a good thing for me, because I definitely had my hands full. My husband was wonderful. He stayed right beside me the whole time, supporting my breathing and rubbing my back. I had some back labor for a while and he helped to ease the pain with pressure. From 9 to 11:45 A.M., I dilated from 3 to 10 centimeters.

By the time I got to transition the contractions were very difficult to manage. I would shut my eyes and scream during the most intense parts. Actually, I don't remember this very well at all, but the people who were there have told me. It seems to me now that I was screaming not so much out of pain, but that in screaming I was less in touch with the pain and more focused on the noise I was making. My husband kept asking me to open my eyes and look at him, which I did as much as I could. His eyes are absolutely beautiful, big and blue, and that day they were so full of love and compassion and support that I wouldn't have traded him for anyone. He was absolutely present with me.

Apparently my screams clued the midwives that transition had completed and it was time to push. This was the point where having remembered my own birth was invaluable. I was thinking how much I wanted to just forget this whole thing and go do something else, that I didn't know what to do, I didn't know how to push, that I couldn't do it, that I should give up, that no one could make me do it—all the helplessness and force issues I had glimpsed in the rebirthing. It was then that Steven (the man who had rebirthed me that day) stepped up and said, "Now Kristin, remember that rebirthing we did together, your force and helplessness issues are coming up and you are wanting someone else to do this for you. There isn't anyone here who can deliver this baby but you, so get to it!"

I knew he was right. I remember telling myself I would do whatever I had to do to get this over with. . . . The next time I felt a contraction coming on I pushed with all my might and yelled at the same time. It was a yell from deep in my throat, and definitely not from pain, but from putting every aspect of my being into that push. I did that for about thirty-five minutes, whenever a contraction would come. Then . . . I felt this horrible burning feeling and I think I shrank back a bit, but then I think someone encouraged me and I pushed harder and the baby's head came out. One more push and her shoulders were delivered. Then the midwives invited me to reach down and pull her out, which I did. . . . It was incredible to me that she was still so tightly lodged. The midwives had slit the sack because she was still inside it, and I pulled her out and laid her on my chest.

Someone said "It's a girl." For me that was irrelevant. She coughed gently once, and then she lay there very peacefully. Someone put a blanket over her and we laid there like that for probably thirty minutes. I have no idea of the time. I was completely transfixed. I think the midwives helped me deliver the placenta, but I did it without paying any attention whatsoever to the process. My husband was behind me where he had been sitting to help me sit up when the contractions came and he stayed right where he was. My universe consisted of him and the baby. Diane took a few pictures and then everyone left us alone.

After a while the baby picked her head up off my chest and began to search for my breast. I helped her find it and she began to nurse. I think then I began to inspect her a little bit, looked at her hands, et cetera. She seemed to be in perfect condition. I was ecstatic. I never felt better in my whole life. I was completely peaceful and joyful at the same time.

According to the midwives Joy was actually about a week overdue. They could tell by her skin and fingernails and toenails. . . . Actually, she was born about the time I originally thought she would be. The obstetrician had told me that date was too early the first time I went to see him. This was more confirmation for me that I can trust myself.

The pregnancy and birth changed my whole view of myself as a woman. I discovered that I had never valued myself as a woman. I valued the masculine aspects of my personality, but I considered my womanly traits weak and counterproductive. Motherhood has been an incredible discovery of the power of my intuition, and of the value of trusting myself.

Comparative Analysis   Tara's kinship with the professional women discussed in the second group of technocratic model adherents is reflected in her early desire for control over the birth process and her belief that she could achieve such control by doing all the "right" things in preparation for the birth. Her wholistic view of birth kept her from wishing to utilize the technocratic forms of control so important to her sisters in the second technocratic group. Unlike them, she was willing to give up her desire for control to the experience that such control was not and had never been hers. Kristin, in keeping with her conscious affiliation with the New Age movement, does not seem to have held control as a value or goal, valuing instead the processes, the experiences of pregnancy and birth, and the insight, wisdom, and spiritual growth that seemed to her to flow from those experiences.

What these two women share are mutual beliefs in the oneness of mother and child, in self-responsibility, and in an association between pain and hard but worthwhile work. Tara, whose beliefs run slightly more parallel to the technocratic model than Kristin's, speaks of the baby as the "product" of that work, whereas Kristin speaks only of the baby as a conscious being with whom she shares her body and with whom she can even communicate before birth. They both clearly see themselves as active doers of birth, sharing greater faith in nature and the inherent abilities of women's bodies to birth babies than in scientific and technological interventions in that process. Tara feels pride in her accomplishment as birth-giver at the same time as she stresses over and over that for her, birth is a miracle—a view that seems to reflect her acceptance of the lesson that indeed, she has no control. She and Kristin both clearly share awe and tremendous appreciation for the miracle and mystery of birth and bonding—a process during which Kristin described herself as completely "transfixed" and which Tara could find no words at all to describe. (Later on, Tara did describe herself, during her second home birth, as being in a "dream state.")

Kristin and Tara are unique and unusual in American society as a whole, representing as they do the 1 percent of American women who choose to give birth at home. This percentage may undergo change as public awareness of the relative safety of home versus hospital birth grows, but, as the stories of Kristin and Tara both demonstrate, the decision to birth at home involves far more than a simple weighing of the evidence. Since birthing at home is so antithetical to mainstream American behavior, such a choice almost always entails a willingness to reject the core values of American society in favor of other values and a different underlying paradigm. In my experience, rare is the woman who makes such a choice for her first birth. Most of the home-birthers I interviewed had their first babies in the hospital, and only then, after confronting the realities of hospital birth, did they decide to reject the technocratic in favor of the wholistic paradigm for subsequent births. The cultural significance of the paradigm shift these women consciously chose to make will be discussed in Chapter 9.

WOMEN-IN-BETWEEN

[Before the birth:]
    It's just such an intense experience you can't be luke-
warm about it. You either have to say oh I'm just so
disappointed because this or that—and it just might be
a minor detail that goes wrong. . . . And if it goes well
I will be up on Cloud Nine about it. But I imagine of
course if something major goes wrong that will be terrible . . . because it's just an intense thing and I have it all
mapped out, all the details, exactly what I want so if
I'm not able to get it that way, I will be disappointed.

[After the birth:] Everything went like I wanted it to!
                                                        —Becky McGee

The majority of women in my study had belief systems that fell in-between the extreme forms of the technocratic and wholistic models. Among these women can be found not only a wide range of beliefs about birth, but also a wide range in types of conceptual outcome of birth, from self-affirming and positive to self-denying and negative—these labels "positive" and "negative" are applied by the women themselves, after the fact, to their experiences. Key elements in determining which label the women will apply are (1) their beliefs and expectations about what the birth should be like and what it actually *is* like; (2) whether or not the knowledge they have accumulated turns out to be sufficient to support them to interpret their birth experiences within their belief systems; (3) the correlation between the degree of control they expect to have and the degree of control they are actually able to maintain; and (4) the degree to which their labor "naturally" conforms to hospital standards.

The beliefs of these women about birth ranged across the spectrum, from strong belief in the powers of technology to strong belief in the integrity of nature. What they do not share with the women in the first technocratic-model category is unquestioning, passive acceptance of modern medicine's way. Unlike the women in the second technocratic-model category, they expected and sought to give birth themselves, but unlike the women who espouse the wholistic model, they hold the belief that the hospital is the safest place to give birth. Some of these women ended up actively demanding highly technological births, some actively rejected them, but all felt that they should have a right to make their own choices, that those choices should include the self-doing of birth, and that education was the key to maximizing that right.

Those women-in-between who actively sought "natural childbirth" based their expectations for achieving a natural birth not so much on trust in the natural process of birth as on the intellectual knowledge they had gathered, which they expected would enable them: (1) to interpret accurately which stage of labor they were in and to assess how well they were progressing (in terms of the technocratic model); (2) to avoid unnecessary intervention; and (3) to participate in deciding what interventions are necessary or at least acceptable. In other words, they expected that this knowledge would enable them to maintain some degree of control over their birthing experiences. Because of that expectation, whether the conceptual outcome of those experiences was positive or negative depended mostly on the woman's perception of the degree of her control over the situation—that is, on the degree to which, *in her perception,* her personal power correlated appropriately with the power of the hospital staff.

For example, even if a woman does not fully accept the belief system in which hospital procedures are grounded, if she has educated herself about these procedures, expects them to be used or chooses that they be used, and is able to control or influence their timing and their manner of application, then the conceptual outcome of her birth can be self-affirming and self-empowering; even if certain individual procedures should arouse in her feelings of anger or humiliation, these will be perceived as peripheral, and not central to the experience, as we will see in the birth stories of Terry Lutzer and Debra Johnson in the following section.

MAINTAINING CONCEPTUAL DISTANCE
FROM THE TECHNOCRATIC MODEL:
ACHIEVING "NATURAL CHILDBIRTH"
IN THE HOSPITAL (15%)

I remember hearing that in Brazil there is a very
high rate of Cesareans, and thinking that there is
something sort of strange about it. I mean, why should
you be so afraid of having a baby if that's what your
organs are there for? If that's part of what your vagina
is for, I mean have it the way you are supposed to have
it!

—Alana Melton

This section contains the birth stories of two women who entered the hospital believing in "natural childbirth" and who came out perceiving their birth experiences as positive and self-empowering. These women also left with their belief in "natural childbirth" as an ideal and in their individual ability to achieve that ideal strengthened and reinforced; in other words, for these two women, the rituals of hospital birth can be said to have failed in their didactic and socializing purposes.

The primary reason for this failure seems to be that, although a number of obstetrical procedures were performed on each of these women, they were able to *maintain conceptual distance* between themselves and those procedures. In other words, they managed to retain their own personal perceptions of their labor experience, their own definitions—the ones they entered the hospital with—all the way through, as we shall see in their stories below.

Terry: "I Was in Charge"

Well, I was very excited to be pregnant and thought it was really neat. I knew it was going to be a great experience. I decided I was going to love being pregnant and I did. I got ahold of every single book I possibly could and read it from cover to cover several times. I was in really good physical shape and I was bound and determined that I would stay really physically fit and that I could teach full time and do this too. . . . And I studied Lamaze and went to the classes with my husband and was sure that I could go the whole way through without any drugs or anything. I went and checked out the hospital, you know, and really knew what the setup was and what it was going to be like and which parts of the "standard hospital procedure" I was going to have to put up with in order to go to the hospital. I never entertained the notion of having the kid at home.

Okay. So I already knew what to expect—that I was going to have an IV, that I was going to have certain kinds of prep that were, you know, hospital policy at the time. I went into labor. . . . I think about nine o'clock in the morning. Nice, easy to control. I just used slow breathing throughout the whole day, took a few walks, crocheted a bit. I was very maternal that day. Um, around five o'clock at night I decided—oh, and I kept eating—I ignored the rule that you are not supposed to eat—I had high protein drinks and stuff like that to keep my energy up—and around five o'clock in the evening I decided I needed a little nap, and I noticed the contractions had been fifteen or twenty minutes apart and very regular for about three hours, easy to manage, and I decided I would take a nap.

Well, I noticed after I laid down my contractions were about two minutes apart and I decided, well, I would check this out for awhile and let it go for about forty-five minutes at two minutes apart. I went out and my husband was reading on the couch and I said, "You know, these contractions have been two minutes apart for about forty-five minutes now" and he freaked. He had just finished medical school at that time and he just totally freaked out. He said, "Oh my God we have got to get to the hospital," blah, blah, blah, and we had a great adventure getting there. I was really starting to get into some hard labor then and I had to really concentrate on my breathing, otherwise it was very, very painful. As long as I could relax and breathe through it, I knew I was doing hard work, but I knew it was working and that felt just fine.

I went through their preps and everything and it seemed that for a good hour-and-a-half my labor slowed down in that the contractions were erratic and were much more painful. . . . They did a partial shave and an enema and put in an IV. That was all. But I knew that it was going to happen and that was part of what made it tolerable was that I knew it was going to happen and that it would be over with quickly and I would be back in control.

That was the way I thought. Part of what happened between 7:30, which was about the time I got into my own room, and 12:45, which was when my son was born, was that they never had a Lamaze-trained woman at that hospital, or they had had so few that most of those interns and residents had not seen such a marvelous phenomenon. So there were people constantly coming in and out of the room to see what I was doing and ask me things like "How are you doing?" you know, right in the middle of breathing through a contraction. That was a little irritating. There was an anesthesiologist who came in five or six times to tell me I didn't have to be a martyr, and why didn't I take something, and I finally yelled obscenities at the man and told him to get his butt out of the room, and he turned around and opened the door and said, "Just 50 cc of Demerol?" And I got really pissed and told my husband who had been in that [hospital] that he was to keep all of those lookielous out, all of those "observers" out, and things just rolled along from then.

The transition was really hard, just that wanting to push and [them] telling me to wait. But it only lasted about half an hour, and I just panted through the whole thing. Then, once I started pushing, I thought it was fabulous and the kid crowned while I was in the bed and then, of course, due to their policy they had to move me over to the delivery room. It didn't bother me though because I knew everything was fine and I knew my kid was going to be born just fine.

I had an episiotomy, which was a shitty one I found out later. It was a lousy episiotomy. I didn't need it, and you see, I was brave enough at the time that I said to the doctor, "Look, just look at the skin down there. You can tell it is totally anesthetized. It is as white as can be. There is no blood in there. I won't do it." You know, because he was trying to give me this tiny little local so I would not feel it. I said, "I am not going to feel it."

So, anyway, my son was born around 12:45. He was incredibly alert, really lively, and it just blew my mind because he was so gorgeous. He was 8 lbs. 2 oz. and he was very, very long. He looked like this gigantic long, skinny kid and he was very vocal right away. They didn't have to do anything, I mean, he got pink in about two seconds. . . .

Right after he was born, they took him over to a crib . . . about eight to ten feet away from me but I could see him and I could see everything that they were doing. I also knew that that was what was going to happen, so it didn't bother me that I didn't hold him right away. That part didn't bother me. It bugged the hell out of me that they turned him upside down and held him by his ankles and measured him, but I thought justice was served because he immediately peed in the face of the nurse that was doing it. I thought it was just wonderful, and I just started cracking up and I shouted over to him, because I knew his name was Rick already, and I said, "All right, Rick! You can show her!" You know, she just got saturated with urine and then he got wrapped up. They put drops in his eyes really early and of course, I wasn't aware at the time the effect that can have. I got to hold him for a few minutes and then they took me to recovery and they took him to the nursery.

But the giving birth itself was really satisfying. . . . I felt incredibly powerful and absolutely delighted. I felt that I knew exactly what was happening, that I was, you know, that it was really a neat kind of letting go, that being totally in control kind of feeling. . . . And I just remember it as being an extremely positive and an incredibly powerful kind of feeling. My perception of it was that I was in charge and these other people were here as my assistants. That was the way I really saw it. I was giving the doctor orders, and he would say to me, "Don't push" and I would say "I am not pushing right now" as if it were my idea not to push right now. I remember there was once he told me to push and I said "No, I am waiting for the contraction." I had no anesthetic at all, so I could really feel everything that was going on, and just a real sense that what was supposed to be happening was happening.

I really—when I try to get a picture in my mind, I can't really see the delivery room. I can see my body, you know. . . . The memories I have are of my body there, you know, and my feet were in stirrups. My arms were not tied or anything. It was hospital policy to do it, but I told them that I wouldn't go to the hospital if they tied my arms. I didn't mind if they tied my legs down because I knew I would still be able to push with the ankles. I checked it out, you know, so it is sort of like what I had given approval for, then I would just let go and I wouldn't worry about it, and the things I didn't give approval for, they didn't do to me. You know, there is that whole issue of why should we even have to fight for such basic rights, but in terms of my own personal experience, I just—my main memory is just a feeling one and it is a feeling of incredible power and of being very very much in charge and being absolutely delighted to see this very strong and incredibly alert baby.

Debra: "I Just Refused to Let Him Ruin It for Me"

We took Lamaze, but about six days past my due date, my water broke, and I would have gone for at least another week if it hadn't, because when I went into the hospital, the cervix was so thick and tough and only a fingertip dilated and my doctor was not on call—the other doctor was on call, and he came in and he checked me—he didn't tell me his name—and he turned to the nurse that was with him and said, "Prep her, we're going to cut it out." I said, "Hold it, hold it—you're not doing anything until you tell me what is going on here." He said, "Baby time. You're not dilating; you need a C-section." I said, "That will be fine as long as you can write down a medical reason why I need a section."

I knew I had twenty-four hours after my water broke to deliver. I knew that I had—I knew that was routine, and he said, "You just need one." I said, "I'm sorry—that's not good enough." He said, "Okay, if you don't make this much progress by this afternoon we'll do tests and do a section." I said, "We'll wait and see" and I laid there all day and hardly did anything. He wouldn't start a drip or anything like that, which I knew he should have because I read some books before I went into labor and he came in that afternoon and was very angry because I wouldn't okay the section, but he couldn't give me a medical reason—he just said, "Because you need one." And about 7 o'clock that evening he finally realized that I was not going to have a section just because he did not want to stay at the hospital. I found out afterwards that I was the only patient in labor on Saturday, and I don't really think he wanted to hang around all night, but we called our Lamaze teacher, Fran, and she came to the hospital. I had supportive nurses but even though they couldn't contradict him they could say, "You're doing fine, the baby's fine, everything's fine." As long as I knew everything was fine, I could last forever.

But he did start a drip that evening, and as soon as he did I picked right up and started going, but I had made little progress, so I had a long way to go until the next morning, which at 4:00 A.M. was twenty-four hours. He was very nasty. He would come in, send my husband out, check me, yell at me because I wasn't doing what he told me to do. He made my husband sign a paper saying that we would take full responsibility for the death of my child and all this. "You know," he said, "you're killing this baby because you won't have a section." I said, "I'll have one if you tell me why." He said, "Just because I say you need one," and I said, "That's not good enough." He was just terrible.

The funny thing was, we were fine. When he was out of the room, labor was wonderful. I enjoyed it. Tremendous Lamaze—it was great. I don't think childbirth is painful, actually. My mother thinks I'm crazy, because she says, "Well, you just don't remember," but using the Lamaze, and with my husband there, I don't really think of pain or anything like that. I had a transition that was twice as long as normal, and then when I did get completely dilated, she was very high, so I had to push for two or three hours to get her down before she could be born. Finally, at 5:36 A.M. she was born.

We were glad we didn't have the section. He just didn't want to hang around. We were glad we didn't have the section because it was fine. When he wasn't there, we were fine.

And when she was born, he cut a radical episiotomy, and I had already made arrangements with Dr. Snyder, my regular doctor, not to have one if I didn't need one. But when her head was barely capping, he just did the old radical by cutting up the vagina and down in the perineum and up into the rectum and her head was only thirteen inches. She just flew out like a cannon ball because he really didn't need to do that—she weighed 8½ pounds, and she flew out and he laid her up there and he didn't even say, "It's a girl or it's a boy, it's a dog, it's a cat"—he didn't say anything. . . . And then when he stitched me up he said—they usually give you a pudendal block, which is no big deal, but they do work, and he stitched me up with nothing. I kept telling him I could feel everything he was doing, and he kept saying "No you can't feel that, you're crazy," and he wouldn't give me anything else, but I knew he did it just for spite . . . because I kept telling him, "Look, I can feel you stitching me up," and it wasn't like he just had a few stitches to go, because he had made a radical incision. . . .

If I can block him out of the picture, then everything is wonderful, 'cause my husband was great. . . . he did everything for me. It was such a long time, because I went in at 6:00 A.M. and I didn't have her until the next morning. He stayed with me the whole time, and then when things really got going, and even though the nurses were supportive, they don't stay with you all the time—everybody has this picture of nurses hovering over your bed—they don't. They come in and look at your monitor and leave. He just did everything. Whatever I needed, he took care of it. I think if it had been our second child, we would have told the doctor to forget it, and let an intern deliver her because that was too much hassle, and it was hard for him to intervene between the doctor and myself because they would send him out of the room. . . . It was distressing because he couldn't intercept, but as soon as he would come back into the room everything would be okay . . . and what was good, too, was Fran was there . . . and the doctor thought she was a nurse, and so when he would send Steve out, she couldn't say anything, but she would stand there and hold my hand and squeeze it all the time he was yelling and screaming and being really nasty, and then as soon as the guy would leave she would hurry Steve back in. That was very good, because she couldn't give us advice, and she couldn't say the doctor was wrong. But the information that she supplied to us helped us make the decision, because we had to make a decision. We had to say, "Yes, we are going to have it," or "No, we are not." So that was a big help—all day and all through the night.

It was very enjoyable when he wasn't there, but like he would come in and check me and leave and scare me to death. . . . He would be checking me during a contraction and I would be blowing my heart out, doing the Lamaze, and I would try to ignore as much of what he said as possible, but as soon as he would leave the room, my body would involuntarily tremble all over. My legs and my arms would just shake all over. I had no control over it. . . . I had that kind of physical reaction to him. It was probably psychological stress that caused the tremors. They would hold my arms and legs down, and they would go away. I wouldn't do it again until he came in and did a little number on me and left.

Comparative Analysis   It becomes apparent from reading Terry's story that she did not internalize the basic tenets of the technocratic model during her birth, in spite of the efforts of the hospital staff to get her to do so. How did she manage to maintain her conceptual distance so successfully? First of all, she did not enter the hospital alone and unaided. She took with her a series of conceptual buffers that she had carefully accumulated before her birth, and which ultimately proved sufficient to prevent any deep degree of fusion between her model of reality and the hospital's.

1. The first of these buffers was the intellectual knowledge with which she equipped herself concerning pregnancy and birth, from

"every single book I could find," from her Lamaze classes, and from the hospital itself. This knowledge taught her exactly what she could expect from the hospital, as well as exactly what she could expect to successfully avoid.

2. She kept herself in good physical shape and cultivated a healthy mental attitude toward her pregnancy, both of which are excellent means to avoid being plugged into the "pregnancy as pathology" tenet of the technocratic model, and to stay on the "mind/body integration" side of the wholistic model.

3. During labor she ignored one of the basic rules of the technocratic model, the tabu against eating. This enabled her to keep her energy level high, which in turn enabled her to avoid the kind of physical exhaustion that might have resulted in her conceptual fusion with the defective machine metaphors of the technocratic model. Moreover, her conscious refusal to abide by this basic rule constituted a powerful statement on her part, early on in labor, that she was not going to play the game entirely by the rules of the technocratic model, but rather, would make some of her own.

4. Terry accepted as inevitable the interventions she knew in advance the hospital would insist upon, but she did not accept them as *necessary*. Throughout her narrative, she refers to these hospital routines as "*their* preps and everything," "*their* policy." In other words, she did not buy into the idea that she was conceptually dirty and so needed a shave and an enema, or that her machine was so defective that she needed an IV. As a result, when these procedures were performed upon her, instead of internalizing their messages, she regarded them as temporary nuisances, knowing that soon she would be "back in control."

5. Far from respecting hospital personnel as authority figures, Terry refers to her would-be observers as "lookielous"; when she began to feel conceptually threatened and to feel the need to defend herself, her husband proved to be an effective buffer against their intrusions into the protective conceptual barriers she had thrown up around herself.

6. Terry's labor was well within the parameters of "normal" as defined by the technological model, and her baby was completely healthy; thus she was buffered by the model *itself* from too much intervention.

7. She was not prepared for and was upset by the treatment her baby received; however, her son found his own means of maintaining conceptual distance, thereby restoring Terry's psychological equilibrium.

Terry's conceptual experience of her birth consists of a fascinating series of inversions of the technocratic model. She transformed hospital procedures into silly-but-bearable nuisances, the doctor's orders into her own ideas, the hospital staff into her assistants instead of his, the lithotomy position into something useful for pushing, and her passage into motherhood into a rite of self-empowerment.

Like Terry, Debra took with her into the hospital a set of conceptual buffers that proved sufficient to ward off conceptual fusion between her perceptions of her birth experience and the technological model, although in Debra's case conceptual distance proved considerably harder to maintain. Her most powerful and effective buffers were (1) her own knowledge; (2) her husband and her Lamaze coach, Fran; (3) a supportive nursing staff.

Her own knowledge enabled Debra to use the technocratic model itself against the obstetrician who attended her, as under that model, a woman has twenty-four hours to deliver before the danger of infection to the baby necessitates a Cesarean section. She knew that she had grounds for a suit if the doctor could not put in writing a strong medical indication for a Cesarean section; she also knew that there was no such indication.

Although her husband anchored and grounded her when the doctor was not present, the fact that he was sent out when the doctor came in rendered him ineffective in buffering Debra from the technocratic reality that the doctor brought with him into her labor room. At these times, it was Fran's presence that enabled Debra to distance herself from the doctor's powerful efforts to impose the technocratic model upon her by telling her that she was killing her baby and the like. The pressure of Fran's hand on hers served as a reassuring reminder to Debra that the doctor did not represent the only reality there was. That the doctor was near to succeeding in his efforts to draw her reality model into his is clearly indicated by the way her body would tremble after he left; without the buffering support of her husband, Fran, and the nurses, she might not have been able to withstand his insistence on a Cesarean.

At the actual moment of birth, Debra's knowledge enabled her to conceptually distance the radical episiotomy the doctor cut; she knew she didn't need one, and thus was able to interpret his actions as "spite" instead of incorporating the idea that her machine was defective.

In order to help herself maintain conceptual ownership of her birth, Debra has almost split her labor experience in her mind. When speaking of her labor when the doctor was not there, she dwelt on the pleasure she felt in the physical experience of labor and on the warmth, love, and support she received from her husband. She takes great pleasure in remembering this part of her labor, saying that she wouldn't give that doctor the pleasure of succeeding in his efforts to spoil her birth experience, that, in the end, "I just refused to let him ruin it for me."

Although their presence in the hospital meant that both Terry and Debra did already hold in their belief systems several points of correspondence with the technocratic model of birth, they were both successful in preventing further fusion between their perceptions of their birth experiences and that model. Both were aided in this endeavor by the high degree of conformity between their labors and the hospital standard; Terry gave birth within six hours of arriving at the hospital, and Debra made it within the allowed twenty-four. *Both women were thus buffered by the technocratic model itself.*

On top of that, the knowledge each had accumulated proved sufficient to ward off the unnecessary interventions (in Terry's case, anesthesia; in Debra's, anesthesia and Cesarean section) proffered by hospital personnel, but only when combined with the physical presence of their husbands; in Debra's case, the force of this intervention was so extreme that the additional presence of Debra's Lamaze coach, who brought with her not only a comforting presence but additional, authoritative knowledge as well, was essential.

The birth experiences of Terry and Debra are representative of 15 percent of the birth experiences of the women in my study group; those women whose birth experiences fit into this category (*maintaining conceptual distance in the hospital through achieving natural childbirth*) entered the hospital believing in natural childbirth as an ideal and in their ability to achieve that ideal. They left with those beliefs reinforced and with enhanced pictures of their strength and ability as women and as birth-givers. In other words, for this group of women, the rituals of hospital birth can be said to have failed in their didactic and socializing purposes. These women not only refused to receive the messages sent by these rituals, but also turned those messages back on the hospital, rewriting them with alternative messages of their own.

MAINTAINING CONCEPTUAL DISTANCE FROM THE TECHNOCRATIC MODEL: PLACING TECHNOLOGY AT THE SERVICE OF THE INDIVIDUAL (10%)

In this section, we will hear the birth stories of two women who were able to maintain conceptual distance between themselves and the technocratic model, not through achieving natural childbirth in the hospital, but through the attitudes with which they approached hospital procedures. The critical factor for them seems to be the degree of control which *they felt* they were able to maintain over their birth experiences: in their perceptions, hospital technology was *at their service,* instead of the other way around.

Roxanne: "I Did It My Way"   Sure of her ability to give birth, Roxanne considered having her first baby at home with two midwives as her attendants. She had gone through the initial interviews with the midwives and was very pleased with them; however, her husband objected strongly to the $900 fee (standard for that midwifery service for complete maternity care, the fee included monthly prenatal exams and counseling, and postpartum visits) on the grounds that their medical insurance would make even a Cesarean section completely free. Agreeing that they were in severe financial straits and could not really afford the midwives, Roxanne made a philosophical decision that she was simply going to go to the hospital and "have it my way there":

> Early labor was easy. I was having a great time with the contractions, and teasing my husband that I might just stay and have it at home with only him to catch it. He freaked out, left, and came in a few minutes later to tell me he had the car running and we were ready to go. We headed on in.
>
> Well, what can I tell you? We got there, and they started to prep me. Every time a nurse came in to do something, he would snarl at her and be really rude. I know he was just trying to be my shining knight on a white horse and protect me from all the bad guy hospital procedures—but the way he did it, he just made everything so awful. He made the nurses mad over and over, because he was so rude to them, and then I would have to play peacemaker, and be extra-nice to them so they would be nice to me. I didn't really care if they hooked up all their stupid stuff—I knew I didn't need it, but it didn't bother me all that much. What bothered me more was the way Tom was acting. I just wanted peace and emotional support from him, and here he was playing big macho man warrior.
>
> Then they wanted to hook up the internal monitor, and I didn't want them to do it. I didn't want that for me or my baby. And the contractions were really intense, and I was really in pain, and I didn't feel like hassling it anymore. So I said to myself, "Fuck this—it's not even worth trying. I just want to have this baby right now and get all this over with." So I told the nurse I wanted to see a doctor right away because I wanted a C-section. And she said "Oh, you don't need a C-section—you are progressing fine and you haven't even been here that long." I said, "I want a C-section, and I'm having one right now—GET THE DOCTOR!" So she scurries out of the room and gets him, and I told him what I wanted, and he said I didn't need one, and I said, "Too bad, I'm having one anyway, because that's what I

want to do," and he said, "Okay, okay" and went off to get things ready—and from then on, everybody did just what I told them to.

Louise: "I Want That Epidural" Louise Daniels is a well-known and successful attorney. One of the first women to enter her firm, she was also one of the youngest members of the firm to make full partner. She never thought she would have any trouble giving birth, and she didn't. But she did not espouse the natural ideal; she said she knew some people thought the total experience was really important, but that she had no desire to be in pain, that "what's good for the goose isn't good for the gander":

> Labor and birth was really pretty easy for me. I didn't have any problem with it. I was at the office when I started having contractions, but they didn't bother me too much, so I kept on working for a while. Finally the contractions got noticeable enough for me to decide I should do something about them. So I called Ron and we went to the hospital. I was having contractions all the way there, but they weren't really too bad, not anything really too difficult to deal with. When the doctor checked me, he said, "We're going to have a baby just any minute now!"—I was already 8 centimeters. And I said, "I want that epidural!" and he said "Okay!" and that's about all there was to it. There were no problems with the birth—it was all really easy.
>
> [Question: Have you ever had second thoughts about the epidural?]
>
> No, I haven't. It was exactly what I wanted. I didn't have anything to prove.

Comparative Analysis Roxanne told me her birth story two days after the birth; she was sitting up in her hospital bed enjoying her dinner, and indeed, she looked like a queen bee in her very own hive. She repeated that she had no regrets about not having had her "natural" birth; she felt strongly that, for her, staying in control of the situation had mattered most. In her insistence on a Cesarean, when under the technocratic model she could not be defined as needing one, she turned that model back on itself in a most interesting way. Instead of being the victim of medical technology, she became its conceptual master. Like Terry, Roxanne felt that she had placed the hospital staff and all their technology at her service, instead of herself at theirs.

Roxanne entered the hospital believing in the natural ideal; Louise did not. But Roxanne was able to turn her failure to achieve that ideal into a personal, instead of a medical, victory. Victory was not an issue for Louise, as she did not feel that she had anything to fight against in the first place. Both of these women experienced their births as self-empowering. Neither doubted her ability to give birth for a moment; however, neither considered it necessary to put forth any effort to prove that she could do so. For both of these women, hospital technology was a convenience, something that they could bend to their wills in order to achieve the kind of nontraumatic, self-empowering birth experiences they desired. These women used the technocratic model *without* internalizing its metaphors.

The birth experiences of Roxanne and Louise are representative of 10 percent of the birth experiences of the women in my study (I categorize them as: *maintaining conceptual distance from the technocratic model through placing technology at the service of the individual*). There are obvious similarities between Roxanne and Louise and the women discussed in the second technocratic model category ("Schedule my Cesarean"). The major difference is that for those women, natural childbirth—actively doing birth themselves—was not originally a primary expectation or desire, whereas Roxanne and Louise and the women in this study whom they represent did enter labor expecting to give birth actively themselves. In the end, these women maintained conceptual distance from the technocratic model not through achieving natural childbirth, but through the attitudes with which they regarded obstetrical procedures. Like Terry and Debra, they did not regard these procedures as necessary. Unlike them, they regarded at least some of these procedures as conveniences to them. They regarded the hospital staff, including the obstetrician, and the hospital's wide array of technology, as being at *their* service instead of the other way around. In their cases, hospital birth rituals can be said to have both failed and succeeded: these women's sense of and belief in the core values of our society was strengthened, but *so was their sense of themselves* in relation to these things. In other words, these two women (and the eight others they represent) came out of their birth experiences feeling that science, technology, institutions, and the people who run them are important and valuable, and are there to serve, not society, but birthing women.

CONCEPTUAL FUSION WITH THE
TECHNOCRATIC MODEL: WITH
COGNITIVE EASE (42%)

In this section, we will hear the birth stories of two women who entered the hospital believing in "natural childbirth," but who ended up with, in the first case, a heavily technocratic birth, and in the second case, a Cesarean section. These experiences did not reinforce or confirm the women's original belief in "natural childbirth" as an ideal that they could achieve. Nevertheless, these women both came out of the hospital perceiving their birth experiences as positive and feeling to some extent empowered by them. Even though their birth experiences failed to meet their expectations, these two women did not feel themselves to be failures. The determining factor for them seems to have been their beliefs that the medical interventions they experienced were justified, appropriate, and necessary.

Lydia: "Serenity and Joy"   The following story is from Lydia Smith's written Lamaze story-report (a form she filled out for her Lamaze teacher after the birth):

My eyes flickered open just as the first rays of sunlight filtered through the clouds. I watched the world from our window as it awakened, and I knew this was a special day. Just at that moment a trickle of water ran down my legs. Suddenly my entire body was filled with butterflies. Our baby was really on his way. I rolled over and quickly nudged Ken and said, "My water broke, it's really time!!" and we both smiled. The next half-hour was quite a rush. I sat in the bathroom for a while letting more fluid flow out while Ken ran around gathering things. He called Dr. Owens and told him our water had broken, and Dr. Owens asked if our bags were packed and then told us to start for the hospital. I took a shower and shaved my legs and put up my hair, and we were off.

The drive to Dunlap was the most beautiful imaginable. It was 6:30 A.M. and no traffic. The air smelled so clean, and there was the fresh calm feeling one finds only at that time of day. The mountains and trees soaring to the heavens made me think of our wedding day and how much love we shared. I could feel us both moving closer to each other with our entire beings as I sat next to Ken and gazed into his eyes. As we neared Dunlap, our hopes and expectations grew, and tears filled both our eyes.

We arrived, and I was ushered into an examining room where three nurses checked my dilation. It was a messy process and no dilation at all. Just a slight disappointment. Just after that, I felt my first contraction. It was very mild, and I was so thrilled that it was there. An hour later, Dr. Owens appeared, and had us moved to the labor room. We began to move things in. Ken was sent away for a few minutes while they "prepped" me. A very friendly nurse gave me a "poodle" shave and an enema. (I had given myself an enema at home, but put up no argument because I had doubts as to its complete effectiveness, besides, the excitement outweighed any inconvenience.) Ken joined me again, and we talked and giggled and began to write down the contractions even though they were mild. My mother and grandmother came in a few hours and were in and out, making this birth quite a family affair. The next time I was checked for dilation was quite some time later and still no progress. The doctor had hoped that because of the excellent condition I was in, that we would have our baby by 7:00 or so that night. Seven came and went and still no progress with dilation but the contractions were getting rougher. Ken and I had been using Lamaze breathing techniques. The slow breathing with effleurage worked well until late that night, then we began to use pant-blow. The contractions had still not stabilized into a pattern. Susan Jones came and added another bright face and warm conversation. She was there to photograph the entire miracle of our child's birth.

Everyone was beginning to fade as the hours dragged on . . . [but] Ken stayed by my side constantly. He knew he was the only one that really knew the way to help me. Not only with the breathing and such, but he was helping me to the bathroom constantly which always worsened my contractions. The best help he gave, of course, was emotional. He gave everything I needed, and more.

Dr. Owens came in again and I had begun to dilate a bit but not enough and it was now more than twenty-four hours past the time my water had broken, so he felt it necessary to speed up the contractions with a pitocin drip. My greatest dread of all was coming to a reality—I had to have an IV and of course, they had a hard time finding a vein. Then the needle slipped out and my arm was a bit swollen. This was only a temporary setback and they put it in the other arm. (The IV made the trips to the bathroom more hazardous.) The drip made the contractions more intense but not regular. Dilation was not progressing rapidly enough either. We discovered later that my bag of waters had resealed so we broke it again. By this time we were well into our second day and contractions were very difficult. We all needed sleep so Ken crawled into bed with me and we caught quick naps (one to ten minutes) between contractions. . . .

With still very little progress, Dr. Owens ordered an x-ray. Our baby's head was not engaged and not moving very quickly to the correct position so he wanted to check to see if there were any unexpected complications. There were none, and we saw that he was perfectly shaped, which put our minds at ease. By this time we had begun to worry. Forty-five hours had passed and my contractions were almost unbearable especially since there was little progress. The doctor began to talk of Cesarean section. . . . Ken and I discussed it and had almost decided to go through with it. Just before they rolled me into delivery, the doctor checked me one last time for dilation. I had dilated a lot more and the baby's head was almost completely engaged. We decided to take him out with low forceps. By this time I was obviously much too tired to be much help during delivery so I agreed to a saddle block and I am very glad I did. Ken was then free to stand over Dr. Owen's shoulder and watch our baby emerge from his soon to be former home, and I was free to see him appear calmly rather than with any sort of pain. Ken said that it was so beautiful to see our baby come out and to be able to look at my face filled with only serenity and joy. All of a sudden, almost before I knew it, there was a beautiful baby boy on my tummy. He did not cry until the mucus was sucked from his mouth. He was perfect. They took him over to a table to perform the circumcision and Ken nearly died. That was the worst part of all. The next thing I knew, I was being rolled down the hall to my room and lifted onto the bed. Ken and the baby were right by my side and we all fell comfortably and happily asleep together! Our beautiful Kenneth was really here to become part of this world.

Beryl: "We Had to Do a C-Section"

My first baby was an emergency C-section. The cord was around the neck. I was connected up to a fetal heart monitor. His heartbeat was dropping so low that it was going off the chart. And they said, "We are going to have to take it." I said, "Oh." I didn't know what they were talking about. So, they took it.

It was a real long, hard labor. I was in labor three days. I was at home the first two days, because they say don't call the doctor unless they are at least five minutes close together. So we didn't call the doctor. They would be five minutes for about half an hour and then jump back up to twenty and then ten and fifteen. I started Thursday morning and then Saturday morning I was real tired so we called the doctor and he said, "Well, you can come in and let me check you." I went in, and he said, "You are 2.5 centimeters. We can either induce you or send you home." I said, "Well, I don't want to go back home, I'm too tired." So they induced. I was on the pit drip from 9 to 5:30. Then they did the C-section.

[Question: Would you do that any differently now?]

I really feel like, well what we knew, we felt like we were very well read. We read everything that we could get our hands on before the birth of Jim, but we didn't read anything on C-sections. We even went through the natural childbirth classes, but nobody tells you about C-sections. . . . I just really feel that we were with the doctor that we should have been with and that it was in the Lord's hands. I just feel like He took care of things. I feel like we had to do a C-section with that one, simply because I was right there and saw the fetal heart monitor and I saw the little thing, whatever it is, going off the chart. Of course they say now that fetal heart monitors half the time don't tell the truth. I don't know if we would have done anything different. That's a hard question, I think. . . . See, when I first asked my obstetrician about having natural birth after one C-section, he said—he cussed me out and told me he wanted to talk to my daddy because he knew my daddy loves me. He said he had been down in Texas where they were trying that out. You know, closely monitoring someone with C-sections and he had witnessed a close friend of his—the lady ruptured, the baby died, and then she went into shock and died, which I know is a rarity, but he was using that to scare me. It did scare me. I didn't want anything to happen to the baby. I guess going back to your question, would I have done anything differently, I almost would have to say no because I simply don't think I would want to jeopardize losing the baby. If they came in and said that his heartbeat is so low that it is going off the monitor, we *have* to do a C-section.

[Question: You were asleep the first time, and awake the last three times? What were the differences in those experiences?]

Asleep—well it is like your mama tells you when you are little and they say, "We are going to have a birthday party next week." And the whole seven days you are built up for a big birthday party, and then comes the day of the birthday party, and they say, "We are not having it anymore." And they even have had the decorations and the cake up, and they say, "No. We are not having your birthday party." And I found that very very hard after—you know, you go to your childbirth classes, and that is all it is, is a wonderful, wonderful experience—and then you do a C-section, and for a while I thought, well, I really did question what was wrong with me. I am not the natural kind of woman that I am supposed to be. The baby is o.k., so, you know. It took me about three months to think through things in my mind as far as what I thought, and then with I guess, the last . . . three C-sections, they were really neat. . . . The first and second one—the first was a boy and the second was a girl, and with the third one I just knew it was going to be a boy and I wanted a girl and they pulled her out and said, "It's a girl!" and I just was on cloud nine. I was just ecstatic.

Comparative Analysis   Although Lydia's avowed intention was to have her baby "as naturally as possible," it becomes apparent early on in her story that she did not enter the hospital with a belief system radically different from the technocratic model of birth, that, indeed, her belief system shared several crucial tenets with the technocratic model: for example, that when the waters break one must head for the hospital whether labor had started or not; once there, one should stay there, and labor should proceed and steady dilation should occur; if it does not, remedial measures are appropriate and should be taken. None of these are givens under the wholistic model.

Like Terry and Debra, Lydia hoped for a "natural birth." Like them, she took with her into the hospital a set of conceptual buffers between her perceptions of her birth experience and the technocratic model: the knowledge she had gained from the Lamaze classes she took, her husband, and her relatives and friends. However, both Terry and Debra had labors that conformed to the hospital standard and were thus buffered by the technocratic model itself. Lydia's labor was very far out of conformity with the hospital norm; when it became subject to intervention under the technocratic model, her buffers proved insufficient to maintain conceptual distance between her perceptions of her birth experience and the technocratic model. Nor did she particularly endeavor to use her buffers as such. Because of the high degree of conformity between her belief system and the technocratic model, she *herself* felt that her labor was simply not proceeding as it should have (i.e., she had internalized the message that her machine was defective). She accepted the 24-hour time limit as appropriate (indeed, in many other hospitals a Cesarean would have been performed long before her obstetrician suggested one), and thus was open to her doctor's suggestion that it was "necessary to speed up the contractions with a pitocin drip"—her greatest dread. Her acceptance of the pitocin cemented her acceptance of the notion that her machine was defective; it took an X ray of the baby to convince her that the baby himself remained undamaged.

Under the wholistic model, the resealing of the bag of waters is interpreted as an indication that the baby is not ready to be born and often entails a redefinition of the woman's experience as being "early labor," during which the woman should stay home, eat as much as possible, rest as much as possible, and assume that she is in for a lengthy labor—a perfectly normal condition. In contrast, Lydia's obstetrician had engendered in her and her husband the expectation that the baby would be born by 7:00 P.M.; when that hour came and went, she began to see herself as making "very little progress" and to define her labor as dysfunctional, *because she was interpreting it under the technocratic model.*

Within that cognitive matrix, the subsequent interventions were appropriate; thus Lydia did not find them conceptually overwhelming, since she herself accepted them as appropriate to the circumstances of her "dysfunctional" labor. Given her complete acceptance of this dysfunctionality, she was lucky to avoid the Cesarean that she and her husband had already accepted as appropriate. It is significant that she did not yet consider Cesarean section absolutely *necessary*—the baby was fine, but she felt that she had reached the end of her own endurance, and that given *her* limitations, and the high value placed on Cesarean birth under the technocratic model, a Cesarean section would have been *appropriate.*

Lydia was proud that she and her husband had handled themselves so well under the circumstances and was happy with the outcome of her birth. She attributes this happiness in large part to her successful use of the Lamaze breathing rituals, to the enhanced closeness and trust in her husband which resulted from both the emotional and technical support he provided to her, to the perfection of her baby, and to the saddle block that enabled her to watch her baby appear with "serenity and joy."

In Lydia's case, to the extent that they reinforced her already-held beliefs in our core value system, the rituals of hospital birth can be said to have succeeded in their didactic and socializing purposes. Their success, however, was not personally traumatizing to Lydia, because her failure to achieve the natural childbirth she had desired was not perceived as personal failure but as circumstance, as the simple and inevitable result of mechanical malfunction. The rituals performed upon her did not overthrow her belief system; they strengthened it. At the same time, her perceptions of herself were made more positive through her birth. She perceived her birth as self-empowering both because it had brought her husband closer to her, because she had grown a healthy and beautiful baby, and because, in spite of all obstacles, she felt she had behaved with dignity in the face of a bewildering, chaotic, and painful labor process, and in front of the numerous hospital personnel who had participated in that process. As a result, her opinions of science and technology, *and* her opinions of herself and her family, were simultaneously strengthened by her birth experience.

Like Lydia, Beryl entered the hospital believing in "natural childbirth"; the classes she took engendered in her the expectation that birth was "a wonderful, wonderful experience." Like Lydia, Beryl's conceptual buffers proved ineffective to prevent conceptual fusion between Beryl's perceptions of her birth and the technocratic model, because she too shared a number of basic beliefs with that model. For example, she believed, at the time of her birth, in the accuracy of fetal monitors and in the appropriateness of their use on her body during labor.

Fusion with the technocratic model began, in Beryl's case, when she stayed at the hospital on Saturday morning and let the doctor induce her because she was "too tired." She thus defined herself from the beginning of her hospital birth experience as weak and in need of technocratic assistance to give birth. The pitocin put additional pressure on her baby and his umbilical cord during contractions for eight and a half hours, pressure that may well have led to the fetal distress that registered on the monitor and resulted immediately in the emergency Cesarean. Once called into conceptual play, the technocratic model has a powerful way of shaping physiological reality to the template it provides.

Beryl was indeed psychologically affected by her birth experience, not so much because she had a technocratic birth, but because she was not there to witness that birth. She had entered the hospital expecting to be an active agent in a "wonderful, wonderful" experience, but she would have settled, as did Lydia (and most of the women in this category), for simply being "present" to her experience, to witnessing the birth of her child. Her enforced absence made her question her competence and her very identity as a woman, a conceptual trauma that she was ultimately able to reconcile because her conceptual fusion with the technocratic model was so complete that she really believed that the Cesarean was necessary. This fusion was later cemented by her obstetrician, who told her a scare story to keep her from even considering vaginal birth after Cesarean; not only did that story serve the purpose for which it was intended, but also it reinforced in Beryl's mind the necessity and appropriateness of the original Cesarean. Her belief in this necessity ensured that Beryl, although not empowered by her birth experience, would not experience long-term trauma as a result of that experience. She was aided in her reinterpretation of that experience as simply necessary by her subsequent Cesareans, during which she was awake and thus was able to conceptually reestablish herself as "present" to her births. (The reinterpretation of negative birth experiences through subsequent births will be discussed in the following chapter.)

Lydia felt self-empowered by her birth; Beryl did not. Lydia believed that the medical interventions were the necessary results of simple mechanical malfunction and thus did not question her adequacy as a woman and birth-giver after her forceps delivery. Beryl, on the other hand, did question her personal adequacy as a woman and birth-giver after her Cesarean, but was able to arrive at a fairly rapid reconciliation of the self-image of inadequacy and absence given to her through her birth, and the self-image of strength, competence, and presence she needed to hold as a mother. The positive conceptual outcomes both women were able to reach after their births seemed to stem primarily from the deep beliefs held by these women that the hospital interventions they experienced were right and appropriate.

Beryl and Lydia are representative of 42 percent of the women in my study, who entered the hospital believing to some degree in the natural childbirth ideal, but who did not feel like personal failures when their actual births turned out not to fit that ideal. (I have labeled this category *conceptual fusion with the technocratic model during birth, with cognitive ease.*) For these women, the rituals of hospital birth can be said to have succeeded in their didactic and socializing purposes. *That success was facilitated by the high degree of prior correspondence between the mother's belief system and the technocratic model.* (In other words, the women in this category already believed in many of the basic tenets of the model on which these rituals are based.) Although that success meant that these women thoroughly internalized messages of their own inadequacy as birth-givers and of the inherent dysfunctionality of their machines, they were not permanently traumatized over the long term because that success *confirmed,* instead of undermined, the belief systems with which they entered the hospital. (This category encompasses the experiences of more of the women in my study than any other. The sociocultural significance of that fact will be considered in Chapter 8.)

CONCEPTUAL FUSION WITH THE
TECHNOCRATIC MODEL DURING BIRTH:
WITH COGNITIVE DISTRESS (9%)

In this final category, we will look at the birth stories of two other women in my study who went into the hospital believing in "natural childbirth" and came out feeling like failures. For these women, at least over the short term, the rituals of hospital birth can be said to have succeeded in their didactic and socializing purposes. But because the belief systems with which these women entered the hospital contained few points of correspondence with the technocratic model (they both believed passionately in "natural childbirth" as an ideal that they could and should achieve), the undermining of these cognitive matrices by the rituals of hospital birth resulted in long-term psychological trauma and rage (and eventually, for one of them, in the total rejection of the technocratic model and its messages, as we will investigate in Chapter 6).

Charisse: "I Lied to You"

I exercised all through my pregnancy, every single day. I felt totally in tune with my body. And I thought I was gorgeous being pregnant. I felt really good and I really enjoyed it. Then one night we were watching the Blue Lagoon on HBO and I was feeling a little just like cramps. It was incredible. You never know what they are going to feel like. It wasn't—like I thought it was going to be . . . just vague and general. But they were very regular. So I went to the nursery and got this stopwatch and Garrett went, "Oh, come on. You are not going to get me out of here tonight." But then, we started timing them and they were thirty seconds long and five minutes apart—just like clockwork. It was amazing that they were so timed. He got his long trenchcoat out and took me for a long walk, thinking it would get rid of them, because the doctor said to take a long walk, and if they still persist, to call him. So we stayed home a long time. . . . but then we knew this was it and I just started shaking, just shaking in excitement and I had

just packed my bags two days before, and had my Lamaze stuff and everything. But—I had—Blair wasn't in the right position. I knew she wasn't. We
knew that a week before, but of course, we thought she might turn. But anyway, at the hospital I had been checked out [turns head away]—I had a
C-section [looks back, smiles cheerfully]. But I was ready for it. I was still
very disappointed but I had read about it and talked to the girls in my
Lamaze class about it . . . and anyway, I wish, certainly, I could vaginally
deliver. But at any rate, so we went to the hospital and she just wasn't turning, I wasn't dilating and I had a C-section at 3 in the morning. . . .

I think I had started in labor around 5 in the afternoon. It wasn't bad. I
didn't really start my breathing until around 11 and I knew I could handle
it, and on the heart monitor, I was watching it to see and I was having some
pretty good contractions. I was handling it. I was a very good breather. I
had been practicing and everything and I was very disappointed—but it was
still beautiful, really. . . . Because Garrett was with me and we were into it
and I just—I don't know . . . she was just so beautiful and everything and
it was just nice and I recovered gorgeously. I don't know, it is like you feel
very uncomfortable the next day, but you also have this beautiful little baby
and you don't even think about it. . . .

I was awake for the C-section. No, I didn't get to watch. I really didn't
care about it that much. But then they brought her to me immediately. . . .
They let her lay with me cheek to cheek.

One year later, over dinner together at an elegant restaurant, Charisse took a deep breath and said to me:

I lied to you about Blair's birth. It wasn't true, all those things I said about
how beautiful it all was and everything. I was devastated by the whole experience. Just totally devastated. I wanted to burst into tears the whole time
I was talking to you. And she wasn't breech. It was herpes. They thought I
might have had herpes—maybe—and so they did the C-section. Garrett and
I had both had herpes before we married, and I had gone to the doctor two
weeks before the birth thinking I might be having another outbreak—but I
hadn't had it at all before that, not once the entire pregnancy. And they
couldn't tell for sure at the doctor's office, and I felt stupid for going in.
And they didn't tell me that they were for sure going to do a C-section.

But then when I got to the hospital, the doctor said we would have to
do a section just to make sure. I was embarrassed and humiliated. And I
was crushed that I didn't get to give birth vaginally, because I'm sure I could
have done it. I didn't want you or anyone else to know. I'm sorry now that
I lied, because maybe it would have helped you with your work to know
the truth.

My response to Charisse was that I had known all along that she
was lying—not about the breech per se, but about the anguish the
Cesarean had caused her—because she was so quick to skip over to the
baby in her narrative, and because I could (and can still) see the pain
in her eyes as she smiled.

Elise: "I Didn't Know Enough"   In contrast to Lydia's story earlier, in the following story we will hear the experience of a woman who entered the hospital believing passionately in the desirability of totally "natural" childbirth—so much so that she had considered home birth but had been discouraged from trying it by her much-trusted obstetrician, so she opted for the new birthing center he had helped to start at a large, local hospital.

Achieving "natural childbirth" was important to Elise because she felt that she had never been "really in touch with her body," and she wanted to use pregnancy and birth as a means of rediscovering the physical and uniquely feminine nature that she had spent years denying. She said she had always hated any kind of rigid authority systems and was determined to avoid the imposition of "arbitrary rules" upon her personal birth experience. She had read all the books she could find about pregnancy and birth and had taken Lamaze classes with her husband, thereby accumulating "a lot of knowledge" about hospital procedures—knowledge that was enough to convince her that she wasn't going to need any of them. Moreover, she felt that this knowledge, combined with her "personal power" and her husband's assistance, would enable her to hold all would-be hospital interventions at bay. She also felt that she was a pansy when it came to pain, and she wanted to prove to herself that she "could handle it." Most of all, she said, she believed that birth was a natural process, that her body was healthy and quite capable of giving birth, and that the birth of her baby would be the means she sought of reintegrating her body and her mind. It became clear that Elise was in the process of reformulating her belief system about herself and her abilities in relation to her body, and that she was hoping to use her birth to cement in actual experience the new set of beliefs she wanted to hold:

> So, I went into labor around 10 in the morning on Saturday, and I remember it was a beautiful day, and I sort of puttered around doing housework because I wanted everything to be perfect when we came home. I was in a really good mood, laughing and talking. Skip was sitting in the bedroom timing the contractions and I would yell out to him when one started, and then I would forget to tell him when it stopped, and he would say, "have you been having a contraction for the last seven minutes?" "Oh, no!" We had a good time and then around 6 at night, the contractions were pretty regular by then—I think they were like four or five minutes apart—I wasn't in any pain but he said, "Well, let's go on in." So we just sort of got it together and went on in because we kind of wanted to get there to make sure that we had the birth center, because, you know, it is first come, first serve in the birthing room. We thought we would go on in and make ourselves at home, so we did.

And around 10:00 P.M. the contractions started to get really serious, and there was this nice long hall, and I felt really good walking down it. . . . but the nurses said, "You are going to exhaust yourself and you should go to bed". . . and I said, "I don't want to, it feels better when I walk" but they kept insisting, and finally they just really laid it on me, they said, "You've got to get in bed—you're going to wear yourself out"—and it's so strange because now I know that walking is the best thing you can do in labor. Well at the time, I wasn't—I sort of knew that, but I didn't know it *enough* to turn around and say, "Leave me alone, it's the best thing I can do"—so I could not be in labor and fight the nurses all of the time telling me, so I got into bed.

Umm—and a friend of mine, a girlfriend, had come from Washington D.C. and she had stayed to be with me for the birth. So I got in bed, and she started massaging my back each time I had a contraction. I was on my side, she would massage my back, and Skip would do breathing with me, and my focal points became either the design on his T-shirt or else his eyes, and I remember this intensive, cocoon-like feeling, as if I were in this cocoon, you know, and the whole world became sort of narrowed down to this little tiny space, you know, and it was a really fine feeling. The contractions were really strong, and we were really strong with them. . . . It was great, you know, and everything was great.

Well, at some point during the night the nurses decided that they would start checking the dilation evey hour—they had been doing it every two hours—and they would—I mean, it started to get incredibly painful. They would do that, and I would scream while they were doing it cause it would hurt like hell, and then it would take me twenty minutes to get it back together again. As long as they left us alone, it was just great, you know, and then they would come in and start bugging me. And then some doctor came in and said, "I'm going to give you some Demerol so you can rest in between the contractions and to take the edge off the pain." I didn't feel tired, but he said, "Well, it will just make you feel better" you know? And I didn't know that what the Demerol would do was put me to sleep after a contraction, and then I would wake up in the middle of night with this blinding, I mean it would be damn blinding pain. It was like waking up to this flash of pain in the dark, you know, and it was awful, because—if you're awake, you know it's coming, and you start to get ready and you kind of get into it, you kind of build up to it, and then it reaches a peak and you're breathing right along there with it, and you come back down, and it's fine. Well, my God, you wake up to it, and there is only pain. But still, in spite of that, Skip and I really did pretty well. I mean, I would wake up, and I would look at him, and he would see that I was in terrible pain, and he would just start counting and I would just start breathing and you know, we did fine for a good long time like that.

Then around 7 in the morning, the nurse came in and checked me, and told me I was only 2 centimeters. They had told me before that I was 4. And I started getting really freaked out because it seemed like I was going backwards after all that work, and it was very discouraging—and if they never told me, I didn't think about it. I was just in labor, and dealing with that, and that was all I wanted to think about, one contraction at a time. Um, so at 7:00 the doctor said, "Well, you're only 2 centimeters, so I'm going to give you a paracervical shot, which will, which might relax your cervix and help it dilate." Well, I knew I didn't want any anesthesia and didn't need it, but when he put it that way, I thought, well, maybe he's right. You know it might help to do that. I don't know whether it will. I didn't have enough information to say, "Go away," you know? I hadn't read medical textbooks at that point, and I didn't know that a paracervical slows down labor and reaches the baby. So I said, "Okay—it sounds reasonable— go ahead."

So he gave me the paracervical. For an hour, I felt no pain at all. In that hour, I felt so peaceful and so happy. "I thought, I'm in labor; I'm having my baby. It's just wonderful. Skip is with me. Julie is here." The sunlight was pouring in the windows. It was beautiful. I went to the bathroom. I combed my hair. Skip took a nap. I felt so calm and so peaceful. There was a joyful feeling about it all. It was great.

Well, the paracervical wore off in exactly forty-five minutes, and in five minutes I was right back in the heavy labor, which was very difficult—but we picked it up again. For three hours, you know, we kept it up, and we were doing fine you know, except when they would check me—every time they would touch me, I would scream, and I would scream for fifteen minutes after that until I could relax again and get it back together again. The pain when they checked me was so overwhelming that I found no recourse but to scream. But it was interesting that when I did that, there was also this little core in me somewhere that said, "I'm in labor, I'm having a baby. They just checked me for dilation. It hurt like hell. I'm screaming because it hurts, because it's a nice release. I'm here and I'm watching—everything is cool. I'm just fine." You know? I wasn't afraid of anything, and I wasn't afraid of myself, and I understood some things—very important—about social etiquette in the hospital. I understood that I wasn't supposed to scream because of the nurses. Skip didn't care, and Julie didn't care. They seemed to understand. But the nurses, everytime, would just flip out. "Oh, she's screaming," you know, "This is terrible," and I understood that I had to make a lot of effort to be quiet in order not to freak them out. I thought, "That's ridiculous. What the hell do they care? It's not their baby. It's not their labor. If they would just go out and close the door, they wouldn't have to listen to me. I don't need them in here anyway."

But they kept coming in and checking me, and now they were doing it every half-hour, because they were concerned because I had been in labor for such a long time—but it wasn't really that long—16 hours in the hospital—I know now it wasn't long at all, but they told me it was too long to still be only 2 centimeters dilated. I didn't know—and then the doctor came in and said, "I'm going to put you on pitocin, because that will help your cervix dilate." Well, I knew I didn't want pitocin, but I didn't know that you could use pitocin to help your cervix dilate. That was a piece of information I wasn't prepared to deal with intellectually. I had, once again, to take his word for it. Well, that was the big mistake. Because I think the first mistake was going to bed, and the second mistake was to let them put me on pitocin—and that was probably the worst mistake, because they— in order to put me on pitocin, they had to take me out of the birthing room. . . . I was in a county hospital, and labor and delivery is the pits. Had I known better, I would have gone to a different hospital, where the birthing center was not quite as nice, but labor and delivery was okay. But I never dreamed that I would be out of the birthing center. It was so nice. It had a double bed so that Skip and I could be in the bed together. It was all just nice.

I remember, now that I think of it, that before the doctor said that about pitocin—like an hour or two before, this friend of mine who was a nurse had come in to see how I was doing. And she had told me to visualize my cervix opening, to just see it opening in my mind and to focus on that. But I really didn't get it—I didn't know what she was talking about. Then she came in again when they were about to take me out, and as I walked past her I looked at her and I started crying, and I said, "I can't do it, Susan. I just can't do it." And she said, "It's okay."

Well, they marched me down the hall to labor and delivery, and I mean, it was—watching these big double doors swing open, it was like walking through the gates of hell. I mean—just literally like that. I walked in, and there was just green everywhere and noise everywhere, and clanging and shouting and women screaming. It was awful. They put me into this narrow little stretcher in this room, and they strapped the fetal monitor and the belt around my waist. They put an IV in my arm, and then they gave me pitocin. My contractions had been, you know, serious up to that time, but once they put me on that pitocin, I would have maybe fifteen to forty seconds between contractions, and the contractions would be the double-peak type. You know, they would peak and then they would go down a little, and then they would peak again without ever really stopping. Then I would rest for fifty seconds, and then it would come again.

And the first nurse that came in was a bitch. Skip told her we needed something, and she said, "I give the orders around here." So Skip said, "Get out of here—we don't need you." So she left and this other nurse came in— very nice. She stood there and looked at me and said, "Breathe in very slowly and out very slowly." So we chucked Lamaze, and I breathed in very slowly and out very slowly . . . and it was amazing. In spite of the hideous room, in spite of the fact that this orderly was taking apart this bed right next to mine and making a clanging and banging, in spite of the people that kept coming in and out and checking the charts and da-da-da—in spite of all that, we made the cocoon again. Julie rubbed my back. . . . As long as I didn't move, the monitor didn't go crazy. So I stayed on my side, and she rubbed my back, and Skip and I did the breathing. Skip and Julie had this thing going. Skip would look at the needle and he could tell when the contraction was about to start just a little before I could. So he would look at her and say, "Get ready" . . . and then we would start breathing, in very slowly and out very slowly. It was amazing. We made the cocoon, and we were just into it. We were flowing right along and everything.

But then, every half hour they would come and check me. And we couldn't sustain it—we kept repairing the cocoon, but it got harder and harder. And then some orderly came at me with a long hook and broke my waters. Apparently, they said that would help. And I didn't know. I just didn't know. Well, that for me was one of the worst moments of the whole experience. It was like all my hopes and dreams of how it was going to be just sort of floated out with the waters. I'll never forget that. It was just an awful feeling. Warm and sad, it was like tears flowing out, you know? And I couldn't walk, I couldn't do anything. I was stuck, you know? By that time, I was totally humiliated. I was incapable of—and then some orderly came in with those electrodes to stick in the baby's scalp—I looked up and I saw him come at me with it between my knees. Skip and I both screamed at him that we didn't want that. He looked kind of shocked and went away. That's the one thing we managed to avoid. And I'm proud of that, because it would have hurt my baby. At least I managed to protect her from having that horrible thing screwed into her scalp.

Then the doctor, who was at church, sent word that I would have to have a Cesarean. By then, that sounded like a great idea—Skip and I agreed we would do that. At *least*, we thought, it will get us out of here. We just gave up—we knew we couldn't do it anymore. So they gave me another paracervical, and we all just waited for the doctor to come. And it wore off, and he still didn't come. So I had a whole 'nother hour of contractions, waiting for him, and that was bad, because there was no reason to try anymore.

Then they wheeled me down the hall—I still remember the feel of the wind in my face and impressions of everything passing me by upside down. They did the Cesarean, and it felt like somebody stepping on my stomach with a boot and pulling up my skin for laces. And I was cold, so cold. And my mouth was dry, but they wouldn't give me any ice chips. I begged for ice chips, and they said no. And the anesthesiologist tried to strap my hands down, but I wouldn't let him. That was too much. I still had some dignity left, and I would not let them take it away completely. And so when they handed me the baby, I could hold her right up by my neck. And she was so beautiful. She looked just like a little monkey, but she was beautiful. I knew right away that she was mine, completely and totally my baby. But I couldn't sit up, couldn't hold her like that for very long, so after five minutes with her, Skip took her out to see Julie and our parents, and they took me to the recovery room.

After the birth I felt just miserable, agonizingly miserable. When I was relating to the baby, I was totally happy—I was so thrilled with her. But all the rest of the time, I felt so sad—like—gray around the edges. Just sad and gray. And I couldn't really put my finger on why. And ashamed. I felt so ashamed of myself for screaming, and for not being able to do it. And you know, I had a friend who gave birth a few days later, and her labor was longer than mine, and she ended up with a perfectly normal labor. And I spent months and months comparing our experiences—going over the times and what happened to each of us step by step. And it just didn't make any sense to me. The doctor said it was "CPD" [cephalo-pelvic disproportion, a condition in which the baby is too large to fit through the mother's pelvic structure] and "failure to progress." But her baby was bigger than mine, and I'm bigger than she is, and she was in labor a lot longer than me. And then I had so many questions that I started to read some more. More and more. And I started to admit to myself that I felt humiliated by my birth. And then when I realized that I probably hadn't even needed a Cesarean, I started to realize that I felt raped, and violated somehow, in some really fundamental way. And then I got angry.

Comparative Analysis   According to the technocratic model, delivery of a baby through a vagina infected with herpes will result in the baby contracting the herpes and eventually dying. Midwives familiar with the delivery of herpes patients at home, however, say that infection of the baby is caused by frequent cervical checks, by the use of internal fetal monitor and/or forceps, and by delivery in the lithotomy position. Some midwives like to cover any active herpes lesions with thick vaseline for birth; others say no such technique is necessary. None of the six midwives I have asked—who between them have attended the births of over 5,000 babies—have ever had a baby born with herpes, even when the mother gave birth with active lesions present.

Charisse did not know all of that when she entered the hospital. But she did know that she didn't think that she had herpes. She had exhibited no symptoms since her last visit to the obstetrician, and she was truly stunned when she was told of the impending Cesarean. Although she did not ever believe that it was really necessary, she had just enough uncertainty to be open to conceptual fusion with the technocratic model in spite of her disbelief: this uncertainty centered around her concern for the safety of the baby and around the issue of responsibility. If she had rejected the C-section, and the baby had been infected, she would have been responsible for seriously damaging her child. She believed that the Cesarean itself would harm only her, and she preferred self-sacrifice to responsibility for the perceived risk to her baby's life and health, small though she believed it to be. Although Charisse took with her into the hospital a strong set of conceptual buffers (her knowledge, her healthy body, her husband), these proved insufficient to counteract the slight possibility that her baby might be damaged if she did not have the Cesarean. This argument is recognizable as the same one the obstetrician used against Debra, that she would be "killing her baby" if she did not have a Cesarean—but Debra was able to avoid internalizing this message because intellectually she *knew* it was not true, whereas Charisse did not have that certainty. Obstetricians know that concern

over fetal safety is the number one point of linkage between the technocratic model and the belief systems of the vast majority of women
giving birth in the hospital—and are generally quick to utilize that
point.

A far more common means of utilizing this strong linkage point than
the threat of herpes is the medical dictum that the breech position is
too dangerous for vaginal birth, so that all breech babies must be delivered by Cesarean section. Instead of Charisse's story, for example, I
could have included Jennifer Evin's birth narrative, which is very similar
except that Jennifer's baby really was breech. Jennifer was devastated
by her Cesarean, because she knew there was an alternative: she had
read that midwives on The Farm in Summertown, Tennessee commonly
deliver breech babies in the hands-and-knees position (Gaskin 1990).
She hoped and prayed that the baby would turn in time; when he did
not, she begged her obstetrician to let her deliver vaginally, but he
adamantly refused. Obstetricians generally have no idea how to handle
vaginal breech deliveries; most of them, especially the younger ones, do
not hold a category that vaginal breech birth is even possible, because
they are only taught in medical schools to do Cesareans for breech and
so have never even seen a vaginal breech delivery.

In Charisse's case, conceptual fusion with the technocratic model
was sudden; in Elise's, it occurred gradually through a pinpointable
series of steps. As she later came to see it, Elise's first "mistake" was
to go to the hospital too soon. She learned through subsequent births
that she has a pattern of long labors, and she realized that she plugged
herself into the technocratic model by entering the hospital while still
in "early labor" (as opposed to what she now conceptualizes as "active
labor," which she learned from her midwives to define as *beginning*
at 6 centimeters), thereby ensuring that her labor would run off the
time chart, thus rendering her subject to the full gamut of technocratic
treatment.

Elise's second "mistake" was allowing herself to be convinced by the
nurses that she should stop walking and go to bed. As she later learned,
her friend walked the halls for most of her successful thirty-six-hour
labor, which provided Elise with her first clue that she had instinctively
been right to want to walk (as we saw in Chapter 2, walking increases
the effectiveness of contractions).

The next two "mistakes," or points of linkage between Elise's cognitive matrix for birth and the technocratic model, as Elise herself sees
it, were the cervical checks and the Demerol. The analgesia rendered

her considerably less able to cope with the contractions, whereas the cervical checks, which she experienced as painful, played a major role in convincing her that her labor was dysfunctional. As with Lydia, the constant news that she was making no progress, even regressing, served to convince Elise that something was terribly wrong with her body, that she was way behind schedule, and ultimately, that she simply could not "do it."

Throughout her labor, it is apparent that Elise lost considerable conceptual ground in her effort to maintain her belief in her ability to achieve "natural childbirth" every time she was confronted by hospital personnel with a suggestion that she was not intellectually prepared to rebut. Her knowledge proved an insufficient buffer because, as she puts it, "The obstetrician and the nurses kept finding a way around what I knew." She knew, for example, that pitocin increases the strength and painfulness of the contractions, so she was sure she didn't want it until her doctor presented it to her as helpful in cervical dilation. She desperately wanted her cervix to dilate, so this particular presentation of the advantages of pitocin achieved even further fusion of her belief system with the technocratic model, through this mutually held linkage point.

As Elise herself sees it, her acceptance of the pitocin was the "beginning of the end." The pitocin entailed removal from the birthing center, an environment that had to some extent buffered her from technocratic reality. When she walked through those big double doors, she had the literal sensation that she "was lost." In the labor and delivery unit, technocratic reality was all around her; its messages became impossible to ignore for any length of time.

Like Beryl, Elise was conceptually prepared only for vaginal birth; she had no cognitive preparation for Cesarean birth. Unlike Beryl, Elise was never able to point to any one factor that could validate the medical necessity of her Cesarean, although she tried very hard to do so. At the time, she had accepted the Cesarean because she had "given up": she truly believed that she was simply incapable of giving birth to her baby—she had internalized the message that her machine was defective. She was able to maintain that belief until she talked to her friend on the telephone the following morning; when she heard the details of her friend's experience, she was suddenly seized with "a physical feeling of shakiness and doubt." In the months that followed, she went over and over the details of the two experiences, trying unsuccessfully to understand why she had had a Cesarean, whereas her friend, whose labor was much longer than Elise's, with an equally slow rate of dilation (and an extremely supportive, wholistically oriented obstetrician), had not.

When Elise finally accepted the conclusion, about ten months after the birth, that she had not actually needed a Cesarean, her first reactions were intensified feelings of guilt, helplessness, weakness, and failure. She lived with these feelings until about one year after the birth, at which point she began reading everything she could find on hospital interventions, in a concerted effort to develop a cognitive matrix in terms of which she could, in her words, "make sense out of" her birth experience. Gradually, as this matrix developed, Elise began to perceive that she had been "tricked," and her self-blame turned into a burning rage against the medical establishment which, in her view, had physically and intellectually "raped" her.

Elise and Charisse are representative of 9 percent of the women in my study who entered the hospital believing strongly in "natural childbirth," and who came out feeling like failures. In their cases, the rituals of hospital birth can be said to have succeeded in communicating their cognitive messages. These women did indeed internalize the images of themselves as defective, as lacking, as helpless in the face of science, technology, patriarchy, and institutions.

On a nationwide scale, it is the women whose birth experiences fit into this category who sent over 40,000 letters of anguish and protest to Nancy Cohen, a leader of the national Cesarean prevention movement, after the publication of her first writings on unnecessary Cesareans and on vaginal birth after Cesarean (Cohen and Estner 1983).

All of the women in this category in my own study experienced postpartum depression, which later turned into rage at the medical establishment. This depression seemed to be the result of their inability to merge the new, devalued self-images and sets of meanings arising out of their birth experiences with the self-images of enhanced competence and ability which they needed to foster as mothers. As well, their depressions resulted from the painful cognitive restructuring these women had to undergo in order to reconcile the cognitive matrix thrust upon them in childbirth with the contradictory sets of beliefs and meanings in terms of which they consciously wished to live their daily lives.

Further insight into the complex causes of postpartum depression (experienced primarily by the women in this category of my study, and by some of the women who espouse the technocratic model) is provided by Janis and Victor Catano in their 1981 paper, "Mild Post-Partum De-

pression: Learned Helplessness and the Medicalization of Obstetrics."
The Catanos cite Seligman's (1975, 1978; Abramson, Seligman, and
Teasdale 1978) "learned helplessness model" as shedding considerable
light on the psychological processes that lead to mild postpartum depression. This model proposes:

> that if an organism perceives that it has no control over a situation, that its
> responses have no effect on outcome, *the organism will learn to be helpless,*
> resulting in depression. . . . The central and defining feature of the learned
> helplessness model is "the expectation that highly desirable outcomes are of
> low probability or that highly aversive outcomes are of high probability *and*
> *that their occurrence is independent of the individual's actions."* (Seligman
> 1981:3–15; emphases mine)

The Catanos hypothesize that mild postpartum depression "is a form
of learned helplessness which results from a woman's perceived lack of
control over events surrounding childbirth" (1981:3). They suggest that
"the more numerous the ways in which the woman perceives herself
to be in control, the less likely that [mild postpartum depression] will
occur" (1981:20–21). Certainly this finding is confirmed in the postpartum experiences of the women in my study group. Those who gave
birth at home, as well as those who felt that *they* controlled the use of
technology, experienced little or no postpartum depression, in contrast
to those who tended to interpret their experiences as Liza Findeisen did:

> I had been all prepared for natural childbirth and we had been through
> twenty-six hours of labor and the whole business. So I was very involved
> with my body and expected to participate in the experience and had been
> in control. I didn't like losing control. You know, when you are in there flat
> on your back with an epidural and can't even feel your toes, you know that
> you are out of control.

Liza, Charisse, and Elise, and the other women in this category
(*conceptual fusion with the technocratic model, with cognitive distress*)
whom they represent overtly rejected the technocratic model of birth
as an ideology while at the same time placing themselves under its sway
by entering the hospital—a conceptual double bind. They had educated
themselves to espouse *some* of the components of the wholistic model—
for example, that most medical procedures are unnecessary, that their
bodies could deliver babies without medical intervention, and that birth
is something a woman does. They entered the hospital armed with the
intellectual knowledge that they expected would augment their control
over their births, and thus their sense of personal power—and so would

TABLE 3. THE SPECTRUM OF WOMEN'S RESPONSES TO
THEIR BIRTH EXPERIENCES

My categorizations of the women's responses to their birth experiences
are summarized here for the reader's convenience:

Full acceptance of the technocratic model of birth

Expecting that the doctor will take care of everything 9%

Rejecting biology in favor of technology 9%

Full acceptance of the wholistic model of birth

Seeing birth as a natural aspect of womanhood 3%

Seeing birth as a spiritual process of growth 3%

Women in-between

Maintaining conceptual distance from the technocratic model:

Through achieving "natural childbirth" in the
hospital 15%

Through placing technology at the service of
the individual 10%

Conceptual fusion with the technocratic model:

With cognitive ease 42%

With cognitive distress 9%

enable them to impose and maintain the "natural" model in the face
of the medical one. Yet once in the hospital, because their labors did
not conform to technocratic standards, these women were confronted
with an escalating loss of control and a steady erosion of their sense of
personal power, along with the complete disappearance of the natural
model as a conceptual base. As mentioned above, the triumphs they did
experience during their births were minor successes at avoiding this procedure or that, as is evident in Elise's narrative. The prep, IV, analgesia,
pitocin, fetal monitor, anesthesia, and final Cesarean—each procedure
performed on each of these women both added to and created the growing dissociation between herself as a person and her body as a machine
and challenged in major ways her normal conceptions of her autonomous personhood and its meaning, in the same ways that a rape or a
robbery can. And each procedure directly circumvented her efforts to
associate a sense of enhanced competence and power with the birth of
her motherhood. This conceptual conflict, between the belief system

these women wished to partially espouse/sense of competence they wished to enhance, and the belief system that was imposed on them through the rituals of hospital birth, with its near-total negation of that sense of competence, became for this group of women the basis of a profound alienation.

However, for many of these women the internalization of such negative messages was not permanent. The internal cognitive conflict engendered by their technocratic births led most of them to a major cognitive restructuring over time, and eventually to the complete reinterpretation of the meaning of their births, as we will investigate in the following chapter.

CHAPTER 6

Scars into Stars

The Reinterpretation of the Childbirth Experience

> Even in the short run encompassed by the ritual itself,
> the communication can be appropriate to the temporarily
> retrogressed structure of the ordinarily complex commu-
> nicator. . . . [T]he cognitive content [of the ritual] can be
> manipulated and fleshed out after it returns to the habitual
> level of functioning. This may take place with relatively little
> effort, be compartmentalized, or initiate further epistemic
> exploration. In the last case, conflict between the cognitive
> content of ritual (and its attendant affective state) and the
> more complex reality model of the individual may institute
> a discrepancy thought to initiate intrinsically motivated be-
> havior. . . . This might lead to further attempts to understand
> or elaborate the model. If the attempt leads [a Roman Catho-
> lic] to a study of Teilhard de Chardin, it will elaborate and
> reinforce the work of ritual. If it leads to Sartre, however, the
> work of ritual may be undone, as it so often is in contem-
> porary Western society.
> —John McManus, "Ritual and Human Social Cognition"

The possibilities outlined in the above quotation are as applicable to
the long-term effects of birth rituals as to the Catholic mass about
which the quotation was written. Many of the women in my study did
indeed continue to "flesh out" the cognitive content of their ritualized
births. As we saw in Chapter 5, for those women who felt self-empowered by their births, or for whom the cognitive content of hospital
birth rituals was not radically divergent from their own, more complex
reality models, this took "relatively little effort." Those women who
found a great discrepancy between the cognitive content of hospital
birth rituals and their own reality models did indeed tend either to
"compartmentalize" the experience or to initiate "further epistemic
exploration" of its meaning. And this attempt did indeed lead some of
these women "to Teilhard de Chardin" (that is, to an intensified search
for meaning in their birth experiences within the interpretive frame-

work provided by the technocratic model) and others "to Sartre" (i.e., to a complete conceptual rejection of that model, and to the development of an alternative belief system). I was not able to follow all the women in my sample through subsequent births, and so I cannot say here what proportion of women in each birth category went on to engage in further epistemic exploration or to compartmentalize their birth experience. This chapter is intended simply to illustrate the range of long-term postbirth responses and transformations experienced by those thirty-two women in my study whom I was able to follow.

COMPARTMENTALIZATION

The "compartmentalizers" among the women in my study tended to be the ones who were most thoroughly effaced during their hospital births. Those who gave birth under total anesthesia, like Toni, or Mary's mother, simply placed the experience completely outside the rhythms and flow of their everyday life, seeing in that experience no meaning at all. As Gladys said, birth was "what you had to do to have a baby."

Those who were awake and aware, in terror or extreme pain, like LeAnn, or who felt like failures after their births—in other words, those who could find few points of correspondence between the reality models and self-images they wished and needed to hold, and those imposed on them through their births—if they chose to compartmentalize, would do their best to "put it all behind" them. As Marie said, "I cannot live with the thought of my birth experience. It gives me the shudders, and I start to cry every time I think about it. So I don't think about it. It's over and done, and life goes on." Psychotherapeutically speaking, of course, this presents a problem, as unresolved traumas tend to resurface in various ways. One woman whom I asked to interview became very angry when I mentioned birth, said she had agonized over her recent Cesarean all she was going to, that she never wanted to think about it again, asked me please not ever to call her back, and hung up the telephone. In "The Value of Narrative in the Representation of Reality," White provides an interpretation from narrative theory of the significance of her refusal: "Narrative ceaselessly substitutes meaning for the straightforward copy of the events recounted. . . . [R]efusal of narrative indicates an absence or refusal of meaning itself" (1980:2).

For many women, compartmentalization only works until they become pregnant again. At that point, they must choose whether to have another birth to compartmentalize, or whether to initiate further epistemic exploration of their traumatic birth, with the goal of having a birth experience whose meaning they can easily integrate with the flux and flow of their daily lives, this time around.

"FURTHER EPISTEMIC EXPLORATION": "TEILHARD DE CHARDIN" VERSUS "SARTRE"

GOING TO "TEILHARD DE CHARDIN"

Some of those women disturbed by the discrepancy between the cognitive messages of birth rituals and their own reality models were not content either to find meaningless or to compartmentalize their birth experiences. The "further epistemic exploration" in which they engaged meant eventual confirmation of the medical necessity of their technocratic births and intensified acceptance of the technocratic model. LeAnn, for example, went on to schedule a C-section with her next child, so that she would not again be confronted with her fear of natural birth. After an emergency Cesarean, Marianne, like Beryl, spent some time questioning her worth as a woman. Her need to fully understand the causes of her Cesarean led her to a literature search, from which she came away satisfied that the Cesarean was indeed medically justified. This recognition gave her an enhanced appreciation of medical technology, as well as the ability to conceptually reconcile with her experience and to stop feeling like a failure. As a result of her epistemic exploration, she realized that what she had learned might help other women too with their Cesarean births, so she began speaking to various childbirth groups and postnatal Lamaze classes on the topic of "Having a Cesarean Is Having a Baby." Her talks were very well received by the Cesarean mothers who heard them, because her theme validated their conceptual need for the right to consider themselves as fully women, as fully birth-givers, and as fully mothers as their friends who had achieved "natural childbirth." Her talks thus became a vehicle through which other women could reinterpret the meanings of their Cesarean births.

GOING TO "SARTRE"

Elise sat in her office late into the night reading the NAPSAC (National Association of Parents and Professionals for Safe Alternatives in

Childbirth) books (Stewart and Stewart 1976, 1977, 1979, 1981). As she was confronted with "overwhelming evidence, procedure by procedure," of the unnecessary and harmful nature of the technocratic interventions in her birth process, her rage and frustration mounted; says she:

> Several times, like when I read about how much better it is to walk during labor, and how paracervical anesthesia slows labor and reaches the baby, I threw the book across the room and burst into tears. For a whole year I had blamed myself. Then for another year I blamed the doctors. Now I blame our entire medical system. I have no trust in it any more. I have seen how all its premises are false.

Elise did not stop at this point in her efforts to cognitively restructure her birth experience. She eventually emerged from her "victim mentality" (her words), transforming her anger and her hurt into acceptance of her own responsibility for her technocratic birth. Realizing that a lifetime of mind-body disconnection is hardly adequate preparation for natural childbirth, she began to seek ways in which to reconnect her "disconnected self" through rewriting the extremely clear messages she felt she had received from her Cesarean about the extent of that disconnection. Like all of the women in my study who sought to rewrite the messages of their hospital births, she utilized the medium of narrative. She also attended the births of friends, became involved in the New Age movement, and actively engaged in a process she saw as a transformation in consciousness to the wholistic model and its stress on self-responsibility (discussed in Chapter 9). As a part of this process, she gave birth to her two subsequent children at home, in order to "turn her scars into stars," as Julie liked to put it. Julie, who had two Cesareans and later became a childbirth educator and birth attendant, said, "I had such a horrible experience with my first baby, and I believe in taking anything that is that bad and making something beautiful out of it if you can."

As we will investigate below, narrative provided such women with the most accessible and often-utilized means for further epistemic exploration of the meanings of their births; those who were not content with the results went on to explore the literature on childbirth far more thoroughly than they had done before, often becoming professionally involved in childbirth education or midwifery. But, after narrative and further self-education about birth, by far the most common technique for further epistemic exploration utilized by these women was birth itself: subsequent births became both the catalysts and the means for the complete reinterpretation of the cognitive content of their earlier hospital births, as well as for the transformation of their own reality models—for, in other words, getting "to Sartre."

"Further Epistemic Exploration" Through Narrative   The importance of childbirth narratives as a women's speech genre cannot be overstated. Intensive exploration of their utilization by women for the interpretation and reinterpretation of their birth experiences would provide an excellent focus for further anthropological and sociolinguistic research, which has heretofore only occurred on a very limited scale (Bromberg 1981; Jencson 1982; Keeler 1984; Lamb 1990).

Although my data are rich in samples of the women's use of narrative for the "further epistemic exploration" of their births, I will confine myself here to three brief examples. I include them chiefly in the hope of stimulating further research on this subject.

When women share their birth experiences with others, they select out of those formless, inchoate experiences certain elements to communicate; the elements they choose will give form and structure to what was lived as a far more undifferentiated flow. By the time they have narrated their births to four or five people, they will have selected out a certain number of elements to narrate; these will then begin to constitute the essence of their birth experiences for them, whereas the other, unnarrated elements will fade into the background and sometimes out of conscious memory. However, when another woman narrates her birth to them, this new story will often remind them of some of those forgotten elements, which can then be pulled back into conscious recall and utilized for the reinterpretation of the overall meaning of their births.

For example, one day after the birth of her second child, I arrived in Betsy's hospital room to record her birth story, to find her friends Alicia and Susan also present. Alicia told us the story of her long, painful and extremely difficult labor, in which the baby was in a transverse position and did not turn until shortly before the birth, concluding that she had achieved natural childbirth but that it was so painful she wished she had had a Cesarean instead. Susan responded flatly,

> Oh no you don't. I had a Cesarean. You don't wish that you had one. It's an awful experience. And now if I have another baby, I'm going to have to fight the whole world to have it vaginally—you know, they have that rule, "Once a Cesarean, always a Cesarean."

To which Alicia replied,

> Oh, wow. I hadn't even thought of that. Well. A baby when it's not facing
> the right direction, the pressure will cause you to have really bad backache,
> it feels like fire burning in your back. But this went all the way through my
> hips and into my legs. It was just horrible.
>   But I'd do it again. You forget so fast. And it was really something that
> I was able to do that, to get through it. And holding her and nursing her
> on the delivery [table]—that was the greatest. It was marvelous to hold her,
> and I just touched her for a really long time.

The conversation then turned to the overwhelming benefits of having
a nurse-midwife attend one's birth, as Alicia did.

A second example of the possibilities for reinterpretation of one's
birth experience through narrative is contained in a conversation between Debra (whose birth story appears in Chapter 5) and an airline
stewardess during a flight. Here is how Debra described that conversation to me:

ROBBIE: Are you glad you didn't have a Cesarean?

DEBRA: Very glad! That's major surgery. It wasn't necessary.

ROBBIE: Did you know what a narrow escape you had?

DEBRA: I don't think I really did until later. At the time you just did what
          you had to do to get through. Telling him no and trying to handle
          the labor and the delivery and the postpartum and all that. You
          were too busy to reflect and think about it. But then afterward,
          after she was five or six months old we would both look at her
          and look at each other and say we're so glad that we had done
          it. It wouldn't have been any good for me or for her, so I felt kind
          of triumphant. You know, victorious. We didn't give in to this
          doctor and the hospital routine, "the system." At first we didn't
          really—we were *glad* but we didn't really have time to *reflect.*
              I was on an airplane when Emily was about four or five months
          old and I don't know how I started talking to her, but the stew-
          ardess asked me how my childbirth was and she was contemplat-
          ing getting pregnant. When I told her about having this close call
          with the Cesarean, she was just amazed—"How could you have
          done that after that doctor told you?" She was talking about a
          book called *Immaculate Deception* and I had read only bits and
          pieces but I hadn't read the whole thing, but she said, she men-
          tioned how that was a kind of prime example—"You didn't let
          the doctor pull the wool over your eyes." But I think that was
          really the first time that it really hit me that I had really done
          something, when she said, "How could you do that?" My mother
          told me I was kind of crazy, that I should have had a C-section.

ROBBIE: How long after the birth was this conversation with the stewardess?

DEBRA: Emily was about four or five months old.

ROBBIE: And that was the first time that it hit you that you—

DEBRA: That was really the first time that anybody had ever expressed that other than my husband and myself—"Wow, that's really something—you stood up to this doctor." My family was very reserved about it—they thought maybe I should have had the section and listened to the doctor. . . . That was the first time anybody other than family had made much of a comment. And so that's why, I guess, really looking back on it, it really hit me that maybe I had done something. Stood up for myself and maybe he wouldn't do that to somebody else, because I had given him a hard time.

ROBBIE: Do you think that that realization made any difference with you later on?

DEBRA: Oh, yes. In the first place, when I got pregnant again, I went back to [the doctor who wasn't on call the day of her birth] and I said things to him that I never would have said. . . . I walked in and I just laid it on the line. I said, "Look. Like I told you before, the care that I had the last time was lousy. I love *you*"—you know, he was great, he was a good doctor—and I said "I'll come back to this practice if you promise me that I'll never have to lay eyes on that man again." He said, "I'm sorry, I can't do that." I said, "I'm sorry, I can't be your patient and I won't waste your time." I think that's when I started realizing I could talk to a doctor like a person and not have to sit down and listen to what they tell me and not say anything back. . . . So it changed me because I started having more confidence as far as getting what I want, and that's important.

ROBBIE: Did that carry over into any other realms of your life besides the medical?

DEBRA: I am not intimidated any more. . . . I think it gave me more confidence about expressing what I know. I have friends that get pregnant or have babies or are nursing call me and ask me, "What is this?" I say, "Have you called your doctor?" And they say, "No, you're the first person I thought of." Before, I would have said, "Don't ask me!" It gave me more confidence to express myself and not be intimidated. When you're lying there flat on your back and somebody is pointing their finger in your face and screaming and yelling at you and telling you that you're going to kill your baby, still to make a decision and not give in, and make the right decision and be perfectly happy and sure of yourself that it is the right thing to do, it definitely carries over into other areas!

One last example of the role of the childbirth narrative in the reinterpretation of the birth experience is provided by Terry. Because her

overall perceptions of her birth were so positive, for several years after the birth Terry both narrated and remembered only the positive
elements of those experiences. But when she began the fieldwork for a
dissertation on childbirth narratives, as she encountered a number of
women who focused on the negative in their hospital births, she found
that

> the more I let go of myself, the more I am getting a variety of experiences
> from the women. More negative sayings than I did at first, more ambivalence
> than I did at first. And what is this doing for me? It is making me begin
> to identify negative aspects of my experience that I had forgotten, and am-
> bivalent aspects of my experience that I had forgotten, which I now have to
> reconcile.

For example, Terry said that she had forgotten how her labor slowed
down during the "prep"

> in that the contractions were erratic and much more painful. And I re-
> member that now, having talked to other women. I hadn't really remem-
> bered that. . . . Then afterwards, I was running a slight fever—this is where
> the hospital policy comes in—they wouldn't let me have anything to drink
> because I was on an IV. They wouldn't give me anything to drink. I was
> famished and they wouldn't give me anything to eat . . . And it is only in
> listening to a lot of other women several years later that I realized how shitty
> some of these things were. At the time, the only thing that really bothered
> me was that I wanted to eat a huge steak and I couldn't have one. I ended
> up with gingerale and saltines about an hour after I gave birth. The other
> thing that really bothered me was that they did not bring my son to me until
> twelve o'clock the next day.

*"Further Epistemic Exploration" through Further Involvement with
Childbirth*   Marianne gave talks to Cesarean groups. Julie, Francine,
and Elise became childbirth educators; Julie also started a consumer advocacy group and became an activist in the Cesarean prevention movement. Susan and Kathleen became midwives. Rima, whose first birth
was highly technocratic and whose next three births were at home in
the water, wrote a book, *The Healing Power of Birth* (Star 1986), and
founded a school for birth attendants. Margaret started a business
teaching exercise classes for pregnant women. July and Debra became
resources of knowledge on parenting, birthing, and babies for their
friends, and Debra was in the process of becoming a La Leche League
leader.

Those women who seemed most deeply touched—with grief or
with joy—by their birth experiences (if they did not compartmentalize)

seemed to be the most likely to pursue their search for meaning through intensifying their involvement with childbirth as a social and individual process—a pattern readily identifiable among many of the past and present leaders of the national consumer movement for childbirth reform (e.g., Arms 1975; Cohen and Estner 1983; Hazell 1976; Karmel 1965; Noble 1982, 1983; Rothman 1982).

Those who had traumatic births wished to empower others to avoid such psychological devastation; those who had joyous births wished to empower others to do the same. As Elizabeth said,

> Every time you help a pregnant woman to achieve a happier pregnancy and a better birth, you empower her, you validate your own experience, you reeducate her health care providers, you help her baby to be born healthy, and you help make this world a better place for all of us to live in.

"Further Epistemic Exploration" Through Subsequent Births Joanne's second birth, a scheduled Cesarean, reflected the continued commitment to avoid "dropping into biology" that her first birth, also a scheduled Cesarean, had expressed. Lila and Gretchen, who both gave birth "naturally" the first time around, went in the opposite direction the next time, requesting epidural analgesia early on in labor. Explained Lila:

> I proved what I had to prove, learned what I wanted to learn. I lived the whole, real experience. And once was enough! Now I'm older, and I don't have anything to prove anymore. This time, I want the baby, but not the pain.

In contrast to these "Teilhard-de-Chardiners," for her second birth Mary went a good bit of the way "to Sartre," stopping short of arriving at his doorstep. After her first birth (described in her letter in Chapter 5), she was told that she could not have any more babies. So she changed doctors. She says, "I placed my faith in another doctor because I felt that it was not medicine that was the bad guy but the individual doctor. . . . I never even thought that the entire field of medicine could be wrong." With her second pregnancy,

> I was determined that I was not going to let any doctor dictate to me like with my first child. . . . I did not believe that a salt-free diet was the way to go and I did not believe that it mattered how much weight I put on. I was not going to let the doctor dictate to me on those accounts. I at age thirty-five sailed through the pregnancy. I attended college up until I was seven-and-a-half months pregnant. I never felt better.

Charisse delivered vaginally her second and third times around. Terry's second birth entailed even fewer interventions than her first, and an attentive French obstetrician repaired her "lousy" episiotomy. Although Toni's first two births occurred under general anesthesia, after her husband came back from Vietnam she delivered her third child "naturally" in the hospital. For Debra's second birth she found a female obstetrician who could offer her a far more humane delivery; for her third delivery she switched to a certified nurse-midwife and delivered in the labor room instead of having to move to the delivery room. July's hands were strapped with her first delivery; they were free with her second, and her third was in the new birthing room at a local hospital, with no interventions at all.

To some extent this pattern of decreasing interventions with each subsequent birth may be due to the simple physiological fact that second and third labors are generally shorter and easier and are thus buffered by the technocratic model itself (in the form of "Friedman's curve") from excessive intervention. But it should also be noted here that each of these women actively and often aggressively pursued for herself this pattern of decreased intervention in subsequent births:

> A lot of the other things I'm doing with my birth experience this time are going to be different, because I'm not going to have the standard prepping that they do, all that sort of stuff that really doesn't make a *drastic* difference, but one of the things I think that caused my labor to be longer the last time was that I was just *uncomfortable* with all the things they made me do. Not terrified, but uncomfortable. I just didn't like it, and this way I'm going to wear my own nightgown instead of that silly hospital gown that they make you wear with the hole up the back and I'm not going to be hooked up to the IV right away so that I can walk around if I want to—you see that's just another thing—they just put you right in the bed and hook you up to all this stuff and shave you and the whole bit. . . . And I'm wanting to have the baby in the labor room, and I don't want an episiotomy. I think my skin will stretch. (Betsy Yellin)

> Then when I got pregnant with this one, I wasn't going to stop for anything but what I wanted. I was going to change doctors again and go to the birthing room at a different hospital, until I found out about [the certified nurse-midwife] who had joined the practice where I already was. (Debra)

> No prep. No enema. No hourly checks by nurses coming in and taking my temperature and stuff because that used to throw off my breathing. No vaginal exams except on request by me. . . . I wanted a room by myself . . . and of course, not being strapped down. . . . And no anesthesia unless I requested it, and nobody asking me if I wanted any. No episiotomy. (Terry)

In rejecting hospital routines, these women were rejecting many of the basic messages of hospital birth. They were making conscious use of subsequent births to invert and subvert the cognitive matrix provided to them by the technocratic model the first time around, and to redefine themselves as powerful and as causative in relation to science and technology, patriarchy and institutions: they sought through their births to send their *own* messages back to the medical system.

The hospital personnel who attend such women are not unmoved by the experience: medical attendants often receive the alternative messages sent by these women—messages of the strength and power of women as birth-givers, of the integrity of the birth process, of the sanctity of the family, of the delicacy and beauty of the interactions between mother and newborn child—and sometimes alter their own beliefs and practices accordingly. Here, for example, is the reaction of an OB/GYN intern to witnessing his first Lamaze birth, as recorded in a letter given to his Lamaze instructor:

> [My first] Lamaze delivery was one in which I assisted an OB intern because the private OB was too late. The image of that lady "pant-pant-blowing," joyfully pushing her baby into the world supported by her sweating, joyful husband, remains as one of my most vivid medical memories, and I shall treasure always these moments as an entire roomful of doctors, nurses, and parents stood around laughing, shaking hands, with tears streaming down every face—my own included.

In the following chapter, we will consider the process by which these medical practitioners are themselves socialized both into the core belief and value system of our society and into their roles as the maintainers and perpetuators of that system.

CHAPTER 7

Obstetric Training as a Rite of Passage[1]

> Why is medical school the way it is? I think it's part of
> the idiocy that goes on with the good ol' boy approach—
> "We did this back in my day, by God, and you've got to do
> the same thing"—it's like the Marine Corps and that sort of
> thing. It's a crazy thing that's gotten in the habit of perpetu-
> ating itself.
>
> —Stephen Saunders, M.D.

In this chapter I shall examine obstetric training in the United States as an initiatory rite of passage. The theories from symbolic anthropology utilized previously in this book to interpret birth as a rite of passage for the woman will be applied to certain aspects of medical school train- ing and obstetrical residency in order to bring to light the deep and often covert sociocultural processes at work in the transformation of medical students into obstetricians.

Obstetrical education during residency has been well and thoroughly documented by feminist researchers Oakley (1984), Scully (1980), and Shaw (1974), and by women physicians Carver (1981) and Harrison (1982) who have recorded their personal experiences of this process. In this chapter, following Turner's (1979) analytic lead, I shall focus both on the messages or "gnosis" encoded in obstetrical training and on the processes that work to effect the obstetrical student's internal- ization of this gnosis. Thus, after describing the methods used in collect- ing and presenting the data in this chapter, I utilize the characteristics of ritual (described in the Introduction) that facilitate such internal- ization to frame my analysis of the process of psychological transfor- mation through which fledgling medical students become full-fledged obstetricians.

METHODS

Data for this chapter were obtained from interviews conducted be- tween January and March 1987 with twelve obstetricians, ten male and two female. Two of the male obstetricians were in their senior years of residency. Interviews with these two were conducted question-and-answer style over the telephone, as attempts to match schedules for face-to-face meetings were unsuccessful. The other ten obstetricians in my study had been in private practice over time spans ranging from one to twenty-three years, in locations from Texas to New York. The names of these physicians and their cities of residence have been left unmentioned. Most of the interviews with these physicians were conducted in their offices; average duration was about one hour and fifteen minutes. I worked from a written list of questions (which can be found in appendix B), but was careful to proceed informally, following the flow of the obstetrician's thoughts and emotions. I conducted informal repeat interviews (over lunch) with two of the ten.

My methods for selection were simple: in each of the three cities where I conducted the interviews, I asked obstetrical nurses and local childbirth educators for names of physicians who might be willing to talk with me. Several whom I called were not available for interview. I sought and ended up with a fairly broad spectrum: three of the obstetricians interviewed considered themselves "conservative," three saw themselves as "radical," and the other six (including both the two residents and the two women in my sample) saw themselves as "middle-of-the-road." All interviewees were told that I was a medical anthropologist doing research about obstetric training. From these interviews, I have tried to choose for inclusion here the quotations most representative of the opinions and experiences of the majority of interviewees, except where my aim was to demonstrate their differences.

A recent body of social science research clearly demonstrates the importance of recognizing such differences. Good et al. (1985), Hahn (1985), Lock (1985), Helman (1985), and others have recently carried out detailed investigations of the differing attitudes, beliefs, and working models developed by individual physicians. Certainly more research is needed in this area. Although I do not question the existence of profound differences among individual physicians, my analysis in this chapter and in this book as a whole concentrates on what I have come to see as a hidden "core curriculum," as it were, that is taught in medical schools in myriad ways, and perpetuated by example in residency training. *Basic aspects of this core curriculum include the practitioner's systematic objectification and mechanization of, and alienation from, the patient.* Most nascent physicians are heavily exposed to this medical gnosis; those who thoroughly absorb and accept it may develop individual stylistic differences, but these will be variations on a theme. Those who do not will often organize their practices in conscious reaction to this gnosis. My task in this chapter is to clearly present this hidden curriculum, so that its impact on physicians and on birthing women can become clear.

PROCESSES OF PSYCHOLOGICAL TRANSFORMATION: MEDICAL SCHOOL AND RESIDENCY

In the rite of passage that constitutes medical training in American society, the separation phase begins as soon as the initiate departs for medical school and gradually merges into the transitional phase, which lasts for eight full years—four years of medical school and at least four years of residency. The first two years of medical school are essentially the same for all initiates, no matter what their eventual specialty: the basic sciences are intensively studied, animal and human corpses are dissected, and countless quizzes and exams are taken. Initiates "rotate through" the various specialties in their third and fourth years, choosing one and finally specializing in it during residency. Elevated to physician status upon graduation from medical school, the initiate must now learn to define himself in terms of the interactional, attitudinal, core value and belief system of his specialty—a rite within a rite. First-year residents (sometimes known as interns) must begin again at the bottom of the status hierarchy with enormous amounts of "scut work" to perform; responsibility and status levels among residents increase with the acquisition of increasing skill during each advancing year of residency. Movement to the integration stage is gradual, as the fourth-year resident phases into personal responsibility for patients approaching that of Board-certified obstetricians. After graduation from residency, he[2] may stay for a few years with an HMO (which may serve as a sort of cultural buffer zone between residency and private practice).

MEDICAL TRAINING AND COGNITIVE SIMPLIFICATION

Ritual forms part of the matrix that organizes
people into the social structure, and provides the
glue that holds the social and cognitive structures
together. . . . Its principal function . . . is to provide
what we have termed the stage one state: the state that
maximizes a single, univariate orientation to reality
at any level of analysis—physiological, psychological,
or social.

—John McManus, "Ritual and
Human Social Cognition"

Straightforward didactic communications must take differing intellectual levels into account, but, as discussed in the Introduction, ritual may overcome this problem by reducing all participants, at least temporarily, to the same lower cognitive level, which McManus (1979a) describes as "stage one"—thinking in either/or patterns of low cognitive complexity that do not allow for the consideration of options or alternative views. Such simplification in cognitive structure is a necessary precursor to the conceptual reorganization that accompanies true psychological transformation. In medical school, this ritual process of cognitive simplification leads to the development by the initiates of a kind of tunnel vision in which the gnosis of medicine becomes all-important.

During medical school and again in residency, ritual techniques of hazing, strange-making, and symbolic inversion are applied with great effectiveness to bring about this transformation. Medical school initiates—formerly at the top of their classes in college, some already successful in another career—are reduced to lowly status:

> The first two years are like backtracking. No fun. Your last two years in college, you tend to do more graduate level work in smaller classes and you have more freedom about what you learn and how you learn it, and you are suddenly popped back into an environment like first year basic science courses in college, where you kind of get what's thrown at you. . . . There's no freedom about what you learn—everybody learns the same thing. (female obstetrician, age 35)

Primarily studied during the two initial years of medical school are the "basic sciences": biochemistry, neurophysiology, anatomy, histology, bacteriology. Often taught not by physicians but by research scientists, these courses are usually presented as pure science, divorced from explanation of any practical function. "Learning" in biochemistry, for example, often consists of endless rote memorization of chemical formulas, with little or no sense of why or how these might be useful to a physician. Physician/author Charles LeBaron recalls his first year as a medical student at Harvard:

> Introductory lectures on the "Embden-Myerhof Glycolytic Pathway" . . . What is it? Are we synthesizing something, breaking it down? Does it take place in the ocean, outer space, crayfish, where? Does it start things off, end them? In short, what's it all about? Silly concerns. Just plunge right in and start getting it all down cold:
>
> > Rabbit muscle adolase—Class I, Type A, MW 160,000, four sub-units of MW 40,000; Formula: Alpha-2, Beta-2, but isozymes of varying ratio Alpha/Beta are found. . . . See handout. Consider reaction in direction of synthesis of hexose-P. (1981:62–63)

The apparent irrelevance of much of this material to clinical medical work is a source of great discontent to many medical students, especially to those who entered medical school with ideals of "helping humanity."

> Most of us look on the basic sciences as something you put up with until you get to the real heart of the issue. I don't know why they even had a lot of courses. We took bioengineering and biostatistics—even a lot of biochemistry is extremely detailed and really has no relevance. The Krebs cycle is a classic example—a biochemical cycle where you have to learn all these enzymes and then when you get through you never use it. My sister in med school now tells me the same thing. She can't understand why she is going through all these detailed analyses of DNA structures and things like that. (obstetrician, age 38)

The enormous quantity of much of this irritatingly irrelevant material adds to its effectiveness as a hazing technique. One obstetrician's assessment is that

> medical school is not difficult in terms of what you have to learn—there's just so much of it. You go through, in a six-week course, a thousand-page book. The sheer bulk of information is phenomenal. You have pop quizzes in two or three courses every day the first year. We'd get up around 6, attend classes till 5, go home and eat, then head back to school and be in anatomy lab working with a cadaver, or something, until 1 or 2 in the morning, and then go home and get a couple of hours sleep and then go out again. And you did that virtually day in and day out for four years, except for vacations.

One result of such overload is the increasing isolation of the initiates. It is characteristic of rites of passage that the initiates are separated as a group from the rest of society, in order to ensure their removal from the everyday conceptual world. This social separation is a prerequisite for the achievement of the necessary cognitive retrogression.

> Every day, I try to trot a couple of times around the Fenway, a park a block or two from the medical school. How amazing it is to me now that nature still exists out there. . . . But how long I can continue to find the time for even these small excursions is becoming questionable. . . . The day no longer has enough minutes in it; I race through dinner, throwing frozen foods into my toaster oven so I won't waste valuable moments cooking. A close friend gets married in New York—no question of being able to attend. (LeBaron 1981:62)

In the first two years of medical school, pressures of threat and uncertainty mount. A competitive emphasis on grades and tests, the unpredictability of pop quizzes, the overwhelming bulk of the work at hand,

and the increasing isolation of the initiates—all combine to narrow the initiates' range of cognitive functioning. In this process medical students do not become less intelligent; rather, the span of their intellectual capacities and concerns becomes constrained. A kind of tunnel vision develops: the cognitive overload that first- and second-year medical students experience forces them to focus only on what is immediately in front of them. Progressively less capable of reflexivity (Babcock 1980) and the conceptual distance from the socialization process that would accompany it, students gradually lose sight of the idealistic goals they may have had on entering medical school. If the rite of passage is successful, the new goals medical students eventually develop will be structured in accordance with the technocratic and scientific values of the dominant medical system. The emotional impact of this cognitive retrogression is aptly summarized by a former resident:

> Most of us went into medical school with pretty humanitarian ideals. I know I did. But the whole process of medical education makes you inhuman. . . . I've seen people devastated when they didn't know *an* answer. . . . The whole thing can get you pretty warped. I think that's where the feelings begin that somebody owes you something, 'cause you really, you know, you've blocked out a good part of your life. People lost boyfriends and girlfriends, fiancees and marriages. There were a couple of attempted suicides. . . . So you forget about the rest of life. And so by the time you get to residency, you end up not caring about anything beyond the latest techniques you can master and how sophisticated the tests are that you can perform.

REDUNDANCY, ORDER, AND AFFECTIVITY AS TRANSFORMATIVE AGENTS IN MEDICAL TRAINING

For maximum effectiveness, a ritual will concentrate on sending one basic set of symbolic messages that it will repeat over and over again in different forms; emotional and physical reception of these messages is enhanced by the heightened affectivity often generated by ritual. Repetition and the hazing process of physical exhaustion, intensified during residency, work together to ensure that the resident will internalize the "set, established routine" of standard obstetrical procedures so thoroughly that he can perform them on "automatic pilot":

> When I was on call every other night, and I had six hours at home every two days to sleep, I was out of my mind. I didn't feel that I took it out on my patients, but I did feel as if my personality was *gone*—my person was not even inside me anymore—it had flown out the window somewhere, and

I really wondered if I'd ever get it back. I was sort of robotlike. (Kim Stearns, M.D., quoted in Harwood 1984:48)

When your beeper wakes you after two hours sleep (having not let you rest for thirty hours before that) and you roll out of your cot and rush to the bedside, you will be faced with decisions no person should have to make. . . . The fatigue and stress make you care a little less; they enable you to make the decisions. You do it in a daze. After doing this hundreds and then even thousands of times, they are no longer deliberate or even confused, but reflexive. You have learned to bypass existential moralizing. . . . Eventually, you do this even when you are well rested and not under any stress. And when that happens you have become a doctor. (Konner 1987:373)

To understand one of the communicative functions the repetitive patterning of obstetrical procedures has for residents and their mentors, we must appreciate the value that adherence to form has in ritual. Moore and Myerhoff (1977:8) observe that order or exaggerated precision in performance, which sets ritual apart from other modes of social interaction, serves to impute "permanence and legitimacy to what are actually evanescent cultural constructs." This establishment of a sense of "permanence and legitimacy" is particularly important in the performance of obstetrical procedures because of the limited power the obstetrician's technocratic model gives him over the events of birth. Obstetrical residents who have experienced the agony and confusion of maternal or fetal death or the miracle of a healthy birth when all indications were to the contrary know at some level that ultimate power over birth is beyond them and may well fear that knowledge. Resort to ritual in such circumstances is an adaptive evolutionary development for finding the courage to carry on. The format for performing standard obstetrical procedures provides a sense of cultural order imposed on and superior to the chaos of nature:

"In honest-to-God natural conditions," [the obstetrician] says [to the students observing the delivery he is performing], "babies were *sometimes* born without tearing the perineum and without an episiotomy, but without artificial things like anesthesia and episiotomy, the muscle is torn apart and if it is not cut, it is usually not repaired. Even today, if there is no episiotomy and repair, those women quite often develop a rectocoele and a relaxed vaginal floor. This is what I call the saggy, baggy bottom." Laughter by the students. A student nurse asks if exercise doesn't help strengthen the perineum. . . . "No, exercises may be for the birds, but they're not for bottoms. . . . When the woman is bearing down, the leveator muscles of the perineum contract too. This means the baby is caught between the diaphragm and the perineum. Consequently, anesthesia and episiotomy will reduce the pressure on the head, and hopefully, produce more Republicans." More laughter from the students. (Shaw 1974:90)

Upon reading this quotation, an obstetrician in my study commented, "It is this type of humor, so common as a teaching technique, that stamps the impression on the soul. The humor feeds into the discomfort the medical students feel over trying to deal with 'perineums,' and allows them to detach in a derisive way."

To say that obstetrical procedures are "performed" is true both in the sense that they are "done" and in the sense that they can be "acted" and "staged," as we can see from the quotation above. Such ordered, acted, and stylized techniques serve to deflect questioning of the efficacy of the underlying beliefs and forestall the presentation of alternative points of view (Moore and Myerhoff 1977:7). Speaking as eloquently to the obstetrical personnel who perform the procedures as to the women who receive them, these "routine" procedures ensure that the more nascent obstetricians see birth "managed" this way, and the more they themselves actively manage birth this way, the stronger becomes their belief that birth *must* be managed this way:

> Why don't I do home births? Are you kidding? By the time I got out of residency, you couldn't get me *near* a birth without five fetal monitors right there, and three anesthesiologists standing by. (female obstetrician, one year in practice)

In "Ritual and Ontogenetic Development," McManus provides physiological groundwork for the feeling of inevitability which can be generated by ritual:

> Habituation is the consequence of a mechanism for consolidating input into the existing model for assimilation. This appears to occur through repetition. . . . The locus of occurrence seems to be among the interneurons rather than in the input neurons of the system (Pribram 1971). Repeated activation of the habituation process, repeated matching of the internal reality model, consolidates the incoming data into that model. The effect of habituation is to create information redundancy, conceptual certainty, and a feeling of necessity. (1979a:199)

Habituation to the redundancy of obstetrical rituals works to create conceptual homogeneity in hospital birth, as well as the certainty that this homogeneity is necessary and valuable, since it so effectively reduces the uncertainty that might otherwise surround the physician's perception of birth. Any change in the rituals through which hospital birth is reduced to such homogeneity is thus equivalent to a reduction in certainty, whereas continued performance of the rituals affirms, in the hearts and minds of the medical personnel involved, the technocratic model of reality upon which these procedures are based.[3] The driving need to reduce uncertainty (Fox 1957) explains why the medical community exhibits such reluctance to alter their standard procedures for birth, for they are taught to regard these procedures as the direct cause of the general success of the birth process in modern times.[4] One physician in my sample put it this way:

> My philosophy of birth is using what I've been taught to use and what I've seen in my experience works, keeping in mind safety above all else and not compromising safety for social reasons. If women put demands on me where I can't monitor the baby, or have an IV in them when they suddenly abrupt and go into shock, start hemorrhaging and go into shock before I can get an IV in—no, I can't live with that, I can't put myself or wouldn't put them in that kind of jeopardy. They can go to somebody else. There are guys out there that will do anything they ask, who make birth a social event. And I think they jeopardize the woman's safety and the baby's safety.

Despite the thoroughness of the learning that stems from intensive physical repetition of obstetrical procedures, there are certain kinds of physical lessons that are far more thoroughly absorbed than others. As discussed in the Introduction, the higher the emotional affectivity of an event, the more deeply it will be imprinted on the psyche of the individual. "Through careful and precise manipulation of symbols and sensory stimuli" (Moore and Myerhoff 1977:7), ritual can create the kind of highly charged emotional experience that can lead to long-term memory storage. Some of the procedures of the delivery room have just this highly charged quality. For example, performing an episiotomy for the first time carries a certain amount of the kind of affectivity that enhances memorization, whereas performing it for the fiftieth time works to reinforce patterns already learned. The great majority of births attended by obstetrical residents are channeled through the same procedures, and most of these births turn out well. Thus, once the resident has internalized the pattern for performing these procedures, this learning (and the successful births that accompany it) become generalized.

Against this generalized background, unusually complicated and dangerous births stand out. The obstetricians in my study seemed always conscious of the relatively few highly emotional "disasters" they had experienced:

> The things that stand out most in your mind are the real disasters. Probably the one that stands out the most in my mind was a supposedly healthy woman who walked in to have her baby and she was laboring way down the hall because she'd had two kids before and no one expected any problems from her. And she suddenly arrested—what she'd done was throw an

embolism. Most people die immediately from that. But this lady—we resus-
citated her and got the baby delivered and she lived to tell about the experience and so did the baby. And that was—I mean, it's a terrifying kind of
experience, because people just don't usually arrest in the middle of labor—
cardiac and respiratory arrest. That lady wouldn't have lived in any other
setting. And she really wouldn't have lived if there hadn't been anesthesia
and respiratory therapy and a neonatologist right there close together like
there is in a county system where everybody could work on her. A nurse
just happened to pass her room at the right moment. You know, she wasn't
just ignored, it was just that she wasn't a high priority patient like everybody
else; we thought she was normal. We had all these other people who were
sick. So you pay more attention to them.

[Question: What was this incident's effect on the way you practice?]
Well, I think it had a lot of effect. It makes me much more conservative.
Like when people ask me about home delivery or going to a birthing center
or something like that—I mean, *it really drove the point home* [emphasis
mine] that you can't predict who's going to have trouble in labor. So it really
makes me tell my patients that I can't go along with a policy like that.

These highly specific details of disaster stand in sharp contrast to
this same physician's far more generalized memories of the happy times
during her training:

Happy-wise, I was most pleased about my last year of residency, because as
a chief resident you can see private patients of your own. And I was very
pleased when I'd follow someone through and they'd have a normal delivery
and be real happy about it. That's real rewarding.

Another obstetrician provides a further example of the lasting effects
of a highly charged emotional experience:

I'll never forget one I had as a resident—a lady who had pregnancy-associ-
ated diabetes and she'd been followed appropriately and at forty-one weeks
came in and had a dead baby. She came in in labor about three days later,
and dilated to 7 centimeters and stopped. And so we gave her pitocin
and she had some harder contractions and three hours later still hadn't progressed. And I was the junior resident and I said you know this lady's got
a big baby, a 9½ or 10 lb. baby, and the baby's dead, but we don't want
to section her if we can avoid it because we don't have the baby's interests
at heart, and the senior resident said "Well let's give her some more
time." . . . I watched her all night and when her total length of labor got to
twenty-four hours she still hadn't dilated any more. That's not an unusual
length of labor, there are a lot of women who have twenty-four-hour labors.
But hers had been obstructed for ten hours I guess. She developed a fever.
We ultimately had to do a section on her and her uterus was so thin that—I
think if we'd let it go much longer it might have ruptured. Trying to suture

it back together was a real mess. She had high blood loss. She had post-operatively a fever that went on for four or five days. She infected her wound and she broke down the wound[5] so that the muscle planes broke down, and so she had a wound that was basically open for about six weeks while it slowly granulated in. You know, I think about her when I face letting patients labor a little bit longer than usual. . . . I found that whole experience to be pretty traumatic, and I don't want to go through anything like that again. So I tend to be very cautious about longer labors—they make me real uncomfortable—and I wonder how they did it fifty years or so ago. I'm grateful for all the things I can do to keep that sort of thing from happening.

In contrast, this same physician gave me a far more generalized report of the high point of his career as a resident:

Uh—probably the beginning of my senior year [was the high point] because at that point you're essentially responsible individually for a patient's care without having to consult a staff physician, and you're also carrying the responsibility of training junior residents below you. I think that was a big turning point—you're finally getting to the point where you're going to be able to function independently.

Thus we see that one emotionally experienced "disaster" can influence the beliefs and behavior of an obstetrician far more profoundly and powerfully than hundreds of normal deliveries. This single phenomenon goes a long way toward explaining why obstetricians cling so tenaciously to the birth rituals that have been consistently presented to them as the only means of preventing those disasters. It seems philosophically possible that failures of technocratic rituals to prevent maternal or fetal death or damage, such as those experienced by the last obstetrician, might lead doctors to question the appropriateness of their procedures. However, the power of the habituating process discussed above seems to ensure that failures generally will be attributed, not to flaws in the rituals themselves, but to the inherent defectiveness of nature and the female body. *Thus each significant failure experienced by the resident,* as in the case of the diabetic woman described above, *will lead to intensified performance of the rituals designed to prevent such failure, rather than to their rejection.*

Certainly, research is often conducted in obstetrics that weighs the efficacy of various procedures. But the obstetricians in my study seemed consistently to take seriously research that validated their standard practices or expanded their technological repertoire, while explaining away research results that challenged those practices or the basic philosophy that underlies them. For example, one thirty-seven-year-old obstetrician stated,

I know that there's been a lot of discussion in the lay literature and in the medical literature too about the utility of monitoring. I read a couple of studies that said the clinical outcome is no different from electronically versus clinically monitored patients. And my gut feeling is that it's not true. Because several times, if we hadn't had the monitor on, we never would have recognized the heart rate decelerations that were going on—and even though you don't, you might not see a depressed baby—it might be more of a long-term than an acute problem.

In an even more convoluted manner, an older obstetrician explained away evidence he had been told about by a colleague on the benefits of walking during labor, saying that such studies came

> not from mainstream medicine, but from childbirth educators and Lamaze people, telling physicians that this is a helpful thing to do, to send people walking. Well, we used to send people walking who came in in false labor, 'cause it would help the false labor, okay? . . . Labor is going to continue whether you're walking or not, dependent on the release of prostaglandins from the uterus. And I don't think walking has ever been shown to increase the release of prostaglandins during labor. If anything, it might decrease it! And that's why we send people in false labor walking. And people tell you, when you send them walking, that that's relieved and then it goes away, and if it *were* releasing prostaglandins then it would *increase* their labor. So I don't know that there's any scientific evidence at all to support walking as a helpful thing in labor.[6]
>
> Now, whether it's more *comfortable* for a woman to be up walking than it is for her to be confined to a bed, I think depends on a lot of factors—whether you put that in her mind or not, whether you've programmed her to believe that, or programmed the nurses to believe that. And I think it varies a lot with the patients. I see some very strange things done today, that just amaze me that people will do. I still don't find—I don't change what I do without some good scientific reasons to change, just 'cause it's socially popular, you know, at the moment.

The authors of *Science as Cognitive Process* offer a means of understanding such convoluted reasoning. They explain that once a scientific paradigm becomes accepted, the general assumption is that this paradigm is correct, so that implicit in the activities of the scientists who espouse it is the expectation that the paradigm will be confirmed. The paradigm itself "admits no disconfirmation—only errors in meaning, data collection, or analysis," so that any encountered disconfirmations of the paradigm are generally "not fed back into the core of the model," but left at its edges, resulting at most in "minor modifications in patterns of scientific behavior." "Normal science," these authors continue, "is something of a closed loop, rarely, if ever, open to serious modifications at the core" (Rubinstein et al. 1984:65).

COGNITIVE TRANSFORMATION IN
MEDICAL TRAINING

Cognitive transformation occurs in ritual when "symbols and awareness become integrated in experience" (MacDonald et al. 1989). The
following quote from a fifty-three-year-old obstetrician presents the
outcome of such transformative learning:

> I think my training was valuable. The people who trained us, and their
> philosophy, were unbeatable. Dr. Pritchard—he's *the* man in obstetrics to-
> day in this country. And his philosophy was one of teaching one way to do
> it, and that was *his* way. And it was basically the right way....I like the set
> hard way. I like the riverbanks that confine you in a direction. Later on . . .
> you can incorporate a little bit of this or that as things change, but you learn
> one thing real well, and that's *the* way.

In medical schools and on hospital wards, this cognitive transformation of the initiates, this perceptual fusion with "the way" occurs when
reality as presented by the technocratic model, and reality as the initiate
perceives it, gradually become one. The intellectual overload of the first
two years plays a significant role in this transformational process.

Most of the intellectual content of the courses taught in the first two
years carries emotional affectivity (in the form of grade anxiety) only
until the course is completed and the grade received and so is quickly
forgotten.

> I was thinking yesterday that I must be a lot dumber than I was when I went
> to medical school, because I don't remember any of the stuff that we learned.
> You remember the things that you use clinically, that's all. (female obstetri-
> cian, age 39)

In contrast, the last two years of medical school, and all four years of
residency, are spent primarily in just the sort of clinical hands-on experience that *is* remembered. A practicing obstetrician recalls,

> I had delivered maybe thirty babies as a medical student. When I was a first-
> year resident . . . on my first day I was thrown in as the Chief of Labor and
> Delivery. I had an intern and six medical students under me. A lady came
> in off the elevator abrupting, we had to do an emergency Cesarean on her.
> I had never even seen one, much less done one! And I had to go in there,
> scared. Well, the second-year resident comes in and walks me through it.
> It's a "see one, do one, teach one" program, and that's how medical schools
> are generally run. Somebody shows you how, they walk you through it once
> or twice. And the next few times, you do it, with them still watching you
> and guiding you. You do that a few times, and then you start teaching
> others. And that's the basic philosophy of how you learn. It's not a bad sys-

tem. I don't know of anything that can replace it. And you learn pretty quick!

Given the effectiveness for learning of the emotional and physical involvement described above, we might well ask why, in a transformative rite of passage whose last six years consist largely of just such emotional and physical learning, the first two years consist primarily of intellectual overload? A rite-of-passage perspective reveals a function, if not a purpose, underlying this educational method. Two years of nothing but science, besides serving to separate the nascent physician from the person that he was, also serve very effectively to separate him from the people whom he will treat. Before he begins to deal with real people as patients, he learns conceptual distance from them, an essential step in his transformational process, as LeBaron demonstrates:

> I held the slide up against the light again. Yes, that had once been someone's finger. It had felt coffee cups and pieces of paper and buttons, scalded itself, shook hands, gestured in excitement, caressed faces. Now it lived between pieces of glass in a box. A small chill ran through me. "Strange," I said. "Yeah, isn't it? Here's a piece of penis. A little later, you'll get to a salivary gland from someone's tongue." I looked at him, my eyes widening. Phil shrugged. "After a while, you just don't think about it anymore." I started again, a little more slowly. If this was human flesh, however sliced, dried, or stained, I should at least show it the courtesy of adequate attention. Soon people began to leave for lunch. It was almost one, I was hungry, and another class started at one-thirty. I sped up: esophagus, testicle, intestine . . . Where are those crazy terminal bars they said I should see? The heck with them. . . . I'm getting something to eat.
>
> You get used to things fast around here, I thought as I locked up the microscope. (LeBaron 1981:40)

Growing detachment from both the diseases studied and the people who have them leads fairly rapidly in the first year of medical school to the development of the kind of cynicism and intellectual arrogance that can only arise from such detachment. LeBaron documents this process, describing one of his first-year Harvard class's rare contacts with an actual patient, a multiple sclerosis victim. The class's first reaction was dismay at the actual physical presence of a "CPC—clinical-pathological correlation, as disease victims were named," but soon:

> "Shit, I'd love to do a coronal section on his frontal lobe," said someone behind me. "You'd see demyelinated plaques the size of golfballs." Some knowing snickers. People hadn't started off talking that way; initially everyone had approached our occasional CPC sessions with an almost reverential awe—the word actually made flesh. But now after a year of dog labs,

corpses, continual memorization, and no patients, that kind of conversation was part of the background noise. And those expressions of flippancy, cynicism, the sarcastic smiles that had been so conspicuous by their absence back at orientation were already starting to spread through the class like some sinister psychological tide. (LeBaron 1981:213)

The Cartesian philosophical separation of mind and body inherent in the scientific medical view does not permit the interaction of individual consciousness with the molecules and atoms that comprise the stuff of "scientific" inquiry:

> The first two years of medical school . . . are not taught in a framework of how *people* function. The students are taught about bodies as though the minds, emotions, and lives associated with those bodies were irrelevant. They are also taught about hundreds of pathological conditions and processes as though they were all equal: equal in importance, equal in outcome, equal in incidence. (Carver 1981:132)

Actual clinical experience is withheld until after the initiates have internalized the basic attitudes and values underlying this scientific worldview. The conceptual distance from their patients thus achieved is intensified when the students begin clinical work, usually in the second semester of the second year. Because this work consists primarily of the highly routinized tasks of doing physicals and taking medical histories, it tends to widen the gap between medical students and the people they are learning to heal, encouraging them to regard these individuals as "cases"—"the gall bladder in 133" or "the section in 214."

This objectification of the patient is further intensified in residency:

> As interns, we lose why we went into medicine—whatever humanistic interest we had. It's very hard to sit there and listen to someone tell his life story when you've got six other admissions, bloods to draw, you've got to be up all night. Every second you spend being compassionate means that much less time to sleep. So you become very efficient at not really listening to people—just getting the information you need, and shutting them off. (second-year resident, quoted in Harwood 1984:70)

Melvin Konner, an anthropologist who recently completed medical school and documents his experiences in *Becoming a Doctor: A Journey of Initiation in Medical School*, feels that doctor-patient separation in medical training does not stop with the objectification of the patient:

> It is obvious from what I have written here that the stress of clinical training alienates the doctor from the patient, that in a real sense the patient becomes the enemy. (*Goddamit, did she blow her IV again? Jesus Christ, did he spike*

a temp?) At first I believed that this was an inadvertent and unfortunate concomitant of medical training, but now I think that it is intrinsic. Not only
stress and sleeplessness, but a sense of the patient as the cause of one's distress contributes to the doctor's detachment. This detachment is not objective but downright negative. To cut and puncture a person, to take his or
her life in your hands, to pound the chest until the ribs break . . . these and
a thousand other things may require something stronger than objectivity.
They may actually require a measure of dislike. (1987:373)

Once early internalization of objective science has been accomplished
during the first two years of medical school, in their third year initiates are offered choices for finding a sense of individual identity within
the medical paradigm through clinical rotations that expose them to
the active practice of various medical specialties. The reasons given
for choosing obstetrics were quite consistent among the obstetricians
interviewed—most often, the happy nature of obstetrical practice:

I really do like delivering babies and taking care of female patients and having happy times being involved. Basically I like healthy people who have a
short-term problem and they're going to get well. I don't like to deal with
elderly patients or dying patients. And then I really love to operate. And you
get to operate as a gynecologist. Those are the real reasons that I chose it.
I didn't choose it until my fourth year of medical school, after I had rotated
through a lot of different things.

In obstetrics as in other branches of medicine, the highest values are
placed on the acquisition of skills, especially surgical skills, as the previous OB/GYN (a female) has indicated. Unlike many other specialties,
in obstetrics most of the technological skills acquired are applied with
great success, as most births will turn out well no matter where or how
they happen. Not having to confront the technological failures of termi-
nal illness or old age on daily rounds, the obstetrician does not experience the limitations of technology as often as do his medical colleagues.
Rather, his experience of technology is more positive, as for him, most
of the time the technology really "works." Thus the application of technology to obstetrics uniquely qualifies obstetricians to acquire and to
pass on a strong sense of the value of the technology which they experience as successful most of the time.

The incorporation of both a sense of the value of technology and of
her own sense of value to society are evident in the same obstetrician's
response to a query about her philosophy of birth:

Birth is a process where you're adding a new life to the world, and hopefully you're enriching the world and the people who are involved with that

child. . . . There's so much we can do now to help mothers and babies that might have died before.

In seeing herself, the obstetrician, as the active agent in the birth process, this physician is not alone. A fourth-year resident states:

Well, I sort of see my role at birth this way: I am the captain of the team, and the mother and the father and the nurses—they are all players. If somebody is going to call the shots, it's going to be me. Sometimes the mother calls the shots, but mostly it's me.

These two statements reflect the nearly complete acceptance of the technocratic model of birth by these two physicians; in this model the obstetrician, not the mother, is the "deliverer," the active agent responsible for "enriching the world" with "perfect babies." I asked an obstetrician who does not share this attitude to put in writing what he sees as the primary characteristics of the residents emerging from the obstetrical program in his Eastern city. He responded as follows:

The residents I am seeing today are very consistent in their attitudes and philosophies about birth. That's why I can't find anyone to hire around here. These are the characteristics that they all seem to me to share:

1. *It is always the patient's fault.* This woman came to me recently—she had been told by a resident in the clinic that she would never get rid of her chronic vaginal infection because she was too fat. She wasn't obese or anything like that—only weighed about 160. Finally she came to me and all she had was a simple yeast infection that he had misdiagnosed. I gave her some Monistat and she was fine the next day. The worst thing was that she believed him for a while, so of course she was feeling terrible about herself because of what he had said.

Here's another example, told to me by a patient I saw yesterday:

Woman to OB/GYN: I have been keeping track of my symptoms and I think I have PMS.

OB/GYN (just out of residency): The problem with you is that you have an obsessive compulsive neurosis, evidenced by the way you keep track of your menses.

And she went back to him! But finally she came to me, and she was right—she does have PMS and it's responding to treatment.

2. *Aloofness.*

3. *Heavy reliance on technology.*

4. *General paternalistic approach.* I'll give you an example of a conversation I heard recently:

Female Patient (to OB after hysterectomy): It hurts more on the left side, doctor. Should I be worried?

OB (to Female Patient): No, dear, we did more work on that side.

Resident (to OB outside of patient's room): Why did you tell her that? I was there, and I didn't see you do more work on that side.

OB (to resident): Of course not, son, but look how much better she feels now!

This is how these residents learn to treat women!

5. *Disdain for paraprofessionals.*

6. *Disdain for nutrition.*

7. *No holism in approach, no consideration of emotional needs.*

8. *Lack of respect for consequences of surgery—time is money or the super-doctor approach—"I can do anything."* One of the teachers most respected by the residents here is so respected because he can do a Cesarean in twelve minutes. His complication rate is horrendous because you can't help but butcher the woman when your emphasis is speed, but the residents don't seem to notice that.

9. *Reverence for the "I'm in control" M.D.*

10. *Disdain for anyone who is willing to relinquish complete control—* they can't understand why I have nurse-midwives doing "my" deliveries.

11. *Disdain for anyone who doesn't rely on technology.*

No residents scrub in on my deliveries because I don't do much, don't use the machines, so they think they have nothing to learn from me—they don't want to know about truly normal birth.

And he summed up the cognitive transformation that occurs:

It doesn't seem to matter—male or female, young or old, wealthy or poor—it is only the most unusual individual who comes through a residency program as anything less than a technological clone. This rite of passage that you are talking about is an assembly line to the adoration of technology, no matter who starts at the beginning.

ALTERNATIVE TRANSFORMATIONS: THE HUMANISTIC PARADIGM

Dr. Emmanuel Friedman (Harvard Medical School, Beth Israel Hospital, Boston) asserted that the Friedman labor curve, which he developed, "is being abused more than it is being used appropriately." . . . Dr. Friedman termed today's high Cesarean rate an "iatroepidemic" [a physician-caused epidemic] . . . [stating] that 70 percent of Cesareans for prolonged labor and 50 percent of Cesareans for arrest disorders

progress stops] are unnecessary. Dr. Friedman observed
that today's "humanistic" and "technologic" trends in
obstetric care "are in direct conflict and the challenge
for the 1990s is to join the two sides together."
                    —Diony Young and Beth Shearer, "Crisis in
                        Obstetrics: The Management of Labor"

As we saw in Chapter 5, human beings are not automatons; rites of
passage can fail in their generalized goal of transmitting the core value
and belief system of a given society to the initiate. Three of the twelve
obstetricians in my study came by different routes to at least a partial
conceptual rejection of the technocratic model of birth and to the development of an alternative paradigm that can best be described as
"humanistic." Although not as complete a departure from the technocratic model as the wholistic model described in Chapter 4, this humanistic approach still differs from the dominant model in fundamental
ways. Under this alternative model, the patient (still called a patient),
not the rules nor the technology, comes first:

> I guess I can best summarize my philosophy as birth should be what the
> woman wants it to be. I can say that without reservation, except that I feel
> that the woman when she chooses should be well-informed as to what she's
> choosing. So, if you . . . don't want a sonogram, or a hospital test for some
> reason, and you know that there's a 1 out of 10,000 chance that that test
> may actually prevent death or some other complication, and you're willing
> to take that chance, I think it's your right to make the decisions, up to a
> point.
>   Now where is that point? Nobody's been able to resolve this issue, and
> that is, where does the fetus have rights? And that becomes more difficult.
> At this point now, I feel that if the woman truly wants to have the delivery
> her way, and if the risk to the baby is relatively small, if she understands
> what the risks are, I'm still in favor of her doing that. I really can't categor-
> ically say right now that exactly what I believe and what modern medicine
> says is the very best for the baby, across the board, so therefore it has to be
> done that way—we can't say that yet. I don't think we can really prove that
> a hospital birth with a certain structure in which every kind of test is done
> is the very very best for a baby. So I think women *need* to have a choice in
> their experience.

As another one of these "radical" obstetricians expresses his humanism:

> I see birth almost as a re-birth or a continuance. I don't know how many
> deliveries I've been at now—I guess several thousand—but each one just

seems so unique and different. I think birth is a normal natural process, that we have learned some things that we can add to, we can make it better at times, but by and large we should just stay out of the way and enjoy the normal natural thing that's going on. . . . My role, if I have a role in birth, is only when there's a problem—as long as things are going well, I just stand around. A real disservice that medicine has done for people is remove death and birth from the family and turn them into medical events. I'm not quite ready to go for home births because of some of the problems that can come up. But I do like a real homey birthing room–type setting with families there, and we've had deliveries with eight to ten people there—everybody excited and it's a real neat experience. And I often just slip out the door and leave, because I know my role isn't really—I know it's not much, and once I'm sure that things are okay, I'll just kind of slide out, and I'll see 'em later, you know, because they've got more important things to do than gloat over me, which is kind of false, you know.

All three "radicals" in my study are in their early forties. The paths by which they came to the development of such an approach reveal both the power of their socialization processes and the means by which, in spite of this power, conceptual distance from these processes can be achieved, either during the rite of passage itself, or after its completion.

The differences between a nonreflexive and a reflexive response to the first two years of medical education are illustrated by two obstetricians in my study:

[Question: Why do you not see patients until late in the second year?]
I don't know. Mostly it's because you have to have some of the other background before you start playing like you're a doctor. You have to have some basics to work on, and you really have to go back to basic sciences and learn principles about why things work a certain way before you can build clinical medicine onto that.

Here this obstetrician demonstrates the effectiveness of her socialization through her acceptance of the science-before-patients structure of her medical school training. In contrast, one of the "radicals" demonstrates conceptual distance from his own socialization with his thoughts on a "better" way:

By taking clinical rotations early on in medical school, you would break up some of the basic science years, and there would be a lot better attitude and a better idea of what you're trying to learn and of the purpose of the basic sciences. As it is now, the basic sciences really get you off the track of what you're there for. Most of us went in with pretty high humanitarian ideals, but by the time you get through the basic science years, most of the people in my class had developed a pretty cynical attitude.

How did this physician manage to maintain enough conceptual distance from his socialization process to be able to analyze it in this highly reflexive way? Realizing early on that his family would suffer considerably if he did not spend *some* time with them, he made a commitment to take off one night a week for that purpose, accepting in advance that it would mean being "a few answers short" on the next day's test:

> It was a tradeoff, but I think worthwhile in the long run, because I knew that my family would be with me a lot longer than medical school. That difference, whether it's a maturity level or not, was missing in a lot of people. I was older, about twenty-seven; most start at twenty-one or twenty-two.

The cognitive separation achieved by this conscious decision not to participate in the competitive values inherent in medical education was intensified by his first child's birth—a highly medicalized and very unhappy experience that occurred during medical school: "When we kind of figured out that things didn't have to be that way, I guess it made us both into crusaders."

As Cynthia Carver, M.D., points out, the medical school selection process ensures the admission of students with highly competitive instincts and a strong scientific bent, who "generally went straight through, from high school to college to medical school, [managing] to reach the age of twenty-one without having experienced anything much other than academic life" (1981:129). Those students selected *out* by this process include those who, "despite being as bright as the high mark getters, allow themselves to be 'distracted' by . . . volunteer work, music, art, literature" and other careers (1981:129).[7] The difference that such "distractions" can make in the medical school experience is documented by writer Charles LeBaron. In *Gentle Vengeance: An Account of the First Year at Harvard Medical School* (1981), LeBaron describes the tremendous cognitive struggle he underwent to maintain conceptual distance from the powerful socialization process he was undergoing. Thirty-four years old, with twelve years' experience as a paramedic and social worker when he entered Harvard, LeBaron's goal was to emerge from medical school with his compassion and involvement with people intact. Well into the first year, aware of a gradual attitude change and afraid that he would succumb, he hit upon the idea of writing a book about his socialization process, in order to "maintain some detachment, give me an objectivity, an independence where none might otherwise exist" (1981:269).

In contrast to LeBaron, the other two physicians in my study group who exhibited considerable conceptual distance from the technocratic model came to this objectivity much later in their obstetrical careers. One of them, known in the Southern city where he practices as the most radical obstetrician in town, was "a good country boy who believed everything they told me," until he reached internship in a military hospital during the Vietnam war. The shock and continuing horror of trying to patch senselessly mutilated bodies back together led him to question all of American society, including its biomedical system. This exploration led him, as it led so many in the early 1970s, to embrace principles of the counterculture, including feminism; this in turn led to a conceptual rejection of the highly patriarchal obstetrical paradigm of birth.

The other "radical" physician in my study group came to the same conceptual rejection through quite a different route. He too "believed everything" they told him, until one day shortly after graduation from residency he attended a debate between one of his favorite professors and Suzanne Arms, author of *Immaculate Deception* (1975) and one of the most radical pioneers of the natural childbirth movement. Expecting the professor to "beat the pants off her," the recent graduate was surprised and shocked when instead "she made him look like an idiot." Eager to redress the balance, he determined to write a book "proving how wrong she was and that my professor was right." Toward that end, he purchased Arms's book and read it straight through. By the time he finished, "She had won again! I realized that, although some of what she said was bullshit, basically she was absolutely right." This realization led to his further exploration of the wide body of nonmedical literature on birth, including works by Kitzinger (1980), Odent (1984), Star (1986), and Stewart and Stewart (1976, 1977, 1979, 1981) and to attending nonobstetrical conferences on childbirth in search of support for the development of a new paradigm to replace the one that had crumbled. He said: "And then I met midwives, and midwives really taught me how to do birth."

In an effort to describe the humanistic paradigm, psychologist and registered nurse Susan McKay states:

> The flip side of dehumanization, humanization, regards people as having inherent worth—without some being more worthy than others—respects the irreplaceability of each individual, avoids stereotyping or treating everyone alike, views the person wholistically, honors freedom of action rather than seeing people as simple objects of action, promotes shared decision-making and responsibility, and communicates with empathy and positive affect. Hu-

manization acts as a counterbalance to the effects of technology; it means tuning in to the person as well as the technology, being present through such acts as sitting with the mother, walking her in the halls, easing her into a hot tub of water, holding her, rubbing her back, and whispering encouragement. (McKay 1990a:14)

McKay points to the perceptive shifts that result from such care as she describes, suggesting that when women are "untethered from the bed, monitor leads and IV lines . . . they [gain] mobility and control, [and are] no longer objects but subjects, no longer machines but birthing women responding to the overtures of caring others."

Correspondingly, the humanistic obstetricians in my study offer their patients some real alternatives. These include the utilization of doulas or monitrices for labor support (Perez and Snedeker 1990),[8] nurse-midwives for prenatal care, for labor support, and for delivery (in hospitals where this is permitted); the options of limited monitoring, no IV, drinking juices and eating their own foods during labor, walking and/or relaxing in water throughout labor, perineal massage instead of episiotomy, and of choosing to squat, stand, or lie on their sides for birth. (Their Cesarean rates are indicative of the benefits of their commitment to such an approach. All three practice in hospitals where the overall Cesarean rate is 21–30 percent, yet their individual rates range from 12–17 percent. Frustrated by his inability to get his Cesarean rate below 12 percent, one of them told me that he is often unsuccessful in convincing women who want to schedule elective repeat Cesareans to try vaginal delivery instead.) Unstartling as these options may seem to the lay person, the extent of their "radicality" is indicated by the response of a more conservative obstetrician practicing in the same city as one of these three. This colleague's comments indicate his bewilderment at the obviously profound philosophical differences between his approach to birth and theirs:

> I put women on a pedestal. I open doors for them. I have a lot of respect for them. In the hospital I have to see them in certain degrading positions, see certain degrading parts of their bodies. So I try to do all I can to maintain their dignity. I heard that one of these younger doctors lets women be naked on his examining table. Can you imagine that? Why would any woman want to do that? I had gowns specially made that conceal all of a woman's body except the part I absolutely have to see in order to preserve their dignity. Once I saw a woman in labor—another doctor's patient—she was crawling around on all fours, stark naked, panting like a puppy. Can you imagine? What kind of respect for women does that show?

When queried as to his policies, this "younger doctor" readily stated that, not finding the female body or any positions women may adopt in labor in any way "degrading," he does indeed let his patients be naked on the examining table and in the labor rooms if they so choose and utilize whatever position and type of breathing they desire for labor and for birth. When I mentioned to him that even the most conservative obstetricians I had interviewed seemed to really like women, he responded vehemently:

> You haven't found any OBs that hate women so far? I can't *believe* that some of these guys like women. They *can't* like women for the things that they do. How can you put some women in the situation they're in during delivery, and like 'em? I mean, why would you put a lady flat on her back, looking up at fluorescent lights, with her arms out like this [demonstrates]—we even used to have their hands tied down! I must admit, I didn't think about it at the time [during residency], that's how insensitive I was—but the minute I heard about alternatives, I grabbed onto 'em. These guys all know the alternatives and they don't grab onto 'em. I mean, I've been trying for years to show these guys that you can turn the lights down, and you don't have to have 'em flat on their backs or use stirrups. . . . They can be the way they want to be to have their babies. When you really let them feel free to choose, it's beautiful to see what they do. But when you never allow them to know that there are options for them—how can you like women, and do that?

Yet these "radicals" share a great deal with their more conservative colleagues: they are trained in the same interventions as are the "conservatives," bound by the same medical rules, and constrained by the same legal system. For example, one of them describes himself as having "one foot in each world," in an attempt to act as a bridge between both. Nevertheless, when a couple desiring home birth interviewed this obstetrician, they ended up leaving in a huff, accusing him of having "not just one, but both feet squarely on the medical side." This statement reflects their sensitivity to the difference in reality models held by homebirthers and even the most humanistic of physicians.

Although the humanistic approach to birth does offer women some real alternatives, it represents not a full rejection but simply a modification of the technocratic model of birth. Women who utilize the services of obstetricians who espouse this approach will still give birth in the hospital and thus will be subject to the same cultural forces as those women who go to the more conservative obstetricians. Any deviations from the norm in labor will still render them subject to a "cascade of interventions" (Brackbill et al. 1984), for the limits to the humanistic approach are defined by the outer boundaries of the technocratic paradigm. Even the patient of the humanistic physician starting out in the birthing room with his full support will wind up on pitocin in a labor room if her cervix fails to dilate to 10 centimeters within the time limit of that hospital (usually twenty-six hours). No matter how compassionate the physician, he is often powerless himself to circumvent hospital rules:

> The fact that I'm even willing to practice in a hospital that won't let women have their babies after birth unless they're in the birthing room just goes to show how much I compromise my principles every day. We don't even give them a choice—no option at all. It's terrible, but if they deliver in the LDR they're just not gonna have their baby. I'm compromising my beliefs to work in this hospital and make good money . . . [and] to ultimately get these things into the hospital, but it's going to take a whole lot longer.

Taking off from Naisbitt (1982), some of the essential distinctions between the models in question here can be summed up this way:

The technocratic model: high tech/low touch

The humanistic model: high tech/high touch

The wholistic model: low tech/high touch

WOMEN IN OBSTETRICS

A new trend in obstetrics is the increasing percentage of women who will be practicing this specialty: half the students in many medical schools today are female. In 1986, 69 percent of U.S. medical school graduates who said they would choose obstetrics were women, compared to 34 percent in 1982 (*Wall Street Journal* 1987). Nevertheless, most female obstetricians practicing today went through medical training as a decided minority and so often felt constrained to overcompensate for being female:[9]

> Women in obstetrics are, as a group, more in philosophical agreement with their male medical colleagues than with female midwives. They are not even necessarily more polite to patients or more willing to accept the patient's having a more active role in her own care. This may be due to a number of factors: the selection process of medical schools; the socialization process during medical education; psychological factors related to the choice of obstetrics as a specialization; the stress inherent in obstetric residency programs; and the fact that women in medicine comprise a small minority . . . they may

feel that they have to outdo the dominant group—males—on male terms. (Lichtmann 1988:139)

Thus far female obstetricians have made no significant changes in the conduct of American birth. What differences the power of increasing numbers will make remains to be tracked by students of the American way of birth. One "radical" obstetrician offered this observation:

I was recently amazed when several OB residents who are female stated that they wanted their epidurals by the third contraction. It's so interesting that these women, usually placed on a pedestal by feminists . . . really don't know what it is to give birth and don't stand a chance of finding out. They learn from their experience in the hospital that birth is only okay if it is technologically controlled. Rarely if ever will they participate in a truly normal birth. That's perceived as boring because they don't learn any skills from it. . . . If a female resident never sees normal, of course she's going to want an epidural!

OBSTETRICS AND AMERICAN SOCIETY

Innovations in technology make it increasingly amenable to humanistic uses—for example, epidurals have been improved to the point where women can "still feel to push, can still push their babies out real well, but without the pain"; women walking in labor can be monitored by telemetry, which will result in less pressure to go to bed to be monitored. When utilized by humanistic physicians, such developments have the potential of being extremely important to women: if technology is truly placed *at the service of the individual,* instead of the individual at the mercy of the technology, then the messages of hospital birth rituals and the focus of obstetric training *could* become profoundly altered.

The changes effected by more humanism in birth—the presence of fathers, the "awake and aware" mother, the "bonding period," however brief, and the growing number of other options available to mothers—do pose a threat to the integrity and the conceptual hegemony of the technocratic model, for the more options the radicals offer, the more options the conservatives, too, must provide. As one conservative obstetrician noted,

It was these other guys that first got fathers into the delivery room in this town. They started doing it, so then we had to. And I think it's nice for the husband to be involved. Of course, some of them fall and hit their heads, say they can't take it. I think their being there has not been a bad thing—but then the tendency is to overlook birth as a real medical problem—uh—I shouldn't say problem, but a medical entity, rather than just a social happening. And making birth into a social event, with all these people around when somebody might end up dying, and all sorts of problems [voice rising], and birth is *not* a social event, but we're being forced into letting it be one!

These humanistic changes are being felt in the residency programs as well. To quote a recent graduate,

> We had some leeway at the medical school where I was doing my training— not everyone there did all the standard things, so the patients weren't always medically slapped with preps and enemas, staying in bed all the time, routine enemas and all that. So I think you get exposed to different people who do things different ways, and you can kind of pick and choose which way you think is the best way to handle a patient. I handle different people different ways. I think you just have to look at the person and see what's appropriate for her at the time.

As birthing women become better-educated consumers of obstetrical services, and residency programs vary their formats, "*the* way" in obstetrics gives way to "which way you think is the best way." This loosening of the conceptual boundaries poses a real danger to the dominant paradigm of our society, a threat especially potent in the medicalization of obstetrics which, unlike other medical specialties, does not deal with true pathology in the majority of cases it treats (most pregnant women are not sick). Thus obstetrics is uniquely vulnerable to the challenges to its dominant paradigm presented by the natural childbirth and wholistic health movements, for these movements rest their cases on that very issue—the inherent wellness of the pregnant woman versus the paradoxical insistence of obstetrics on conceptualizing her as ill, and on managing her body as if it were a defective machine. Aware of this paradox, and wishing to be responsive to consumer demand, many younger obstetricians are trying to increase the number of birthing options available to women. Thus obstetrics is no longer as reliable as it once was in the straightforward transmission and perpetuation of American society's core value system. To deal with this challenge, our society has gone outside the medical system, utilizing the combined forces of its legal and business systems to keep obstetricians in line.

Over 70 percent of all American obstetricians have been sued, a percentage higher than that of any other specialty (Easterbrook 1987). (Obstetrical malpractice insurance costs now average $38,138, soaring to more than $236,000 in some areas [Nazario 1990].) Because this malpractice "crisis" dramatically affects teaching practices, it plays a crucial role in the rite of passage through which nascent obstetricians are channeled. Malpractice insurance premiums in obstetrics began their dramatic rise in 1973, just at the time that the natural childbirth movement was beginning to pose a major threat to the obstetrical paradigm of birth. A common cultural response to this type of threat is to step up the performance of the rituals designed to preserve and transmit the reality model under attack (Douglas 1973:32; Vogt 1976: 198). Consequently, the explosion of humanistic options which challenge the conceptual hegemony of the technocratic model was paralleled by a stepping up of ritual performance, in the form of a dramatic rise in the use of the fetal monitor (from initial marketing in the sixties to near-universal hospital use today [*Ob. Gyn. News* 1982]), accompanied by a concurrent twenty-five-year-long rise in the Cesarean rate, from 5 percent in 1965 to 24.7 percent in 1988, reaching 50 percent in many teaching hospitals (and leveling off in 1989 at 23.3 percent). (In contrast, the Cesarean rate in European nations ranges between 4 percent and 12 percent.)

A number of studies have shown that increased monitoring leads to increased performance of Cesareans (Banta and Thacker 1979; Haverkamp and Orleans 1983; Leveno et al. 1986; Young 1982:110). These dramatic increases in the ritual use of machines in labor and in the ritual performance of the ultimately technocratic birth, delivery "from above," are at least partially attributable to the coercive pressure brought to bear on obstetricians by the constant threat of lawsuit. Most obstetricians interviewed perceived constant electronic monitoring as a means of self-protection and confirmed that they are far more likely to perform a Cesarean than not if the monitor indicates potential problems, because they know that the likelihood of lawsuit is lower if they cleave to the strict interpretation of the technocratic model, whereas if they try the humanistic approach—that is, if they try to be innovative, less technocratic, and more receptive to the woman's needs and desires, they place themselves at greater risk. As one of them puts it:

> Certainly I've changed the way I practice since malpractice became an issue. I do more C-sections, that's the major thing. And more and more tests to cover myself. More expensive stuff. We don't do risky things that women ask for—we're very conservative in our approach to everything. . . . In 1970 before all this came up, my C-section rate was around 4 percent. It has gradually climbed every year since then. In 1985 it was 16 percent, then in 1986 it was 23 percent.

Large numbers of obstetrician/gynecologists (one in eight) are now withdrawing from the obstetrical part of their practice as a direct result of the soaring costs of malpractice insurance (Church 1986; Nazario 1990). Their withdrawal generally works to limit birth options further for many women, as most of the suits that have resulted in huge claims being paid to the plaintiffs by the physician's insurance companies have stemmed from the emergency Cesarean *not* performed, from the doctor's willingness to wait on nature, rather than his manipulation of it. Moreover, our capitalist system articulates our technocratic values and beliefs: high profits result from widespread use of technocratic procedures, so physicians in for-profit institutions experience constant pressure from hospital administrators to utilize as many such procedures as they can (Starr 1982). Such strong financial and legal deterrents to radical change powerfully constrain our medical system, in effect forcing it to reflect and to perpetuate the core value and belief system of American society as a whole. From this symbolic perspective, the malpractice situation emerges as society's effort to keep its representatives, the obstetricians, from reneging on their responsibility for imbuing birthing women with the basic tenets of the technocratic model of reality. In enlisting American obstetricians as guardians of technocracy, and in watchdogging that guardianship with its legal system, American society is doing its utmost to protect our shared cultural dream of transcendence through technology.

CHAPTER 8

The Computerized Birth?

Some Ritual and Political Implications
for the Future

Often I don't like the women I've delivered. I don't like
them for their submissiveness. When I make rounds in the
morning I ask, "When are you going home?" They answer,
"I don't know when my doctor will let me." They have let
themselves be imprisoned. For me, the submissiveness of one
woman becomes my own, as though we were all one organism. . . . I used to have fantasies at Doctor's Hospital about
women in a state of revolution. I saw them getting up out of
their beds and refusing the knife, refusing to be tied down,
refusing to submit—whether they are in childbirth or when
they were forty and having a hysterectomy for a uterus no
longer considered useful. Women's health care will not
improve until women reject the present system and begin
instead to develop less destructive means of creating and
maintaining a state of wellness.
    —Michelle Harrison, M.D., *A Woman in Residence*

THE CULTURAL CONSENSUS

To me personally, one of the most significant results of my research
was that, when I added together the women who either accepted, demanded, or merely did not mind the eventual complete application of
the technocratic model to their births, fully 70 percent of the births
occurred in varying degrees of conceptual harmony with the technocratic model. In other words, the majority of the women I interviewed
either desired, actively sought, or accepted as appropriate the technocratic treatment they experienced. Only 15 percent actually desired and
achieved natural childbirth in the hospital, and only 9 percent who desired natural childbirth but did not achieve it were seriously disturbed
as a result. (The other 6 percent gave birth at home.)

Until I became adjusted to this picture of reality, such results confused me, for they ran contrary to my personal expectations. After

much research and more questioning, I had reached the conclusion that American hospital birth rituals are medically damaging and psychologically disempowering and degrading to women. Once I had arrived at this conclusion, I had a good deal of trouble understanding why anyone would want a technocratic birth. Although it is true that I did not encounter many women who really wanted a highly technocratic birth, I kept running into woman after woman who felt generally comfortable with such a birth. Initially finding this incomprehensible, I had to work very hard to understand it. I hope that my analysis of birth narratives in Chapter 5 has made clear the answers I finally found as to why some of these women were so ready to accept birth under the technocratic model, even when they had originally espoused the ideal of "natural childbirth," namely, that their technocratic births usefully served to strengthen and confirm the basic tenets of the belief systems they already held.

The above results accord well with the expressed perceptions of most of the health care professionals I have interviewed and with Leavitt's (1986) findings that women have been actively involved in making hospital birth what it is today. These results are also in accord with Arney's (1982) conclusions about the collusion between women and obstetricians in developing a system with which both groups are comfortable, and with the conclusion of other anthropologists engaged in similar research who are finding that the majority of their interviewees also desire or at least accept without protest highly technocratic births (McClain 1988, 1989; Nelson 1983; Sargent and Stark 1989). (Indeed it seems that the trend of the 1990s is toward the rapid spread of the "epidural epidemic.") Although my personal views are more in accord with those expressed by Martin (1987),[1] I must take seriously the notion that American women do not rise up in protest against technocratic birth because it is in fact what most of them want.

Why? To ask why women want technocratic births is, in a broader sense, to ask what technocracy has done for women that they should value it so. The answer to that question seems clear: in the early years of this century technology began to give women the power to expand beyond the "natural order" that made many of them, in an industrializing society, appear to themselves to be slaves to their biology. Ever since the invention of the bottle—the "war cry" of a generation of women—technology has increasingly offered women a way out of the home and into participation in the wider social world. And this trend has not slowed. Women's continued expansion beyond the "natural order" that kept them in "women's domain" is increasingly facilitated by technology, which women therefore have special reason to value and to seek. Sadie Johnson puts it this way:

> I just love machines. What would I do without my dishwasher, my washer and dryer, even my hairdryer? I know some studies show that they take up more of your time than they save, but I don't believe it for a minute. And they do so much more than save time! Back when I couldn't use a computer, I felt so isolated from the real world, the world where everybody had instant access to information, where everybody was "with it" except me. Now, even though I'm not working anymore, I don't even think I could parent without a computer—to make lists on, to play games with the kids, to write the little bit that I do when I can snatch a minute. And what about all those toy computers for the kids that teach them to read and do math and keep them occupied for hours? Oh, and just yesterday I learned to use a fax machine. I sent something off to Mexico and got back the information I needed within fifteen minutes. Boy did I feel powerful—I've got "connections"! I suffer no nostalgia for the "simplicity" of our grandmothers' days. I'm a modern woman, and I love modern life.

As Barbara Katz Rothman (1989) reminds us, a society's technology is created out of and in accordance with that society's dominant ideology. And as stated in Chapter 2, the term *technocracy* implies use of an ideology of technological progress as a source of political power (Reynolds 1991). Certainly the political powers that women have been able to achieve in this century are inextricably linked with an ideology of technological progress that, whatever else it has done, has helped to blur the lines between traditionally male and female work domains, offering women boundless opportunities for advancement within technocratic society. At the same time, technocratic competence has become a prerequisite for success. The degree of a worker's familiarity and comfort (both physical and ideological) with machines (and with the machinations of bureaucracy) will often determine not only how well she can perform, but also how much money she can make, and how far she can go in a given organization or on a chosen career path.

I used to be surprised when women reported experiencing technocratic interventions in birth as empowering. But I have come to understand that even if those interventions come in forms that appear to me to disempower women as individuals and as birth-givers, they do nevertheless make women themselves feel not only powerful over the caprices of nature but also most fully participants in their culture.[2] To ask why so many women are so accepting of the hegemonic reality model that devalues them is not merely to ask why *women* behave in

ways that appear to run counter to their own best interests; it is also
to ask why so many of us in this society—female *and* male—engage in
myriad behaviors that appear to run counter to the best interests of
humans and their planetary environment. There is a strong parallel
between our consensual choice of technocratic birth and many of our
other consensual choices—a parallel that demonstrates the manifestation of the same core value system in all aspects of American life. On
a daily basis, we eat processed food that has been stripped of natural nutrients, poison dwindling groundwater supplies with pesticides,
throw away enormous quantities of reusable materials made from non-
renewable resources, pour chemical pollutants into rivers, lakes, and
oceans, and release into the atmosphere enough chlorofluorocarbons to
destroy large portions of the earth's protective ozone layer. Why do we
do all these highly irrational things? As I hope I have shown in Chapter
3, 99 percent of us are socialized into the technocratic model of reality
from birth; consequently, little of our behavior makes rational-technical
sense from a planetary point of view. It does, however, make excellent
sense from within the conceptual confines of the technocratic model,
which holds that whatever predicaments our technocratic ideology gets
us into, our technological skills will get us out of.

These excesses of technocratically driven behavior have thus become
loaded political issues, many of which pit those who espouse the technocratic model (which justifies the exploitation of the earth) against
those who adopt an ecological, systems-oriented approach (which does
not). A key cultural arena for the enactment and transmission of cultural values, birth in the United States today reflects this battle of the
paradigms and has itself become a political battleground in myriad
ways, from abortion to "natural childbirth" to the new reproductive
technologies.

WOMEN'S RITES: THE POLITICS OF BIRTH

> Like all other metaphors, political . . . metaphors
> can hide aspects of reality. But in the area of politics
> . . . metaphors matter more, because they constrain our
> lives.
>
> —George Lakoff and Mark Johnson,
> *Metaphors We Live By*

Of considerable political importance for American women is a major
conclusion of my research: that hospital birth as a rite of passage has

far more in common cross-culturally with male initiation rites than with female ones. This conclusion is foreshadowed by Eliade's insights into the nature of the difference between male and female initiation rites. He feels that when a passage is an arbitrary, socially decided-upon crossover from, for example, boyhood to manhood, "initiation represents an introduction to a world that is not immediate—the world of spirit and culture." But when it reflects the cultural acknowledgment of a physiological state, as in menstruation and childbirth, then "initiation involves a series of revelations concerning the secret meaning of a natural phenomenon" (1975:27–32). I have found this distinction of Eliade's between male and female initiation rites to be fundamental to an understanding of what has happened in hospital birth. The medical establishment, by its takeover of what had always been a quintessentially female rite involving "revelations concerning the secret meaning of a natural phenomenon," has changed the conduct and management of that rite in order to make it "an arbitrary, socially decided-upon crossover" introducing the initiate to the world of technocratic culture—making it resemble, in other words, the rites of male, not female, initiation.

In his analysis of female initiation rites in five different cultures, Bruce Lincoln states:

> Regardless of the specifics, the resolution of opposites [in female initiation rites] always involves a move from separation to unity, tension to harmony, and limitation to totality. By becoming a part of this process, an immature girl—incomplete and imperfect—becomes an adult, as the nature of her very being is radically transformed. (1981:98)

From a woman's perspective, I fail to see any move toward unity, harmony, or totality in the rituals of hospital birth. On the contrary, it seems to me that hospital birth both reflects and works to create the separation and segmentation (better known as "specialization") so pervasive in our society today. Lincoln finds that one of the chief purposes of all female rites of initiation is "to make a girl ready and willing to assume the traditional place of a woman as defined within a given culture." However, in low-technology cultures these same initiation rites also work to imbue the female initiate with a strong sense of the *cosmic importance* of that traditional place: "each time a woman is initiated, the world is saved from chaos, for the fundamental power of creativity is renewed in her being" (Lincoln 1981:107).

In the rituals of birth in the American hospital, there is no such renewal; in its place, there is complete denial of the fundamentally female power of creativity. Women in American society have been deprived, not only of social "equality" but also of their cosmic significance as birth-givers, transformed even in the transformation of giving birth into mere machines to be manipulated and repaired.

In the feminist view, women function for the larger society as signifiers of the Female Principle in cultural life. This principle signifies women's procreative power—a signification inseparable from women's reproductive processes. When women are conceptually integrated into the technocratic model in childbirth, the entire Female Principle is denied, leaving complete conceptual hegemony over both cultural and individual reproduction to the institutions that represent society's dominant value system.[3]

THE TECHNOCRATIC MODEL OF BIRTH: FUTURISTIC EXTREMES

In "Childbirth 2000," Gena Corea (1979) presents a frightening view of the possibilities inherent in such hegemony. She tells the imaginary story of a pregnant woman living in a remote rural area, who decides on home birth with a midwife for her first pregnancy. Unbeknownst to this woman, on her one and only visit to the obstetrician at the nearest regional health care facility, an electronic "homing device" was implanted in her uterus. As soon as she goes into labor, this homing device emits a signal picked up by the computers at this regional hospital. A short time later, a helicopter descends down out of the skies and whisks the bewildered and terrified woman and her husband off to the hospital. Labor "fails to progress," fetal distress is diagnosed, and an emergency Cesarean is performed.

Could such an eventuality come to pass? A 1986 national survey of heads of maternal-fetal medicine teaching programs reported twenty-one attempts to obtain court orders to force obstetrical interventions on pregnant mothers, fifteen of which were for Cesarean sections (Kolder, Gallagher, and Parsons 1987). According to Beth Shearer (1989), four more court-ordered Cesareans have been ordered since then. For example:

> In a 1981 Georgia case, doctors told the court there was a 99% chance of fetal death and a 50% chance of maternal death unless a scheduled Cesarean section was performed, since two ultrasounds indicated a complete placenta praevia [a potentially life-threatening situation in which the placenta lies under the baby, blocking the entrance to the birth canal]. The mother stead-

fastly believed in her ability to give birth safely. After the court order was granted, a third ultrasound showed no praevia at all. (Shearer 1989:7)

In Denver, in 1982, a judge and an attorney were actually summoned to the hospital room where an obese woman was in labor and was adamantly refusing a Cesarean. The baby still in her womb was officially declared a ward of the state until birth, the woman was anesthetized, and the Cesarean was performed. The doctor had insisted there was fetal distress, but the baby was born perfectly healthy. This incident, recently analyzed by Jordan and Irwin (1989) along with eight other similar cases, was reported to me in 1983 by one of the obstetricians whom I interviewed in Centertown. He said that the obstetrician who performed the Cesarean had been bragging about it at a recent obstetrical convention. Even more alarming, the Centertown obstetrician whom I interviewed did not personally see anything wrong with such an approach.

Many more extremes in human "reproduction" are potentiated by the technocratic model, including test-tube fertilization, surrogacy, egg and embryo flushing and freezing, superovulation of women, sex preselection, artificial hormones, artificial insemination, genetic engineering and more. They are thoroughly reported and analyzed from a feminist perspective by Arditti et al. in *Test-Tube Women* (1985), by Corea in *The Mother Machine* (1985*b*), by Spallone in *Beyond Conception* (1989), and by Rapp (1988*a,b*), Rothman (1986, 1989), and others. Such writers argue that the result of these new reproductive technologies is the subordination of women to the interests of medical science, population planners, and the burgeoning biotechnology industry. Although it is commonly assumed in American society that these technologies enhance women's freedom of choice, such critics show that choices to use or not use these technologies are seldom freely made, but are strongly shaped and influenced by cultural values and norms.

For example, Rothman points out that even as technology opens up some choices, it closes down others. Asking, "Is there any meaningful way one could now choose horses over cars as a means of transportation?" she goes on to show that as the new reproductive technologies give us more and more information about the quality of our fetuses so that we can "choose" to abort "defective" fetuses, such abortions begin to seem socially desirable, even necessary, and we begin to lose the choice *not* to abort, *not* to know, the choice to simply accept our children as they are: "Choices open and choices close. For those whose choices meet the social expectations, for those who want what the society wants them to want, the experience of choice is very real. . . . Society, in its ultimate meaning, may be nothing more and nothing less than the structuring of choices" (1985:32).

Feminists, Rothman reminds us, thought that increased access to information would give women more choices and more power to make those choices. "What we perhaps overlooked," Rothman continues, "is that it is *power* which gives one control over both information and choice":

> The question then for feminism is not only to address the individual level of "a woman's right to choose," but also to examine the social level, where her choices are structured. . . . We must not get caught into discussions of which reproductive technologies are "politically correct," which empower and which enslave women. They ALL empower and they ALL enslave, they all can be used by, for, or against us. We will have to lift our eyes from the choices of the individual woman, and focus on the control of the social system which structures her choices, which rewards some choices and punishes others, which distributes those rewards and punishments along class and race lines. (1985:32–33)

It is important to remember that the new reproductive technologies—all thoroughly logical extensions of the technocratic model—are envisioned, invented, and "chosen" in a sociocultural context that values them more than the women's bodies such technologies act upon. Our cultural core value system works to ensure that scientists and technicians are not engaged in reproductive research simply to help women give birth, but to make possible the technocratic creation of new life and the perpetuation of society independent of reliance on women's procreative power. The prevailing belief system in the United States today so values technology that it encourages technology's extension into all possible realms, making the conquest of human reproduction seem worthy of attempting just because we have the technology with which to attempt it—a cultural drive that I call the technocratic imperative. And this imperative seems relentless. The February 1989 issue of *Life* magazine's cover story, "The Future and You," predicts "Birth Without Women," stating:

> By the late 21st century, childbirth may not involve carrying at all—just an occasional visit to an incubator. There the fetus will be gestating in an artificial uterus under conditions simulated to re-create the mother's breathing patterns, her laughter and even her moments of emotional stress. (1989:55)

Few of the individuals to whom I have shown that article did more than blink in amazement at the limitless possibilities of technology. We have known since the days of the orphanage that newborn babies die if they are not held and touched, that children's emotional growth is stunted in impersonal environments. And yet we can blithely contemplate the possibility of incubating babies in machines. The easygoing cultural acceptance of this Frankensteinian option for our future indicates more clearly than anything else I can say that our core value system centers around science, technology, patriarchy, and institutions. Only out of such a core value matrix could artificial wombs—even in imagination—emerge. What form will this technocratic nightmare take? Should such babies survive and grow into adulthood, what sort of human beings would they become? No one knows. What we do know is that there is far more involved in the growth of a human being from a cluster of cells than we even begin to understand. And we know that every time we rely on technology to get us out of one predicament we have created, a whole new set of problems gets generated by that technology for which another set of technological remedies must be constructed, which generates yet another set of problems. . . .

The electronic fetal monitor is a case in point. Hailed at first as a device that would alleviate some of the perceived problems of birth by allowing early detection of fetal distress, the EFM proceeded to generate its own new set of problems, including misdiagnoses leading to unnecessary Cesareans and the complications that result from imprisoning women in bed. This latter problem is now being addressed with more technology—remote sensing devices that allow a woman to walk around in labor while still being continuously monitored. Such devices will no doubt entail their own problems (more misdiagnoses? detrimental effects of the ultrasound waves? increased reliance on the machines at the expense of the woman's own perceptions?). Meanwhile, the EFM has been shown to be less reliable as a source of information than periodic manual monitoring by people. Yet such machines continue to dominate hospital labor rooms. Given this reality, it is not surprising that a reputable national magazine like *Life* would speak confidently of a future replete with artificial wombs. I must stress once again that this scenario is an absolutely logical futuristic extension of our contemporary technocratic model.

Such technocratic fantasies have other insidious ramifications. For example, no matter how highly technology may be valued in the future, it is unlikely that such extreme reproductive options, even if they should

become socially desirable, would ever be available to all. Their ex-
pensive nature would make them, along with many other technology-
based reproductive options, exclusively available to those who can af-
ford them, as is the case with one such option now on the market—the
renting of natural wombs in the growing surrogate industry. Typically,
today's surrogate mothers are of lower socioeconomic status than those
who pay for their services; some enterprises have begun to import Third
World women to serve as surrogate incubators for the embryos of the
white American middle class (Sault 1989:18).[4] Moreover, studies in
every health care setting repeatedly show that nonwhite racial or ethnic status, lower socioeconomic class, and female gender "powerfully
and irrationally bias diagnosis, rapidity and type of response to patient
needs, type of treatment, length of treatment, and so forth" (McKay
1990a:13). Correspondingly, one of the most tragic aspects of the technocratization of American birth, as reported by Gertrude Fraser (1988),
is manifested in the medical treatment of poor black women in some
American hospitals. Left alone to labor and birth with little assistance,
these women scream for the technology that they see as a high cultural
good. No one tells them that some would consider them lucky to be so
ignored. All they can see is that the best that American society has to
offer is consistently withheld from those on the lowest rungs of the
class/caste/gender ladder.

Given the prevailing inequities of the technocratic socioeconomic
hierarchy and their sociopolitical consequences, it becomes clear that
the cultural conduct of childbirth is an issue of unsurpassed political
import for all women. In "Women and Political Power," the editors of
Women's Realities, Women's Choices point out that a

> close connection exists between public and private matters. For example,
> public laws, made and enforced largely by men, have determined women's
> rights to say no or yes to a prospective partner . . . and to decide whether
> or not to continue a pregnancy. Public policy, made largely by men, deter-
> mines women's rights and obligations to our children and women's ability
> to carry out our wishes with regard to our children's care and education,
> nourishment and safety. Public policy also restricts and shapes women's
> rights and capacities to select ways to support ourselves, and it determines
> the conditions under which we work. In other words, nearly everything we
> have been brought up to regard as personal and private turns out to be a
> matter of public concern. To the extent that the private sphere has been the
> domain of women, and the public sphere has been the domain of men, poli-
> tics has been a means to control women's lives. (Hunter College Women's
> Studies Collective 1983:531–542)

As has medicine. As we have seen, our medical system is society's representative no less than our political system, and actually more so, for in our political system, women's oppressions or victories are often overt, whereas in the medical system they remain hidden, disguised as the hysterectomy or the Cesarean section performed under the mantle of scientific necessity, when what is really happening is simply that women are being stripped of their reproductive powers and of the body parts that connote those powers. Women's hegemony over society's reproduction so strongly signifies the power of the Female Principle that it is easy to see that denial of that principle takes form in the surgical removal of its core from the bodies of the women who house it.

Shifting needs in our society enable women to work in a man's world, sometimes for equal pay, but no matter how early in life a woman begins her career, nor how successful she is, she will still be living and working under the constraints of the technocratic model of reality—a paradigm that defines her body-machine as inherently defective. Based as it is on this assumption of her inherent physiological inferiority to men, and for as long as it holds conceptual hegemony over this nation, that model will guarantee her continued psychological disempowerment by the everyday constructs of the culture at large, and her alienation both from political power *and* from the physiological attributes of womanhood.

CHAPTER 9

—Or Birth
as the Biodance?

Most people cannot truly comprehend all of the unin-
tended consequences of their actions, either on their physical
or social environment. The lack of systems consciousness is,
in our opinion, the single greatest danger to this planet. . . .
The emergence of systems consciousness may prove pivotal
to [our] future.

—Sheila Richardson, "The Future of
Human Consciousness"

The preceding chapter discussed the social consensus on the technocratization of birth, as well as potential directions in birth's further
technocratization and some of the political implications of those directions. This chapter will investigate several aspects of individual and social resistance to those trends, and some of their political and futuristic
implications.

BIRTH AS A MEANS FOR ACCOMPLISHING
A PARADIGM SHIFT

If women have a role to play, it is only in assuming
a negative function: reject everything finite, definite,
structured, loaded with meaning, in the existing state
of society. Such an attitude places women on the side
of the explosion of social codes: with revolutionary
movements.

—Julia Kristeva, Interview in *Tel Quel,*
translated in *New French Feminisms*

We have never been the masters of others or of ourselves. We don't have to confront ourselves in order to
free ourselves. We don't have to keep watch on ourselves, or to set up some other erected self in order to

understand ourselves. All we have to do is to let the
body flow, from the inside . . .
            —Madeleine Gagnon, "Corps 1," in *New
            French Feminisms: An Anthology*

Although 70 percent of the women in my study either wanted or
were comfortable with their technocratic births the first time around,
30 percent were not. Of those 30 percent, 15 percent were active birth-
givers in the hospital, 9 percent were devastated when their desires to
be so were overridden, and 6 percent had their first child at home. In
subsequent births, another eight women in my study switched from hospital to home birth through an arduous process of personal commitment and choice.

The most common pattern among these eight women was as follows. Their first births entailed a high degree of medical intervention,
usually culminating in forceps delivery or Cesarean section. After their
births, they either experienced severe postpartum depressions that lasted
for months, or else compartmentalized the experience until about ten
months after the birth, at which point they would begin to verbalize
intense feelings of grief, rage, and psychological anguish over their hospital treatment. For their second births, they would be a good deal more
prepared, and would either fight for and usually achieve significantly
fewer interventions in the hospital, as we saw in Chapter 6, or would
reject the medical establishment completely, and choose to give birth
at home.

I became interested in the process through which some of these
women shifted their conceptions of birth-place appropriateness from
hospital to home, and in the accompanying changes I thought I detected
in their conceptions of reality in general. I noticed that as they switched
from hospital to home birth, they not only fired their obstetricians and
searched for midwives, but also developed decided affinities for naturo-
paths, massage therapists, recycling, herbs, and whole wheat bread. It
seemed that something farther-reaching than a simple change in birthplace was going on with these women. It seemed, in fact, that they were
actually using their births as means to change their personal belief systems—undergoing on an individual level what Thomas Kuhn, speaking
of changes in scientific models of reality, has called a paradigm shift
(1962).

Just as society's core values and beliefs come together in birth, so do
a woman's individual values and beliefs. By the same token, if a woman

wishes to change those individual values and beliefs, birth is an excellent place to begin. By assuming personal responsibility for her physiological transition into motherhood, instead of assigning that responsibility to the larger society, a woman can consciously utilize the opening process of pregnancy to send herself messages about the rightness and validity of the beliefs she *wishes* to hold. As psychotherapist Gayle Peterson says, "Birth is a doorway for the integration of body and mind" (1984:205).

To that end, most of the home-birthers in my study engaged in a conscious process of both the de-ritualization of subsequent pregnancies and births under the technocratic model, and the re-ritualization of these experiences under the wholistic paradigm. These home-birthers tended to have explicit and conscious ideologies that included very strong notions about the nature and significance of the birth process. Thus, the rituals they developed for their home births, although consciously meaningful, tended to be far less elaborate, less structured, and more diffuse than hospital birth rituals. These home birth rituals included formalized interactions with midwives, the performance of prenatal Blessingway ceremonies, candle ceremonies, singing, chanting, the creation of specially marked sacred space where the birth was to occur, and the elaboration of specially marked artifacts (a birthing dress worn by many women as they gave birth, a quilt from the bed where a grandmother gave birth, etc.).

Where hospital birth rituals provide a strong sense of cultural order as opposed to natural chaos, the rituals of home birth work to nurture and enhance the natural biological rhythmic imperatives of nature and birth. Where hospital rituals seek to impose a belief system often alien to the woman, today's home birth rituals develop out of the belief system that she consciously chooses to espouse. Where hospital birth rituals focus the energy of birth away from the mother and toward her birth attendants, the rituals of home birth work to keep the birthing energy focused on the mother. In a future work, I hope to give as much attention to home birth rituals as I have in this book given to the rituals of hospital birth.[1]

WHOLISM IN BIRTH: FUTURISTIC EXTREMES

> New metaphors are capable of creating new understandings and, therefore, new realities.
>
> —George Lakoff and Mark Johnson,
> *Metaphors We Live By*

As we have seen, the hegemony of the technocratic model, though deeply entrenched, is far from totalitarian. The switches to home birth and a wholistic paradigm undergone by eight women in my study are not isolated events. A diverse array of social movements seek to ensure that a wide range of options to technocratic hegemony will exist in American society as we move into the twenty-first century. A number of these movements—including the home birth, home schooling, wholistic health, environmental, and transpersonal psychology movements—base themselves on premises fundamentally different from those of our dominant core value system. Although diverse, these movements intersect in systems theory. They all have in common a wholistic view of reality—an alternative system of values and beliefs that coexists with our dominant system, and whose underdog proponents seek to garner increasing amounts of cultural territory vis-à-vis the dominant model. In their turn, defendants of the dominant model often seek to cut back on the amount of territory allowed to the proponents of this alternative worldview. Many of the turf wars, for example, between physicians and wholistic health practitioners, obstetricians and midwives, the legal system and homeschoolers,[2] and industrialists and environmentalists can be understood in this light.

Tara, whose home birth story appeared in Chapter 5, makes this connection explicit:

> How do we change this trend toward more drugs for birth, more machines? I think it starts with the way we raise our kids. I think the environmental movement could help as much as anything. That movement is in vogue, and it's nonpartisan—it's for everyone. It encourages us to love Mother Earth, and to teach our children—boys and girls—to be emotional, feeling, and caring. The environmental movement can help us to change our sex role stereotypes. Men have been moving in that direction, but society has not been very accepting. There is a passion and emotion that comes out in the environmental movement, that both men and women feel and accept as good. And that will influence birth. It will take both parents seeing things differently to change birth. As men open up to their emotional, caring selves, they will begin to feel strongly about natural birth. Mother Earth has historically been seen as feminine. If we get back to caring about the Earth, being caretakers, it would be difficult not to translate that into other parts of our lives. Sooner or later people will ask themselves how they can give birth drugged and hooked up to machines, when they are trying to stop treating their own Mother Earth that way.

This gestalt, relationship-oriented model of reality shared by many wholistic health practitioners, midwives, homeschoolers, and environmentalists is hardly new. For centuries in the West, it has provided a conceptual basis for underground social movements and groups, from the female lay healers of the Middle Ages to the modern lay midwife. What *is* new is the contemporary grounding of this ancient model in modern scientific understanding. Although the technocratic model manifested in modern scientific obstetrical practice is derived from the Newtonian mechanical view of the world, the conceptual basis of the "old physics," the "new science" of the "new physics" (Bohm 1951, 1980; Prigogine 1980) is based on systems theory, which assumes the fundamental interconnectedness of all things. Such an assumption, carried to its furthest extensions, can take us to an extreme of difference from conventional understandings of reality, as is clearly illustrated by some excerpts from Dossey's (1982) chart of the primary differences between the conventional view and the systems approach. In many ways, Dossey's formulation of the differences between what he terms the "traditional view" (which I take the liberty of re-labeling the "conventional view") and the "modern physical view" can be seen as an extension of the technocratic and wholistic paradigms of birth presented in similar contrasting form in Chapter 4.

It should be clear from the comparisons in table 4 why social movements based on systems theory (such as the wholistic health and home birth movements) are often perceived as socially and politically subversive by those with a vested interest in maintaining the stability of the hegemonic model. Systems theory in its most extreme form (which itself is but a model of "reality" just as is the technocratic model) blends our cherished and clearly demarcated cultural hierarchies and oppositions (up/down, good/bad, man/woman) into a boundless "biodance." It becomes difficult to organize individuals in society in any meaningful way if we are all to be conceptualized as specks waltzing around in an undifferentiated universe. Whatever the value of such notions, it should be clear that one reason why systems theory provides an appropriate conceptual basis for so many groups engaged in assaulting the technocratic model is that it so fundamentally diverges from the basic tenets of that model, stressing consciousness and integration instead of mechanicity and separation.

Proponents of a paradigm tend to create the world in its image. Just as the technocratic model's emphasis on separation potentiates the behavioral extremes discussed in Chapter 8, so systems theory's emphasis on interconnectedness leads to a number of very different sorts of behavioral extremes in the cultural arena of birth. These include Marilyn Moran's "New Nativity," a philosophy espoused by

TABLE 4. A SPACETIME MODEL OF BIRTH,
LIFE, HEALTH, AND DEATH*

Conventional View	Modern Physical View
The body is an object, localized to a specific space.	The body is not an object, and cannot be localized in space.
The body is an isolated, self-contained unit.	The body is in dynamic relationship with the universe and with all other bodies through actual physical exchange—"the biodance."
The body is comprised of individual building blocks, the atoms.	"Building blocks" and atoms are inaccurate descriptions, since all particles can only be understood in relation to all other particles.
Birth and death are demarcations at the poles of life.	No demarcations in time exist.
Time flows.	The flow of time is a psychological, not a natural event. No physical experiment has ever detected the flow of time.
The matter that comprises the body is an absolute.	Nothing of the body's matter is absolute. All matter, as well as space and time, are relative.
Disease is molecular misbehavior and is thus an objective affair.	Objective theory is an illusion. Intervention in nature, as well as scrutiny of all types, changes what is observed. The observer cannot separate himself from the outcome of the observation, so that objectivity in its pure sense is an impossibility.
Disease is a body affair.	The influence of consciousness on the physical processes occurring in the body obliterates this distinction.

*Excerpted from Dossey 1982:148–149.

some home-birthers which holds that birth is an intimate sexual expression of love between partners and should only happen at home with no one else present to interfere with its intimacy (Moran 1981). They also include facilitating psychic communication between mother and unborn child through visualization and other techniques (Jones 1989; Peterson 1981; Peterson and Mehl 1984); "preconception bonding" (communicating with the child before conception [Clymer 1950; Parvati-Baker 1986a]); and the practice of "shamanic midwifery" (Parvati-

Baker 1992). Other such extremes involve attempting to create more psychically aware, "healed" human beings through "conscious conception" (Parvati-Baker 1986a; Ray 1985) and conscious preparation for birth (Alzugaray 1992; Chamberlain 1988; Dansby 1987; Parvati-Baker 1986b; Ray 1985; Sidenbladh 1982; Star-Cunningham 1992a,b); and birthing in the ocean with dolphins to tap the potentials of "dolphin consciousness" and interspecies communication (Sidenbladh 1982) in the interests of "birthing peace on earth" (Star-Cunningham 1992a,b).

Such extremes, although desired and striven for by only a tiny minority of those involved with birth, play an important role in defining the outer edges of the possible. However "far out" they may appear, those at the extreme of conceptual opposition to a society's dominant belief system—the "radical fringe"[3]—do create much more room for growth and change within that society than would exist without them. By their utter rejection of the dominant "sacred cows" of their society, such radicals foster new ways of thinking that could not exist if everyone in that society believed in the same sacred cows. What if there were no midwives or mothers in this country insisting that women can be trusted to give birth, that there is an inner knowing that can be tapped, that human skills are more trustworthy than medications and machines—so trustworthy, in fact, that the home—the environment that best nurtures such knowing and such skills—is the safest place to give birth? How much more technocratic might even hospital birth look, if *no one* believed all those things? Just as those engaged in genetic research and developing artificial wombs define, and thus create, the outer boundaries of the possible under the technocratic model, so those who strive to be conscious at the moment of conception and to birth in the ocean with dolphins define, and thus create, the outer edges of the possible under the wholistic model.

When asked to predict the future of American birth, Ellen Lawson, who had both of her children at home, stated:

> I think birth is going to become much more technological, more geared toward more testing, early intervention, genetic selection. But I would prefer that birth remain as natural as possible. There's something emotional, psychological involved. If we lose that, we will regret it in the future, because we're missing out on something that links us to life in a very fundamental way. Birth is what ties us to other forms of life, creates a bond between human women that goes back hundreds of generations, and bonds us to other species as well. The more technological birth becomes, the more it differentiates us, and the more unlike other species—and other members of our own species—we become.

Her remarks point toward what seems in fact to be a primary aim of those at the extreme of technocratic futurism: to become more unlike other species, to culturally and deliberately take the next evolutionary step. Fascinatingly, this impulse to deliberately seek the next evolutionary step also seems to be at the root of the wholistic futurists' attempts at conscious conception and birth. Such futurists speak glowingly of the human potential that would be unleashed if conception, gestation, and birth were consciousness-enhancing processes carried out with psychic awareness and conscious love:

> If babies are born into an environment that honors and recognizes them as conscious beings prior to conception, at conception, and during pregnancy, birth, and infancy, they will have the opportunity to bring with them into this life tremendous wisdom and experience gained over the whole of their existence, and not be reduced to beings that become recognized as conscious (at best) at age 5. We vastly underestimate the evolutionary leaps we can make as a species simply by recognizing the transcendent intelligence in our preborn and newborn babies. (Star-Cunningham 1992b)

Such futuristic visions notwithstanding, the contemporary fact remains that fewer than 3 percent of American women choose to give birth in wholistically grounded free-standing birthing centers; fewer than 1 percent choose to give birth at home; and fewer still engage in the extreme sorts of extensions of the wholistic model described above. Yet the importance to American society as a whole of these alternative-model women is tremendous, for they are holding open a giant conceptual space between the technocratic model and the wholistic extreme—a space in which women and their babies can be not mechanistic antagonists but unified energy fields, complementary co-participants in the creative mysteries, entrained and joyous dancers in the rhythms and harmonies of life, natural beings birthing each other—child to mother, mother to child. As the metaphors of systems theory speak of webs, networks, holograms, waves, rhythms, synchrony, and the dance, so the wholistic model of birth is ripe with metaphoric conceptualizations of pregnancy, labor, and birth that can work to humanize, personalize, feminize, and naturalize the processes of procreation. If this wholistic model ceases to be lived out to its fullest extent by those who birth at home (or at sea), then the conceptual possibilities for mothers and babies will shrink back to a grounding in the technocratic core. Free-standing birth centers, instead of being seen as a sensible compromise between hospital and home, will become the radical extreme, and the efforts that for all of the twentieth century have been aimed at stamping out home birth (DeVries 1985; Litoff 1978; Mathews 1990; Susie 1988), may be redirected at such centers. Because such centers must be formally organized and licensed, they are more subject to regulation and control than home-birthers, and thus are generally less able to hold open the total alternatives to the technocratic model than can be held open in home birth.

Home-birthers in the United States are an endangered species. (As part of a fundraising effort, a group of local midwives in Anycity is selling T-shirts with whales painted on the front; the caption underneath reads "SAVE THE MIDWIVES!") Should they cease to exist, the options available in American society for thinking about and treating pregnancy, birth, and the female body would sharply decrease, and our society would be enormously impoverished.

Such a loss would have many pragmatic ramifications, some of which are already in evidence in areas of the nation that suffer a shortage of obstetricians. For one example, in Virginia, according to a recent National Public Radio broadcast, many obstetricians have recently pulled out of rural areas because of heavy work loads with little financial reward. Now many women are left with no prenatal care at all, and with trips of several hours to reach hospitals where there are still obstetricians attending deliveries. This area used to enjoy a strong indigenous midwifery tradition, but that was successfully stamped out over a decade ago by a medical anti-midwifery and anti-home birth campaign.

Likewise, Holly Mathews (1990) describes the systematic efforts of the medical profession in North Carolina to stamp out a thriving localized midwifery tradition—efforts that finally succeeded in 1989, the first year in which there were no official records of any deliveries by lay midwives in North Carolina. Ironically, in that same year, state officials, responding to funding shortages and the highest infant mortality rate of any state in the nation, began to suggest the training of local lay health advocates for pregnant women who could help to compensate for the pervasive lack of physicians in the rural areas of the state.

As the high cost of malpractice insurance drives more obstetricians out of the specialty (Church 1986:20), such scenarios will be repeated around the country. These scenarios, in combination with the rising tide of scientific evidence concerning the safety of home relative to hospital birth, may play a significant role in achieving recognition by the dominant society of the viability of the home birth option. Should home-birthers thrive, our society will continue to be enriched by their alternative visions.

THE COMPUTERIZED BIRTH, *AND* THE BIODANCE: ENVISIONING THE RICHNESS OF DIVERSITY

In response to my question, "Do you have a vision for the future of American birth?" Joanne Moorehouse, the professional who did not want to "drop into biology," stated:

I think people who are procreating will have a much better chance of having a child with no diseases. Rather than look at genetic engineering as a chance to ensure a child with blonde hair and blue eyes, which was flip, I think we will become more and more sophisticated about using genetic engineering to prevent not only birth defects but also proclivities toward certain types of diseases like breast cancer. . . . If anything, I think people in the future are going to expect medicine and science to have more answers.

To the same question, Susan Frye responded:

Unfortunately, I think that our choices are being limited. I recently found out that in California, where I now live, home birth is illegal. You would think that in California, of all places, women would have managed to preserve what I consider to be a very basic right, to have your baby the way that works best for you. The medical associations are working overtime to regulate women's bodies. Legislators all across the nation are getting more and more into midwifery, into telling those midwives who are legal what they can and can't do. So we have fewer and fewer choices.

Home birth brings us back to basics. It's just simply better for moms and babies. So women who want that should be able to choose it. I want to see a society in which it is more and more acceptable to choose home birth. Insurance companies even now are starting to cover it. . . . I think if people would look at the statistics, they'd see that home birth is safer. Thinking that home birth is dangerous is a societal thing, built into us before we were born. In this society we are just not comfortable with our bodies. We expect others to take control, we let legislators and total strangers tell us what to do with our bodies. Home birth matters on a very personal level. When you yourself realize that *you* gave birth, not someone or something else—they didn't grow that baby, they didn't bring it down into the birth canal—you have a much more intense and personal relationship with that baby, and that's a basic feature of growing up as a whole healthy person, not to be born in a drug-induced stupor. The first arms that baby should feel are those of his family.

And Elizabeth Fisher said:

I look forward to a future with room for everybody to do birth in the way that feels best, works best for them. I pray that my daughters will have that right.

My own vision of the future, like Elizabeth's, seeks conceptual room for all of theirs, and finds it in the more moderate form of systems theory described by physicist Fritjof Capra in *The Turning Point* (1983). Capra emphasizes that living systems are integrated wholes whose properties cannot be reduced to those of smaller units. He points out that the systemic properties of individuals, social systems, and ecosystems are destroyed when a system is dissected into isolated elements, as the emergence of organic patterns is fundamentally different from the manufacture of a machine product in precisely programmed steps. Nevertheless, Capra continues, machine-like operations do take place in living systems:

> Although they are of a more specialized and secondary nature, machinelike operations occur throughout the living world. The reductionist description of organisms can therefore be useful and may in some cases be necessary. It is dangerous only when it is taken to be the complete explanation. Reductionism and holism, analysis and synthesis, are complementary approaches that, used in proper balance, help us obtain a deeper knowledge of life. (1983:266–267)

We will, without doubt, continue for many years to come in our reductionist and analytic approach to reality, driven by the technocratic imperative, even as national and international awareness focuses increasingly on the need for understanding and nurturing the fragile ecosystem that nurtures us. So strong seems this imperative that I cannot look ahead to a twenty-first century in which the majority of women will reclaim their procreative powers and their bodies under a systems-based ideology of self-empowerment; the trend of the entire twentieth century has not been for women radically to redefine technocratic reality, but to seek increasing participation in that reality, and in so doing, to transform it in subtle ways. What I *can* envision with hope is a twenty-first century replete with real, discussable, and occasionally transcendent options and alternatives that span the spectrum from technocratic reductionism to the biodance.

In the twenty-first century, I envision nuclear, extended, traditional, gay or lesbian, single-parent, and friend-based families forming matrices for multiple work-and-home lifestyles facilitated by new reproductive and communicative technologies (Footlick 1990). In my vision, the existence of so many options for family life will provide a new framework within which infertile women who desire children can freely choose between such options as intensive involvement in raising children borne by relatives or friends (English 1988), adoption, and technologies whose benefits, risks, and purposes they clearly understand. I envision certain ethical decisions we must make at the end of this century forestalling the defeminization of birth and shifting reproductive research toward the true empowerment of mothers, fathers, and children. Rather than developing technologies to intervene in natural processes like birth, I envision technological experts studying the birth process to invent devices not to control but to assist—a better birthing chair that makes it easy for women to move around, the perfect nutritive food and drink for labor. I envision a society in which those who wish to take responsibility for their own health and births are empowered to do so, and those who wish others to take that responsibility are cared for by a compassionate and humanized medical system. I envision ever more sophisticated technologies, applied with loving hands, available to women like Joanne who do not want to "drop into biology"; and for those who do, no matter what their economic status, I envision a wide-open range of true alternatives. As we rise above our planet and look back at its wholeness, I envision that we will also rise above our hierarchical categorizations, allowing conceptual equality and freedom of choice in birth and in life to all human beings.

In my vision of the future, spreading awareness of the nature of systems will spawn a widespread acceptance among researchers and technicians that mother, baby, and family form a whole that can only be harmed by dissection into individual parts. Such awareness will form the conceptual basis of all government-sponsored clinical programs, leading directly to high funding priority for prenatal nurturance and nourishment of the mother and increased efforts to provide an optimum environment for parent-child bonding at birth. (One immediate result would be an enormous decrease in the number of babies needing the high-tech intensive care environment; one long-term result would be healthier families building a healthier society.) Respect and appreciation for the interactive flow between mother and baby of hormones, nutrients, energy, rhythm, emotion, movement, sound, spirit, and love will make unthinkable both institutionalized surrogacy and attempts to grow babies in mechanical incubators. So great will be this respect and appreciation that physicians will redefine their roles from managers to facilitators of the pregnancy/birth process. Midwives will become the primary birth attendants and they will be able to move between paradigms, providing the technology when the woman desires it and supporting her with hands-on skills when she doesn't. As society's conceptual emphasis shifts from part to whole, from unit to system, the technocratic paradigm itself will transform: science, technology, and institutions will be ideologically redefined as the servants of organic systems that link nature, individuals, and families in an emergent eco-culture. When patriarchy ceases to form any part of our core value matrix, the medical treatment and conceptualization of women's bodies as inherently defective machines will transform into their redefinition as integrated systems to be understood on their own terms.

As we have seen, the efforts of modern medicine to manipulate and control birth and other aspects of female physiology stem from a basic insecurity in American society about the viability of our mechanistic worldview. Once more of that worldview becomes systems-based, improved understanding of the physiology of birth, combined with a new respect for what women know, feel, and desire, will define a new field—the ecology of birth—whose practitioners will find their fulfillment not in manipulating but in honoring and safeguarding birth's delicate ecocycle. The Cesarean rate will stabilize at 4 percent.

As long as the technocratic model holds conceptual hegemony, few of these options are realizable. But I suggest, in the space allowed me here for dreaming, that expansion of that model into a systems-based paradigm that both emphasizes organic interconnectedness and makes practical use of models of mechanicity and separateness will potentiate these options and more.

Conclusion

In this book, I have applied a model derived from symbolic anthropology to the pregnancy/childbirth process which interprets this process as a year-long initiatory rite of passage. In so doing, I have sought to demonstrate that the same anthropological theory that applies to religious ritual can be utilized to illuminate the underlying cultural significance of modern technology and its uses. I have argued that childbirth is a rite of passage of tremendous cognitive significance for the mother in American society; that the messages conveyed by the rituals of hospital birth both reflect and reinforce the core values of our society; and that these rituals transform the mother in ways that reflect her orientation to those core values and to the technocratic belief system that underlies them.

In short, I have sought to demonstrate that the pregnancy/childbirth process has been culturally transformed in the United States into a male-dominated initiatory rite of passage through which birthing women are taught about the superiority, the necessity, and the "essential" nature of the relationship between science, technology, patriarchy, and institutions. I have shown how this socialization into our society's collective core value system is accomplished through obstetrical procedures—the rituals of hospital birth. I have presented step-by-step demonstrations of how these procedures work to map the technocratic model of reality which underlies our core value system onto the birthing woman's perceptions of her labor and birth experience, with the goal of achieving complete conceptual fusion between this technocratic model and the belief system of the birthing woman.

Through the birth narratives of individual women, I have shown how these birth rituals can fail in their didactic and socializing purposes when women manage during their births to maintain conceptual distance between themselves and the technocratic model, either by (1) achieving natural childbirth in the hospital; or (2) placing science and technology, patriarchy and the institution at *their* service instead of the other way around. I have also demonstrated the process by which, in the majority of births in my study, obstetrical rituals succeeded in completing conceptual fusion between the belief system of the woman and the technocratic model, or in cementing the preexisting correspondence between the two.

I have shown that a woman's ultimate perception of her birth experience as positive or negative, empowering or victimizing, will depend on the degree to which this experience confirms or undermines the belief system with which she enters the hospital. And I have outlined the nature of the process of reinterpretation through which those women who were traumatized by their birth experiences—whose belief systems, in other words, were overthrown through the consistent application of obstetrical procedures to their labor and birth processes—seek to rewrite the messages sent to them by hospital rituals through narrative, through childbirth activism, and through subsequent births.

I have examined medical school as a complementary rite of passage, in order to show how medical practitioners themselves are socialized into the technocratic model, thus ensuring that the system will continue to perpetuate itself in its present form. I have considered the cultural, political, and futuristic significance of most women's choices of technocratic birth, as well as the significance of some women's alternative choices. I have come to believe that the periodic failure of the rituals of hospital birth to socialize birthing women into our dominant technocratic model can be interpreted as success for American culture as a whole, for just as genetic diversity enhances a culture's ability to adapt to rapid environmental change (Rensberger 1981), so also is ideological diversity within one society a source of great strength and resilience, especially in today's rapidly changing times. Therefore, finally, I have sought to indicate some potential directions toward expanded options and sociocultural change inherent in the decisions of a minority of women to utilize their birth experiences both to reflect and to effect individual paradigm shifts from the technocratic model of reality to a more wholistic model based on systems theory.

If it is true, as psychotherapist Gayle Peterson says, that "as a woman lives, so shall she give birth," then perhaps it is also true that as individuals within a society shape birth, so shall they shape social life. The core values and beliefs of both individual women and the wider society in which they live condense into visible, focused form in childbirth, where their perpetuation is either assured or denied. It is both my belief and my hope that in the end—or the beginning—the salvation of the society which seeks to deny women their power as birth-givers will arise from the women who, nevertheless, give that society birth.

Appendix A
Interview Questions
Asked of Mothers

Interviews were usually conducted in the home or office of the interviewee, in a free-flowing style in which I tried to follow her train of thought and emotion. Most of the following questions were asked, in varying forms and at varying times, of most interviewees. Among many other things, I learned that there is a real art to the successful interview. Because I am a mother too (I have two children, ages twelve and eight), and have strong feelings and beliefs about birth and mothering, I had quite a struggle at first to avoid imposing my personal views on the women I interviewed through the questions I asked, and an even harder struggle to really hear what they were telling me when that directly conflicted with my own belief system. I hope that in the end I was able to let them speak their special truths, and to hear those truths, while at the same time sharing enough of myself to keep the interviews warm and interactive. Over time, I noticed that as I developed the ability to listen, I was more and more able to live their experiences as they were narrated to me—to put myself in their shoes, as it were. The better I listened, the better they talked, until I was able to leave most interviews feeling that the woman had really opened her heart and mind to share with me. There was of course a price to pay for being the repository of so many emotions—I wrote some pages with tears flowing down my cheeks. But in the end, I feel honored to have been touched by so many women's lives. What I have learned from the women I interviewed has enhanced my respect, appreciation, and love for them.

For first-time mothers:

Would you describe your primary occupation? Your husband's?

How long have you been married?

This may sound like a strange question, but can you tell me how you think about your body/describe your relationship with your body?

Did you plan the pregnancy? How did you know you were pregnant? How did you feel when you first found out? What did you do then?

Tell me about your experience of being pregnant. (If that question did not elicit much information, I would supplement it with the following:)

> Did you like being pregnant? What was different about it? How did you feel about the changes in your body? How were you treated by others? any differently than usual? How did you feel about that? How did you feel about other pregnant women? What did you do about being pregnant (alter your diet? read books? stop smoking/ drinking? take long naps?)? How did you feel about that?

What sort of prenatal care did you have? What did you think/how did you feel about it? Who was your obstetrician/midwife? How did you select him or her? What sort of relationship did you have? Describe any interactions with your birth practitioners in his/her office that you felt were significant.

What were your expectations for the pregnancy? Were they fulfilled? Why/why not?

Were you given a baby shower? Please describe it. What did it mean to you?

Did you take prenatal classes? Why/why not? Where? What kind? What did they teach you? What did they do for you? Did they make a difference in your birth experience?

What were your expectations for the birth? What did you want/hope/ dream it would be like? What did you plan for? What did you actually think it would be like? Did you have any fears? Why/why not/ of what?

What do you think labor is? Birth? That is, what are your definitions of labor and birth? How do you think about them? How do you feel when you think about them?

Tell me about your labor and birth. (Usually I would cease to ask questions at this point and simply listen to the narrative. But if the woman stopped, or seemed unsure, or gave me a very brief description, then I would look for more detail with the following questions, which I tried to keep as non-leading as possible—in other words, instead of saying, for example, "Did the IV make you uncomfortable?" I asked, "How did you feel about that?")

When did you go into labor? How did it feel? How did you feel about it? Who was with you? What did you do? Then what happened? Did you have anything to eat or drink? Why/why not? How did you decide when to go to the hospital? Tell me about getting there. What happened when you got there? How did you feel about that? Then what happened? How did that make you feel? etc.

How soon did you see the baby? For how long? How soon did you have care of him or her? Was that all right with you?

Did you nurse? When? For how long? Why/why not?

What do you think would have happened if you hadn't had access to a hospital? How did you feel about being in a hospital? Why?

Tell me about the days right after the birth.

What were you doing? How were you feeling? How much time did you spend with the baby? Did people come visit? Send you flowers? Why did people do/not do that? How did it make you feel? What did that time mean to you?

Do you feel that your birth experience was consistent with the rest of your life? Why or why not?

How would you rate your overall birth experience—positive or negative? On a scale of 1–10?

What did you like best about the birth? Least? Is there anything about the birth that you wish had been different? Will you plan to do anything differently if you have another child?

What sort of place and meaning does giving birth have in your life?

Is there anything special you would like others to know about what you have learned about being pregnant and giving birth?

What do you believe birth will be like in the future?

What is your vision for the future of American birth?

For mothers with more than one child, I would also ask:

How many children do you have? When were they born/what are their ages/names/gender?

Tell me about your second/third/etc. birth.

What accounts for the differences between these experiences? How do you feel about those differences? What did you learn?

Appendix B
Interview Questions
Asked of Obstetricians

Following is an abbreviated list of the basic questions asked (not necessarily in this order) of most obstetrician-interviewees. As with the women, I tried while interviewing obstetricians to put myself in their shoes, to feel their feelings and to see the world from their perspective.

When did you know that you wanted to attend medical school?

Did you take pre-med courses in college?

Where did you go to medical school?

Why did you choose that school, and what did you think of it?

What were your professors like? What did they seem to value? How did they present their material?

How much of your basic science courses did you retain?

Did you see patients before your third year of medical school?

If not, why do you think your medical school required two years of basic sciences before students could see patients?

How would you describe your medical school experience? Residency?

Would you tell me about your daily life during medical school and residency?

Did you enjoy medical school? Residency?

What were your personal relationships like during medical school and residency?

313

How did you feel while you were in medical school? Residency?

How did you decide to go into obstetrics?

Where did you do your residency? How did you choose that program? What did you think of it?

What kind of hours did you work? How did you feel about that? Why do you think residents have to work such hours?

What was the high point of your residency? The low point?

What do you see as most valuable about your medical school training? Your residency?

If you could design the medical school curriculum, would you keep it the same, or change it? How and why?

Were you exposed to alternatives in your training? In what ways?

If not, how did you find out about alternatives in obstetrics? (where applicable)

Did you find your medical school and residency experiences different because you were a woman? How so? (where applicable)

Do you think you personally approach obstetrics any differently because you are a woman? (where applicable)

What differences do you think increasing numbers of women will make in obstetrics?

How long have you been in practice?

What do you enjoy most about obstetrics? Dislike most?

What is your philosophy of birth? How did you arrive at this philosophy?

What do you think of women? Babies?

How do you view labor? Birth?

How do you see your role at birth?

How do you perceive yourself in relation to other obstetricians?

How do you perceive yourself in relation to your patients?

How do you perceive other obstetricians in your city?

Where do you place yourself on the scale "conservative to radical"?

Would you do home births?

What do your standing orders consist of?

What do you consider to be standard procedures for birth?

How often do you use these procedures?

To about what percentage of your patients do you give enemas?

About what percentage are shaved or clipped?

On about what percentage of your patients do you use epidurals? Pitocin? External monitor? Internal monitor?

What position do most of your patients deliver in?

Do your patients get to hold their babies after delivery? For approximately how long?

What is your Cesarean rate?

On what do you base your decision to perform a Cesarean?

Have you ever rejected a patient? Why?

Has a patient ever rejected you? Why?

Are you worried about lawsuits? If so, when did these worries begin? What effects does this have on your practice?

Have you ever been sued? If so, will you describe the circumstances and the results?

What were your overall perceptions of your training?

Is there anything further you would like to add?

Notes

INTRODUCTION

1. I am aware of no research on black and Hispanic middle-class women who go to private obstetricians. I suspect that their experiences encompass the range of experiences of the middle-class white women in my study without radical differences. Nevertheless, I want to call attention to the need for further research on the birthing experiences of middle-class members of other-than-Anglo ethnic groups.

2. In their introduction to *Secular Ritual*, editors Sally Moore and Barbara Myerhoff provide a well-considered list of six characteristics of ritual which are integral to its universal use and wide success in accomplishing its purposes (1977:7–8). These characteristics include: repetition, acting, "special" behavior or stylization, order, evocative presentational style and staging, and the "collective dimension" identified by Rappaport (1971) as the fact that the very occurrence of ritual contains a social message. In order to establish an explicit and sufficiently broad model of ritual within which I can interpret the rituals of both hospital and home birth, I have utilized this list, but expanded it to include other works on ritual, specifically recent research on the neurophysiological effects of ritual (d'Aquili, Laughlin, and McManus 1979), as well as the findings of other scholars within the symbolic anthropology tradition.

3. Language that evokes images will also access right lobe properties. The complex relationship between the hemispheres of the human brain is summarized by Laughlin:

> There appears to be an asymmetrical predominance of right hemisphere processing of nonverbal imagery, and of left hemisphere processing of verbal symbolism. But caution must be exercised. . . . The best information we have suggests that the more abstract the meaning associated with nonverbal imagery, the more the right hemisphere predominates (Ley 1983; Paivio 1986) in establishing, retaining in memory,

and processing those cognitive associations. Moreover, the left hemisphere predominates in the processing of analytical and sequential ordering in knowledge, whereas the right hemisphere predominates in processing synthetic, simultaneous spatial relations. Imagery evoking emotional associations would also seem to be processed primarily in the right hemisphere.

Yet the brain works as a unit, and the hemispheres are intimately interconnected across the corpus callosum and other commissures. Complex meaning primarily associated with nonverbal imagery and produced primarily by right hemisphere tissues may become associated with left hemisphere conceptual structures and be expressed via left hemisphere language functions (e.g., written scores of melodies, mythic stories). Likewise, cross-talk between the hemispheres may result in left hemisphere conceptual knowledge being expressed via right hemisphere imagery (e.g., illustrations, metaphors). (Laughlin 1990:16–18)

1: ONE YEAR

1. This chapter describes the wanted pregnancies of white middle-class women. Unwanted pregnancies generate very different sorts of experiences. Analyses of the ritual and symbolic aspects of aborted pregnancies and of the pregnancies and births of women who put their babies up for adoption await future work, as do the ritual and symbolic experiences of parents choosing to adopt their children. These are rich topics that deserve further scholarly attention.

2. This process of social and subsequent self-symbolization has many ramifications and deserves further investigation.

3. Although half of the freshman classes in many medical schools are now female, the vast majority of currently practicing obstetricians are still male (see Chapter 7).

4. Clinics run by nurse-midwives, some wholistically oriented M.D.s, and feminist self-help groups seek to avoid the disparity thus created between the nascent mother's need for increasing self-reliance and self-confidence and her continual disempowerment in the obstetrician's office, by offering women the opportunity to carry and read their own charts, to test their own urine and record the results, to weigh themselves, to watch internal exams in a mirror—in other words, to be active co-creators of their own medical care (Jordan 1977).

5. Yet in a study by Jordan in a women's self-help clinic of women's competence at self-diagnosis of pregnancy:

> Of 28 women who had no objective evidence of pregnancy at the time of the interview, all but one were correct in their assessment of their state. [The one who was wrong had been taking a hormone for weight control that produced feelings of pregnancy.] Almost half of the pregnant women reported that they knew of their pregnancy before they reported a missed period. An additional 44% knew before the time at which laboratory pregnancy tests begin to show results. It can be concluded that the women in this sample were able to make a diagnosis of pregnancy earlier and with greater accuracy than is possible in a physician's office. (Jordan 1977:33)

6. In her 1987 study comparing the social networks of home- and hospital-birthers, Carol McLain (1987a) found that women who chose home birth were far more likely to know the details of the pregnancy and birth experiences of their friends, and to be influenced by those experiences, than hospital-birthers

who chose conventional care. Hospital-birthers who chose the ABC (alternative birthing center) were in-between the home and conventional hospital groups in their involvement in and reliance on their social networks.

7. Some women reported a certain feeling of social pressure to observe this ritual period of seclusion, common across cultures. For example, when Melinda took her three-day-old baby out to an exhibit, she received shocked queries from other women about the baby's age, and thinly disguised disapproving responses, such as, "My, aren't you brave! I would never dream of doing such a thing! I would be afraid it would hurt the baby."

2: THE TECHNOCRATIC MODEL

1. The agrarian-based feudal system of medieval Europe (c. 400–1500) and the medieval Roman Catholic church, patriarchal as they were, still seem to have allowed women more latitude than the industrially based political system that followed (Roddy 1980). There are many instances of women reaching positions of high influence within medieval Catholicism, including sainthood (Alic 1986) and within the feudal system; in addition, some of the folk paradigms of medieval Europe were relatively egalitarian (Merchant 1983). In general, the Industrial Revolution, which replaced the extended with the nuclear family, narrowed women's spheres of activity, placing poor women in confining factory jobs, and limiting upper-class women to the domain of the home. Although some of the new sects that sprang up after the Protestant Reformation (1519 onwards) were egalitarian, most of the forms taken by Protestantism, especially the most influential sects (Lutheranism, Baptism, Methodism, Presbyterianism, Episcopalianism, etc.) were intensely patriarchal. In short, the historical context for the development of science and medicine ensured that these fields would take increasingly patriarchal form.

2. Much of this explication of the technocratic model of birth (earlier versions of which appear in Davis-Floyd 1986a, b, 1987b, 1988, 1990b) is based upon Rothman's (1982) illuminating comparison of the "medical" and "midwifery" models of birth, and parallels Martin's (1987) analysis of medical metaphors and reproductive imagery. In these earlier writings I labeled this paradigm "the technological model of birth." But I have come to realize that "technological" is far too broad a label—"as anthropologists have long recognized, technology, defined as the social organization of tools and techniques, is a universal feature of human society" (Reynolds 1991:10). Thanks to the suggestions of Peter C. Reynolds and Nicole Sault, I have recently switched to the more precise "technocratic." In Webster's (1979), technocracy is defined as "management of society by technical experts." In the hospital, birth is likewise defined by its management by technical experts.

3. This concept of the "uterus as an involuntary muscle" did not articulate with the experience of many of the women in my study, who reported that uterine contractions, although certainly outside of conscious control, seemed very responsive to environmental stresses and psychological shifts. One woman birthing at home, for example, said that her labor, well-advanced and progressing regularly, stopped altogether when her midwives had a traumatic dis-

pute, only resuming when the dispute was resolved. A hospital-birther reported that her desultory contractions became regular and powerful when an unfriendly nurse was replaced by a compassionate one. Martin points out that earlier editions of *Williams* did acknowledge that "labor contractions are affected by a woman's environment and emotional state" (1987:61). The dropping of this acknowledgment in later editions accompanied an increasing obstetrical insistence on the necessity of a steady progression of labor that conforms to what is defined as normal on medical charts, and signifies an intensification of the technocratic perception of birth by medical authorities.

4. According to Reynolds (1983), the rationale for this practice was found in Leviticus 12:1–7:

> The Lord said to Moses, "Say to the people of Israel, If a woman conceives, and bears a male child, then she shall be unclean seven days; as at the time of her menstruation, she shall be unclean. And on the eighth day the flesh of his foreskin shall be circumcised. Then she shall continue for thirty-three days in the blood of her purifying; she shall not touch any hallowed thing, nor come into the sanctuary, until the days of her purifying are completed. But if she bears a female child, then she shall be unclean two weeks, as in her menstruation; and she shall continue in the blood of her purifying for sixty-six days. And when the days of her purifying are completed, whether for a son or for a daughter, she shall bring to the priest at the door of the tent of meeting a lamb a year old for a burnt offering, and a young pigeon or a turtledove for a sin offering, and he shall offer it before the Lord, and make atonement for her; then she shall be clean from the flow of her blood. (The Bible, Revised Standard Version, 1952:111–112)

5. See Chapter 7 for a discussion of the increasing numbers of women entering obstetrics.

3: BIRTH MESSAGES

1. Most of the women in my study were married, and were accompanied during labor and birth by their husbands, and sometimes by other friends as well. But some were unmarried, and were accompanied by their lover, usually the baby's father, and/or by friends. I will use the term "partner" to refer to the laboring woman's primary support person. Since for most of the women in my study, this was a male, I will refer to the partner as "he."

2. Physicians sometimes try to correct for this by administering drugs to reduce gastric volume, or various combinations of antacids and other substances (cimetidine, ranitidine, metoclopramide, etc.) to raise the pH of stomach contents. Although gastric acidity and volume can sometimes be favorably affected by some of these methods (McKay and Mahan 1988a:217), they have made no difference in maternal mortality (Cohen 1979; Moir 1983; Scott 1978) and can themselves trigger other complications: they can cause the woman to vomit when she otherwise might not have (Duffy and Woodhouse 1982) and antacid particulate matter, if aspirated, can be as harmful to the lungs as gastric juices (Pritchard et al. 1985:331).

3. According to Anycity midwives, Recharge and Third Wind contain no artificial chemical compounds and can be found in health food stores. Mixing these juices with protein powder makes an especially delicious, nourishing,

stamina-enhancing drink. (Bananas, apples, strawberries, etc. can be added to make a delicious and energizing "fruit smoothie.")

4. When surgery under general anesthesia is anticipated or planned from the beginning, the NPO (nothing *per os*—by mouth) policy makes sense.

5. Brigitte Jordan contrasts the feeding of the laboring woman by her partner in the hospital with a videotape Jordan made of a home birth, in which the woman, "after a horrendous contraction, reaches over and picks up a glass of water and drinks it" (Jordan, personal communication, 1991). This act, often precluded in the hospital when the woman is allowed ice chips but denied water, is a simple yet powerful statement of autonomy and capability.

6. According to one physician, in the late 1970s the FDA said that elective induction was not an approved use of pitocin. In order to get around this restriction, some physicians in the hospital in which my interviewee practiced began to bring in the women whom they wanted to induce and immediately rupture their membranes, so that since now there were only twenty-four hours left for labor, they could administer pitocin with an indication of "ruptured membranes."

7. Some researchers have demonstrated that babies are conscious at birth and can remember and act upon prenatal and birth experiences (summaries of this research can be found in Chamberlain 1983, 1987b, 1988; Klaus and Klaus 1985; Salapatek and Cohen 1987; Verny 1987; Verny and Kelley 1981). Extrapolating from this base, and noting that the first generation to be generally anesthetized during birth—children born in the late 1940s and 1950s—was also the first generation to widely abuse drugs, some researchers are beginning to postulate possible correlations between drug use at birth and drug abuse later in life (see, for example, "Starting Young: Use of Anesthesia During Delivery Increases Risk of Narcotic Addiction" [*Harvard Health Letter* April 1991, p. 7]). Tentative hypotheses include the suggestion that drugging a child at birth may (1) weaken that child's ability to cope with stress, as the above studies indicate; (2) program that child to resort to drugs in response to increased stress; and/or (3) program the child to believe that important life transitions, like birth, are best accomplished when drugged. Such research is in its infancy. Certainly it would be very difficult to prove such assertions, as controlling for the many other variables that might lead to drug abuse would be well-nigh impossible.

A fourth hypothesis proposes that adult human behavioral patterns can be imprinted by specific risk factors during birth. Dr. Bertil Jacobson and his colleagues, of Sweden's Karolinska Institute, carried out case-controlled studies of 412 suicide victims and drug addicts in Stockholm. They concluded that "suicide involving asphyxiation was associated with asphyxiation at birth, suicide by violent mechanical means was associated with mechanical birth trauma, and drug addiction was associated with opiate and/or barbiturate administration to mothers during labor, [suggesting that the mechanism transferring birth trauma to adulthood is] analogous to imprinting in animals" (Jacobson et al. 1987:364). These researchers stress that "obstetric procedures should be carefully evaluated and possibly modified to prevent eventual self-destructive behavior" (1987:371).

In a second, more recent study, Jacobson et al. (1988) find a strong statistically significant correlation between the use of nitrous oxide during labor and subsequent amphetamine addiction in the children when they become adults. This risk of amphetamine addiction increased along with the duration of nitrous oxide administration: when nitrous oxide was given for 4.5 hours, the risk that the infant would become an addict was 5.6 times greater than if only given for 0.25 hours.

The association between drug use and a mechanistic society can also be metaphoric, as indicated in the following description by one of my college students of drug use during her teenage years:

> Drugs were a way of recognizing that we are in an industrial age, and therefore we should act mechanical and industrial ourselves by manipulating our bodies in a technological manner. It's even more industrial-like that we did the synthetic, factory produced drugs that someone had invented to mimic other naturally derived drugs. Our bodies were machines and doing drugs was a way of seeing whose machine could last the longest without giving out . . . I can't say that I was sad or that this was the worst time in my life . . . because actually I have never felt so in control of who I was and what I was doing.

8. The epidural is referred to in the medical literature as both an analgesic and an anesthetic. *Williams* uses the term *anesthesia* to refer only to general anesthetics that render the mother unconscious, while calling everything else *analgesia*, including epidurals. In the many journal articles on the subject, these words are often used interchangeably, with a notable regional preference in England for epidural *anaesthesia* and in the United States for epidural *analgesia*. *Webster's* (1979) defines anesthesia as "loss of sensation with or without loss of consciousness," and analgesia as "insensibility to pain without loss of consciousness."

9. At a national childbirth education conference in 1981, a Virginia obstetrician stated that in his efforts to return control of the pregnancy to the mother, the lithotomy position had been the hardest thing for him to give up. That position offered him the greatest sense of participation and control: he could put his hands on the baby as the mother pushed, move the baby around, try to ease him out. But if the mother squatted, or knelt on all fours, *she* delivered, while he felt awkward because he had nothing to do but watch and wonder "what am I here for?" (Sheila Richardson, personal communication).

10. Before germs were known to exist, Western physicians often went from post-mortem examinations to births without washing their hands. From the late 1700s on, there was periodic insistence by first European and later American physicians that doctors were the agents of childbed fever. But such radicals were often severely ridiculed for suggesting that physicians, who were gentlemen and healers and therefore clean, could be the agents of disease and death. Not until Pasteur demonstrated in the late 1800s that streptococci bacteria carried on physicians' hands were the cause of this deadly disease did antisepsis come to be standard medical procedure (Wertz and Wertz 1989:120–125).

11. As it becomes increasingly standard in medical practice to treat every birthing woman as if she has AIDS (which can be transmitted through the amniotic fluid), the impersonality of hospital birth is intensifying. An obstetrician practicing in New York reports that some of his colleagues wear goggles, plastic

masks, plastic aprons, and hip boots (like fisherman's boots) to attend births. And no one except the mother is allowed to touch the newborn baby skin-to-skin.

12. This statement, in all likelihood, is true at least for the 99 percent of human history that we have spent as hunter-gatherers (Trevathan 1987:230)—that is, from our evolutionary origins as a species several hundred thousand years ago until we switched to a sedentary agricultural lifestyle some 10,000 years ago. This switch was accompanied by a rise in not only population growth rates (as women went from having babies every four years to every two) but also in malnutrition from periodic food shortages (which hunter-gatherers, who did not depend on single crops, seldom experienced), in infectious diseases, and in infant mortality. In a review of 174 contemporary cultures of "low technology," Trevathan (1987:231) found that in 76 of them, mothers and babies were traditionally separated for at least the first thirty minutes after birth. She suggests that this separation may be a social mechanism for preventing the mother from too-rapidly becoming attached to an infant who might die, as these societies tended to have high infant mortality rates. I would add that perhaps some of these other societies also have reason, as we do, to lay symbolic claim to the newborn.

13. "Tells the baby" can be taken metaphorically. For researchers in the field of pre- and perinatal psychology (e.g., Chamberlain 1983, 1987b, 1988; Verny 1987; Verny and Kelley 1981) who feel assured that newborns are conscious and can remember the events surrounding birth, such a statement is literal, meaning that babies will internalize, remember, and to some extent be cognitively shaped by the symbolic messages they receive at birth. Two of the obstetricians I interviewed who were familiar with this literature had decided to act upon it, and had begun to speak soothing words of wonder and welcome directly to the newborn as he or she emerged from the womb, in spite of being considered "weird" by other hospital personnel. One of them said, "If it's true that babies remember and internalize what is said and done at birth, then maybe I can make a tremendous positive difference in their psychological well-being throughout their life. If it isn't, then at least I have done no harm by welcoming them, and it certainly makes the parents feel good."

14. These technocratic patterns have also been evident in our cultural treatment of breastfeeding, as Ann Millard makes clear in "The Place of the Clock in Pediatric Advice: Rationales, Cultural Themes, and Impediments to Breastfeeding" (1990). Analyzing the works of eighteen medical authors published in thirty-six volumes from 1897 to 1987 (twenty-seven volumes are editions of two major pediatric textbooks), Millard shows that although all sources advocate breastfeeding, the advice they give on how to do it actually undermines the process:

> The clock has provided the main frame of reference, creating regimentation reminiscent of factory work, segmenting breastfeeding into a series of steps, and emphasizing efficiency of time and motion. Feeding schedules were advocated in former days as a matter of discipline for the infant, but nowadays they are viewed as biologically innate to normal infants and to breast milk production. . . . Cultural themes besides the factory model of breastfeeding include the extension of professional advice to family mat-

ters, the subordination of lay women to professional expertise, mistrust of women's bodily signals including the let-down reflex . . . mistrust of signals from infants as well. . . . The relegation of control in breastfeeding to medical experts denies the validity of mutual bodily and emotional responses within the mother-infant dyad. . . . Ironically, the clock remains the major reference point in most pediatric sources today. (Millard 1990:211)

15. The entire technocratic birth process is a fine example of what Peter Reynolds (1991:1–3) calls the "one-two punch." Take a highly successful natural process (e.g., salmon swimming upstream to spawn). Punch One: render it dysfunctional with technology (dam the stream, preventing the salmon from reaching their spawning grounds). Punch Two: fix it with technology (take the salmon out of the water with machines, make them spawn artificially and grow the eggs in trays, then release the baby salmon downstream near the ocean). Reynolds identifies this "one-two punch"—destroy a natural process, then rebuild it as a cultural process—as an integral result of industrial society's supervaluation of science and technology over nature (1991:3–5).

4: BELIEF SYSTEMS ABOUT BIRTH

1. In her book *In Labor: Women and Power in the Birthplace* (later published in paperback under the title *Giving Birth: Alternatives in Childbirth* 1985) sociologist Barbara Katz Rothman describes and documents these two paradigms, which she labels the "medical" and "midwifery" models of pregnancy and birth (1982:134–140). Although I am indebted to Rothman for her carefully detailed explications of these models, I have chosen the label "the technocratic model of pregnancy and birth" instead of "the medical model" to emphasize the point that the medical model of birth is but a condensation of the larger technocratic model upon which our society is now conceptually based. Likewise, I have chosen the term "wholistic" instead of "midwifery" to name the emerging conceptual alternative to the technocratic model of birth, to emphasize that this alternative model comes out of the same systems theory upon which the entire "wholistic health" movement is based, and is but a reflection specific to birth of the larger view of reality encompassed by systems theory, which challenges the limitations of the still-dominant technocratic model (as will be further discussed in the final chapter).

2. A brief explication of this wholistic model appears in my "Afterword" to Rima Beth Star's *The Healing Power of Birth* (1986); parts of it are included here with permission of the author.

3. To the home-birthers in my study group, "family" seems generally to mean householders living together—usually partners and children, sometimes including certain relatives and even close friends.

4. The first Dick-Read groups were formed in various cities around the country in the early 1950s.

5. The major hospitals in Anycity report epidural rates averaging 70 percent (including epidurals used for Cesarean sections) for 1991. Assuming that about 10 percent of women use other types of anesthesia, this figure implies that perhaps about 20 percent of women birthing in Anycity hospitals in 1991 opt

for and achieve drug-free natural childbirth—a number lower than the 25–30 percent who receive Cesareans.

6. I owe part of the title of this section to Lois-Anne Hanson Arnold, who entitled a section of her recent master's thesis "Medical Safety as the Organizing Ideology of Birth" (1989:52).

7. Most authors writing about safety and home versus hospital birth cite this study not only because of its revelations but also because there are so few studies to cite. There is a crying need for more large-scale matched-sample comparisons between planned, midwife-attended home birth, planned physician-attended hospital birth, planned nurse-midwife attended hospital birth, and planned free-standing birth center births in the United States. Unless many more such careful studies demonstrate the relative safety of home birth, medical claims for the safety of hospital birth and the dangers of birth at home will continue to be unquestioningly accepted by both state legislatures and the majority of American citizens, home-birthers will continue to be regarded as taking untoward risks, and midwives across the country and in Canada (James-Chetelat 1989) will continue to be unfairly persecuted by the medical and legal systems (Litoff 1978; Sullivan and Weitz 1988).

8. Fear of postpartum hemorrhage is the bugaboo that drives many women who might otherwise choose the safer alternative of home birth into the hospital. As the studies cited in this section indicate, postpartum hemorrhage is more common in the hospital than at home. Hospital practices that contribute to postpartum hemorrhage include, according to *Williams*: use of pitocin during labor, midforceps delivery, forceps rotation, incisions of the uterus or cervix, uterine atony resulting from anesthesia, and too much haste in removing the placenta (Cunningham et al. 1989:415). To these Mehl (1977) adds too early cutting of the cord, pulling on the cord, and manual removal of the placenta.

While postpartum hemorrhage sometimes does occur in planned, midwife-attended home deliveries, midwives have a number of techniques for coping with it. Marimikel Penn, whose statistics are cited earlier in this section, reports that her first move is to tap the powers of mind-body integration by asking the mother to focus on visualizing her uterus hardening and the blood flow stopping (personal communication). She makes sure that the placenta is out and the bladder empty. She finds uterine massage, nursing the baby or breast stimulation, and tincture of shepherd's purse tea effective at aiding uterine clamping. Eating a piece of the placenta (sometimes ground up in a blender with tomato juice for palatability) is extremely effective. (Penn points out that animals who eat their placentas have no trouble with postpartum hemorrhage, theorizing that the placenta may be full of oxytoxic hormones.) Further technologies she utilizes include intramuscular injections of pitocin or methergen, or oral methergen, and occasional use of IV fluids in hypovolemia (low blood volume, which can lead to shock). In rare cases she has utilized bimanual compression (a fist pushing upwards in the vagina and another downwards on the uterus) to halt blood flow until the pitocin can take effect. In eighteen years of practice (1974–1991) and over 1,000 deliveries, only three of her clients have required transfer to the hospital and blood transfusions. (Two were cigarette smokers; Anycity midwives are finding that most of their clients who have trouble with postpartum bleeding are smokers.)

9. Addressing the argument that doctors' statistics are worse than midwives' because they handle more high-risk cases, Tew points to the statistically significant results cited here, asserting that high-risk cases do not occur often enough to account for such wide differences in outcome (1990:267). However, epidemiologist Kenneth C. Johnson (1991) finds methodological problems with Tew's interpretations of the data, most specifically (1) in her failure to highlight the fact that most of the most dangerous births—those of premature infants—are attended by physicians and not midwives; and (2) in her failure to present the data by intended place of delivery. In other words, if a birth that was planned to happen at home ends up taking place in the hospital, the statistics on that birth should stay in the home birth sample to avoid making home birth look good just because many complications end up in the hospital. Tew, however, feels that once a woman is transferred to the hospital and is subsumed under the technocratic system, it would not be fair to register the outcome as part of the home birth sample, as the outcome of that birth will have been strongly influenced by the technocratic model and so can no longer be appropriately registered with the births that do take place in a wholistic context. Nevertheless, Johnson concludes that because correcting for such interpretive flaws would significantly reduce the outcome gap between physicians and midwives, "it is not possible therefore to conclude who are the safest birth attendants from this recent Dutch evidence" (1991:5). (It is also not possible to conclude that midwife-attended home birth is any riskier than physician-attended hospital birth.) It is my understanding that Tew is under some pressure to revise her interpretive methods for future publications.

10. As Carol McClain (1983) shows in a fascinating study, the same decision-making processes operate for both home- and hospital-birthers. To interpret these processes, McClain utilizes the psychological bolstering theory of Janis and Mann (1977), which holds that a decision-maker confronted with competing options will select the least objectionable alternative and then enhance its appeal by maximizing its benefits and discounting its risks. McClain found that both home- and hospital-birthers "bolster" their choices by playing up the risks of the rejected alternative while at the same time discounting the risks of the chosen alternative. Thus, hospital-birthers stressed the dangers of home birth while minimizing the hospital's iatrogenic and psychosocial risks— risks upon which home-birthers placed great emphasis. Also in consonance with bolstering theory, both home- and hospital-birthers in McClain's study, once their decision had been made, actively avoided exposure to dissonant information or negative feedback about that decision. (Certainly this is also true for both home- and hospital-birthers in my study.) McClain points out that her findings not only should alert childbirth professionals to potential influences on a client's decisions, but should also enable professionals to assess their own risk biases and how these could shape their communications with clients.

7: OBSTETRIC TRAINING AS A RITE OF PASSAGE

1. This chapter is a revised version of an article by the same title that first appeared in *Obstetrics in the United States: Woman, Physician and Society,* a

special edition of the *Medical Anthropology Quarterly* 1(3):288–318, edited by Robert A. Hahn and Alan Harwood.

2. Because most of the practicing obstetrician/gynecologists in the country, as well as in my study, are male, it seems appropriate to use the gender-specific pronoun "he" in this chapter, except, of course, where the referent is a woman. All obstetricians quoted without mention of their sex are male.

3. It might be argued that my emphasis on the redundancy of obstetrical rituals ignores the high value placed in residency on mastery of "the latest" techniques. I would like to suggest, however, that no matter which new techniques are incorporated into the obstetrical management of birth, as long as they are technocratic in method and orientation, "the latest," symbolically speaking, is just "more of the same."

4. In contrast to this view, proponents of home birth point to improvements in the standard of living and nutrition as the major causes of the decline of the infant mortality rate. They further claim that this rate, as well as the number of birth injuries and infections of mother and child, would be far lower if birth were de-technologized (Odent 1984, 1986; Stewart and Stewart 1976, 1977, 1979, 1981). The midwifery statistics cited in Chapter 4 support this claim.

5. These phrases ("she infected her wound," "she broke down the wound") are common medical parlance (Konner 1987:373). They reveal how this physician, perhaps unconsciously, assigns blame to the woman for her physical malfunctions.

6. See Chapter 3 for references to studies on standing and walking during labor.

7. Reflecting back on twenty years of teaching medical students at three different universities, Robert Glew is pleased to see a downward trend in the test scores of today's applicants. He feels that these students, admitted in a less competitive atmosphere than previously, will have a beneficial effect on the medical profession because they

> are, on the whole, nicer people, more well-rounded, less self-absorbed, and possessed of a more wholesome motivation regarding their professional goals, when compared with the generation of tunnel-visioned egotists who preceded them, and whom I hold largely responsible for having wrecked the medical profession in this country. . . . I am confident despite the very real risks that the wart-hogs who control clinical training may quench medical students' enthusiasm and altruism, that most of our students will emerge from the gauntlet battered and bruised but with their values and high standards of personal behavior intact. If they do, then within a decade their impact on this profession in decline is certainly going to be felt in a very substantial and positive way. So let us [reassure] the admissions committee members . . . that there is no reason to be frightened or ashamed when they admit a new freshman class whose mean QPA is 3.2. It is unlikely they will foul the medical profession the way their 3.87 predecessors have been doing for the last twenty years. (1989:4)

8. A doula is a supportive female companion; a monitrice is a registered nurse specially trained to give labor support. So that the benefits of human caring in childbirth, as in other aspects of modern health care, can become rational-technical matters of objective observation, a number of prominent researchers have attempted to quantify the benefits of such humanized care. For one example, Sosa, Kennell, Klaus, and their associates, working first with

Guatemalan women, and more recently with women in a large charity hospital in Texas, have proven the physiological value of the humanization of
childbirth (1980, 1986, 1988). Their studies all involve comparison of results
of normal hospital labors with labors of women attended one-on-one by a
doula. Somewhat caustically, Kennell summarizes their dramatic results in technocratic context:

> If I told you today about a new medication or a new electronic device that would
> reduce problems of fetal asphyxia and the progress of labor by two-thirds, cut labor
> length by one-half, and enhance mother-infant interaction after delivery [as does the
> presence of the doula], I expect that there would be a stampede to obtain this new
> medication or device in every obstetric unit in the United States, no matter what the
> cost. Just because the supportive companion makes good common sense does not de-
> crease her importance. (1982:23)

I present here the important results of this project—a randomized controlled
study at Jefferson Davis Hospital in Houston, Texas, where mothers routinely
labor without family support (Kennell et al. 1988). Four hundred two healthy
first-time mothers in active, normal labor were randomly assigned to the Supported (S) or the Observed (O) group on hospital admission. Supported patients
were accompanied by a doula from admission through delivery. Observed
women received routine obstetric care with no additional support but were observed throughout labor by an observer ten feet away. To control for the effects
of the observer, postdelivery information was obtained on a Control group (C).
Epidural anesthesia and forceps use were much lower in the Supported group
compared to the Observed and Control groups, and Cesarean section rates were
halved compared to the Control group.

	S (n = 210)	O (n = 192)	C (n = 204)
C/sec (% of all deliveries)	8.1	13.0	18.1
Forceps (% of vag. deliveries)	8.3	22.2	26.9
Epidural (% of all deliveries)	11.4	28.6	60.8

The researchers were surprised to find that Cesarean rates were significantly
lower in the Observed group as compared to the Control group, as were the
use of forceps and epidurals. They concluded that support during labor, even
in the form of the presence of a silent observer, has a therapeutic effect. Most
of the women in the Observed group commented how much they appreciated
"that woman who stayed in the labor room throughout the entire labor and
who checked [my] chart to be sure everything was all right" (Klaus 1989:2).

9. A recent incident in a Pennsylvania medical school, described in the
school newsletter *Murmurs* (May 1989:1), illustrates the tremendous strength
of the male biases that female students still must cope with. A male professor
opened a lecture on female anatomy with a cartoon depicting a butcher shop
named for him filled with items for sale by the pound drawn to represent parts
of female reproductive anatomy and labeled "Fried Ovary," "Fallopian Sau-
sage," and "Whole Cooked Uterus." Another cartoon "depicted a woman lying
on her back on an examining table naked and undraped with a flower growing

from her vagina. Standing beside her was a male doctor. The caption read, 'When was the last time you douched?'" The authors of the article (written in the form of a letter to the Dean) in the newsletter, who list themselves as "Concerned Members of the Class of 1991," were angry that no action had been taken against this professor in spite of his "dehumanizing attitude towards women." Instead, in a show of support for this professor, a majority of the class had voted to honor him with the Golden Apple Award for excellence in teaching. But after a protest, a runoff was held and the second-place candidate won (Guo, *Pittsburgh Post-Gazette* 1989:5).

8: THE COMPUTERIZED BIRTH?

1. In her award-winning *The Woman in the Body*, anthropologist Emily Martin stresses women's resistance to demeaning and dehumanizing medical metaphors for and treatment of their bodies.

2. Certainly there is much more to be said on the subject of why women "choose" technocratic births, but further analysis of the factors feeding into the cultural construction of women's reproductive choices is beyond the scope of this book. Such analysis has begun (e.g., Arditti et al. 1985; Corea 1985*b*; Rapp 1988*a*, *b*; Rothman 1982, 1986, 1989; Spallone 1989) and must become an increasingly important facet of sociocultural research. Many feminist writers have already provided profound and valuable insights into the cultural forces at work in women's socialization (e.g., Woolf 1966; de Beauvoir 1970; Morgan 1970, 1982; Rich 1977; Daly 1973, 1978; Griffin 1978; Mackinnon 1979; McNulty 1981; Jones 1980; Hull et al. 1981; Rothman 1982, 1989; Spender 1982; Frye 1983; Walker 1983; see also Graebner 1975; Beuf 1979; Derber 1979). Such works have made great strides in identifying powerful forces at work in modern society which are not consciously articulated by its individual members, showing how patriarchy works to oppress women *and* men in fundamental and largely unconscious ways. For example, both Merchant (1980) and Dubois (Dubois et al. 1985) have demonstrated how male hegemony over ideas and their dissemination has operated to control the paradigms of reality in terms of which most members of Western society, male and female, perceive, live, choose, and interpret the meaning of their lives.

3. I am indebted to Beverly J. Stoeltje for this insight.

4. In other cultures, nontechnocratic solutions have been found for the problem of infertility. Anthropologist Nicole Sault compares American surrogacy with the Mexican system of *compadrazgo*, or godparenthood, in which the godparents sponsor the child's baptism, thereby participating in the child's social birth into the community. During the baptismal ceremony, the godmother holds the child in her arms and the godfather places his hand on the child; thus they impart some of their essence to their godchild. Throughout the child's life, the godparents are expected to be intimately involved in their godchild's education, religious development, and medical care. People refer to the godparents as a second mother and father, and godchilden often actually go to live with their godparents for an extended period of time, and sometimes per-

manently. Sault stresses that "in Mexico there is a strong emphasis on sharing, and this includes not only material resources but also the responsibility for raising children and the benefit of their respect and affection. . . . The significant point is that sharing children is seen as natural and beneficial to the children" (1989:22–25).

Sault points out that similar systems of child sharing have been imported into the United States by various immigrant groups, as well as developed in black communities (Stack 1974). Such systems, like *compadrazgo*, emphasize not biological but social parenting. In the United States the emphasis is on biological parenthood, meaning individual ownership. Thus couples who cannot physically have children feel they are being deprived of the right to have "children of their own" (Sault 1989:33). So valued is biological parenting by middle-class America that entire industries (surrogacy, IVF, artificial insemination) have sprung up to attempt to create it when nature does not.

9: —OR BIRTH AS THE BIODANCE?

1. I wish to stress again that this book deals with mainstream American paradigms of birth and the rituals that enact them. The wide variety of folk and ethnomedical paradigms of birth active in the United States are not considered here.

2. I am thinking here not of religious fundamentalist homeschoolers but of those homeschoolers who reject the educational system because they believe that it stifles individuality and creativity, teaches technocratic values they do not wish their children to absorb, and ignores the spiritual and emotional needs of the whole child (Farenga 1989). These wholistically oriented homeschoolers (often readers of *Mothering* magazine) believe in both mind-body and parent-child integration, and decry the separation of the family fostered by the educational system (Clark 1988). Their systems-based wholistic ideology is antithetical to the technocratic model, a situation that has led to their occasional persecution by the legal system (Shepherd 1988), which, like the medical system, is a major cultural defender of that model.

3. About being on "the radical fringe," Jeannine Parvati-Baker, author of *Hygeia: A Woman's Herbal* (1978), *Conscious Conception* (1986a), and *Prenatal Yoga* (1986b), has this to say (personal communication):

> Some years ago, I wrote a visualization . . . which led the participants in gradual steps to a door, and encouraged them to open it without giving any hints as to what might be on the other side. Experimenting, I tried it out on myself, and found that when I opened the door, I stepped out into the starry night sky, which began to swirl and swirl. . . . The next time someone told me that I "hang out on the fringe," something I've been hearing for most of my life, I suddenly saw that yes, I am on the fringe—on the fringe of the skirt of the goddess as she dances around the universe. That starry sky, that's the fringe of her skirt, and it swirls and swirls as she dances. And that's my place, and it's a wonderful place to be, full of movement and excitement and joy.

References

Abitol, M. M.
1985   "Supine Position in Labor and Associated Fetal Heart Rate Changes." *Obstetrics and Gynecology* 65:481–486.

Abrahams, Roger D.
1973   "Ritual for Fun and Profit (or The Ends and Outs of Celebration)." Paper delivered at the Burg Wartenstein Symposium No. 59, Ritual: Reconciliation in Change.

Abrahamson, E. M., and A. W. Pezet
1977   *Body, Mind, and Sugar.* New York: Avon Books.

Abramson, L. Y., M. E. P. Seligman, and J. D. Teasdale
1978   "Learned Helplessness in Humans: Critique and Reformulation." *Journal of Abnormal Psychology* 87:49–74.

Abramson, Milton, and John R. Torghele
1961   "Weight, Temperature Change, and Psychosomatic Symptomatology in Relation to the Menstrual Cycle." *American Journal of Obstetrics and Gynecology* 81:223.

Alic, Margaret
1986   *Hypatia's Heritage: A History of Women in Science from Antiquity through the Nineteenth Century.* Boston: Beacon Press.

Allison, A. C.
1955   "Danger of Vitamin K to Newborn." (Letter to the Editor.) *Lancet* 1:669.

Alten, D. Van, M. Eskes, and P. E. Treffers
1989   "Midwifery in the Netherlands, The Wormeveer Study: Selection, Mode of Delivery, Perinatal Mortality, and Infant Morbidity." *British Journal of Obstetrics and Gynecology* 96:656–662.

Alzugaray, Marina
1992   "Fluid Birth." Unpublished manuscript.
Amighi, J. K.
1990   "Some Thoughts on the Cross-Cultural Study of Maternal Warmth and Detachment." *Pre- and Perinatal Psychology Journal* 5(2): 131–146.
Arditti, Rita, Renate Duelli Klein, and Shelley Minden, eds.
1985   *Test-Tube Women*. Boston: Pandora Press.
Arms, Suzanne
1975   *Immaculate Deception*. New York: Bantam Books.
1977   "Why Women Should Be in Control of Childbirth and Feminine Health Services." In *21st Century Obstetrics Now!* ed. D. Stewart and L. Stewart. Marble Hill, Mo.: NAPSAC.
Arney, William Ray
1982   *Power and the Profession of Obstetrics*. Chicago: University of Chicago Press.
Arnold, Lois-Anne Hanson
1989   "Cultural Dynamics in the Interaction of Primigravid Women and Orthodox Medicine." Master's thesis, Dept. of Anthropology, University of Calgary, Alberta.
Arx, Walter von
1978   "La Benedicion de la Mere apres la Naissance: Histoire et Significacion." *Concilium* 132.
Ashford, Janet Isaacs, ed.
1984   *Birth Stories: The Experience Remembered*. Trumansburg, N.Y.: The Crossing Press.
1986–   *The Childbirth Alternatives Quarterly*, Winter.
1987
1988a   *Natural Love*. Solana Beach, Calif.: Janet Isaacs Ashford.
1988b   *George Engelmann and "Primitive" Birth*. Solana Beach, Calif.: Janet Isaacs Ashford.
Babcock, Barbara, ed.
1978   *The Reversible World: Symbolic Inversion in Art and Society*. Ithaca, N.Y.: Cornell University Press.
1980   "Reflexivity: Definitions and Discriminations." *Semiotica* 30:1–14.
Baggish, M. S., and S. Hooper
1974   "Aspiration as a Cause of Maternal Death." *Obstetrics and Gynecology* 43(3):327–336.
Balaskas, Janet, and Arthur Balaskas
1983   *Active Birth*. New York and London: McGraw-Hill.
Banta, H. David, and Stephen B. Thacker
1979   *Costs and Benefits of Electronic Fetal Monitoring: A Review of the Literature*. (U.S. Dept. of Health, Education, and Welfare, National Center for Health Services Research, DHEW Pub. No. (PHS)79–3245.) Washington, D.C.: U.S. Government Printing Office.
Barker, C. S.
1945   "Acute Colitis Resulting from Soapsuds Enema." *Canadian Medical Association Journal* 52:285.

Beattie, John
1966   "Ritual and Social Change." *Man* 1:60–74.
Beecham, Clayton T.
1989   "Natural Childbirth: A Step Backward?" *Female Patient* 14:56–60.
Benditt, M.
1945   "Gangrene of the Rectum as a Complication of an Enema." *British Medical Journal* 1:664.
Benson, Ralph C.
1980   *Handbook of Obstetrics and Gynecology.* 7th ed. Los Altos, Calif.: Lange Medical Publications.
Beuf, Ann Hill
1979   *Biting Off the Bracelet: A Study of Children in Hospitals.* Philadelphia: University of Pennsylvania Press.
Bing, Elisabeth
1967   *Six Practical Lessons for an Easier Childbirth.* New York: Grosset.
Bing, Elisabeth, and Libby Coleman
1977   *Making Love During Pregnancy.* New York: Bantam Books.
Bing, Elisabeth, and Marjorie Karmel
1961   *A Practical Training Course for the Psychoprophylactic Method of Childbirth.* New York: American Society for Psychoprophylaxis in Obstetrics.
Birnbaum, David
1977   "The Iatrogenesis of Damaged Mothers and Babies at Birth." In *21st Century Obstetrics Now!* ed. D. Stewart and L. Stewart. Marble Hill, Mo.: NAPSAC.
The Birth Book: Your Guide to Vaginal, Cesarean, and VBAC Deliveries. San
1991   Bruno, Calif.: Krames Publications.
Blanchet, Therese
1984   *Meanings and Rituals of Birth in Rural Bangladesh.* Dhaka, Bangladesh: University Press Ltd.
Bleicher, N.
1962   "Behavior of the Bitch During Parturition." *Journal of the American Veterinary Medical Association* 140:1076–1082.
Bluebond-Langner, Myra
1978   *The Private Worlds of Dying Children.* Princeton: Princeton University Press.
Bohm, David
1951   *Quantum Theory.* New York: Prentice-Hall.
1980   *Wholeness and the Implicate Order.* London: Routledge and Kegan Paul.
Borgatta, Lynn, Susan L. Piening, and Wayne R. Cohen
1989   "Association of Episiotomy and Delivery Position with Deep Perineal Laceration During Spontaneous Delivery in Nulliparous Women." *American Journal of Obstetrics and Gynecology* 160(2): 294–297.
Bowen, Evlyn M.
1983   *Pre-Birth Bonding.* San Diego: HeartStart/LoveStart Publications.

Brackbill, Yvonne, Karen McManus, and Lynn Woodward
1988   *Medication in Maternity: Infant Exposure and Maternal Information.* Ann Arbor: University of Michigan Press.
Brackbill, Yvonne, June Rice, and Diony Young
1984   *Birth Trap: The Legal Low-Down on High-Tech Obstetrics.* St. Louis: C. V. Mosby.
Bradley, Robert A.
1981   *Husband-Coached Childbirth.* 3d ed. New York: Harper and Row.
Braude, Morris
1935   *Life Begins: Childbirth in Lore and Literature.* Chicago: Argus Books.
Brazelton, T. B.
1973   "Effect of Maternal Expectations on Early Infant Behavior." *Early Child Development Care* 2:259–273.
Brennan, Barbara, and Joan Rattner Heilman
1977   *The Complete Book of Midwifery.* New York: E. P. Dutton.
Brewer, Tom
1966   *Metabolic Toxemia of Late Pregnancy: A Disease of Malnutrition.* Springfield, Ill.: Charles C. Thomas.
Brewer, Tom, and Gail Brewer
1977   *What Every Pregnant Woman Should Know: The Truth about Diet and Drugs in Pregnancy.* New York: Random House.
Broach, Jeanine, and Niles Newton
1988   "Food and Beverages in Labor, Part I: Cross-Cultural and Historical Practices." *Birth* 15(2):81–85.
Bromberg, Joanne
1981   "Having a Baby: A Story Essay." In *Childbirth: Alternatives to Medical Control,* ed. Shelly Romalis. Austin: University of Texas Press.
Brunvand, Jan
1978   *The Study of American Folklore.* New York: W. W. Norton and Co.
Burnett, C., J. Jones, J. Switzer, G. Davenport, and A. Miller
1977   "Home Delivery and Infant Mortality in North Carolina." Paper delivered at American Public Health Association Conference.
Burnett, Claude, James Jones, Judith Rooks, Chong Hwa Chen, Carl Tyler, and C. Arden Miller
1980   "Home Delivery and Neonatal Mortality in North Carolina." *Journal of the American Medical Association* 244:2741–2745.
Burns, Tom, and Charles D. Laughlin
1979   "Ritual and Social Power." In *The Spectrum of Ritual,* ed. Eugene d'Aquili, Charles D. Laughlin, and John McManus. New York: Columbia University Press.
Cafferata, John
1975   *Rites.* New York: McGraw-Hill.
Caldeyro-Barcia, Roberto
1975   "Supine Called the Worst Position for Labor and Delivery." *Family Practice News* 5:11.

1978   "The Influence of Maternal Position During the First Stage of Labor." In *Kaleidoscope of Childbearing: Preparation, Birth, and Nurturing*, ed. P. Simpkin and C. Reinke. (Highlights of the 10th Biennial Convention of the International Childbirth Education Association, Inc.) Seattle: Penny Press.

1979   "The Influence of Maternal Position on Time of Spontaneous Rupture of Membranes, Progress of Labor, and Fetal Head Compression." *Birth and the Family Journal* 6(1):10–18.

Calvert, J. P., R. G. Newcombe, and B. M. Hibbard
1982   "An Assessment of Radiotelemetry in the Monitoring of Labour." *British Journal of Obstetrics and Gynecology* 89:285–291.

Campbell, Rona, I. Macdonald Davies, Alison J. Macfarlane, and V. Beral
1984   "Home Births in England and Wales: Perinatal Mortality According to Intended Place of Delivery." *British Medical Journal* 289: 721–724.

Campbell, Rona, and Alison Macfarlane
1987   *Where To Be Born? The Debate and the Evidence*. National Perinatal Epidemiology Unit, Radcliffe Infirmary.

Campbell, Ross
1988   "Homeschooling: State by State." *Mothering* 47:88–91.

Capra, Fritjof
1975   *The Tao of Physics*. Boulder: Shambala Publications.
1983   *The Turning Point: Science, Society and the Rising Culture*. New York: Bantam Books.

Carver, Cynthia
1981   "The Deliverers: A Woman Doctor's Reflections on Medical Socialization." In *Childbirth: Alternatives to Medical Control*, ed. Shelly Romalis. Austin: University of Texas Press.
1984   *Patient Beware: Dealing with Doctors and Other Medical Dilemmas*. Scarborough, Ontario: Prentice-Hall Canada.

Catano, Janis W., and Victor M. Catano
1981   "Mild Post-Partum Depression: Learned Helplessness and the Medicalization of Obstetrics." Paper delivered at the meetings of the Eastern Psychological Association, New York.

Cetrulo, C. L., and R. K. Freeman
1975   "Problems and Risks of Fetal Monitoring." In *Risks in the Practice of Modern Obstetrics*, ed. S. Aldajem. St. Louis: C. V. Mosby.

Chalmers, Ian
1978   "Randomized, Controlled Trials of Intrapartum Fetal Monitoring." In *6th European Congress of Perinatal Medicine, Vienna, Austria*. Stuttgart: Georg Thieme Verlag.

Chamberlain, David
1983   *Consciousness at Birth: A Review of the Empirical Evidence*. San Diego: Chamberlain Communications.
1987a   "The Cognitive Newborn: A Scientific Update." *British Journal of Psychotherapy* 4(1):30–71.
1987b   "Consciousness at Birth: The Range of Empirical Evidence." In *Pre-*

and Perinatal Psychology: An Introduction, ed. Thomas R. Verny. New York: Human Sciences Press.

1988   *Babies Remember Birth.* San Diego: Chamberlain Communications.

Chapple, E., and C. Coon

1942   *Principles of Anthropology.* New York: Holt, Rinehart and Winston.

Chestnut, D. H., G. F. Vanderwalker, C. I. Owen, J. N. Bates, and W. W. Choi

1987   "The Influence of Continuous Epidural Bupivacaine Analgesia on the Second Stage of Labor and Method of Delivery in Nulliparious Women." *Anesthesiology* 66:774.

Church, George G.

1986   "Sorry, Your Policy Is Canceled." *Time,* 24 March 1986:16–26.

Cixous, Helene

1975   "Sorties." In *La jeune nee,* ed. Caterine Clements and Helene Cixous. Paris: Union Generale d'Editions.

Clark, Edward

1988   "Nature or Nurture?" *Mothering* 47:79–81.

Clark, Nancy, and Anita Bennets

1982   "Vital Statistics and Nonhospital Births: A Mortality Study of Infants Born Out of Hospitals in Oregon." In *Research Issues in the Assessment of Birth Settings,* ed. Committee on Assessing Alternative Birth Settings. Washington, D.C.: National Academy Press.

Clifford, James, and George E. Marcus, eds.

1986   *Writing Culture: The Poetics and Politics of Ethnography.* Berkeley, Los Angeles, London: University of California Press.

Clymer, Swinburne

1950   *Prenatal Culture: Creating the Perfect Baby.* Quakertown, Penn.: Philosophical Publishing Company.

Cohen, L. B.

1979   "Our Developing Knowledge of Infant Perception and Cognition." *American Psychologist* 34(10):894–899.

Cohen, Nancy, and Lois Estner

1983   *Silent Knife: Cesarean Prevention and Vaginal Birth after Cesarean.* South Hadley, Mass.: Bergin and Garvey Publishers, Inc.

Cohen, S. E.

1979   "Aspiration Syndromes in Pregnancy." *Anesthesiology* 51(5):375–377.

Collias, N. E.

1956   "The Analysis of Socialization in Sheep and Goats." *Ecology* 37:228–239.

Collier, Jane, Michelle D. Rosaldo, and Sylvia Yanigisako

1982   "Is There a Family? New Anthropological Views." In *Rethinking the Family,* ed. B. Thorne and M. Yalom. New York: Longuran.

Concerned Members of the Class of 1991

1989   "When Jokes Go Too Far: A Letter to the Dean." *Murmurs* (Newsletter of the University of Pittsburgh School of Medicine), May:1–4.

Condon, W. S., and L. W. Sander
1974   "Neonate Movement Is Synchronized with Adult Speech: Interactional Participation and Language Acquisition." *Science* 183:99–101.
Corea, Gena
1979   "Childbirth 2000." *Omni*, April.
1980   "The Cesarean Epidemic." *Mother Jones*, July.
1985a   *The Hidden Malpractice*. New York: Harper and Row.
1985b   *The Mother Machine: Reproductive Technologies from Artificial Insemination to Artificial Wombs*. New York: Harper and Row.
Cotton, D. B., et al.
1984   ".Intrapartum to Post-Partum Changes in Colloid Osmotic Pressure." *American Journal of Obstetrics and Gynecology* 149(2): 174–176.
Coulton, G. G.
1922   "Infant Perdition in the Middle Ages." *Medieval Studies* 16.
Cox, S. M., J. E. Bost, S. Faro, and R. J. Carpenter
1987   "Epidural Anesthesia During Labor and the Incidence of Forceps Delivery." *Texas Medicine* 83:45.
Crawford, J. S.
1979   "Continuous Lumbar Epidural Analgesia for Labour and Delivery." *British Medical Journal* 1:72.
1985   "Some Maternal Complications of Epidural Anesthesia for Labour." *Anesthesia* 40:1219.
Cruse, M. D.
1977   Obstetrics and Gynecology Newsletter. *Journal of Continuing Education Ob/Gyn*, December:9.
Culler, Johnathan
1981   *The Pursuit of Signs: Semiotics, Literature, Deconstruction*. Ithaca, N.Y.: Cornell University Press.
Cunningham, F. Gary, Paul C. MacDonald, and Norman F. Gant
1989   *Williams Obstetrics*. 18th ed. Norwalk, Conn.: Appleton & Lange.
Daly, Mary
1973   *Beyond God the Father*. Boston: Beacon Press.
1978   *Gyn/Ecology*. Boston: Beacon Press.
Dansby, Binnie
1987   "Underwater Birth: The Ultimate Alternative." In *Pre- and Perinatal Psychology: An Introduction*, ed. Thomas R. Verny. New York: Human Sciences Press.
d'Aquili, Eugene G.
1979   "The Neurobiology of Myth and Ritual." In *The Spectrum of Ritual: A Biogenetic Structural Analysis*, ed. Eugene d'Aquili, Charles D. Laughlin, and John McManus. New York: Columbia University Press.
d'Aquili, Eugene G., Charles D. Laughlin, and John McManus, eds.
1979   *The Spectrum of Ritual: A Biogenetic Structural Analysis*. New York: Columbia University Press.

Davis, Elizabeth
1983 *A Guide to Midwifery: Heart and Hands.* New York: Bantam Books.
1989 *Women's Intuition.* Berkeley, Calif.: Celestial Arts.
Davis-Floyd, Robbie E.
1983 "Pregnancy and Cultural Confusion: Contradictions in Socialization." In *Cultural Constructions of Woman,* ed. Pauline Kolenda. Salem, Wis.: Sheffield Press/Sage Publications.
1986a "Afterword." In Rima Beth Star, *The Healing Power of Birth.* Austin, Texas: Star Publishing.
1986b "Birth as an American Rite of Passage." Ph.D. diss., Dept. of Anthropology/Folklore, University of Texas at Austin.
1986c "Routines and Rituals: A New View." In *NAACOG* (Nurses Association of the American College of Obstetrics and Gynecology) *Update Series.* Princeton: Continuing Professional Education Center, Inc.
1987a "Obstetric Training as a Rite of Passage." *Medical Anthropology Quarterly* 1(3):288–318.
1987b "The Technological Model of Birth." *Journal of American Folklore* 100(398):93–109.
1987c "Hospital Birth Routines as Rituals: Society's Messages to American Women." *Pre- and Perinatal Psychology Journal* 1(4):276–296.
1988 "Birth as an American Rite of Passage." In *Childbirth in America: Anthropological Perspectives,* ed. Karen Michaelson. Beacon Hill, Mass.: Bergin and Garvey.
1990a "Ritual in the Hospital: Giving Birth the American Way." In *Anthropology: Contemporary Perspectives,* ed. Phillip Whitten and David Hunter. 6th ed. Glenview, Ill: Scott Foresman.
1990b "The Role of American Obstetrics in the Resolution of Cultural Anomaly." *Social Science and Medicine* 31(2):175–189.
1992 "Mind Over Body: The Pregnant Professional." In *Many Mirrors: Body Image and Social Relations in Anthropological Perspective,* ed. Nicole Sault. Philadelphia: University of Pennsylvania Press.
Daviss-Putt, Betty Anne
1990 "Rights of Passage in the North: From Evacuation to the Birth of a Culture." In *Gossip,* ed. Mary Crnkobich. Canadian Arctic Resources Committee.
de Beauvoir, Simone
1970 *The Second Sex.* New York: Bantam Books.
DeLee, Joseph B.
1920 "The Prophylactic Forceps Operation." *American Journal of Obstetrics and Gynecology* 1:34–44.
Derber, Anton
1979 *The Pursuit of Attention: Power and Individualism in Everyday Life.* Cambridge, Mass.: Schenckman Publishing Co.

Derrida, Jacques
1981 *Positions: Three Interviews on Marxism, Psychoanalysis, and Deconstruction.* Chicago: University of Chicago Press. (Originally published in French. Paris: Minuit, 1972.)
DeVries, Raymond G.
1985 *Regulating Birth: Midwives, Medicine, & the Law.* Philadelphia: Temple University Press.
Diaz, A. G., R. F. Schwarcz, and R. Caldeyro-Barcia
1980 "Vertical Position During the Course of the First Stage of Labor, and Neonatal Outcome." *European Journal of Obstetric and Gynecological Reproductive Biology* 11:1–7.
Dick-Read, Grantly
1933 *Natural Childbirth.* London: Heinemann.
1959 *Childbirth without Fear: The Principles and Practice of Natural Childbirth.* New York: Harper and Row.
Doering, Paul L.
1983 "Obstetrical Analgesia and Anesthesia." In *Obstetrical Interventions and Technology in the 1980s,* ed. Diony Young. New York: The Haworth Press.
Doering, Paul L., and R. B. Stewart
1978 "The Extent and Character of Drug Consumption During Pregnancy." *Journal of the American Medical Association* 239:843.
Donegan, Jane B.
1978 *Women and Men Midwives: Medicine, Morality and Misogyny in Early America.* Westport, Conn.: Greenwood Press.
Donnison, Jean
1977 *Midwives and Medical Men: A History of Inter-Professional Rivalries and Women's Rights.* New York: Schocken Books.
Donovan, Debbi
1989 "Exposing Epidurals: The Cadillac of Anesthesia." *The Cesarean Prevention Clarion* 7(2):6.
Dossey, Larry
1982 *Space, Time and Medicine.* Boulder and London: Shambala Press.
Douglas, Mary
1966 *Purity and Danger.* London: Routledge and Kegan Paul.
1973 *Natural Symbols: Explorations in Cosmology.* New York: Vintage Books.
Dubois, Ellen C., Gail P. Kelly, Elizabeth L. Kennedy, Carolyn W. Korsmeyer, and Lillian S. Robinson
1985 *Feminist Scholarship: Kindling in the Groves of Academe.* Urbana: University of Illinois Press.
Duffy, B. L., and P. C. Woodhouse
1982 "Sodium Citrate and Gastric Acidity in Obstetric Patients." *Medical Journal of Australia* 2:37–38.
Duffy, John
1979 *The Healers: A History of Western Medicine.* Urbana: University of Illinois Press.

Dundes, Alan
1980   *Interpreting Folklore.* Bloomington: Indiana University Press.
Dungey, Kim
1991   "ICEA Certifies One Thousand ICCE's." *International Journal of Childbirth Education* 6(2):20.
Durkheim, Emile
1954   *The Elementary Forms of the Religious Life.* New York: The Free Press.
Dworkin, Andrea
1974   *Woman Hating.* New York: E. P. Dutton.
1976   *Our Blood.* New York: Harper and Row.
1982   "For Men, Freedom of Speech; For Women, Silence Please." In *Take Back the Night: Women on Pornography,* ed. Laura Lederer. New York: Bantam Books.
1983   *Right Wing Women.* New York: Perigee Books.
Eagan, Andrea
1985   *The Newborn Mother: Stages of Her Growth.* Boston: Little, Brown and Co.
Eakins, Pamela S., ed.
1986   *The American Way of Birth.* Temple University Press.
Easterbrook, Gregg
1987   "The Revolution in Medicine." *Time,* 26 January 1987:40–74.
Eckstein, K. L., and G. F. Marx
1974   "Aortocaval Compression and Uterine Displacement." *Anesthesia* 40(1):92–96.
Edwards, Margot, and Mary Waldorf
1984   *Reclaiming Birth: History and Heroines of American Childbirth Reform.* Trumansburg, N.Y.: The Crossing Press.
Ehrenreich, Barbara, and Deirdre English
1973a   *Complaints and Disorders: The Sexual Politics of Sickness.* Old Westbury, N.Y.: The Feminist Press.
1973b   *Witches, Midwives, and Nurses: A History of Women Healers.* Old Westbury, N.Y.: The Feminist Press.
Einstein, Albert, B. Podolsky, and Nathan Rosen
1935   "Can Quantum Mechanical Description of Reality Be Considered Complete?" *Physical Review* 47:777ff.
Eisenhart, R. Wayne
1983   "You Can't Hack It, Little Girl: A Discussion of the Covert Psychological Agenda of Modern Combat Training." In *Feminist Frontiers,* ed. Laurel Richardson and Verta Taylor. Reading, Mass.: Addison-Wesley Publishing Co.
Eliade, Mircea
1958   *Rites and Symbols of Initiation: The Mysteries of Birth and Rebirth.* New York: Harper and Row.
1959   *The Sacred and the Profane: The Nature of Religion.* New York: Harcourt, Brace, Jovanovich.

1975 "Modern Man's Need to Understand the Rites of Passage." In *Rites*, ed. John Cafferata. New York: McGraw-Hill.

Elkins, Valmai H.
1980 *The Rights of the Pregnant Parent*. New York: Schocken Books.

Ellul, Jacques
1965 *The Technological Society*. New York: Alfred A. Knopf.

Engelmann, George
1977 *Labor among Primitive Peoples*. New York: AMS Press.

English, Jane
1985 *Different Doorway: Adventures of a Cesarean Born*. Mt. Shasta, Calif.: Earth Heart Publishing.
1988 *Childlessness Transformed: Stories of Alternative Parenting*. Mt. Shasta, Calif.: Earth Heart Publishing.

Entwisle, D. R., and S. G. Doering
1981 *The First Birth: A Family Turning Point*. Baltimore: Johns Hopkins University Press.

Ettner, Frederic
1976 "Comparative Study of Obstetrics—with Data and Details of a Working Physician's Home O.B. Service." In *Safe Alternatives in Childbirth*, ed. D. Stewart and L. Stewart. Marble Hill, Mo.: NAPSAC.
1977 "Hospital Obstetrics: Do the Benefits Outweigh the Risks?" In *21st Century Obstetrics Now!* ed. D. Stewart and L. Stewart. Marble Hill, Mo.: NAPSAC.

Eyer, D.
1992 *Maternal-Infant Bonding: A Scientific Fiction*. New Haven: Yale University Press.

Farenga, Patrick
1989 "Homeschoolers and College." *Mothering* 53:77–81.

Feeley-Harnik, Gillian
1981 *The Lord's Table: Eucharist and Passover in Early Christianity*. Philadelphia: University of Pennsylvania Press.

Feldman, G., and A. Freiman
1985 "Prophylactic Cesarean Section at Term?" *New England Journal of Medicine* 312(19):1264–1267.

Ferguson, Marilyn
1980 *The Aquarian Conspiracy: Personal and Social Transformation in the 1980s*. Los Angeles: J. P. Tarcher, Inc.

Field, Mary
1985 "The Jewel in the Crown: Clitoral Massage as an Analgesia for Labor." *Childbirth Alternatives Quarterly* 6(4):4–5. (First published in the Newsletter of the Association of Radical Midwives, Winter 1984/1985, Great Britain.)

Finger, S., and D. Simons
1976 "Effects of Serial Lesions of Somatosensory Cortex and Further Neodecortication on Retention of a Rough-Smooth Discrimination in Rats." *Experimental Brain Research* 25:183–197.

Firth, Raymond
  1967   *Tikopia Ritual and Belief.* Boston: Beacon Press.
Fiske, Shirley
  1975   "Pigskin Review: An American Initiation." In *The Nacirema: Read-ings on American Culture,* ed. James P. Spradley and Michael A. Rynkiewich. Boston: Little, Brown and Co.
Flynn, A. M., J. Kelly, G. Hollins, and P. F. Lynch
  1978   "Ambulation in Labor." *British Medical Journal* 5:591–593.
Footlick, Jerrold K., with Elizabeth Leonard
  1990   "What Happened to the Family?" *Newsweek* Special Edition, Winter/Spring, pp. 14–20.
Fortes, M., and E. E. Evans-Pritchard
  1940   "Introduction." In *African Political Systems,* ed. M. Fortes and E. E. Evans-Pritchard. London: Oxford University Press for the International African Institute.
Fox, Renee
  1957   "Training for Uncertainty." In *The Student Physician: Introduc-tory Studies in the Sociology of Medical Education,* ed. Robert K. Merton, George G. Reader, and Patricia L. Kendall. Cambridge, Mass.: Harvard University Press.
Fraser, Gertrude
  1988   "Afro-American Midwives, Biomedicine, and the State: An Ethno-historical Account of Birth and Its Transformation in Rural Vir-ginia." Ph.D. diss., Dept. of Anthropology, Johns Hopkins Univer-sity.
Freak, M. J.
  1962   "Abnormal Conditions Associated with Pregnancy and Parturition in the Bitch." *Veterinary Record* 74:1323–1335.
Freud, Sigmund
  1938   *The Basic Writings of Sigmund Freud.* New York: Modern Library.
  1953   *A General Introduction to Psychoanalysis.* New York: Perma-books.
Frye, Marilyn
  1983   *The Politics of Reality: Essays in Feminist Theory.* Trumansburg, N.Y.: The Crossing Press.
Gagnon, Madeleine
  1980   "Corps 1." In *New French Feminisms: An Anthology,* ed. Elaine Marks and Isabelle de Courtivron. Amherst: University of Massa-chusetts Press.
Gaines, Atwood D., and Robert A. Hahn
  1985   "Among the Physicians: Encounter, Exchange, and Transforma-tion." In *Physicians of Western Medicine: Anthropological Ap-proaches to Theory and Practice,* ed. Robert A. Hahn and Atwood D. Gaines. Boston: D. Reidel Publishing Co.
Gardosi, Jason, Noreen Hutson, and Chris B. Lynch
  1989   "Randomised, Controlled Trial of Squatting in the Second Stage of Labour." *Lancet,* July 8:74–77.

Gaskin, Ina May
1990   *Spiritual Midwifery.* 3d ed. Summerton, Tenn.: The Book Publishing Company. (First published in 1977)
Geertz, Clifford
1957   "Ritual and Social Change: A Javanese Example." *American Anthropologist* 59:32–54.
1971   *Myth, Symbol and Culture.* New York: W. W. Norton and Co.
1973   *The Interpretation of Cultures.* New York: Basic Books.
Geiger, J.
1975   "The Causes of Dehumanization in Health Care and Prospects for Humanization." In *Humanizing Health Care,* ed. J. Howard and A. Strauss. New York: Wiley.
Gellhorn, E.
1968   "Central Nervous System Tuning and Its Implications for Neuropsychiatry." *Journal of Nervous and Mental Diseases* 147:148–162.
1969   "Further Studies on the Physiology and Pathophysiology of the Tuning of the Central Nervous System." *Psychosomatics* 10:94–104.
1970   "The Emotions and the Ergotrophic and Trophotropic Systems." *Psychologische Forschung* 34:48–94.
Gellhorn, E., and W. F. Kiely
1972   "Mystical States of Consciousness: Neurophysiological and Clinical Aspects." *Journal of Nervous and Mental Diseases* 154:399–405.
1973   "Autonomic Nervous System in Psychiatric Disorder." In *Biological Psychiatry,* ed. J. Mendels. New York: Wiley.
Gendlin, Eugene T.
1980   *Focusing.* New York: Bantam Books.
Gerth, H. H., and C. Wright Mills
1958   *From Max Weber: Essays in Sociology.* New York: Oxford University Press.
Ginsburg, Faye
1989   *Contested Lives: The Abortion Debate in an American Community.* Berkeley, Los Angeles, London: University of California Press.
Glew, Robert
1989   "A New Breed of Medical Student." *Murmurs* (Newsletter of the University of Pittsburgh School of Medicine) May:1–4.
Gluckman, Max
1954   *Rituals of Rebellion in South East Africa.* Manchester: Manchester University Press.
Goffman, Erving
1961   *Asylums.* New York: Anchor Books.
1974   *Frame Analysis: An Essay on the Organization of Experience.* New York: Harper and Row.
Golding, J., M. Paterson, and L. J. Kinlen
1990   "Factors Associated with Childhood Cancer in a National Cohert Study." *British Journal of Cancer* 62:304–308.

Gonik, B., and D. B. Cotton
    1984   "Peripartum Colloid Osmotic Pressure Changes: Influence of Intravenous Hydration." *American Journal of Obstetrics and Gynecology* 150(1):99–100.
Good, Byron J., Henry Herrera, Mary-Jo DelVecchio Good, and James Cooper
    1985   "Reflexivity, Countertransference, and Clinical Ethnography: A Case from a Psychiatric Cultural Consultation Clinic." In *Physicians of Western Medicine: Anthropological Approaches to Theory and Practice*, ed. Robert A. Hahn and Atwood D. Gaines. Boston: D. Reidel Publishing Co.
Goyert, Gregory L., Sidney F. Bottoms, Marjorie C. Treadwell, and Paul Nehra
    1989   "The Physician Factor in Cesarean Birth Rates." *New England Journal of Medicine* 320(11):706–709.
Graebner, Alan
    1975   "Growing Up Female." In *The Nacirema: Readings on American Culture*, ed. James R. Spradley and Michael Rynkiewich. New York: Little, Brown and Co.
Griffin, Susan
    1978   *Woman and Nature*. New York: Harper and Row.
Grylack, L. J., S. S. Chu, and J. W. Scanlon
    1984   "Use of Intravenous Fluids Before Cesarean Section: Effects on Perinatal Glucose, Insulin, and Sodium Homeostasis." *Obstetrics and Gynecology* 63:654–658.
Guo, David
    1989   "Medical Class Gets Apology for Lectures." *Pittsburgh Post-Gazette*, May:1, 5.
Hafetz, E. S., ed.
    1962   *The Behavior of Domestic Animals*. Baltimore: Williams and Wilkens.
Hahn, Robert A.
    1985   "A World of Internal Medicine: Portrait of an Internist." In *Physicians of Western Medicine: Anthropological Approaches to Theory and Practice*, ed. Robert A. Hahn and Atwood D. Gaines. Boston: D. Reidel Publishing Co.
    1987   "Divisions of Labor: Obstetrician, Woman and Society in *Williams Obstetrics*, 1903–1985." *Medical Anthropology Quarterly* 1(3): 256–282.
Hahn, Robert A., and Atwood D. Gaines, eds.
    1985   *Physicians of Western Medicine: Anthropological Approaches to Theory and Practice*. Boston: D. Reidel Publishing Co.
Haire, Doris
    1977   *The Cultural Warping of Childbirth*. Minneapolis: International Childbirth Education Association.
Hall, Edward T.
    1977   *Beyond Culture*. New York: Anchor Books.
Hallpike, C. R.
    1979   "Social Hair." In *Reader in Comparative Religion*, ed. W. A. Lessa and E. Z. Vogt. 4th ed. New York: Harper and Row.

Hand, Wayland, ed.
1975   *The Frank C. Brown Collection of North Carolina Folklore,* vols.
        6, 7. Durham, N.C.: Duke University Press.
Hand, Wayland, Anna Cassetta, and Sondra B. Thiederman, eds.
1981   *Popular Beliefs and Superstitions: A Compendium of American
        Folklore.* 3 vols. Boston: G. K. Hall and Co.
Handwerker, W. Penn, ed.
1990   *Births and Power: Social Change and the Politics of Reproduction.*
        Boulder: Westview Press.
Harrison, Michelle
1982   *A Woman in Residence.* New York: Random House.
Harvey, O. J., D. E. Hunt, and H. M. Schroeder
1961   *Conceptual Systems and Personality Organization.* New York:
        Wiley.
Harwood, Michael
1984   "The Ordeal: Life as a Medical Resident." *New York Times Maga-
        zine,* 3 June 1984:38–46, 70–82.
Hathaway, Jay
1990   "Reaction to 'Medications for Labor' Article" (Letter to the Edi-
        tor). *International Journal of Childbirth Education* 5(2):3.
Haverkamp, Albert D., and Miriam Orleans
1983   "An Assessment of Electronic Fetal Monitoring." In *Obstetrical In-
        tervention and Technology in the 1980s,* ed. Diony Young. New
        York: The Haworth Press.
Hawkes, Terence
1977   *Structuralism and Semiotics.* Berkeley, Los Angeles, London: Uni-
        versity of California Press.
Hazle, Nancy R.
1986   "Hydration in Labor: Is Routine Intravenous Hydration Neces-
        sary?" *Journal of Nurse-Midwifery* 31(4):171–176.
Hazell, Lester Dessez
1976   *Commonsense Childbirth.* New York: Berkeley Medallion Books.
Helman, Cecil
1985   "Disease and Pseudo-Disease: A Case History of Pseudo-Angina."
        In *Physicians of Western Medicine: Anthropological Approaches to
        Theory and Practice,* ed. Robert A. Hahn and Atwood D. Gaines.
        Boston: D. Reidel Publishing Co.
Henslin, J., and M. Biggs
1971   "Dramaturgical Desexualization: The Sociology of the Vaginal
        Exam." In *Studies in the Sociology of Sex,* ed. J. Henslin. New
        York: Appleton-Century-Crofts.
Hertz, Robert
1960   *Death and the Right Hand.* Trans. Rodney and Claudia Needham.
        New York: The Free Press.
Hocart, A. M.
1939   "Ritual and Emotion." *Character and Personality* 7:201–211.

Hoff, Gerald Allen
1985 "Having Babies at Home: Is It Safe? Is It Ethical?" *Hastings Center Report,* December.
Hon, Edward H.
1974 "Fetal Heart Rate Monitoring." In *Modern Perinatal Medicine,* ed. L. Gluck. Chicago: Year Book.
Howard, J., and A. Strauss
1975 *Humanizing Health Care.* New York: Wiley.
Hugo, M.
1977 "A Look at Maternal Position During Labor." *Journal of Nurse-Midwifery* 22:26.
Hull, Gloria T., et al.
1981 *All the Women Are White, All the Blacks Are Men, But Some of Us Are Brave.* Old Westbury, N.Y.: The Feminist Press.
Humphrey, M., A. Chang, E. C. Wood, S. Morgan, and D. Hounslow
1974 "A Decrease in Fetal pH During the Second Stage of Labor, When Conducted in the Dorsal Position." *Journal of Obstetrics and Gynaecology of the British Commonwealth* 81:600–602.
Humphrey, M., D. Hounslow, S. Morgan, and C. Wood
1973 "The Influence of Maternal Posture at Birth on the Fetus." *Journal of Obstetrics and Gynaecology of the British Commonwealth* 80: 1075–1080.
Hunt, J. M.
1963 "Motivation Inherent in the Processing of Information and Action." In *Motivation and Social Interaction,* ed. O. J. Harvey. New York: Ronald.
Hunter College Women's Studies Collective
1983 "Women and Political Power." In *Women's Realities, Women's Choices,* Hunter College Women's Studies Collective. New York: Oxford University Press.
Illich, Ivan
1976 *Medical Nemesis: The Expropriation of Health.* New York: Bantam Books.
Inch, Sally
1984 *Birth-Rights: What Every Parent Should Know About Childbirth in Hospitals.* New York: Pantheon Books.
Iseroff, A.
1980 "Facilitation of Delayed Spontaneous Alternation Behavior in Adult Rats Following Early Hydroxyzine Treatment: Differential Sensitivity in Late Infancy." *Psychopharmacology* 69:179–181.
Jacobson, Bertil
1987 Abstract in the *Syllabus of Abstracts* of the Third International Congress on Pre- and Perinatal Psychology, 9–12 July 1987, San Francisco, p. 13. Toronto, Ontario: Pre- and Perinatal Psychology Association of North America.

Jacobson, B., G. Eklund, L. Hamberger, D. Linarsson, G. Sedvall, and M. Valvereius
1987   "Perinatal Origin of Adult Self-Destructive Behavior." *Acta Psychiatrica Scandinavica* 76:364–371.

Jacobson, B., Karin Nyberg, Gunnar Eklund, Marc Bygdeman, and Ulf Rydberg
1988   "Obstetric Pain Medication and Eventual Adult Amphetamine Addiction in Offspring." *Acta Obstetrica Gynecoliga* 67:677–682.

James-Chetelat, Lois
1989   "Reclaiming the Birthing Experience: An Analysis of Midwifery in Canada from 1788 to 1987." Ph.D. diss., Dept. of Sociology and Anthropology, Carleton University, Ottawa, Ontario.

Janis, I. L., and L. Mann
1977   *Decision-Making: A Psychological Analysis of Conflict, Choice, and Commitment.* New York: The Free Press.

Jawalekar, S., and G. F. Marx
1980   "Effect of IV Fluids on Maternal and Fetal Blood Glucose." *Anesthesiology* 53(3):3115.

Jencson, Linda
1982   "Birth Narratives." Unpublished paper.

Johnson, Kenneth C.
1991   "Safest Birth Attendants: Recent Dutch Evidence." *MIDIRS* (Midwives Information and Resource Service, London) 1:4.

Johnstone, F. D., M. S. Abaedmagd, and A. K. Harouny
1987   "Maternal Posture in Second Stage and Fetal Acid Base Status." *British Journal of Obstetrics and Gynaecology* 94:753–757.

Jones, Ann R.
1980   *Women Who Kill.* New York: Holt, Rinehart and Winston.
1985   " 'Writing the Body': Towards an Understanding of L'Ecriture Feminine." In *The New Feminist Criticism: Essays in Women, Literature and Theory,* ed. Elaine Showalter. New York: Pantheon Books.

Jones, Carl
1989   *From Parent to Child: The Psychic Link.* New York: Warner Books.

Jones, J. J., and D. Koldjeski
1984   "Clinical Indicators of a Developmental Process in Phlebitis." *NITA* 10:279–285.

Jordan, Brigitte
1977   "The Self-Diagnosis of Early Pregnancy: An Investigation of Lay Competence." *Medical Anthropology* 1(2):1–38.
1983   *Birth in Four Cultures: A Cross-Cultural Investigation of Childbirth in Yucatan, Holland, Sweden and the United States.* Montreal: Eden Press.
1984   "External Cephalic Version as an Alternative to Breech Delivery and Cesarean Section." *Social Science and Medicine* 18(8):637–651.
1986   "The Hut and the Hospital: Information, Power and Symbolism in the Artifacts of Birth." *Birth* 13(2).

1989   "Cosmopolitical Obstetrics: Some Insights from the Training of Traditional Midwives." *Social Science and Medicine* 28(9):925–944.

1990   "Technology and the Social Distribution of Knowledge." In *Anthropology and Primary Health Care,* ed. J. Coreil and D. Mull. Boulder: Westview Press.

Jordan, Brigitte, and Susan Irwin
1989   "The Ultimate Failure: Court-Ordered Cesarean Section." In *New Approaches to Human Reproduction,* ed. Linda Whiteford and Marilyn Poland. Boulder: Westview Press.

Kaminski, H. M., A. Stafl, and J. Aiman
1987   "The Effect of Epidural Analgesia on the Frequency of Instrumental Obstetric Delivery." *Obstetrics and Gynecology* 69:770.

Karmel, Marjorie
1965   *Thank You, Dr. Lamaze.* New York: Dolphin Books.

Kearl, Michael C.
1989   *Endings: A Sociology of the Dying and the Dead.* New York: Oxford University Press.

Keeler, Teresa F.
1984   "Narrating, Attitudes and Health: The Effects of Recounting Pregnancy and Childbirth Experiences on the Well-Being of the Participants." Ph.D. diss., Dept. of Folklore and Mythology, University of California, Los Angeles.

Keller, Trudy
1990   "From the President." *International Journal of Childbirth Education* 5(1):4.

Kennell, John
1982   "The Physiologic Effects of a Supportive Companion (Doula) During Labor." In *Birth: Interaction and Attachment,* ed. Marshall H. Klaus and Martha O. Robertson. Johnson and Johnson.

Kennell, John, and Marshall Klaus
1984   "Mother-Infant Bonding: Weighing the Evidence." *Developmental Review* 4:275–282.

Kennell, John, Marshall Klaus, Susan McGrath, Steven Robertson, and Clark Hinckley
1988   "Medical Intervention: The Effect of Social Support During Labor" (Abstract #61). *Pediatric Research,* April:211.

Kennepp, N. B., et al.
1980   "Effects on Newborn of Hydration with Glucose in Patients Undergoing Cesarean Section with Regional Anesthesia." *Lancet* 1(8169):645.

Kennepp, N. B., W. C. Shelley, and S. G. Gabbe et al.
1982   "Fetal and Neonatal Hazards of Maternal Hydration with 5% Dextrose before Cesarean Section." *Lancet* 1(8282):1150–1152.

Kitzinger, Sheila
1972   *The Experience of Childbirth.* 3d ed. Baltimore: Penguin Books.
1979   *Birth at Home.* New York: Penguin Books.

1980   Women as Mothers: How They See Themselves in Different Cultures. New York: Vintage Books.
1985   "The Sexuality of Birth." In S. Kitzinger, Women's Experience of Sex. New York: Penguin Books.

Klaus, Marshall
1989   "Medical Intervention: The Effect of Social Support During Labor." Lecture given at the Conference on Innovations in Perinatal Care, March, San Francisco.

Klaus, Marshall H., and John H. Kennell
1982   Parent-Infant Bonding. St. Louis: C. V. Mosby Co.
1983   "Parent to Infant Bonding: Setting the Record Straight." Journal of Pediatrics 102(4):575–576.

Klaus, Marshall H., and Phyllis Klaus
1985   The Amazing Newborn. Reading, Mass.: Addison-Wesley.

Klein, Norman
1979   Culture, Curers, and Contagion: Readings for Medical Social Science. Novato, Calif.: Chandler and Sharp Publishers, Inc.

Kleinman, Arthur
1980   Patients and Healers in the Context of Culture: An Exploration of the Borderland between Anthropology, Medicine, and Psychiatry. Berkeley, Los Angeles, London: University of California Press.

Klopfer, P.
1971   "Mother Love: What Turns It On?" American Science 49:404–407.

Kolder, V., J. Gallagher, and M. Parsons
1987   "Court-ordered Obstetrical Interventions." New England Journal of Medicine 316:1192–1196.

Konner, Melvin
1987   Becoming a Doctor: A Journey of Initiation in Medical School. New York: Viking.

Kramer, Heinrich, and Jacob Sprenger
1972   Excerpts from the Malleus Maleficarum (The Hammer of Witches, orig. pub. 1486). In Witchcraft in Europe, 1100–1700: A Documentary History, ed. Alan C. Kors and Edward Peters. Philadelphia: University of Pennsylvania Press.

Kristeva, Julia
1980   "Oscillation du 'pouvoir au refus.'" Interview by Xaviere Gauthie in Tel Quel, trans. in New French Feminisms: An Anthology, ed. Elaine Marks and Isabelle de Courtivron. Amherst: University of Massachusetts Press.

Kruse, J. C., and C. P. Gibbs
1978   "Aspiration and Obstetrical Anesthesia." Journal of the Florida Medical Association 65(10):819–821.

Kuhn, Thomas S.
1962   The Structure of Scientific Revolutions. Chicago: University of Chicago Press.

Kurz, C. S., H. Schneider, R. Huch, and A. Huch
1982   "The Influence of Maternal Position on Fetal Transcutaneous Oxygen Pressure (tcPo2)." *Journal of Perinatal Medicine* 10 (supplement 2):74–75.

Labov, William, and Joshua Waletzky
1967   "Narrative Analysis: Oral Versions of Personal Experience." In *Essays in the Verbal and Visual Arts*, ed. June Helm MacNeish. Seattle: University of Washington Press.

Laderman, Carol
1983   *Wives and Midwives: Childbirth and Nutrition in Rural Malaysia.* Berkeley, Los Angeles, London: University of California Press.

Laing, R. D.
1976   *The Facts of Life.* New York: Pantheon.

Lakoff, George, and Mark Johnson
1980   *Metaphors We Live By.* Chicago: University of Chicago Press.

Lamaze, Ferdinand
1956   *Painless Childbirth: The Lamaze Method.* New York: Pocket Books.

Lamb, Deborah
1990   "Birth Stories: Psychological Aspects of Labor and Delivery." Diss. proposal, Dept. of Applied Psychology, School of Education, Health, Nursing and Arts Professions, New York University.

Lamb, Michael E.
1982   "The Bonding Phenomenon: Misinterpretations and Their Implications." *Journal of Pediatrics* 101:555.

Lamb, M. E., and C. P. Hwang
1982   "Maternal Attachment and Mother-Neonate Bonding: A Critical Review." In *Advances in Development Psychology*, vol. 2. Hillsdale, N.J.: Lawrence Erlbaum.

Lamb, M. E., R. A. Thompson, W. Gardner, and E. L. Charnov
1985   *Infant-Mother Attachment: The Origins and Developmental Significance of Individual Differences in Strange Situation Behavior.* Hillsdale, N.J.: Lawrence Erlbaum.

Larson, E., S. Lunche, and J. T. Tran
1984   "Correlates of IV phlebitis." *NITA* 7:203–205.

Laughlin, Charles D.
1989   "Pre- and Perinatal Anthropology: A Selective Review." *Pre- and Peri-Natal Psychology Journal* 3(4):261–296.
1990   "Mirror of the Brain." Unpublished manuscript.
1991   "Pre- and Perinatal Anthropology II: The Puerperium in Cross-Cultural Perspective." Unpublished manuscript.

Laughlin, Charles D., and Eugene d'Aquili
1974   *Biogenetic Structuralism.* New York: Columbia University Press.

Laughlin, Charles D., John McManus, and Eugene G. d'Aquili
1990   *Brain, Symbol, and Experience.* Boston: Shambala New Science Library.

Laughlin, Charles D., and Sheila Richardson
1986   "The Future of Human Consciousness." *Futures,* June:401–419.
Lazarus, Ellen
1988*a*   "Poor Women, Poor Outcomes: Social Class and Reproductive Health." In *Childbirth in America: Anthropological Perspectives,* ed. Karen Michaelson. South Hadley, Mass.: Bergin and Garvey Publishers.
1988*b*   "Theoretical Considerations for the Study of the Doctor-Patient Relationship: Implications of a Perinatal Study." *Medical Anthropology Quarterly* 2(1):34–58.
1990   "Falling through the Cracks: Contradictions and Barriers to Care in a Prenatal Clinic." *Medical Anthropology* 12(3):269–288.
Leach, Edmund
1958   "Magical Hair." *Journal of the Royal Anthropological Institute (Man)* 88:147–154.
1976   *Culture and Communication.* New York: Cambridge University Press.
1979   "Ritualization in Man in Relation to Conceptual and Social Development." In *Reader in Comparative Religion,* ed. William A. Lessa and Evon Z. Vogt. 4th ed. New York: Harper and Row.
Leavitt, Judith
1986   *Brought to Bed: Childbearing in America 1750–1950.* New York: Oxford University Press.
LeBaron, Charles
1981   *Gentle Vengeance: An Account of the First Year at Harvard Medical School.* New York: Richard Marek.
Lee, Dorothy
1980   "Codifications of Reality: Lineal and Non-Lineal." In *Conformity and Conflict,* ed. James P. Spradley and David W. McCurdy. 4th ed. Boston: Little, Brown and Co.
Lerner, Gerda
1986   *The Creation of Patriarchy.* New York: Oxford University Press.
Lessa, William A., and Evon Z. Vogt, eds.
1979   *Reader in Comparative Religion: An Anthropological Approach.* 4th ed. New York: Harper and Row.
Leveno, K. J., F. G. Cunningham, S. Nelson, M. Roark, M. L. Williams, D. Guzick, S. Dowling, C. R. Rosenfeld, and A. Buckley
1986   "A Prospective Comparison of Selective and Universal Electronic Fetal Monitoring in 34,995 Pregnancies." *New England Journal of Medicine* 315:615.
Lévi-Strauss, Claude
1963   "The Effectiveness of Symbols." In *Structural Anthropology.* New York: Basic Books.
1969   *The Raw and the Cooked.* New York: Harper and Row.
1976   *Structural Anthropology II.* New York: Basic Books.

Lewis, A. E.
  1965   "Dangers Inherent in Soap Enemas." *Pacific Medical Surgery* 73:
          131.
Lex, Barbara
  1979   "The Neurobiology of Ritual Trance." In *The Spectrum of Ritual:
          A Biogenetic Structural Analysis*, ed. Eugene d'Aquili, Charles D.
          Laughlin, and John McManus. New York: Columbia University
          Press.
Ley, R. G.
  1983   *Imagery: Current Theory, Research, and Application.* New York:
          Wiley.
Lichtmann, Ronnie
  1988   "Medical Models and Midwifery: The Cultural Experience of
          Birth." In *Childbirth in America: Anthropological Perspectives*, ed.
          Karen Michaelson. South Hadley, Mass.: Bergin and Garvey.
Liddell, H. S., and P. R. Fisher
  1985   "The Birthing Chair in the Second Stage of Labor." *Australia-New
          Zealand Journal of Obstetrics and Gynaecology* 25:65–68.
Life
  1989   "The Future and You: Visions of Tomorrow." February 1989:54–
          55.
Lincoln, Bruce
  1981   *Emerging from the Chrysalis: Studies in Rituals of Women's Initi-
          ation.* Cambridge, Mass.: Harvard University Press.
Litoff, Judy Barrett
  1978   *American Midwives: 1860 to the Present.* Westport, Conn.: Green-
          wood Press.
  1986   *The American Midwife Debate: A Sourcebook on Its Modern Ori-
          gins.* New York: Greenwood Press.
Liu, Y. C.
  1974   "Effects of the Upright Position During Labor." *American Journal
          of Nursing* 74:2202–2205.
Lock, Margaret
  1985   "Models and Practice in Medicine: Menopause as Syndrome or Life
          Transition?" In *Physicians of Western Medicine: Anthropological
          Approaches to Theory and Practice*, ed. Robert A. Hahn and At-
          wood D. Gaines. Boston: D. Reidel Publishing Co.
Lucas, A., T. E. Adrian, and A. Aynsley-Green
  1980   "Iatrogenic Hyperinsulinism at Birth." *Lancet* 1(8160):144–145.
Luria, A. R.
  1966   *Higher Cortical Functions in Man.* New York: Basic Books.
MacArthur, C., S. Lewis, T. Knox, and J. S. Crawford
  1990   "Epidural Anesthesia and Long-Term Backache after Childbirth."
          British Medical Journal 301:9–12.
McClain, Carol
  1983   "Perceived Risk and Choice of Childbirth Service." *Social Science
          and Medicine* 17(23):1857–1865.

1986 "The Social Distribution of Elective Repeat Cesarean Section." Paper presented at the Annual Meetings of the American Ethnological Society and the Society for Medical Anthropology, Wrightsville Beach, N.C.

1987a "Some Social Network Differences Between Women Choosing Home and Hospital Birth." *Human Organization* 46(2):146–152.

1987b "Patient Decision-Making: The Case of Delivery Method After a Previous Cesarean Section." *Culture, Medicine, and Psychiatry* 11:495–508.

1988 "Patient Demand for Repeat Cesarean Section." Paper presented at the Annual Meetings of the American Anthropological Association, Phoenix.

McClain, Carol, ed.
1989 *Women as Healers: Cross-Cultural Perspectives*. New Brunswick: Rutgers University Press.

MacCormack, Carol P., ed.
1982 *Ethnography of Fertility and Birth*. New York: Academic Press.

McCutcheon-Rosegg, Susan, with Peter Rosegg
1984 *Natural Childbirth the Bradley Way*. New York: E. P. Dutton.

MacDonald, G. F., J. Cove, C. D. Laughlin, and J. McManus
1989 "Mirrors, Portals and Multiple Realities." *Zygon* 23(4):39–64.

McKay, Susan
1990a "Humanizing Birth in a Technological Society." Unpublished paper, School of Nursing, University of Wyoming.

1990b "Shared Power: The Essence of Humanized Childbirth." *Pre- and Perinatal Psychology Journal* 5(4):283–296.

McKay, Susan, and Charles Mahan
1983 "How Worthwhile Are Membrane Stripping and Amniotomy?" *Contemporary Ob/Gyn* December:173–184.

1984 "Laboring Patients Need More Freedom to Move." *Contemporary Ob/Gyn* July 1984:119.

1988a "Modifying the Stomach Contents of Laboring Women." *Birth* 15(4):213–221.

1988b "How Can Aspiration of Vomitus in Obstetrics Best Be Prevented?" *Birth* 15(4):222–229.

McKay, Susan, and Joyce Roberts
1989 "Maternal Position During Labor and Birth: What Have We Learned?" *ICEA Review* 13(2):19–30.

McKenna, James Joseph
1987 "An Anthropological Perspective on the Sudden Infant Death Syndrome: A Testable Hypothesis on the Possible Role of Parental Breathing Cues in Promoting Infant Breathing Stability, Part 1." *Pre- & Peri-Natal Psychology Journal* 2(2):93–135.

McKenna, James Joseph
1988 "An Anthropological Perspective on the Sudden Infant Death Syndrome: The Neurological and Structural Bases of Speech Breathing

and Why SIDS Appears to be a Species-Specific Malady, Part 2." *Pre- & Peri-Natal Psychology Journal* 2(3):149–179.

McKenna, James Joseph, et al.

1990   "Sleep and Arousal Patterns of Co-sleeping Human Mother/Infant Pairs: A Preliminary Physiological Study with Implications for the Study of Sudden Infant Death Syndrome (SIDS)." *American Journal of Physical Anthropology* 83:331–347.

Mackinnon, Catharine A.

1979   *Sexual Harassment of Working Women.* New Haven and London: Yale University Press.

McManus, John

1979a   "Ritual and Ontogenetic Development." In *The Spectrum of Ritual: A Biogenetic Structural Analysis,* ed. Eugene d'Aquili, Charles D. Laughlin, and John McManus. New York: Columbia University Press.

1979b   "Ritual and Human Social Cognition." In *The Spectrum of Ritual: A Biogenetic Structural Analysis,* ed. Eugene d'Aquili, Charles D. Laughlin, and John McManus. New York: Columbia University Press.

McNulty, Faith

1981   *The Burning Bed.* New York: Bantam Books.

McPhee, John

1989   *The Control of Nature.* New York: Farrar Straus Giroux.

Mahan, Charles S., and Susan McKay

1983   "Preps and Enemas—Keep or Discard?" *Contemporary Ob/Gyn* November:241–248.

1984   "Let's Reform Our Antenatal Care Methods." *Contemporary Ob/Gyn* May:147–158.

Malinowski, Bronislaw

1954   "Magic, Science, and Religion." In *Magic, Science and Religion and Other Essays.* New York: Doubleday/Anchor.

Marcus, George E., and Michael M. J. Fischer

1986   *Anthropology as Cultural Critique: An Experimental Moment in the Human Sciences.* Chicago: University of Chicago Press.

Martin, Emily

1987   *The Woman in the Body.* Boston: Beacon Press.

Mathews, Holly

1990   "Killing the Medical Self-Help Tradition among Afro-Americans: The Case of Midwifery in North Carolina, 1917–1983." Unpublished manuscript.

Mehl, Lewis, et al.

1977a   "Outcomes of Elective Home Births." *Journal of Reproductive Medicine* November:281–290.

1977b   "Research on Childbirth Alternatives: What Can It Tell Us about Hospital Practice?" In *21st Century Obstetrics Now!* ed. D. Stewart and L. Stewart. Marble Hill, Mo.: NAPSAC.

1980   "Evaluation of Outcome of Non-Nurse Midwives." *Women and Health* Summer:17–23.

1981   "The Influence of Belief in Childbirth." In *The Five Standards for Safe Childbearing,* ed. D. Stewart and L. Stewart. Marble Hill, Mo.: NAPSAC.

Mendelsohn, Robert

1979   *Confessions of a Medical Heretic.* New York: Warner Books.

1981   *Mal(e) Practice: How Doctors Manipulate Women.* Chicago: Contemporary Books, Inc.

Mendelson, C.

1946   "The Aspiration of Gastric Contents into the Lungs During Obstetric Anesthesia." *Obstetrics and Gynecology* 52:191–204.

Mendez-Bauer, C. J., C. Aroya, C. Garcia-Ramos, A. Menendez, M. Lavilla, F. Izquierdo, I. Villa Elizaga, and J. Zamariego

1975   "Effects of Standing Position on Spontaneous Uterine Contractility and Other Aspects of Labor." *Journal of Perinatal Medicine* 3:89–100.

Mendiola, J., L. J. Grylack, and J. W. Scanlon

1982   "Effects of Intrapartum Maternal Glucose Infusion of the Normal Fetus and Newborn." *Anesthesia and Analgesia* 61(1):32–35.

Merchant, Carolyn

1983   *The Death of Nature: Women, Ecology, and the Scientific Revolution.* San Francisco: Harper and Row.

Midwives Alliance of North America (MANA)

1991   "Midwives Alliance of North America Statement of Values and Ethics" (working draft). Bristol, Va.: MANA.

Millard, Ann V.

1983   "Perceptions of a Family Planning Campaign in Rural Mexico." In *Women, Health, and International Development,* ed. Margaret I. Aquwa. East Lansing: Office of Women in International Development, Michigan State University.

1985   "Child Mortality and Economic Variation among Rural Mexican Households." *Social Science and Medicine* 20(6):589–599.

1990   "The Place of the Clock in Pediatric Advice: Rationales, Cultural Themes, and Impediments to Breastfeeding." *Social Science and Medicine* 31(2):211–221.

Millard, Ann V., and Margaret A. Graham

1984   "Principles that Guide Weaning in Rural Mexico." *Ecology of Food and Nutrition* 16:171–188.

1985a   "Breastfeeding in Two Mexican Villages: Social and Demographic Perspectives." In *Breastfeeding, Child Health, and Child Spacing,* ed. Valerie Hull and Mayling Simpson. London: Croom-Helm.

1985b   "Abrupt Weaning Reconsidered: Evidence from Central Mexico." *Journal of Tropical Pediatrics* 31:229–234.

Miner, Horace

1975   "Body Ritual among the Nacirema." In *The Nacirema: Readings*

on American Culture, ed. James P. Spradley and Michael A. Rynkiewich. Boston: Little, Brown and Co.

Mitre, I. N.
1974   "The Influence of Maternal Position on Duration of the Active
        Phase of Labor." International Journal of Gynaecology and Ob-
        stetrics, pp. 181–183.

Moir, D. D.
1979   "Anaesthesia and Maternal Deaths." Scottish Medical Journal 24:
        187–188.
1983   "Climetidine, Antacids, and Pulmonary Aspiration." Anesthesiol-
        ogy 59(2):81–83.

Montagu, Ashley
1989   Growing Young, 2d ed. Granby, Mass.: Bergin and Garvey.

Moore, Sally Falk, and Barbara Myerhoff, eds.
1977   Secular Ritual. Assen, The Netherlands: Van Gorcum.

Moran, Marilyn A.
1981   Birth and the Dialogue of Love. Leawood, Kans.: New Nativity
        Press.

Morgan, Robin
1970   Sisterhood Is Powerful. New York: Vintage Books.
1982   The Anatomy of Freedom. New York: Anchor Press/Doubleday.

Morley, Gerald K., Arshag D. Mooradian, Allen S. Levine, and John E. Morley
1984   "Mechanism of Pain in Diabetic Peripheral Neuropathy: Effect of
        Glucose on Pain Perception in Humans." The American Journal of
        Medicine 77:79–82.

Munn, Nancy D.
1973   "Symbolism in a Ritual Context: Aspects of Symbolic Action." In
        Handbook of Social and Cultural Anthropology, ed. John J. Hon-
        igmann. Chapel Hill: Rand-McNally.

Murphee, Alice H.
1968   "A Functional Analysis of Southern Folk Beliefs Concerning Birth."
        American Journal of Obstetrics and Gynecology 102:125–134.

Murphy, Jane
1985   "From Mice to Men? Implications of Progress in Cloning Research."
        In Test-Tube Women, ed. Rita Arditti, Renate Duelli Klein, and
        Shelley Minden. London: Pandora Press.

Murray, Margaret Alice
1921   The Witch-Cult in Western Europe. New York: Oxford University
        Press.

Myerhoff, Barbara
1974   Peyote Hunt: The Sacred Journey of the Huichol Indians. Ithaca,
        N.Y.: Cornell University Press.

Myerhoff, Barbara, and Jay Ruby
1982   "Introduction." In A Crack in the Mirror: Reflexive Perspectives
        in Anthropology, ed. Jay Ruby. Philadelphia: University of Pennsyl-
        vania Press.

Myers, B. J.
1984   "Mother-Infant Bonding: The Status of This Critical Period Hypothesis." *Developmental Review* 4:270–274.
Naisbitt, John
1982   *Megatrends.* New York: Warner Books.
National Center for Health Statistics
1982   "Advance Report of Final Natality Statistics." *Monthly Vital Statistics Report* 31(8).
Nazario, Sonia
1990   "Midwifery Is Staging Revival as Demand for Prenatal Care, Low Tech Births Rises." *Wall Street Journal,* 25 September 1990:B5.
Needham, Rodney
1979   "Percussion and Transition." In *Reader in Comparative Religion,* ed. William A. Lessa and Evon Z. Vogt. 4th ed. New York: Harper and Row.
Needham, Rodney, ed.
1973   *Right and Left: Essays on Dual Symbolic Classification.* Chicago and London: University of Chicago Press.
Nelson, Margaret K.
1982   "The Effect of Childbirth Preparation on Women of Different Social Classes." *Journal of Health and Social Behavior* 23(4):339–352.
1983   "Working-Class Women, Middle-Class Women, and Models of Childbirth." *Social Problems* 30(3):284–297.
Newman, Lucille F.
1965   "Culture and Perinatal Environment in American Society." Ph.D. diss., University of California, Berkeley.
Newton, Niles
1973   "The Interrelationships between Sexual Responsiveness, Birth, and Breastfeeding." In *Contemporary Sexual Behavior: Critical Issues in the 1970s,* ed. Joseph Zubin and John Money. Baltimore: Johns Hopkins University Press.
1977   *Maternal Emotions: A Study of Women's Feelings toward Menstruation, Pregnancy, Childbirth, Breastfeeding, Infant Care and Other Aspects of their Femininity.* Paul B. Hoeber, Inc.
Newton, Niles, Michael Newton, and Jeanine Broach
1988   "Psychologic, Physical, Nutritional, and Technologic Aspects of Intravenous Infusion During Labor." *Birth* 15(2):67–72.
Newton, Niles, D. Peeler, and Michael Newton
1968   "Effect of Disturbance on Labor: An Experiment Using 100 Mice with Dated Pregnancies." *American Journal of Obstetrics and Gynecology* 101:1096–1102.
Niswander, Kenneth
1976   *Obstetrics: Essentials of Clinical Practice.* Boston: Little, Brown and Co.

Noble, Elizabeth
    1982   *Essential Exercises for the Childbearing Year.* 2d ed. Boston: Houghton-Mifflin.
    1983   *Childbirth with Insight.* Boston: Houghton-Mifflin.
Nolen, William A.
    1979   "How Doctors Are Unfair to Women." In *Culture, Curers, and Contagion,* ed. Norman Klein. Novato, Calif.: Chandler and Sharp Publishers, Inc.
Oakley, Ann
    1979   *Becoming a Mother.* New York: Schocken Books.
    1980   *Women Confined: Towards a Sociology of Childbirth.* New York: Schocken Books.
    1984   *The Captured Womb: A History of the Medical Care of Pregnant Women.* New York and Oxford: Basil Blackwell.
O'Banion, Laura
    1987   "Delivering Labor in the 20th Century." Paper in lieu of master's thesis, Dept. of Anthropology, University of Illinois at Urbana-Champaign.
Ob.Gyn. News
    1982   "Every Woman Probably Should be Monitored During Labor." 17(20):1.
O'Connor, S., K. B. Sherrod, M. M. Sandler et al.
    1978   "The Effects of Extended Postpartum Contact on Problems with Parenting: A Controlled Study of 301 Families." *Birth and the Family Journal* 5:231.
O'Connor, S., P. M. Vietze, K. B. Sherrod, H. M. Sandler, and W. A. Altemeier
    1980   "Reduced Incidence of Parenting Inadequacy Following Rooming-in." *Pediatrics* 66:176.
Odent, Michel
    1984   *Birth Reborn.* New York: Pantheon Books.
    1986   *Primal Health: A Blueprint for Our Survival.* London: Century.
Olkin, Sylvia Klein
    1987   *Positive Pregnancy Fitness.* Garden City Park, N.Y.: Avery Publishing Group, Inc.
Ornstein, R. E.
    1969   *On the Experience of Time.* New York: Penguin.
    1972   *The Psychology of Consciousness.* San Francisco: Freeman Press.
Ortner, Sherry
    1974   "Is Female to Male as Nature Is to Culture?" In *Woman, Culture and Society,* ed. Michelle Zimbalist Rosaldo and Louise Lamphere. Stanford: Stanford University Press.
Oxorn, Harry, and William R. Foote
    1975   *Human Labor and Birth.* 3d ed. New York: Appleton-Century-Crofts.
Paivio, A.
    1986   *Mental Representations: A Dual Coding Approach.* New York: Oxford University Press.

Parfitt, Rebecca
1977   *The Birth Primer: A Source Book of Traditional and Alternative Methods in Labor and Delivery.* Philadelphia: Running Press.
Parsons, Talcott
1951   *The Social System.* Glencoe, Ill.: Free Press.
Parvati-Baker, Jeannine
1978   *Hygeia: A Woman's Herbal.* Monroe, Utah: Freestone Publishing.
1986a   *Conscious Conception: Elemental Journey through the Labyrinth of Sexuality.* Monroe, Utah: Freestone Publishing.
1986b   *Prenatal Yoga and Natural Birth.* Rev. ed. Monroe, Utah: Freestone Publishing.
1988   "The Dolphin-Midwife." *Newsletter of the Pre- and Perinatal Psychology Association of North America* Spring:7.
1991   *The Deep Ecology of Birth: Healing Birth Is Healing Our Earth.* Monroe, Utah: Freestone Publishing Co.
1992   "The Shamanic Dimension of Childbirth." *Pre- and Perinatal Psychology Journal,* in press.
Pearse, W. H.
1982   "Trends in Out-of-Hospital Birth." *Obstetrics and Gynecology* 60(3):267–270.
Pederson, H., and M. Finster
1979   "Anesthetic Risk in the Pregnant Surgical Patient." *Anesthesiology* 51:439–451.
Perez, Paulina, and Cheryl Snedeker
1990   *Special Women: The Role of the Professional Labor Assistant.* Seattle: Pennypress, Inc.
Peterson, Gayle
1981   *Birthing Normally: A Personal Growth Approach to Childbirth.* Berkeley: Mindbody Press.
Peterson, Gayle, and Lewis Mehl
1984   *Pregnancy as Healing: A Holistic Philosophy for Pre-Natal Care,* vols. 1, 2. Berkeley: Mindbody Press.
Pike, B. F.
1971   "Soap Colitis." *New England Journal of Medicine* 285:217.
Ploss, Heinrich, Max Bartels, and Paul Bartels
1935   *Woman: An Historical, Gynecological and Anthropological Compendium* (English trans.), ed. Eric John Dingwal. 3 vols. London: William Heineman, Ltd.
Poovey, Mary
1986   "'Scenes of an Indelicate Character': The Medical 'Treatment' of Victorian Women." *Representations,* Spring.
Potts, M. B. S., J. A. Janowitz, and J. A. Fortner, eds.
1983   *Childbirth in Developing Countries.* Boston: MTP Press Ltd.
Prentice, A., and T. Lind
1987   "Fetal Heart Rate Monitoring During Labor—Too Frequent Intervention, Too Little Benefit." *Lancet* 2:1375–1377.

Pribram, Karl H.
   1971   *Language of the Brain.* Englewood Cliffs, N.J.: Prentice-Hall.
   1977   "Holonomy and Structure in the Organization of Perception." In *Images, Perception and Knowledge,* ed. John M. Nicholas. Dordrecht, Holland: D. Reidel.
   1979   "Holographic Memory." Interview by Daniel Goleman, *Psychology Today,* February.
Prigogine, Ilya
   1980   *From Being to Becoming.* San Francisco: Freeman.
Pritchard, Jack A., and Paul C. MacDonald
   1980   *Williams Obstetrics.* 16th ed. New York: Appleton-Century-Crofts.
Pritchard, Jack A., Paul C. MacDonald, and Norman F. Gant
   1985   *Williams Obstetrics.* 17th ed. New York: Appleton-Century-Crofts.
Rapp, Rayna
   1984   "XYLO: A True Story." In *Test-Tube Women,* ed. R. Arditti, R. Klein, and S. Minden. Boston: Pandora Press.
   1988*a*   "Chromosomes and Communication: The Discourse of Genetic Counseling." *Medical Anthropology Quarterly* 2(2):143–157.
   1988*b*   "The Power of Positive Discourse: Medical and Maternal Discourses on Amniocentesis." In *Childbirth in America: Anthropological Perspectives,* ed. Karen Michaelson. South Hadley, Mass.: Bergin and Garvey.
Rappaport, Roy A.
   1971   "Ritual Sanctity and Cybernetics." *American Anthropologist* 73 (1):59–76.
Ray, Sondra
   1985   *Ideal Birth.* Berkeley: Celestial Arts.
Redfield, Robert
   1960   "A Selection from *The Folk Culture of Yucatan.*" In *Anthropology of Folk Religion,* ed. Charles Leslie. New York: Vintage Books.
   1962   *Chan Kom: A Maya Village.* Chicago: University of Chicago Press.
Rensberger, Boyce
   1981   "Racial Odyssey." *Science Digest,* January/February.
Reynolds, Peter C.
   1991   *Stealing Fire: The Atomic Bomb as Symbolic Body.* Palo Alto, Calif.: Iconic Anthropology Press.
Reynolds, Roger F.
   1983   "Churching of Women." In *Dictionary of the Middle Ages,* vol. 3, ed. Joseph R. Strayer. New York: Charles Scribner's Sons.
Rich, Adrienne
   1977   *Of Woman Born: Motherhood as Experience and Institution.* New York: Bantam Books.
Richardson, Sheila
   1986   "The Future of Human Consciousness." *Futures,* June:401–419.
Ridington, Robin
   1979   "The Hunting and Gathering Worldview in Relation to Adaptive Strategy." Unpublished manuscript.

Ritter, C. A.
1919   "Why Pre-Natal Care?" *American Journal of Gynecology* 70:531.
Roberts, Joyce, C. Mendez-Bauer, J. Blackwell, M. E. Carpenter, and T. Marchese
1984   "Effects of Lateral Recumbency and Sitting on the First Stage of Labor." *Journal of Reproductive Medicine* 29(7):477–482.
Roberts, Joyce, C. Mendez-Bauer, and D. A. Woodell
1983   "The Effects of Maternal Position on Uterine Contractility and Efficiency." *Birth* 10(4):243–249.
Roddy, Kevin
1980   "Mythic Sequence in Chaucer's *Man of Laws* Tale." *Journal of Medieval and Renaissance Studies* 10(1):1–22.
Romalis, Coleman
1981   "Taking Care of the Little Woman: Father-Physician Relations during Pregnancy and Childbirth." In *Childbirth: Alternatives to Medical Control,* ed. Shelly Romalis. Austin: University of Texas Press.
Romalis, Shelly, ed.
1981   *Childbirth: Alternatives to Medical Control.* Austin: University of Texas Press.
Romney, M., and H. Gordon
1981   "Is Your Enema Really Necessary?" *British Medical Journal* 282: 1269.
Rooks, Judith P., Norman L. Weatherby, Eunice K. M. Ernst, Susan Stapleton, David Rosen, and Allan Rosenfield
1989   "Outcomes of Care in Birth Centers: The National Birth Center Study." *New England Journal of Medicine* 321:1804–1811.
Rosenberg, Harriet
1987   "Motherwork, Stress, and Depression: The Costs of Privatized Social Reproduction." In *Feminism and Political Economy: Women's Work, Women's Struggles,* ed. H. J. Maroney and M. Luxton. Toronto: Methuen.
Rosengren, W. R., and S. De Vault
1963a   "Impact of Hospital Routines on the Management of the Different Stages of Birth." In *The Hospital in Modern Society,* ed. E. Friedson. New York: The Free Press.
1963b   "The Sociology of Time and Space in an Obstetrical Hospital." In *The Hospital in Modern Society,* ed. E. Friedson. New York: The Free Press.
Ross, W. D.
1955   *Aristotle Selections.* New York: Charles Scribner's Sons.
Rothman, Barbara Katz
1979   "A Sociologic View of Birth: Physiologic Reality vs. People's Interpretations of that Reality." In *Compulsory Hospitalization or Freedom of Choice in Childbirth?* ed. David Stewart and Lee Stewart, Marble Hill, Mo.: NAPSAC.
1981   "Awake and Aware, or False Consciousness? The Cooption of Childbirth Reform in America." In *Childbirth: Alternatives to Medical Control,* ed. Shelly Romalis. Austin: University of Texas Press.

1982   *In Labor: Women and Power in the Birthplace.* New York: W. W. Norton and Co. (Reprinted in paperback under the title *Giving Birth: Alternatives in Childbirth.* New York: Penguin Books, 1985.)

1985   "The Meanings of Choice in Reproductive Technology." In *Test-Tube Women,* ed. Rita Arditti, Renate Duelli Klein, and Shelley Minden. London: Pandora Press.

1986   *Tentative Pregnancy: Prenatal Diagnosis and the Future of Motherhood.* New York: Viking.

1989   *Recreating Motherhood: Ideology and Technology in Patriarchal Society.* New York: W. W. Norton.

Rubinstein, Robert A., Charles D. Laughlin, Jr., and John McManus

1984   *Science as Cognitive Process: Toward an Empirical Philosophy of Science.* Philadelphia: University of Pennsylvania Press.

Russell, Jeffrey B.

1980   *A History of Witchcraft: Sorcerers, Heretics and Pagans.* London: Thames and Hudson, Ltd.

Rutter, N., et al.

1980   "Glucose during Labor." *Lancet* 1(8186):155.

Salapatek, Phillip, and Leslie Cohen, eds.

1987   *Handbook of Infant Perception.* Vol 1. New York: Academic Press.

Sanday, Peggy, and Ruth Gallagher Goodenough, eds.

1990   *Beyond the Second Sex: New Directions in the Anthropology of Gender.* Philadelphia: University of Pennsylvania Press.

Sargent, Carolyn

1989   "Women's Roles and Women Healers in Contemporary Rural and Urban Benin." In *Women as Healers: Cross-Cultural Perspectives,* ed. Carol S. McClain. New Brunswick: Rutgers University Press.

1989   *Maternity, Medicine, and Power: Reproductive Decisions in Urban Benin.* Berkeley, Los Angeles, London: University of California Press.

Sargent, Carolyn, and Nancy Stark

1987   "Surgical Birth: Interpretations of Cesarean Deliveries among Private Hospital Patients and Nursing Staff." *Social Science and Medicine* 25(12):1269–1276.

1989   "Childbirth Education and Childbirth Models: Parental Perspectives on Control, Anesthesia, and Technological Intervention in the Birth Process." *Medical Anthropology Quarterly* 3(1):36–51.

Sault, Nicole

1989   "Surrogate Mothers and Spiritual Mothers: Cultural Definitions of Parenthood and the Body in Two Cultures." Paper presented at the Annual Meetings of the American Anthropological Association, Washington, D.C.

1992a   "Surrogate Mothers and Godmothers: Defining Parenthood and the Body in the U.S. and Mexico." In *Many Mirrors: Body Image and Social Relations in Anthropological Perspective,* ed. Nicole Sault. Philadelphia: University of Pennsylvania Press.

1992*b* "Walking Wombs: Surrogate Motherhood as Political Control." Unpublished manuscript.

Savage, Wendy
1986 *A Savage Inquiry*. London: Virago Press.

Schwartz, R., A. G. Diaz, R. Fescina, and Roberto Caldeyro-Barcia
1979 "Latin American Collaborative Study on Maternal Posture in Labor." *Birth and the Family Journal* 6(1):22–31.

Scott, D. B.
1978 "Mendelson's Syndrome." *British Journal of Anesthesia* 50(10): 81–82.

Scully, Diana
1980 *Men Who Control Women's Health: The Miseducation of Obstetrician-Gynecologists*. Boston: Houghton-Mifflin.

Seel, Richard
1986*a* "Birth Rite." *Health Visitor* 59:182–184.
1986*b* *The Making of the Modern Father*. Bath: Gateway Books.

Seligman, M. E. P.
1975 *On Depression, Development, and Death*. San Francisco: Freeman and Co.
1978 "Comment and Integration." *Journal of Abnormal Psychology* 87: 165–179.

Seropian, R., and B. Reynolds
1971 "Wound Infections after Preoperative Depilatory versus Razor Preparation." *American Journal of Surgery* 121:251.

Shaw, Nancy Stoller
1974 *Forced Labor: Maternity Care in the United States*. New York: Pergamon Press.

Shearer, Beth
1989 "Forced Cesareans: The Case of the Disappearing Mothers." *International Journal of Childbirth Education* 4(1):7–10.

Sheper-Hughes, Nancy, and Margaret M. Lock
1987 "The Mindful Body: A Prolegomenon to Future Work in Medical Anthropology." *Medical Anthropology Quarterly* 1(1):6–41.

Shepherd, Michael S.
1988 "Homeschooling: A Legal View." *Mothering* 47:82–87.

Shy, Kirkwood, David A. Luthy, Forrest C. Bennett, Michael Whitfield, Eric B. Larson, Gerald van Belle, James P. Hughes, Judith A. Wilson, and Martin A. Stenchever
1990 "Effects of Electronic Fetal Heart Rate Monitoring, as Compared with Periodic Auscultation, on the Neurological Development of Premature Infants." *New England Journal of Medicine*, March 1:588–593.

Sidenbladh, Erik
1982 *Water Babies: A Book about Igor Tjarkovsky and His Method for Delivering and Training Children in Water*. New York: St. Martin's Press.

Siegel, E.
    1982   "Early and Extended Maternal-Infant Contact: A Critical Review."
            American Journal of Diseases of Childhood 136:251–257.
Simchak, Marjorie
    1989   "Medications for Labor Pain." International Journal of Childbirth
            Education 4(4):15–17.
    1990   "Response to Jay Hathaway's Letter." International Journal of
            Childbirth Education 5(3):3.
    1991   "Has Epidural Anesthesia Made Childbirth Education Obsolete?"
            Childbirth Instructor 1(3):14–18.
Singhi, S., E. Choo Kang, and J. S. E. Hall
    1982   "Hazards of Maternal Hydration with 5% Dextrose." Lancet
            2:335–336.
Sinsheimer, Robert L.
    1973   "Prospects for Future Scientific Developments." In Ethical Issues in
            Human Genetics, ed. Bruce Hilton. New York: Plenum Press.
Smellie, William
    1756   A Treatise on the Theory and Practice of Midwifery. 3d. ed. Lon-
            don: D. Wilson and T. Durham.
Smith, D.
    1964   "Severe Anaphylactic Reaction After a Soap Enema." British Med-
            ical Journal 4:215.
Smith, W. Tyler
    1847   "On the Utilization and Safety of the Inhalation of Ether in Obstet-
            ric Practice." London Lancet 1:377.
Sosa, R., J. Kennell, S. Robertson, and J. Urrutia
    1980   "The Effect of a Supportive Companion on Perinatal Problems,
            Length of Labor, and Mother-Infant Interaction." New England
            Journal of Medicine 303:597–600.
Spallone, Patricia
    1989   Beyond Conception: The New Politics of Reproduction. Granby,
            Mass.: Bergin and Garvey Publishers.
Spender, Dale
    1982   Women of Ideas and What Men Have Done to Them. London:
            Routledge and Kegan Paul.
Spradley, James P., and Michael A. Rynkiewich
    1975   The Nacirema: Readings on American Culture. Boston: Little,
            Brown and Co.
Stack, Carol B.
    1974   All Our Kin: Strategies for Survival in a Black Community. New
            York: Harper and Row.
Stapp, H. S.
    1971   "Correlation Experiments and the Non-Validity of Ordinary Ideas
            about the Physical World." Physical Review D3.
Star, Rima Beth
    1986   The Healing Power of Birth. Austin: Star Publishing.
Star-Cunningham, Rima Beth
    1992a   "Water and Birth." Unpublished manuscript.

1992*b*   "Birthing Peace on Earth." Unpublished manuscript.

Starr, Paul
1982   *The Social Transformation of American Medicine.* New York: Basic Books.

Stein, Leonard
1967   "The Doctor-Nurse Game." *Archives of General Psychiatry* 16: 699–703. (Reprinted in *Conformity and Conflict,* ed. James P. Spradley and David W. McCurdy. 4th ed. Boston: Little, Brown and Co., 1980.)

Stewart, David, and Lee Stewart, eds.
1976   *Safe Alternatives in Childbirth.* Marble Hill, Mo.: NAPSAC.
1977   *21st Century Obstetrics Now!* Vols. 1, 2. Marble Hill, Mo.: NAPSAC.
1979   *Compulsory Hospitalization or Freedom of Choice in Childbirth?* Vols. 1, 2, 3. Marble Hill, Mo.: NAPSAC.
1981   *The Five Standards for Safe Childbearing.* Marble Hill, Mo.: NAPSAC.

Stewart, P., E. Hillian, and A. A. Calder
1983   "A Randomised Trial to Evaluate the Use of a Birth Chair for Delivery." *Lancet* 1:1296–1298.

Sullivan, Deborah, and Rose Weitz
1988   *Labor Pains: Modern Midwives and Home Birth.* New Haven: Yale University Press.

Susie, Debra Ann
1988   *In the Way of Our Grandmothers: A Cultural View of Twentieth-Century Midwifery in Florida.* Athens: University of Georgia Press.

Sutton-Smith, Brian
1972   "Games of Order and Disorder." Paper presented to Symposium on Forms of Symbolic Inversion. American Anthropological Association, Toronto, December.

Szasz, Thomas
1971   *The Manufacture of Madness.* New York: Delta Books.

Taffel, Selma M., Paul J. Placek, Mary Moien, and Carol L. Kosary
1991   "1989 U.S. Cesarean Section Rate Steadies—VBAC Rate Rises to Nearly One in Five." *Birth* 18(2):73–78.

Talley, Frances
1978   "From the Mystery of Conception to the Miracle of Birth: An Historical Survey of Beliefs and Rituals Surrounding the Pregnant Woman in Germanic Tradition, Including Modern American Folklore." Ph.D. diss., Dept. of Germanic Languages, University of California, Los Angeles.

Tao-Kim-Hai, Andre M.
1979   "Orientals Are Stoic." In *Culture, Curers, and Contagion,* ed. Norman Klein. Novato, Calif.: Chandler and Sharp.

Taylor, Carol
1970   In *Horizontal Orbit: Hospitals and the Cult of Efficiency.* New York: Holt, Rinehart and Winston.

Teresi, Dick, and Kathleen McAuliffe
1985   "Male Pregnancy." *Omni*, December.
Tew, Marjorie
1982   "Obstetrics vs. Midwifery: The Verdict of the Statistics." *Journal of Maternal and Child Health*, May:193–201.
1990   *Safer Childbirth: A Critical History of Maternity Care*. New York: Routledge, Chapman and Hall.
Thacker, Stephen B., and H. David Banta
1983   "Benefits and Risks of Episiotomy." In *Obstetrical Intervention and Technology in the 1980s*, ed. Diony Young. New York: The Haworth Press.
Thayer, Stephen
1988   "Close Encounters." *Psychology Today*, March.
Thomas, Keith
1971   *Religion and the Decline of Magic*. New York: Charles Scribner's Sons.
Thorp, James A., V. M. Parisi, P. C. Boylan, and D. A. Johnston
1989   "The Effect of Continuous Epidural Analgesia on Cesarean Section for Dystocia in Nulliparous Women." *American Journal of Obstetrics and Gynecology* 161(3):670–675.
Toelken, Barre
1976   "The 'Pretty Languages' of Yellowman: Genre, Mode and Texture in Navaho Coyote Narratives." In *Folklore Genres*, ed. Dan Ben-Amos. Austin and London: University of Texas Press.
Trevathan, Wenda R.
1987   *Human Birth: An Evolutionary Perspective*. New York: Aldine de Gruyter.
Tronick, E. Z., G. A. Morelli, and S. Winn
1987   "Multiple Caretaking of Efe (Pygmy) Infants." *American Anthropologist* 89:96–106.
Tronick, E. Z., S. Winn, and G. A. Morelli
1985   "Multiple Caretaking in the Context of Human Evolution: Why Don't the Efe Know the Western Prescription for Child Care?" In *The Psychobiology of Attachment and Separation*, ed. M. Reite and T. Field. New York: Academic Press.
Turner, Victor W.
1967   *The Forest of Symbols*. Ithaca and London: Cornell University Press.
1968   *The Drums of Affliction*. New York: Oxford University Press.
1969   *The Ritual Process: Structure and Anti-Structure*. Chicago: Aldine Publishing Company.
1974   *Dramas, Fields and Metaphors: Symbolic Action in Human Society*. Ithaca, N.Y.: Cornell University Press.
1974   "Liminal to Liminoid in Play, Flow and Ritual." *Rice University Studies* 60:53–92.
1977   "Variations on a Theme of Liminality." In *Secular Ritual*, ed. S. Moore and B. Myerhoff. Assen, The Netherlands: Van Gorcum.

1979 "Betwixt and Between: The Liminal Period in *Rites de Passage.*" In *Reader in Comparative Religion,* ed. W. Lessa and E. Z. Vogt. 4th ed. New York: Harper and Row.

Tyson, Holliday
1991 "Outcomes of 1001 Midwife-Attended Home Births in Toronto, 1983–1988." *Birth* 18(1):14–18.

Ucko, L. E.
1965 "A Comparative Study of Asphyxiated and Non-Asphyxiated Boys from Birth to Five Years." *Developmental Medicine and Child Neurology* 7:643–657.

Ueland, K., and J. M. Hansen
1979 "Maternal Cardiovascular Dynamics, II: Posture and Uterine Contractions." *American Journal of Obstetrics and Gynecology* 103(1): 1–8.

van Gennep, Arnold
1966 *The Rites of Passage.* Chicago: University of Chicago Press.

van Lier, D. J.
1985 "Effect of Maternal Position on the Second Stage of Labor." Ph.D. diss., University of Illinois at the Medical Center Graduate College.

Verny, Thomas R., ed.
1987 *Pre- and Perinatal Psychology: An Introduction.* New York: Human Sciences Press.

Verny, Thomas R., and J. Kelley
1981 *The Secret Life of the Unborn Child.* New York: Summit Press.

Visscher, Harrison C., and Rebecca D. Rinehart, eds.
1990 *ACOG Guide to Planning for Pregnancy, Birth, and Beyond.* Washington, D.C.: The American College of Obstetricians and Gynecologists.

Vogt, Evon Z.
1969 *Zinacantan: A Maya Community in the Highlands of Chiapas.* Cambridge, Mass.: The Belknap Press of Harvard University Press.
1976 *Tortillas for the Gods: A Symbolic Analysis of Zinacanteco Rituals.* Cambridge, Mass.: Harvard University Press.

Walker, Alice
1983 *In Search of Our Mothers' Gardens.* San Diego: Harcourt, Brace, Jovanovich.

Wallace, Anthony F. C.
1956 "Revitalization Movements." *American Anthropologist* 58:264–281.
1966 *Religion: An Anthropological View.* New York: Random House.
1970 *The Death and Rebirth of the Seneca.* New York: Knopf.

Wall Street Journal
1987 "Obstetrics and Gynecology." 26 January 1987:1.

Walter, V. J., and W. G. Walter
1949 "The Central Effects of Rhythmic Sensory Stimulation." *Electroencephalography and Clinical Neurophysiology* 1:57–85.

Wambach, Helen
1979 *Life Before Life.* New York: Bantam Books.

Ward, Martha C.
   1986   Poor Women, Powerful Men: America's Great Experiment in Family Planning. Boulder: Westview Press.
Warner, W. Lloyd
   1959   The Living and the Dead: A Study of the Symbolic Life of Americans. New Haven: Yale University Press.
Webster's New Collegiate Dictionary
   1979   Springfield, Mass.: Merriam.
Weigle, Marta
   1989   Creation and Procreation: Feminist Reflections on Mythologies of Cosmogony and Parturition. Philadelphia: University of Pennsylvania Press.
Weil, Andrew
   1988   Health and Healing. Boston: Houghton-Mifflin.
Wertz, Richard W., and Dorothy C. Wertz
   1989   Lying-In: A History of Childbirth in America. Rev. ed. New Haven: Yale University Press.
White, Hayden
   1980   "The Value of Narrative in the Representation of Reality." In On Narrative, ed. W. J. T. Mitchell. Chicago: University of Chicago Press.
Whitley, N., and E. Mack
   1980   "Are Enemas Justified for Women in Labor?" American Journal of Nursing 80:1339.
Williams, R. M., M. H. Thom, and J. W. W. Studd
   1980   "A Study of the Benefits and Acceptability of Ambulation in Spontaneous Labor." British Journal of Obstetrics and Gynecology 87:122–126.
Woodard, L., et al.
   1982   "Exposure to Drugs with Possible Adverse Effects During Pregnancy and Childbirth." Birth 9:165.
Woolf, Virginia
   1966   Three Guineas. New York and London: Harcourt, Brace, Jovanovich.
Wynn, Ralph M.
   1975   Obstetrics and Gynecology: The Clinical Core. 2d ed. Philadelphia: Lea and Febiger.
Young, Diony
   1982   Changing Childbirth. Rochester, N.Y.: Childbirth Graphics.
Young, Diony, and Beth Shearer
   1987   "Crisis in Obstetrics: The Management of Labor." C/Sec Newsletter 13(3).
Young, Ernle W. D.
   1989   Alpha & Omega: Ethics at the Frontiers of Life and Death. Reading, Mass.: Addison-Wesley.
Zukav, G.
   1979   The Dancing Wu-Li Masters. New York: Morrow-Quill.

Index

Abitol, M. M., 86
Abney, Darlene (interviewee), 103
Abrahams, Roger D., 18, 19, 66–67
Abrahamson, E. M., 93
Abramson, L. Y., 53, 238
Accidental out-of-hospital births, obstetrical restructuring of, 150–152
Active birth, 33
Activists, childbirth, 17, 75, 139
Adams, Georgia (interviewee), 38, 88, 101
Affectivity: of dangerous births, effect of, on obstetricians, 260–263; hospital procedures and, 15, 121, 153, 154; long-term memory and, 260; of medical trainees, 260; of postpartum period, 40–41; ritual and, 14, 15, 257
Alic, Margaret, 319 n. 1
Alicia (interviewee), 245–246
Allison, A. C., 138
Alternative birth centers, 184–186; freestanding, 186, 299–300; in hospitals, 185–186
Alzugaray, Marina, 298
American Academy of Husband-Coached Childbirth, 172, 173
American core values, 46–47
American Society for Psychoprophylaxis in Obstetrics (ASPO), 163, 166, 168, 170, 175
Amighi, J. K., 141
Amniocentesis, 22–23, 57
Amniotic sac, resealing of, 221, 224

Amniotomy, 74, 102–104; official rationale, 102–103; physiological effects, 103; ritual purposes, 104; women's responses, 103–104
Analgesia, 73, 74, 99–102; Lamaze method and, 163; official rationale, 99; physiological effects, 99–100; ritual purposes, 101–102; women's responses, 100–101. See also Epidural/caudal analgesia/anesthesia
Anesthesia, 4; fasting and, 89; feminists on, 72; general, replacement of, 115–116; Lamaze method and, 163; postpartum depression and, 41. See also Epidural/caudal analgesia/anesthesia
Antiseptic. See Disinfectant
Apgar scoring system, 135–138; official rationale, 135; ritual purposes, 135; women's responses, 135
Aquinas, Thomas, 50
Arditti, Rita, 68, 287, 329 n. 2
Aristotelian precepts, 49–50
Aristotle, De Generatione Animalium, 50
Arms, Suzanne, 5, 77, 249, 273
Arney, William Ray, 104, 144, 282
Arnold, Lois-Anne Hanson, 325 n. 6
Arx, Walter von, 68
Ashford, Janet Isaacs, 67, 125
ASPO. See American Society of Psychoprophylaxis in Obstetrics
Assembly-line method, for technocratic birth, 55
Assertive childbirth, 33

Autonomy, loss of, 82; lying down and, 87
"Awake and aware" births, 162, 225–226; Cesarean sections, 167

Babcock, Barbara, 19, 133, 257
Baby(ies): effect of analgesics on, 99–100; enculturation of, through medical rituals, 61, 67–68; as mechanical product, metaphor of, 110–111; mortality rates for home births, 178–180; new mothers as secondary to, 57–58; nursery bassinets for, 148–149; "perfect," 57; as product, 57–58; separation from mothers, 147–148; as separate from mothers, 58; standard medical procedures applied to, 74; Vitamin K injection for, 138–139; washing of, 74, 136
Baby showers, 36–37
Bacon, Francis, 44, 48–49
Baggish, M. S., 89
Balaskas, Arthur, 122
Balaskas, Janet, 122
Banta, H. David, 105, 128, 129, 279
Baptism, 68; postpartum procedures as, 139
Barker, C. S., 84
Barrett, Jacqueline (interviewee), 85
Bassinets/warmers, 148–149
Bauman, Richard, 71
Becoming a Doctor (Konner), 266–267
Bed, 86–88; messages communicated by, 88; official rationale, 86; ritual purposes of, 88; women's responses, 87–88
Beecham, Clayton T., 54
Belief and value system: alignment of, with society, 10; altering through ritual, 8–17; about birth, 6, 154–186; breaking down of, 19–20; comfort in accepting, 27–28; denigrating, getting women to accept, 61, 71–72; ethnography and, 6; imprinting of, during childbirth, 40, 293–294; making birth appear to conform to, 63; mechanistic model, 44–46; obstetrical profession and, 62–65; oppositional paradigm, 46–48; on pain, 102; preservation of, 16; "safety" issue and, 177–184; transmission of, 1, 2, 38–39 (see also Transformation, cognitive); significance of, 154–155; women's hospital birth experiences and, 109, 187–188, 190–191, 226–227. See also Technocratic model of pregnancy/childbirth
Benditt, M., 84

Benin, home births in, 182–183
Bennets, Anita, 179
Benson, Ralph C., 79, 161 n.
Beryl (interviewee), 222–226, 236
Betsy (interviewee), 250. See also Yellin, Betsy
Betts, Susan (interviewee), 80
Beuf, Ann Hill, 30, 47, 329 n. 2
Beyond Conception (Spallone), 287
Bible, 44, 320 n. 4
Biesele, Christine (interviewee), 169
Bing, Elizabeth, 168
"Biodance," 296, 302
Biotechnology, and choice, 287–288
Birnbaum, David, 94
Birth. See Childbirth
Birth Book, The, 177
Birth centers: alternative, 184–186; freestanding, 299–300; in hospitals, 184–185
Birth cushion, 123
Birthing suites, 75
Bleicher, N., 120
Blessingway ceremonies, 294
Body(ies), female: male control of, 30; medical profession's perceptions of, 52–59
Body as machine, 44–46, 48–51; analgesia and, 102; male body as prototype for, 51, 52; female body and, 52–59
Bohm, David, 296
Bonding period, 139–147; integration of mental images during, 141; intense joy of, 146–147; official rationale, 139–140; patriarchal needs served by, 144, 146; physiological effects, 140–142; preconception, 297; ritual purposes, 143–147; women's responses, 142–143
Bonner, Becky (interviewee), 177–178
Boone, Margaret, 95
Borgatta, Lynn, 129
Bowen, Evlyn M., 23
Brackbill, Yvonne, 76, 83, 99–100, 105, 107, 110, 275–276
Bradley, Robert A., 6, 79, 171, 172
Bradley Method, 79, 171–175; versus Lamaze method, 172–173
Brain: rhythmicity and, 11; symbolism and, 9–10, 317 n. 3
Brazelton, T. B., 24
Brazil, 131
Breasts, sexual connotations of, 84
Breasts, stimulation of, during labor, 69
Breathing techniques, Lamaze. See Lamaze method
Brewer, Gail, 193

COMPARATIVE STUDIES OF
HEALTH SYSTEMS AND MEDICAL CARE

General Editor
John M. Janzen

Founding Editor
Charles Leslie

Editorial Board
Don Bates, M.D.,
McGill University

Frederick L. Dunn, M.D.,
University of California, San Francisco

Kris Heggenhougen,
University of London

Brigitte Jordan,
Michigan State University

Shirley Lindenbaum,
The Graduate School and University Center of the
City University of New York

Patricia L. Rosenfield,
The Carnegie Corporation of New York

Paul U. Unschuld,
University of Munich

Francis Zimmermann,
Centre National de la Recherche Scientifique, Paris

Designer: U.C. Press Staff
Compositor: Prestige Typography
Text: 10/13 Sabon
Display: Sabon
Printer: Braun-Brumfield, Inc.
Binder: Braun-Brumfield, Inc.